102 025 333 9

Contesting Transformation

This book is due for return on or before the last date shown below.

D1336305

CONTESTING TRANSFORMATION

Popular Resistance in Twenty-First-Century South Africa

Edited by
Marcelle C. Dawson and Luke Sinwell

PlutoPress
www.plutobooks.com

First published 2012 by Pluto Press
345 Archway Road, London N6 5AA

www.plutobooks.com

Distributed in the United States of America exclusively by
Palgrave Macmillan, a division of St. Martin's Press LLC,
175 Fifth Avenue, New York, NY 10010

British Library Cataloguing in Publication Data
A catalogue record for this book is available from the British Library

ISBN   978 0 7453 3273 4   Hardback
ISBN   978 0 7453 3502 5   Paperback
ISBN   978 1 8496 4832 5   PDF eBook
ISBN   978 1 7837 1213 7   Kindle eBook
ISBN   978 1 7837 1212 0   EPUB eBook

Library of Congress Cataloging in Publication Data applied for

This book is printed on paper suitable for recycling and made from fully managed
and sustained forest sources. Logging, pulping and manufacturing processes are
expected to conform to the environmental standards of the country of origin.

10   9   8   7   6   5   4   3   2

Designed and produced for Pluto Press by Chase Publishing Services Ltd
Typeset from disk by Stanford DTP Services, Northampton, England
Simultaneously printed digitally by CPI Antony Rowe, Chippenham, UK and
Edwards Bros in the United States of America

Contents

List of Figures

Acknowledgements

This book arose out of a symposium on the theme 'A Decade of Dissent: Reflections on Popular Resistance in South Africa, 2000–2010'. The event, which ran from 12–14 November 2010, was organised by the editors of this collection and hosted by the South African Research Chair in Social Change (University of Johannesburg).

We would like to thank John Appolis, long-time activist, unionist and former chairperson of the Anti-Privatisation Forum, for a stimulating opening address, which set the tone for the 20 papers that were presented over the course of the symposium.

While the invitation to participate in the subsequent book project was extended to all presenters, not all of them were able to do so owing to other commitments. Nonetheless, their input contributed to the success of the symposium, and we would like to offer a word of thanks to Noor Nieftagodien, Steven Friedman, Steven Robins, Mazibuko Jara, Llewellyn Leonard, Mzi Mngeni, Tayo Jolaosho and Janeske Botes.

We are grateful to the National Research Foundation and the Faculty of Humanities at the University of Johannesburg for financial assistance, without which we would not have been able to put this collection together.

Although this book has given us an opportunity to recognise the critical engagement and intellectual production of our contributing authors, it required a great deal of 'behind the scenes' administrative and technical assistance. In this regard we would like to acknowledge Lucinda Becorny, finance and administration officer at the South African Research in Social Change, and Alex Potter whose proofreading, editing skills and meticulous attention to detail took a large burden off our shoulders.

We would like to thank the team at Pluto Press. Roger van Zwanenberg and David Shulman initially took an interest in the book and David in particular worked closely with us to secure peer reviewers and guiding us through the publication process. Robert Webb oversaw the editorial and production process and Melanie Patrick created the superb cover design. Chase Publishing Services appointed Tracey Dando to copy-edit the manuscript and we are grateful for her sharp eyes and professionalism. We would like to acknowledge the anonymous reviewers whose comments and suggestions helped to clarify and strengthen our arguments. Such work – although labour-intensive and time consuming – often goes unnoticed and unrewarded and we are tremendously grateful for their intellectual insight and rigour.

Finally we would like to thank those who willingly shared their stories and struggles, which are reflected in these pages. *Aluta continua*!

Marcelle C. Dawson
Luke Sinwell
University of Johannesburg

List of Abbreviations

AbM	Abahlali baseMjondolo
ADR	Apartheid Debt and Reparations
AEC	Anti-Eviction Campaign
ANC	African National Congress
APF	Anti-Privatisation Forum
ASGISA	Accelerated and Shared Growth Initiative for South Africa
CBO	community-based organisation
CCMA	Commission for Conciliation, Mediation and Arbitration
CDM	Clean Development Mechanism
CJN	Climate Justice Now
CJNSA	CJN South Africa
COP	Conference of the Parties
COPE	Congress of the People
COSATU	Congress of South African Trade Unions
DA	Democratic Alliance
DLF	Democratic Left Front
EJNF	Environmental Justice Networking Forum
FOSATU	Federation of South African Trade Unions
GEAR	Growth, Employment and Redistribution
GJM	Global Justice Movement
IEC	Independent Electoral Commission
IFP	Inkatha Freedom Party
IMATU	Independent Municipal and Allied Trade Union
IRP	Integrated Resource Plan
Khulumani	Khulumani Support Group
LPM	Landless People's Movement
MEC	member of the executive council
MP	Mpumalanga Party
NCGLE	National Coalition for Gay and Lesbian Equality
NDR	National Democratic Revolution
NEDLAC	National Economic, Development and Labour Council
NEHAWU	National Education, Health and Allied Workers' Union

NERSA	National Energy Regulator of South Africa
NFP	National Freedom Party
NGO	non-governmental organisation
NPA	National Prosecuting Authority
NSMs	new social movements
OKM	Operation Khanyisa Movement
PAC	Pan Africanist Congress
POPCRU	Police and Prisons Civil Rights Union
RDP	Reconstruction and Development Programme
REDD	Reducing Emissions from Deforestation and Forest Degradation in Developing Countries
SACP	South African Communist Party
SADTU	South African Democratic Teachers' Union
SAMWU	South African Municipal Workers' Union
SANCO	South African National Civics Organisation
SANDF	South African National Defence Force
SANDU	South African National Defence Union
SAPS	South African Police Force
SASCO	South African Students' Congress
SCM	Socialist Civic Movement
SCR	Soweto Concerned Residents
SDCEA	South Durban Community Environmental Alliance
SECC	Soweto Electricity Crisis Committee
SECCP	Sustainable Energy and Climate Change Project
SERI	Socio-Economic Rights Institute of South Africa
SKPRC	Schubart and Kruger Park Residents' Committee
SMI	Social Movements Indaba
SMO	social movement organisation
SRC	Student Representative Council
TAC	Treatment Action Campaign
TCC	Thembelihle Crisis Committee
TRC	Truth and Reconciliation Commission
UDF	United Democratic Front
UNFCCC	United Nations Framework Convention on Climate Change
WSF	World Social Forum
WSSD	Word Summit on Sustainable Development

1
Transforming Scholarship: Soberly Reflecting on the Politics of Resistance

Marcelle C. Dawson and Luke Sinwell

THE GLOBAL JUSTICE MOVEMENT: A LENS THROUGH WHICH TO ASSESS RESISTANCE MOVEMENTS IN AFRICA

On a summer day in Durban, South Africa, on 3 December 2011, a global day of action against the crisis of climate change was held at COP 17,[1] the meeting at which elites and other world leaders came together to discuss how to combat climate change. In contrast to their suggestion that carbon trading is the solution, many of the thousands of protesters held the view that this would only benefit the richest countries and would leave the crisis intact. In an attempt to have their concerns addressed through non-institutionalised means, they refused to be silenced, renaming COP 17 'The Conference of the Polluters'. Some of the more striking slogans were displayed by the Democratic Left Front (DLF), a new umbrella social movement intent on unifying the left in post-apartheid South Africa. Some 500 DLF protesters marched forcefully, wearing T-shirts reading 'Africa is Burning, Transform the System' and 'Listen to the People', thereby pointing to what they saw as the root cause of the problem: the pursuit of profit by the few at the expense of the many in Africa and the rest of the global South.

Resistance efforts such as the global day of action against COP 17 arguably form part of developments from the late 1990s onwards that constitute the Global Justice Movement (GJM).[2] 'The Battle of Seattle' – the mass protests that successfully shut down World Trade Organisation conference proceedings in that city – marked the beginning of a new era of resistance to neoliberalism.[3] Slogans such as 'Our World is not for Sale' and 'People before Profit' became commonplace in the spate of protests that have spread across the globe since 1999. The World Social Forum (WSF), which is defined as 'an event and an open space for debate and discussion',[4] is widely regarded by some as the organised and sustained form of these struggles.[5]

The GJM and WSF have been celebrated and lauded globally in academic and activist circles. As embodied in the WSF's slogan, 'Another World is Possible', these initiatives provided a sense of hope that neoliberal globalisation could be contested from below through mass action. As quickly as these protests were unfolding, a body of scholarship emerged to capture what was happening on the ground. Initial accounts of the GJM were written in a way that arguably inspired more people to become part of the larger struggle against capitalism.[6] These texts proved useful in publicising the work of the different movements and garnering sympathy for them. However, many authors – particularly those rooted in the academy – failed to interrogate, from the viewpoint of movement activists, what an 'alternative' or 'transformative politics' actually entailed. From scholarly writings, it was clear that an alternative was desirable; some authors suggested that the alternative was decidedly anti-capitalist. But it was not clear whether the millions that made up the movements desired the same and, if so, how they sought to achieve this or a different outcome. Internal documents drawn up by activists themselves may have been clearer about movement ideals, objectives, strategies and tactics, but these were not always reflected in scholarly writing. Relying largely on definitions of transformation that were imposed from the outside rather than those that were generated by activists themselves, scholarship was out of tune with the reality on the ground. However, alongside these overly sanguine texts, some scholars began to reflect on the shortcomings of the GJM and it was not long before its ability to provide a concrete alternative to neoliberal globalisation began to be questioned by activists and sympathetic scholars alike.[7] Spaces like the WSF were criticised as being very expensive talk shops with no direction, no clear strategies on how to stop neoliberal globalisation and no viable alternatives to capitalism.[8]

Similar realities are reflected on the ground and on paper in the South African context. In this book, we assess the state of social movements in post-apartheid South Africa and the attendant scholarship after more or less a decade of dissent. In the South African context, the term 'social movement' has largely excluded trade unions, whereas elsewhere, in North American and European literature for example, organised labour is theorised as part of the social movement milieu. As some of the chapters indicate (see

Ngwane and Ceruti in particular) this narrow definition of social movements has precluded any significant engagement between community-based and workplace struggles.

South Africa is an interesting context in which to contest transformation and problematise resistance, since it is one of the most unequal countries in the world and has recently been dubbed 'the protest capital of the world'.[9] While some scholars suggest that protest sits comfortably alongside a dominant ruling party that has been in power for nearly two decades and that unfaltering party loyalty is one of the biggest resources of the African National Congress (ANC),[10] others (notably Alexander, this volume) suggest that ANC hegemony is beginning to crumble.

From the late 1990s social movements such as the Anti-Privatisation Forum (APF), the Anti-Eviction Campaign (AEC), the Landless People's Movement (LPM) and Abahlali baseMjondolo (AbM) forged alliances with community-based organisations in poor communities in order to provide a non-institutional space in which activists could contest the legitimacy of the ANC and fight against the effects of neoliberalism. In addition, the Treatment Action Campaign (TAC) put pressure on the ANC to provide anti-retrovirals to people living with HIV/AIDS. Despite having achieved some concessions from the state and capital, many of these movements have waned over the years; for example, the TAC is now regarded by some as a well-funded non-governmental organisation than a grassroots social movement, the APF has lost the public face it once had, and several scholars have criticised AbM for failing to live up to the grandiose expectations of transformation, formulated largely by the scholar-activists who were involved in the movement.[11] In this collection, we offer a sober reflection on the politics of a wide array of social movements such as these about ten years after their emergence on the post-apartheid political landscape.

Although the collection focuses on resistance efforts in South Africa, useful comparisons can be made with other countries, both globally and especially on the African continent. Indeed, the ongoing work of scholars like David Seddon, Leo Zeilig, Peter Dwyer and Miles Larmer continues to contribute to a growing body of research on past and present popular resistance on the African continent.[12] Although these authors reject the 'Afro-pessimism' of the 1990s, their Marxist analysis offers a considered reflection on popular protest and working-class struggle in Africa. While Seddon and Zeilig acknowledge that the chief motivation behind the resistance efforts in Africa, Asia and Latin America is still 'the establishment of more-representative governments',[13] they astutely point out that

> there is now emerging a cluster of movements and groupings which are explicitly – ideologically and politically – linked to similar movements of protest elsewhere in the world and which draw strength and vitality from international links to form the beginnings of a truly global movement of dissent against the dominant form of global capitalism – specifically US and more generally 'Western' imperialism.[14]

Like scholarship on the GJM, the writings of these authors in the early 2000s reflected a fair amount of optimism about a 'global integration of anti-capitalism',[15] but from the mid 2000s onwards their work acknowledges the limitations of popular resistance amid a context of continuing 'liberalisation and privatisation ... as part of the globalisation project'.[16] Nonetheless, they suggest that 'there are signs of new forms of struggle emerging'.[17] As we outline below, this pattern of 'hope–celebration–critical reflection' – although not in linear sequence – is embedded in the activist and scholarly writing on South African resistance movements in post-apartheid South Africa. This book reflects the third aspect of this pattern. Although it is not the first comprehensive text to provide a critical appraisal of resistance efforts in this context,[18] it is not limited to an analysis of what was termed South Africa's 'new social movements'.

In their assessment of the extent to which 'Northern' scholarship on social movements is useful for understanding these movements in Africa, Habib and Opoku-Mensah draw our attention to some important shortcomings in existing Northern debates, particularly those emanating from Europe.[19] The American tradition of social movement scholarship centred initially on collective behaviour theories.[20] Later, in response to the limitations of these approaches, which regarded activists and their actions as deviant and disorganised, intellectual endeavours began to focus on resource mobilisation and political processes as important aspects of working-class or nationalist movements.[21] European scholars turned their attention to what they called 'new social movements' (NSMs), choosing to emphasise middle-class activism that centred on 'quality of life and life-style concerns',[22] as opposed to economic redistribution. However, in light of the emergence of the GJM, even NSM scholars could not deny that global protest had entered a new phase in which the insidious consequences of privatisation, commodification, and capitalist greed were being felt and vehemently challenged by the working class and that this emerging movement had significant middle-class support. Commenting on the trajectory of Northern social movement scholarship, Ellis and van Kessel note that authors of NSM theory 'also perceive new patterns of collective action that are significantly different from the familiar characteristics of largely middle-class-based movements. Working-class action, they observe, seems to be back with a vengeance.'[23]

Commenting on these shifts in Northern debates, Habib and Opoku-Mensah point out that on the African continent there was never a moment in which labour struggles faded into obscurity. They challenge the idea that 'the fulcrum of mobilization and anti-hegemonic political activity is shifting from the realm of production to that of consumption'[24] by arguing that trade unions play an indispensible role in social movement activism, despite the Congress of South African Trade Unions' (COSATU's) alliance with the ANC, and they claim that 'COSATU may not phrase its agenda and activities in counter-hegemonic terms but this has not completely disarmed the federation'.[25] Ceruti's work in this volume underscores this point, and this book as a whole makes a concerted effort to locate industrial action more firmly within the social movement lexicon in South Africa, paying particular attention to instances of both cooperation and contestation between unions and movements. As such, we agree with the assertion that 'movements in the arena of production not only continue to retain vibrancy, but also are crucial to the sustainability of struggles of consumption' and vice versa.[26]

Habib and Opoku-Mensah develop a critique of the work of South African academics and activists whom they claim have bought into the idea that resistance occurs mainly at the point of consumption rather than production.[27] The trouble with their assertion is that they have selectively chosen to cite works that reflect an earlier phase of social movement scholarship in South Africa, which – whether rightly or wrongly – as we suggest below, was written in an over-celebratory tenor. Moreover, the scholars whom they criticise were writing at a time when trade union activity in South Africa was ebbing,[28] while their own writing was able to reflect the resurgence of industrial action. Like others, Habib and Opoku-Mensah have failed to engage with literature that reflects how, over time, authors – including the very same activist-intellectuals with whom they find fault – reconsidered material that was produced through the optimist lens. As a result, they brand certain South African literature on social movements, as well as the authors who produced it, as 'extreme'[29] and do not pick up on the contestations and nuances within the literature.

The second limitation that Habib and Opoku-Mensah identify in early NSM literature is its tendency to focus on identity issues or recognition struggles as the key driving force within movements. Based on their assessment of the nature of a range of movements in post-apartheid South Africa and other African countries, they conclude that material concerns remain central to movements in Africa and that 'distributional issues need to be an explicit component of the theory-building agenda of social-movement scholars'.[30] Indeed, most of the chapters in this volume offer grounded analyses of popular protest and resistance movements in South Africa that highlight the salience and continued significance of theoretical explanations that grant primacy to the issue of economic redistribution. Their interest in redistribution, as opposed to recognition, places many of the movements in a relationship with the state and political parties; they are not anarchic and many of them seek to engage with the state (and state institutions) to win incremental gains. Some movements might still harbour hopes of overthrowing the state and replacing it with a more equitable, democratic socialist regime, but to do this, movements must interact with, and arguably also accept concessions from, the state.

Narrowing the lens even further, the next section evaluates the non-linear and uneven shifts in social movement scholarship in South Africa. We argue for the need to move into a phase of critical reflection, allowing scholars to take stock of what has been written about the 'new social movements' and what it means for transformation and democracy.

TOWARDS A CRITICAL SYMPATHETIC APPROACH TO THE STUDY OF SOCIAL MOVEMENTS

To grasp more adequately how social movement scholarship in post-apartheid South Africa has evolved over time, as well as its implications for transformation, we identify three approaches to thinking about and studying transformation (in Africa and perhaps even globally). These approaches are not necessarily separate and distinct, but rather reflect specific ways of understanding social movements, especially scholars' understanding of their relationship to the state and capital. The approaches are also significantly dependent on the individual scholar's perception of the limitations and potential of social movements and popular resistance to challenge or transform the status quo. In contrast to conventional approaches to social science that view scholars as objective observers of social phenomena, a non-neutral and reflexive approach to social science enables one to see that scholars' understanding of the politics of social movements may change over a period of time, even though the fundamental nature and make-up of movements may remain relatively constant. Attempting to understand the worldviews of both scholars and activists provides novel and important insights into readers' understanding of popular resistance in post-apartheid South Africa and beyond.

The first of the three approaches taken by scholars is to largely ignore the question of popular resistance and instead focus on an analysis of structural problems. In the South African context, this scholarship has taken on the form of a radical critique of the political economy of the transition to democracy.[31] The primary focus of the investigation in this type of approach lies in a critique of oppressive structures and social problems rather than of social movements themselves, but, nevertheless, resistance is given secondary attention. This body of work was enormously valuable in that it scrutinised the underlying structural factors and criticised dubious policy choices that continue to marginalise the poorest and most vulnerable sections of the population. It provided plausible explanations for the emergence of resistance movements and the outbreak of community unrest.

In Africa more broadly, Harrison notes a 'striking decline in academic attention paid to struggle'.[32] His book offers a 'different "angle" on the political analysis of a continent which is principally represented as a place of repression, authoritarianism and generalized decline'.[33] His starting point is that much of the available scholarship on the African continent is 'misleading because it ignores the capacity of African societies and social groups to innovate, resist, challenge and elaborate new ideals of liberation in the face of the dire forces that produce the orthodox images of Africa'.[34] However, as the discussion above shows, contemporary analyses of popular resistance have become a more central part of stories of transformation on the continent.

The second approach is the tendency in both scholarly and activist writing to romanticise resistance. Dominant representations of social movements in the media and by the state depict them as illegitimate, and the alternative approach (of romanticisation) produces overly optimistic accounts of movements in order to counteract these dominant views. The latter approach risks creating a sharp binary between social movements, which may be projected as bottom-up and therefore inherently 'good', and the state, which is regarded as necessarily neoliberal, top-down and 'bad'. According to Pointer, '[i]n writing about the struggle in order to inspire, "human potential" becomes an article of faith; something we believe in, whatever the reality'.[35] In line with her critique of this type of scholarship, we argue, among other things, that while this approach is potentially useful for inspiring new activists and scholars and providing solidarity to flowering movements, it has certain limitations in terms of contributing towards significant sociopolitical and economic transformation. Romantic accounts centre on scholars' desire to see a form of resistance that challenges neoliberalism (both in South Africa and elsewhere) by providing a bottom-up alternative to top-down conceptions of democracy.

A renowned book by Ashwin Desai reflects one of the first, and most detailed and romantic accounts of community struggles in a place called Chatsworth, Durban.[36] Seeking to contribute to and build new forms of resistance that had begun to emerge from 1999 after the ANC's adoption of neoliberal policies in 1996, which led to deepening inequality, Desai's book provides an insider's perspective on 'how the downtrodden regain their dignity and create hope for a better future in the face of a neoliberal onslaught, and show the human faces of the struggle against the corporate model of globalization in a third world country'.[37] As we will see below, the same author later revisited these kinds of accounts that elevated the poor.

Pointer put forward the first wave of critique of such an approach, arguing as follows:

> In South Africa, those who have already written about 'the new social movements' have described 'the poors' (Desai 2002) ... 'the community' (Weekes 2003) ... the resistance of 'pensioners' (Pithouse 2001) ... the 'aunties' (Pithouse 2001) ... and so on, in an optimistic and glorifying way; they have selected descriptions of the movement by its participants, but without any deep and meaningful critique of whether or not that self description matches action. Part of the reason for this may be that current writers on these movements sought to attract attention to these struggles in the world-at-large [and build solidarity] but do not seem to have considered the need for their work to constitute a movement talking to itself.[38]

Paying particular attention to the politics of representation about and within movements, she further suggests that '"activist intellectuals" have served as publicists for the movements, but have not sought to critique and challenge the shape of these existing forms of insurgency'.[39]

Authors such as Desai and Pithouse responded to Pointer's critique by defending their romantic accounts of the AEC on the grounds that '[its] campaign had received no academic attention and only hostile observation from the State and Corporate Media'.[40] They add that they wrote the article with two goals in mind:

> to provide uncompromising academic legitimation for this struggle in an elite public, from which so much ideological delegitimation of this and other struggles is produced … [and] to use the example of this struggle, including the conditions that have produced it and repressed it, to mount an attack on the academic common sense that works to reinforce these conditions.[41]

Responding to the labelling of movements as counter-revolutionary and ultra-left by the ANC and in the mainstream media, Miraftab and Wills argue for the legitimation – rather than stigmatisation – of agency that falls outside the parameters of the government as an active form of citizenship.[42] Echoing these sentiments, an edited collection by Nigel Gibson, for example, suggests that new social movements in post-apartheid South Africa

> are not only challenging neo-liberal capitalist globalization, but also attempting to articulate alternatives and raise the question of what it means to be human. Whether reconnecting electricity, or struggling for housing or for HIV/AIDS anti-virals [sic], these social movements are a challenge, in the most human of ways, to the mantra that 'there is no alternative' to capitalist globalization.[43]

This kind of scholarship is relevant and necessary, but it does not provide insight about the limitations of movements. Scholars interested in the prospects of 'another world' are bent on the notion that grassroots resistance efforts necessarily challenge the dominant neoliberal framework.[44] Sinwell argues that this type of approach simplifies and homogenises movements rather than uncovering the complexity of their political and internal dynamics.[45] Also critical of the orthodox literature on social movements in the global South, Thompson and Tapscott point out that 'Marxist scholars have portrayed … multiple protests as the manifestation of ongoing class struggle, [but these protests] do not necessarily represent a direct challenge to the legitimacy of the state'.[46]

Moving forward, we advance a position that goes beyond those scholars who continue to call solely for an amplification of the voices of the poor.[47] We argue that the way in which academics relate to movements must begin to evolve in such a way that they do not act merely as megaphones for movement activism and exacerbate the false binary between top-down and bottom-up approaches to social change. As Hickey and Mohan cogently argue, one 'can no longer juxtapose the alleged benefits of bottom-up, people-centred, process-oriented and "alternative" approaches with top-down, technocratic, blueprint planning of state-led modernisation'.[48] More nuanced analyses are necessary and, indeed, as several of the chapters in this collection point out, popular agency can be co-opted or embedded within the dominant development paradigm. Thus, conservative (and sometimes regressive) elements are apparent in bottom-up movements that openly advocate progressive transformation.

Coming to grips with the limitations not only of social movements in post-apartheid South Africa, but also of the overly sanguine accounts that had existed until the mid 2000s, Desai provided one of the earliest critical reflections on intellectual production on social movements.[49] He suggests that scholars had imposed their own worldviews onto movements by depicting them as the next 'revolutionary subject' or associating them with a particular theoretical school. He concludes that it is the scholars who must now be questioned, in particular their political, career and academic motivations for writing about the movements in the ways that they do. Indeed, as the present collection shows, the analytical lens that authors bring to their research and the particular meanings of transformation that they implicitly or explicitly adopt significantly shape the kinds of analyses that they present.

Our aim is to advance beyond a binary between critical and sympathetic accounts of movements, and we suggest that it is possible and necessary to move between the two in such a way as to avoid the romantic register of earlier writings, but not fall into the trap of vanguardism or, even worse, delegitimising and destroying movements[50] (see the chapters by Tissington and Walsh in this volume). This is, of course, not a new challenge. In a classic text on poor people's movements in America in the 1900s, Piven and Cloward were heavily criticised for purportedly not reflecting on the limitations of social movements in their study of lower-class groups.[51] Their response was that scholars must beware of discrediting movements on the basis that they do not meet the expectations of ideologues. Fundamental to their response was the inability of scholarship to provide a critical but sympathetic perspective on the potential and limitations of movements that are bound within certain institutional and historical frameworks – something that each chapter of this book seeks to do.

Taking this lead, we suggest that *critical and sympathetic* approaches to the study of social movements are not mutually exclusive, but in fact can be complementary. Furthermore, while knowledge is clearly produced in movements and through struggle, we maintain that the academy is also an important site for linking knowledge production to social change.[52] In our view, contesting transformation thus also involves reimagining and redefining the relationship between scholarship and activism. We have written elsewhere that scholars must transform how they relate to movements and in so doing 'subvert the institutional logic of academia itself'.[53] We agree with Pointer that 'representation of a "social movement" serves as a contested space of power',[54] one that is influenced by so-called outsiders (including academics) who themselves may wield power within or over social movements. We maintain that scholars must be honest about their ideological commitment. The critical, yet sympathetic approach is enabled by a methodological strategy that does not draw a stark divide between scholarship and activism. For example, Lichterman argues that it is possible to remain somewhere in between the extremes of the detached researcher and the participant observer. He emphasises that 'closeness and analytic distance are not mutually exclusive'[55] and argues:

> We learn more when we are willing to keep an analytic lens focused on the groups we study. We learn less if we surrender that lens to the notion that we already agree with the group's cause and therefore understand what they are doing, or we already disagree with the group's cause and therefore understand – to our chagrin – what they are doing. Keeping the conceptual lens at hand hardly precludes other lenses, other relationships to the group that arise doing a project: occasional helper, fellow activist, friendly critic.[56]

The approach adopted in this book is that researchers can be involved with the movements they are studying, but at a certain distance. However, it should not be assumed that being an activist in a movement necessarily makes one biased or less critical of that movement. Rather, involvement and even sympathy for a movement can enable one to come to grips with its internal contradictions or the structural limitations that it is faced with. None of the authors in this collection claims to be detached, apolitical or neutral, as orthodox academic discourse would have it. As we have indicated above, this is undesirable and, we would argue, impossible. The authors of the subsequent chapters are embedded researchers who position themselves – to varying degrees – as participant observers and agents within the social movements that they have investigated.

Another aspect of this third approach is the relationship of social movements to the powerful actors and authorities that they seek to challenge. As Goldstone astutely points out, social transformation is often the result of a complex interplay among states (at all levels), social movements and political parties, among other social actors.[57] The contributors to this book accept that there is no pure revolutionary subject that is completely separate and distinct from the state, political parties and capital; instead, they view any assumption along these lines as counterproductive.

This book comes to terms with why the ANC still forms part of the identity of millions of South Africans. Any study that attempts to understand contested meanings of transformation and problematise resistance must explain the political space within *and* outside the ANC-led Alliance, and this book marks an important step in that direction.[58] For instance, some chapters deal with the relationship between social movements and trade unions, while others address popular protest and electoral politics. Some authors consider the relationship between the state and grassroots resistance, while others address interactions between movements and 'outsiders', such as academics and lawyers. As such, the book is not narrowly focused on the resistance efforts of organised or recognised social movements in South Africa. Instead, it takes into account a broad spectrum of 'contentious politics', defined by Tarrow as 'what happens when collective actors join forces in confrontation with elites, authorities, and opponents around their claims or the claims of those they claim to represent'.[59]

OUTLINE OF CHAPTERS

In his chapter, **Dale McKinley** argues that the South African left is in crisis in that it remains 'numerically small and politically weak' and unable to challenge and alter capitalist relations. He points to the adoption of the neoliberal Growth, Employment and Redistribution (GEAR) policy as one the major roots of the crisis and suggests that the ANC's efforts to absorb much of the left into Alliance structures substantially weakened left forces. He also points out that the inability – or perhaps unwillingness – of COSATU and the South African Communist Party, as junior partners in the ANC-led Alliance, to cut ties with the ANC places them in the invidious position of not being able to challenge 'the systemic nature of the inequalities and injustices of the deracialised capitalism of which the ANC has long been a champion'. His chapter introduces us to the new social movements that began to appear on the political scene in the late 1990s, partly in response to the shortcomings of the 'traditional left' to achieve substantive gains for the working class. Although he is generally optimistic about the social movements – himself a founding member of one of South Africa's largest movements to date – McKinley is also realistic about what they have achieved thus far and can still attain in the future. He alerts us to four main weaknesses in the 'new left', namely unrealistic expectations, limited resources, a social base that is largely poor and unemployed, and 'rising social conservatism' within the broad working class. Plotting the way forward for left politics, McKinley suggests that 'unionised workers [must] ... respond politically to intensifying mass struggles from the very communities of which they are also part'.

Amid claims that the administration of President Jacob Zuma has been a more sensitive, 'listening government' towards workers and the poor, **Jane Duncan** questions the degree to which having Zuma at the helm has in fact opened up spaces for political dissent by social movements and political organisations. She uses the state of protest action as an indicator of the state of health of the country's democracy under Zuma's leadership and reflects on three case studies in her analysis, namely struggles against the re-demarcation of provincial boundaries, the control of dissent in the South African National Defence Force and the regulation of protest action in the build-up to the 2010 FIFA World Cup. Duncan's research shows that despite increased 'points of access to the decision-making system', protesters' demands and grievances have fallen on deaf ears. Moreover, she suggests that the Zuma administration has exerted greater control over the security cluster, thereby increasing the coercive capacities of the state. Based on these findings, her work paints a bleak picture of the state of democracy in post-apartheid South Africa.

Peter Alexander analyses the 2011 local government elections through the lens of some of the most militant community-based social movements in the country (including those in Balfour and Thembelihle), which received national media attention and in some instances a direct response and visit from President Zuma. In terms of electoral behaviour, Alexander argues that protesting communities – the youth in particular – do not necessarily fall back on a sense of loyalty towards the ANC, but rather resort to other electoral tactics, such as spoiling ballot papers and standing as independent or socialist candidates, and he views this as a sign that ANC hegemony is crumbling and looks to the possibility of these community-based movements seeking a transformative left alternative to the party. He suggests that, '[e]specially at Polokwane, community and trade union struggles left their mark, but so too have self-aggrandisement and factionalism, with the effect that the ANC is now deeply divided and incapable of commanding unbridled loyalty in its urban heartland'.

Malose Langa and **Karl von Holdt** provide an alternative viewpoint to Alexander in their case study of 'Kungcatsha', which was also wracked by service delivery protests mainly in 2009. By investigating the interface between political parties and community organisations, they show how these two local actors are embedded in one another. They illustrate that

> [t]he trajectory of the protest movement in Kungcatsha provides a dramatic instance of the way in which the ANC remains the hegemonic political and social force at the local level, occupying both the political space structured by town-level politics and the broader social space beyond the political domain, and preventing the emergence of an autonomous civil society at the local level.

They explore the internal dynamics of the protest movement in Kungcatsha and its relationship to internal contestations within the local ANC and town council. They also point to some of the common limitations that 'service delivery' protests are faced with, since they tend to be focused on holding local government councillors accountable to their demands and, once they are heard, the movement dies out and there is no organisation left to press for the other demands of the wider community. Challenging available scholarship that tends to romanticise popular protest (and service delivery protests in particular), Langa and von Holdt also point to what they call some of the darker sides of citizenship, such as xenophobia and patriarchy, patronage networks, and a quest for power by individual leaders of the ANC. In contrast to conventional approaches to the study of social movements and political parties in South Africa, which look at how the ANC at the national level structures its relationship to the grassroots,[60] their focus on the internal dynamics of protest and the ANC reveals the ways in which this 'domination over civil society is constructed from below by the agency of local elites and subalterns, rather than by instructions from above'.

Claire Ceruti considers the two largest strikes in South African history, namely the public sector strikes in 2007 and 2010, and asks why the potential of these significant resistance efforts to bring about transformation was stalled. She suggests that one of the main reasons is that 'the strikes were a (missed) opportunity for social movement activists who were critical of the ruling party to build links with the union movement, despite its ties to the ruling party'. Thus, in a similar fashion to McKinley – albeit with a different emphasis – she is suggesting that substantive transformation depends on making connections between strikes (trade unions/the workplace) and community protests (social movements/home). In her examination of the public sector strikes, Ceruti highlights the 'development of contradictions in the ANC-led Alliance, which were pushed explosively to the surface in the confrontational atmosphere of these strikes' and suggests that the connections that hold the Alliance together have started to fray, especially since in the 2010 strike unionised workers began to see the parallels between their own experiences and those of the scores of protesting unemployed workers.

Reflecting on the vibrant and diverse popular resistance in post-apartheid South Africa, **Trevor Ngwane**, like McKinley and Ceruti, argues that there has been little connection, unity or solidarity between community and workplace struggles. He explores instances in which social movement organisations and trade unions have cooperated with and supported each other in struggles during the post-apartheid era. One of these instances occurred in the lead-up to the formation of the APF. For Ngwane, who played a leading role in shaping South Africa's post-apartheid social movements, the APF's formation 'united workplace and community action targeting the capitalist class and the government'. However, he argues that, over time, 'the different parts of the workers' movement were hardened' and that '[e]ach section was left to move into struggle alone rather than in unity with the rest of the class'. Ngwane is adamant that the only way that capitalism will be defeated is if the different sections of the working class come together. He also sets up a challenge for social movement researchers whose work thus far has served to reinforce and exacerbate the divisions between community and workplace struggles. In other words, he is suggesting that activists and academics alike have a role to play in forging greater unity among labour struggles, social movement activism and community protests.

Fiona Anciano reflects on earlier scholarly writing on social movements and assesses the achievements of two quite different movements in terms of four dimensions that are evident in the literature, namely the extent to which these movements challenge ANC hegemony, the degree to which they put forward 'explicit and progressive economic and political agendas', their potential to generate mass support, and the extent to which they act as agents of democracy. The movements that she assesses in her chapter include the Soweto Electricity Crisis Committee and Sikhula Sonke, the latter of which she describes as 'neither a traditional trade union nor a conventional social movement, but a unique hybrid of both'. As far as the first three analytical themes are concerned, she shows that the movements have had limited success, either because their intentions differed from what scholars projected in their writings or because movement leaders and supporters had different motivations that drove their actions, leading to a mismatch between intention and outcome. In terms of the final dimension, Anciano unpacks a number of ways in which movements have played a significant role in promoting substantive democracy. Echoing other authors, she suggests that existing movements could be strengthened by linking up with other forms of community resistance that do not seem to be orchestrated by organised social movements.

In contrast to conventional Northern analysis that views social movements as coherent and unified, **Carin Runciman** analyses some of the contradictions and tensions thrown up in the relationship between the APF and its local affiliates, showing how conflict and tension 'exist not only between movements and the wider political environment, but also within movements themselves'. She shows that, while the APF may not be able to unite in order to provide a counter-hegemonic force that is capable of challenging the power of the ANC, this and the fact that APF affiliates buy into the ANC are not necessarily a weakness per se. Looking specifically at the internal dynamics of the APF, from her perspective, she makes the important point that the APF provides an important political home for organisations that are faced with evictions, and water and electricity cut-offs.

Jacklyn Cock addresses the issue of ecological transformation in post-apartheid South Africa, arguing that climate change hits poor and marginalised communities the hardest. She criticises the state's efforts to bring about 'green capitalism' and questions whether local environmental organisations are able to effectively challenge the 'technocist' and market-oriented logic of green capitalism. She assesses the emerging environmental justice movement, reflecting not only on its historical roots in the form of the Environmental Justice Networking Forum, but also on one of the key drivers of the movement in the contemporary period, namely Earthlife Africa, which has served to 'globalise local resistance'. She alerts us to three initiatives that have the potential to radically transform the terrain of environmental activism and spur on 'a powerful environmental justice movement': the emerging climate justice movement, the formation of the Democratic Left Front and the mobilisation of labour. As far as the last of these initiatives is concerned, she notes that 'the labour movement is beginning to explicitly challenge green capitalism'. Like some of the other authors, Cock points to the possibility of different social actors, such as trade unions and community movements, coming together to fight for a common goal, in this case environmental justice. In light of the fact that the actions of different social groups are triggered by different motivations, she stresses the importance of devising a 'master frame of environmental justice' to coordinate the activities of the different groups and bring some coherence to the disparate and fragmented struggles. For her, the central message that this master frame must convey is that 'the climate crisis is caused by the expansionist logic of the capitalist system'.

The next three chapters shift from the internal dynamics of movements to the role of so-called 'outsiders' in them. Drawing from participant observation in the Socio-Economic Rights Institute, (SERI) which works with social movements on issues of housing and evictions, **Kate Tissington** views legal recourse as one tactic in the repertoire of social movements that often have few options by which to have their concerns addressed by the state. The suggestion is that institutions or policies are potentially transformative, but that they just need to be reformed. Responding to radical critiques presented by authors such as Ashwin Desai and Heinrich Böhmke, she highlights 'a tendency of the frustrated left to criticise community-based movements because they are either un-strategic, not vanguardist enough or, at worst, counter-revolutionary'.

Like Walsh, **Tshepo Madlingozi** suggests that there has been a shift from a power discourse to a rights discourse. His starting point is that 'post-apartheid legal norms, discourses, procedures and institutions have provided significant discursive and institutional political opportunities and threats that have structured the emergence of social movements, their trajectory and outcomes' and he shows that 'law functions as a resource *and* constraint for social movements'. In contrast to Walsh and Tissington, Madlingozi examines some of the nuances regarding the relationship between social movements and the legal route. He reminds us that we must also evaluate the transformative politics of movements on the basis of their own definitions. Drawing from movement scholar Bert Klandermans, he points out that 'success at a policy level is not the only way to assess the effectiveness of a social movement' and suggests that what is 'truly transformative' in this movement occurs in public spaces rarely written about by academics.

Despite good intentions, 'outsiders' may have a great deal of power and resources that affect strategies and tactics in possibly negative ways. **Shannon Walsh** takes this position in her analysis of the role of lawyers, and more specifically, academics in social movements. She uses the term 'radical chic', a term coined by Tom Wolfe in the 1970s to describe how members of the academic left, in their ivory towers, to suggest that academics do not have 'any real intention to disrupt the status quo or hegemonic order'. In doing so, she provides a further critical appraisal of social movements in post-apartheid South Africa more broadly by arguing that there has been a decline in anti-capitalist struggles over the past decade, that the left has largely misunderstood the political and social dimensions of anti-capitalist struggles, and that the left and other actors have internalised capitalist logic.

Across the chapters, the authors interrogate the implications of contentious collective action for democracy and social change and, although they point to some of the shortcomings of resistance efforts over the last decade and seek to unpack why these movements have not reached their full potential, they also pick up on signs of fragmentation in the ANC's hegemony. Some authors suggest that the diverse and seemingly disparate struggles characterising twenty-first-century South Africa are beginning to find common ground and realise common purpose, and that, in concert, these struggles have the potential to alter the political playing field as we move into the next decade, in a direction where the legitimacy of the ANC and loyalty to the party are thrown into question. In no way are we intimating that a revolution is imminent – such an assessment, after all, would be just as romanticised as earlier scholarship's views on social movements – but we are suggesting that, on their own, the different strands of struggle constitute little more than loose threads, while together they can weave new tapestries of resistance that have the potential to bring about substantive social transformation.

NOTES

1. 17th Conference of the Parties to the Kyoto Protocol.
2. The resistance efforts that comprise the GJM are alternatively referred to as the Movement of Movements, the Global Solidarity Movement or the Anti-Globalisation Movement.
3. A few months prior to the Battle of Seattle, the 'Carnival Against Capitalism' took place in cities across the world, but it is the events in Seattle that stand out as marking a new era of resistance on a global scale.
4. I. Santiago, 'A fierce struggle to re-create the world', in J. Sen et al., *World Social Forum: Challenging Empires*, New Delhi: Viveka Foundation, 2004, p. xiv.
5. Sen et al., *World Social Forum*.
6. D. Solnit, *Globalize Liberation: How to Uproot the System and Build a Better World*, San Francisco: City Lights Books, 2004. See also A. Starr, *Global Revolt: A Guide to Movements against Globalization*, London and New York: Zed Books, 2005; F. Houtart and F. Polet (eds), *The Other Davos: The Globalization of Resistance to the World Economic System*, London and New York: Zed Books, 2001.
7. See A. D. Morton, 'The antiglobalization movement: juggernaut or jalopy', in H. Veltmeyer (ed.), *Globalization and Antiglobalization: Dynamics of Change in the New World Order*, Aldershot: Ashgate, 2004.
8. It should, however, be noted that some of its more ardent supporters have argued that the intention behind the WSF was merely to create an open space for debate and that such spaces should be protected, rather than being turned into vehicles for transformation.
9. A. Kota, 'SA, we cannot say we are free', *Mail & Guardian*, 6 May 20011.
10. S. Booysen, *The African National Congress and the Regeneration of Political Power*, Johannesburg: Wits University Press, 2011.
11. See, for example, S. Walsh, '"Uncomfortable collaborations": Contesting constructions of the "poor" in South Africa', *Review of African Political Economy*, Vol. 35, No. 116 (2008). See also L. Sinwell, 'Defensive social movements need to engage with politics', *South African Labour Bulletin*, Vol. 34, No. 1 (March/April 2010); H. Böhmke, 'The branding of social movements', *Dispositions*, Vol. 1, No. 1 (1 May 2010).
12. A useful starting point for anyone interested in social movements in Africa is M. Mamdani and E. Wamba-dia-Wamba (eds), *African Studies in Social Movements and Democracy*, Senegal: CODESRIA, 1995. Contemporary Marxists accounts include P. Dwyer and D. Seddon, 'The new wave? A global perspective on popular protest', paper presented at the 8th International

Conference on Alternative Futures and Popular Protest, Manchester Metropolitan University, 2–4 April 2002; L. Zeilig (ed.), *Class Struggle and Resistance in Africa*, Cheltenham: New Clarion Press, 2002 (a revised edition of this book was published by Haymarket Books in 2009); D. Seddon and L. Zeilig, 'Class and protest in Africa: New waves', *Review of African Political Economy*, Vol. 32, No. 103 (2005); D. Renton, D. Seddon and L. Zeilig, *Congo: Plunder and Resistance*, London: Zed Books, 2006; M. Larmer, P. Dwyer and L. Zeilig, 'Southern African social movements at the 2007 Nairobi World Social Forum', *Global Networks*, Vol. 9, No. 1 (2009); P. Dwyer and D. Seddon, 'The role of popular movements in Africa today', paper presented at the 5th International Conference on Alternative Futures and Popular Protest, Manchester Metropolitan University, 29–31 March 2010; L. Zeilig, M. Larmer and P. Dwyer, 'An epoch of uprisings: Social movements in post-colonial Africa, 1945–1998', *Journal of Socialist History* (2012, forthcoming); P. Dwyer and L. Zeilig, *Social Movements and Anti-globalization in Africa*, Chicago: Haymarket Books, 2012.

13. Seddon and Zeilig, 'Class and protest', p. 22.
14. Ibid., p. 23. See also Seddon and Dwyer, 'Popular protest', p. 20.
15. Seddon and Dwyer, 'Popular protest', p. 20.
16. Ibid.
17. Ibid., p. 28.
18. See, for example, D. McKinley and P. Naidoo (eds), *Mobilising for Change: The Rise of the New Social Movements in South Africa*, Development Update Series, Johannesburg: Interfund, 2004.
19. A. Habib and P. Opoku-Mensah, 'Speaking to global debates through a national and continental lens: South African and African social movements in comparative perspective', in S. Ellis and I. van Kessel (eds), *Movers and Shakers: Social Movements in Africa*, Leiden: Brill, 2009.
20. See, for example, H. Blumer, 'The field of collective behavior', in A. M. Lee (ed.), *Principles of Sociology*, New York: Barnes and Noble, 1951; N. J. Smelser, *Theory of Collective Behavior*, New York: Free Press, 1962.
21. See, for example, J. D. McCarthy and M. N. Zald, *The Trend of Social Movements in America: Professionalization and Resource Mobilization*, Morristown: General Learning Press, 1973; J. D. McCarthy and M. N. Zald, 'Resource mobilization and social movements: A partial theory', *American Journal of Sociology*, Vol. 82 (1977).
22. N. A. Pichardo, 'New social movements: A critical review', *Annual Review of Sociology*, Vol. 23 (1997), p. 414.
23. S. Ellis and I. van Kessel, 'Introduction: African social movements or social movements in Africa', in S. Ellis and I. van Kessel (eds), *Movers and Shakers: Social Movements in Africa*, Leiden: Brill, 2009, p. 15.
24. Habib and Opoku-Mensah, 'Speaking to global debates', p. 48.
25. Ibid., p. 57.
26. Ibid., p. 44.
27. Here they are lambasting Richard Pithouse and Ashwin Desai; see Habib and Opoku-Mensah, 'Speaking to global debates', p. 49.
28. See Seddon and Zeilig, 'Class and protest', p. 24.
29. Habib and Opoku-Mensah, 'Speaking to global debates', p. 49.
30. Ibid., p. 57.

31. P. Bond, *Elite Transition: From Apartheid to Neoliberalism in South Africa*, London: Pluto Press, 2000. See also, P. Bond, *Against Global Apartheid: South Africa Meets the World Bank, IMF and International Finance*, Cape Town: UCT Press, 2003; H. Marais, *South Africa: Limits to Change: The Political Economy of Transition*, London: Palgrave Macmillan, 2001; H. Marais, *South Africa Pushed to the Limit: The Political Economy of Change*, London: Zed Books and Cape Town: UCT Press, 2011.

32. G. Harrison, *Issues in the Contemporary Politics of Sub-Saharan Africa: The Dynamics of Struggle and Resistance*, Basingstoke and New York: Palgrave Macmillan, 2002, p. 1.

33. Ibid.

34. Ibid., p. 2.

35. R. Pointer, 'Questioning the representation of South Africa's "new social movements": A case study of the Mandela Park Anti-eviction Campaign', *Journal of Asian and African Studies*, Vol. 39, No. 4 (2004), p. 272.

36. A. Desai, *We Are the Poors: Community Struggles in Post-apartheid South Africa*, New York: Monthly Review Press, 2002.

37. Ibid., back cover.

38. Pointer, 'Questioning the representation', p. 271.

39. Ibid., p. 272.

40. A. Desai and R. Pithouse, 'Sanction all revolts: A reply to Rebecca Pointer', *Journal of Asian and African Studies*, Vol. 39, No. 4 (2004), p. 300.

41. Ibid., pp. 300–1.

42. F. Miraftab and S. Wills, 'Insurgency and spaces of active citizenship: The story of the Western Cape Anti-Eviction Campaign in South Africa', *Journal of Planning Education and Research*, Vol. 25, No. 2 (2005), p. 200.

43. N. Gibson (ed.), *Challenging Hegemony: Social Movements and the Quest for A New Humanism in South Africa*, Trenton and Asmara: New World Press, 2006, back cover.

44. For examples, see F. Polet and CETRI (eds), *Globalizing Resistance: The State of Struggle*, London: Pluto Press, 2004; T. Mertes, *A Movement of Movements: Is Another World Really Possible?*, London: Verso, 2004; D. Harvie et al., *Shut Them Down: The G8, Gleneagles 2005 and the Movement of Movements*, West Yorkshire and New York: Dissent! and Autonomedia, 2005.

45. L. Sinwell, 'Is "another world" really possible? Re-examining counter-hegemonic forces in post-apartheid South Africa', *Review of African Political Economy*, Vol. 28, No. 127 (2011). See also Böhmke, 'The branding of social movements' and Walsh, '"Uncomfortable collaborations"' for insightful critiques of the romanticised accounts of social movements in South Africa.

46. L. Thompson and C. Tapscott, *Citizenship and Social Movements: Perspectives from the Global South*, London and New York: Zed Books, 2010.

47. Miraftab and Wills, 'Insurgency and spaces of active citizenship'.

48. S. Hickey and G. Mohan, 'Towards participation as transformation: Critical themes and challenges', in S. Hickey and G. Mohan (eds), *Participation from Tyranny to Transformation: Exploring New Approaches to Participation in Development*, London and New York: Zed Books, 2004, p. 4.

49. A. Desai, 'Vans, autos, kombis and the drivers of social movements', Harold Wolpe memorial lecture, 28 July 2006, http://ccs.ukzn.ac.za/files/DN072006desai_paper.pdf (accessed 1 August 2011).

50. Böhmke, 'The branding of social movements', p. 47.

51. F. F. Piven and R. A. Cloward, *Poor People's Movements: Why They Succeed and how They Fail*, New York: Vintage Books, 1977.
52. M. C. Dawson and L. Sinwell, 'Ethical and political challenges of participatory action research in the academy: Reflections on social movements and knowledge production in South Africa', *Social Movement Studies*, Vol. 11, No. 2 (2012).
53. Ibid.
54. Pointer, 'Questioning the representation', p. 1.
55. P. Lichterman, 'Seeing structure happen: Theory-driven participant observation', in B. Klandermans and S. Staggenborg (eds), *Methods of Social Movement Research*, Minneapolis: University of Minnesota Press, 2002, p. 143.
56. Ibid., p. 127.
57. J. A. Goldstone, *States, Parties and Social Movements*, Cambridge: Cambridge University Press, 2003.
58. In R. Ballard, Adam Habib and Imraan Valodia (eds), *Voices of Protest: Social Movements in Post-apartheid South Africa*, Scottsville: University of KwaZulu-Natal Press, selective chapters in this collective took the Alliance seriously at a time when much scholarship on social movements had written it off. See, for example, the chapters by E. Zuern, 'Elusive boundaries: SANCO, the ANC and the post-apartheid South African state', pp. 179–202, and A. Habib and I. Valodia, 'Reconstructing a social movement in an era of globalisation: A case study of COSATU', pp. 225–54.
59. S. Tarrow, *Power in Movement: Social Movements and Contentious Politics*, New York: Cambridge University Press, 2011, p. 4.
60. See P. Heller, 'Moving the state: The politics of democratic decentralisation in Kerala, South Africa, and Porto Alegre', *Politics and Society*, Vol. 29, No. 1 (2001).

2
The Crisis of the Left in Contemporary South Africa

Dale T. McKinley

HARSH REALITIES

Seventeen years into the post-apartheid era, the left[1] in South Africa needs to face two harsh realities: firstly, despite a long and often-courageous history, it has failed to capture the social imagination and political/organisational loyalty of the vast majority of South Africa's inhabitants; and, secondly, no anti-capitalist (socialist[2]) vision and strategy exists that has the potential to fundamentally challenge and change South African capitalism and unite left forces.

From the mid 1980s to the mid 1990s the organisational and political state and direction of mass-based class struggle were very much on the left agenda. An intellectual willingness and much practical activity existed directed at forging a strategy that would be able to politicise and organise these class struggles towards a possible anti-capitalist future. Unfortunately for the left, and for the millions of South African workers, the broader urban and rural working class, and the youth, the revolutionary promise of that period has foundered to a large degree on the rocks of a strategic sterility among the South African left. While struggles against the intensified ravages of global and South African capitalism have continued, these have taken place in spite of the strategic impasse that the South African left has found itself in for the last 15 or so years.

The ideological, political, organisational and socioeconomic realities of contemporary South Africa do not paint a flattering picture of the left. The neoliberal variant of capitalism as a social, political and economic system is not only practically dominant, but generally in a phase of ideational triumphalism, despite its recent setbacks in some corners of the globe. The state has rapidly become the 'public arm' of a slowly deracialising capitalist ruling class (both bureaucratic and corporate). The African National Congress

(ANC), which is in political and administrative possession of the state, is under the effective control of this ruling class and is fully committed to serving its interests. Despite the recent growth of a crisis of ideological 'identity' and political division, the ANC's own leadership layers, as well as those of its Alliance partners, the Congress of South African Trade Unions (COSATU) and the South African Communist Party (SACP), have become sub-agents of such class rule.

Further, the socioeconomic situation of the majority of people, but particularly that of the formal working class and those outside of formal capitalist employment, has worsened.[3] Large sections of these oppressed classes are increasingly embracing the social and economic logic/consciousness of capitalist consumerism and individualism (see Walsh, this volume). Regardless of the growing legitimacy crisis of bourgeois democracy and its concomitant electoral system,[4] no mass-based and national political/organisational alternative has arisen either in relation to participating within or in creating the conditions for an alternative system of democratic participation and process outside of, and against, bourgeois democratic electoralism. Lastly, despite their historical centrality to the struggle against apartheid and their continued presence in both the ANC-led Alliance and the independent sociopolitical struggles of the poor/working class, left forces remain numerically small and politically weak, characterised by organisational sectoralism, disjointed resistance struggles and a lack of ideological confidence.

Besides the ongoing struggles of the organised working class for better living and working conditions, as well as those of social movements and a wide range of community organisations around the socioeconomic conditions of existence,[5] the dominant form and content of left struggles since the late 1990s have revolved around issue-oriented social and political struggles such as those that focus on HIV/AIDs, privatisation, water/electricity/housing, the environment, and so on. While these struggles are in and of themselves necessary and important, they have proven unable to grapple with the demands and actual forging of a meaningful left strategy that has the potential to radically change the organisational and political face of anti-capitalist politics and struggle in South Africa (and, implicitly, Southern Africa).

Simply put, left politics in South Africa has to a large degree become ideologically balkanised, and to a lesser extent strategically and politically declassed. Additionally, most left forces (particularly in the realm of leadership) continue to suffer from the age-old problems of personal egoism, organisational sectarianism, power-mongering, and political dishonesty and opportunism.[6]

ROOTS OF THE CRISIS

When South Africa's first ever one-person, one-vote election in 1994 resulted in an overwhelming victory for the ANC, the majority of South Africans understandably celebrated the arrival of a new democracy. After all, the ANC and its liberation movement allies were now in political control of the state thanks to the votes of those who had, throughout South Africa's modern history, been denied the right of institutionalised democratic participation simply because of their racial categorisation.

Accompanying this, however, there still remained a broad-based (but ultimately mistaken) expectation among the black majority – and also among most sections of the left – that the new ANC state would immediately begin to pursue a more anti-capitalist – or at the very least, radically redistributive – political economy. The basis upon which such expectation had been built derived from the militant, mass-based political and socioeconomic struggles that had been waged by trade unions and community organisations (and supported by more radical non-governmental organisations (NGOs)) since the mid 1980s, alongside the continued 'socialist' rhetoric of the ANC itself.[7] 'As has happened so often in newly liberated countries, the euphoria of political transition led many to expect that the need for adversarial social struggle with the state was over.'[8]

Even if it had been long apparent to some on the left that the ANC was never going to follow even a proto-socialist developmental path once in power,[9] the bubble was clearly and publicly burst with the ANC state's 1996 unveiling of the neoliberal GEAR (Growth, Employment and Redistribution) macroeconomic policy. Instead of supporting and strengthening the plethora of community and civic organisations (along with progressive unions) that had formed the backbone of the anti-apartheid struggle in the 1980s, the ANC called on all civics and community structures to become part of ANC branches or to join the newly launched South African National Civics Organisation (SANCO), which, it was announced, would become the 'fourth' member of the ANC-led Alliance. Simultaneously, the ANC further formalised its political and organisational alliance with COSATU – and the main left political party, the SACP – by setting up numerous (consultative) Alliance structures and drafting key leadership figures into its electoral list for all levels of government.

Consistent with the sociopolitical thrust of GEAR, the ANC government also set about forming national structures to give institutional form to its corporatist commitments. The National Economic, Development and Labour Council (better known by its acronym, NEDLAC) was formed, in which 'civil society' was represented by a 'development chamber' consisting of chosen NGOs and community-based organisations (CBOs), a labour component consisting of recognised union federations, and a corporate component consisting of representatives from capital and big business. At the same time, legislation was passed, for example, the Non-Profit Act of 1997, and institutions set up like the Directorate of Non-profit Organisations (which required NGOs and CBOs to officially register with the state) and the National Development Agency 'to direct financial resources to the sector'.[10] All of this fitted comfortably within the ANC government's push 'for a more formalised civil society constituency as part of a developmental model where formally organised groups participate in official structures to claim public resources' and where 'the role of such organised groups is constructed along the lines of official government programmes, without space to contest the fundamentals of those programmes'.[11]

To their eternal discredit, the leadership of both COSATU and the SACP eagerly bought into the ANC 'nation building' and 'corporatist consensus' sales pitch, rationalised by constant reference to the Stalinist era-inspired theory of the 'National Democratic Revolution'. This placed the key components of the political left in a classic strategic cul-de-sac, in other words, into a situation where the pursuit of an anti-capitalist struggle is effectively co-determined by capital and by a state already wholly committed to securing the core interests of capital. When, as they did throughout the better part of the 1990s, COSATU and SACP leaders tell the workers and poor that the best (and only) strategic option is to better manage their own exploitation and hope that somewhere down the road it will lead to 'socialism', the entire meaning of the concept of 'the left' is put into question.[12]

Cumulatively, these developments meant that by the mid to late 1990s the vast majority of what had constituted a previously vibrant and predominately independent South African left, rooted in broad working-class politics and struggles and sustaining the hope of millions for an anti-capitalist transformation of South

African society, had effectively been neutered. Whether swallowed by the ANC, absorbed into other Alliance structures, hobbled by the co-option of key leaders into the state and associated corporatist institutions, or starved of financial resources, the bottom line was that the political and organisational terrain for active and militant resistance to the ANC's creeping neoliberalism, elite deal-making and wholesale acceptance of the institutionalised framework of bourgeois democracy had been largely contained.

THE 'TRADITIONAL' LEFT: COSATU AND THE SACP

It might well be argued (and, indeed, it has been[13]) that the 'transitional' presence of COSATU and the SACP as part of both a formal alliance with the ruling ANC and the 'broad left' in South Africa would translate into a collection of vibrant anti-capitalist forces capable of and willing to contest fundamentally the politics, policies, and overall developmental agenda of both capital and the state. However, the 'transitional' reality has been that the acceptance of an unequal and essentially subservient political and organisational relationship within an ANC-dominated alliance[14] – which is supposed to act as the political master of the state – and participation in corporatist institutionalism have served to tie organised workers and large numbers of community activists with historic ties with and/or sympathy for the Alliance into a false sense of ideological and strategic unity with the ANC-led state and – even if to a much-lesser extent – with corporate capital.

Unfortunately for the broad left in South Africa, the SACP and COSATU have been fiddling with the same strategic and political choices since the beginning of the 'transition'. Their first choice is to be junior partners in an alliance they will never control (but might have key positions in) and thus to practise a politics of offering critiques of existing policy implementation and arguing for policies that have a more pro-poor character or more state involvement, and to engage in occasional campaigns and activities designed to 'show' that the working class is still a force to be reckoned with, while simultaneously continuing to be part of an ANC electoral machine and to participate in an ANC-run state through its various institutional mechanisms. Their second choice is to go back to the basics of organising and mobilising the poor and working class (which means real, practical alliances with community organisations and new social movements) based on a radical programme of demands for the redistribution of ownership and wealth that will act as an organisational and political base to both shift ANC and government policy – not through insider bargaining or politicking, but through mass mobilisation and class struggle – and to rebuild a genuinely independent left political and organisational base to contest power relations within South African society (something that is not simply reducible to elections and running as an electoral force separate from the ANC).

The problem is, however, that the fiddling has been just that – the second choice has never really been on the agenda. As a result, both COSATU and the SACP have continued to play the Alliance political 'game'. While this has contributed to minor policy shifts and occasional genuflections by the ANC government towards the mitigation of rising inequalities and poverty, these have not happened in isolation from the myriad protests and mobilisations that have taken place outside the SACP–COSATU nexus and that have arguably been just as responsible for various policy shifts and the recent rise in political fragmentation and contestation within the Alliance. Indeed, the ANC is arguably more wary of uprisings in poor communities over corruption and poor service delivery and the accompanying disillusionment (read: electoral abstentionism) with ANC 'rule' than with the regular sniping and critiques of the SACP and COSATU. In this respect, the ANC's liberation pedigree (and the corresponding loyalty quotient which flows from that), alongside the fact that it has been the ruling party since the demise of apartheid, has not meant that its overall popularity has increased or even remained at the same levels (see also Alexander, this volume).

The politics and practical work of the SACP and COSATU have become – over the last few years in particular – tied directly to what is going on inside the ANC Alliance in direct proportionate relation to intensifying personal, positional and factional power struggles. Confirmation of this state of affairs could be seen at the ANC Policy Conference, the SACP Twelfth Congress and the ANC National Conference at Polokwane (all in 2007) in the form of the dictates of the personal and political battle between the 'camps' of former South African president (and at the time still ANC president) Thabo Mbeki and former deputy president (and at the time ANC deputy president) Jacob Zuma. Since those conferences, the ANC and its Alliance partners have done little to challenge and/or change such a politics. Indeed, at its most recent 2010 National General Council meeting, most of the time was spent in circular debates centred on the ANC Youth League's ongoing (opportunistic) campaign for the 'nationalisation' of South

African mines and ANC leadership succession issues. There was also lots of navel gazing around the rampant corruption among ANC politicians and state employees[15] and, not surprisingly, continued affirmation of the overall macroeconomic growth path, while once again repeating the need to 'prioritise' the needs of the poor and effect better distribution of socioeconomic opportunity.

The SACP and COSATU have been ensnared in the 'left' political game that the ANC has constructed. Any slight change in ANC and/or government policy that has occurred or might occur – and which could provide some additional succour to the broad working class – is interpreted as a 'victory' for the 'left', precisely because to interpret it otherwise would be to undermine the larger claim and position that it is necessary and imperative for the SACP and COSATU to remain in alliance with the ANC. Also, any deeper and more realistic interpretations would undermine the entire theoretical construct of the 'National Democratic Revolution' on which the Alliance rests, as well as the present and ongoing organisational and ideological positioning of both the SACP and COSATU.[16] Because the leadership of the SACP and COSATU refuse to cut the long-standing umbilical cord with the ANC, the core of their 'left' critique and struggle centres on contesting the character of the Alliance and ANC governance, not the systemic nature of the inequalities and injustices of the deracialised capitalism of which the ANC has long been a champion. As a result, they have no other option but to propagate the idea that the sidelining of specific individuals and selected class forces (within the ANC Alliance) alongside continued political participation within the state constitutes the main strategic 'path' for anti-capitalism.

In reality, then, the core struggles of the SACP and COSATU have over time become a battle to politically and organisationally 'cleanse' the ANC of its historic and more contemporary progeny; in other words, a battle to politically and organisationally defeat those who want what former ANC secretary general A. B. Xuma called their 'fair share' of the capitalist system.[17] This would mean nothing less than a complete political and ideological revolution within and through the ANC – something that is clearly not going to happen simply because certain SACP and COSATU leaders want it to happen and proclaim its possibility as the fundamental basis for their own organisational strategy.

While more recent (and resuscitated) moves by COSATU to form a 'new UDF' (United Democratic Front) in partnership with various elements of 'civil society' might appear to signal a potentially radical shift, the reality is that such moves fit more than comfortably into the ANC- and state-centred macro strategy. No further confirmation of this is needed other than COSATU general secretary Zwelinzima Vavi's remarks at the opening of the Civil Society Conference in October 2010 where he stated: 'Let us right from the onset state that we are not an anti-ANC and anti-government coalition ....'[18]

What all this represents is a crisis of confidence of, and in, the SACP and COSATU at its most acute: a crisis of confidence in the 'traditional left's' ability to forge an independent political and organisational opposition to what it stands against and what it stands for; and a crisis of confidence in the ability and willingness of its claimed constituency (that is, the poor and the formal working class) to embrace a political, organisational, and ideological alternative to the ANC's deracialised and elitist capitalism and to identify with the class lines and struggles that so clearly divide South African society.

THE 'NEW LEFT': SOCIAL MOVEMENTS AND COMMUNITY ORGANISATIONS

Not surprisingly, the subjective politico-strategic choices on the part of COSATU and the SACP – alongside SANCO – has done little to stem the increased socioeconomic inequality, poverty and political marginalisation that have been experienced by most workers and all poor communities across South Africa since the late 1990s. Indeed, it was the ongoing results of such political and strategic choices and socioeconomic realities that eventually saw the rise of a range of new social movements and community organisations from the late 1990s onwards.

Due to the implementation of the state's neoliberal policies, massive job losses were visited upon those members of the South African working class who had been fortunate enough to be employed; the 'experience' being accompanied by all the attendant social and economic devastation of already poor families and communities. To make matters worse, the ANC-led state also implemented basic needs policies that effectively turned such needs and related services into market commodities, to be bought and sold on the basis of private ownership and the profit motive. This was facilitated by a drastic decrease in national government subsidies to local municipalities and city councils, and support for the development of financial instruments for privatised delivery. In turn, this forced local government to turn towards the commercialisation and privatisation of basic services as a means of generating the revenue no longer provided by the state.[19]

The logical result of these developments was a huge escalation in the costs of basic services and a concomitant increase in the use of cost-recovery mechanisms such as water and electricity cut-offs that necessarily hit poor people the hardest. By the turn of the century, millions more poor South Africans had also experienced cut-offs and evictions as the result of the ANC's neoliberal orgy.[20] Similarly, the state's capitalist-friendly land policies, which ensured that apartheid land ownership patterns remained virtually intact, meant that South Africa's long-suffering rural population continued to taste the bitter fruits of labour exploitation and landlessness. It was the cumulative result of such experiences, combined with the failure of the main traditional forces of the left (for example, COSATU and the SACP) and 'civic' structures like SANCO to lead and sustain counter-mobilisations and active class resistance that eventually saw the rise of new social movements and community organisations,[21] at first in the main urban centres and then also in some rural areas.

From their inception, these 'new' left forces that emerged outside of, and often in consequent opposition to, the 'traditional left' within the Alliance have been largely ignored, treated with thinly disguised contempt, and regularly and actively opposed by the SACP and COSATU.[22] Despite the fact that these social movements and community organisations have been subject to a consistent state campaign of rhetorical vitriol and physical assaults,[23] the various leaderships of the SACP, COSATU and other ANC 'civil society' allies have often given tacit support to the state's actions and have consistently failed to seriously engage with, politically support and provide material solidarity to their struggles against the state's service delivery policies and suppression of political dissent. Even during the numerous public and private sector workers' strikes that have taken place over the last several years, there has been little if any effort and/or practical work by COSATU and the SACP around linking worker struggles for better wages/working conditions and those of poor communities for basic services and freedom of expression. One notable exception to this has been the South African Municipal Workers' Union (SAMWU). Having been a member of the Anti-Privatisation Forum in its early phases, SAMWU has regularly given political support to community struggles around basic services and occasionally sought to form organisational and campaign links with urban-based social movements.

The positioning of the SACP and COSATU demands that they play the role of organisational and ideological gatekeepers of left forces in South Africa. The practical goal of this role is to politically and organisationally control the 'anti-ANC' and, to a lesser extent, the 'anti-state' politics and mobilisations of the new movements and organisations so as to ensure that these social forces do not pose any ongoing or future threat to the 'left' dominance of the SACP and COSATU and the self-anointed 'left' forces in the ANC-led state. This is the main reason why the SACP and COSATU find the 'new left' to be a 'problem' (instead of seeing it as constituting allies to build a viable and grounded anti-capitalist movement). It is precisely because the SACP and COSATU refuse to cut their umbilical ties to the ANC that they must adopt this wholly contradictory position, so much so that they are more apt to be accepting of closer relations with capitalists and liberals than with most poor communities and their struggles. To a large extent, it has been such an organisational and ideological gatekeeping role that has ensured that the possibilities of a united left capable of fundamentally contesting the state and establishing broader power relations within society as a whole have remained stillborn.

Despite the obvious organisational and leadership weaknesses and politically incipient and often transitory nature of the 'new' movements and struggles, they broadly represent those who increasingly desire to push beyond the enforced boundaries of institutionalised bourgeois democracy; who are actively engaged in grassroots struggles against specific state policies and for the basic necessities of life; and who seek to pursue an independent, mass-based mobilisation outside of the confines of state institutionalism as the only meaningful and realistic option for resisting global neoliberalism and planting the seeds for an ideological and organisational alternative to existing political party politics. While these movements do not represent some kind of homogeneous entity, and while there have been (and continue to be) substantive organisational differences and political and ideological debates within their ranks, they have become inextricably bound together by the levelling content and common forms of the neoliberal onslaught, both nationally and, to a lesser extent, internationally.[24]

Regardless, the new movements and organisations have their own Achilles' heel – the accumulation of unrealistic and misplaced expectations of singular (or dominant) leadership of sociopolitical struggles within poor communities and a consistent lack of appreciation of the practical means (both human and in terms of resources) by which any such leadership role could even begin to approach reality. Such a serious weakness is somewhat understandable, given the trajectory that such movements have followed since the 'big events' of 2001/02,[25] combined with the abject failure on the part of the 'traditional left' to fill the political and organisational gap created by growing impoverishment, inequality, and hugely unpopular government policies and attitudes towards the poor majority. But it is a severe weakness nonetheless and one that, unfortunately, remains impregnated in the general psyche of many leading movement activists; it can only and always lead to disillusionment and rationalisations for turning social movements into prefigured vanguardist political entities.

As has become very clear over the last few years, movements can be 'in touch' with the mood of the 'masses' and can define the political and socioeconomic conditions and their subsequent impact on poor communities, but if they do not have serious and committed activists who respect democratic structures and collective decisions to mobilise resources, enjoin open debate and discussion, and support and sustain organisation within communities, then the ability to do so is not much more than an intellectual exercise.

Linked to this is a stark, but often ignored reality that impacts on the ability of the new movements to be part of a strategically unified left. The social base of such movements has remained dominated by the 'other' working class, that is, those whose work is not measured as part of the formal economy and whose ranks are populated by a majority of women. While such a social base has allowed a collectivisation of the hard-nosed survival skills and experience of those who form the ranks, it has also made the organisation of such collectivities into a coherent and sustainable political and social movement that encompasses all layers of the working class extremely difficult. In classic 'left' parlance, for these movements, the 'community' has come to replace the 'workplace' as the epicentre of organising collective resistance to the dominant capitalist political and socioeconomic system (see Ceruti and Ngwane, this volume).

Besides the highly fractured social and productive relations within poor communities, there is the additional challenge of engaging and overcoming a rising social conservatism among the ranks of the broad working class, driven by the growth of (right-wing) Christian evangelical churches and 'culturally' enforced patriarchy, as well as intensified ethnic and national chauvinism. Much of this social conservatism[26] has come to the political and social surface since the rise of the current South African president, Jacob Zuma, whose thinly disguised misogyny and homophobia, and open embrace of patriarchal 'traditional values' and religion have provided a trickle-down, socially backward 'role model' to the ANC's and left's core constituency – the broad working class. Further reinforcement has come from the ANC-led state's consistent championing of a narrow nationalism that has framed and encouraged xenophobia.[27] When combined with the structurally derived material desperation and widespread social dysfunction in poor communities, the overall and unfortunate impact has been that sizeable sections of social movement membership have imbibed such social conservatism and allowed it to permeate their own politics.

A STRATEGIC IMPASSE

Even if differentially experienced, the combined characters and actions of both the 'traditional' and 'new' left in South Africa have produced the effective institutionalisation of a left anti-politics, grounded in an essentially reactive, issue-based and personality-driven strategic framework as the best means to confront capital, 'engage' the state, mobilise the 'masses' and transform societal power relations under capitalism. While this kind of politics can – and does – provide an ongoing vehicle for left activism, it can only go so far. It is essentially a defensive politics, and while degrees of such a politics have been necessary, there is no ideological, political or organisational basis from which to move onto the offensive. This has, in turn, seriously obscured seeing (and acting upon) the possibilities for those implicitly anti-capitalist battles to give birth to more explicitly socialist politics/class struggle and organisational forms that have the potential to contest capitalist power and social relations on a terrain and on terms that are not reflective of the demands and needs of capitalism itself, as well as to forge a lasting left unity.

The question that the entirety of the South African left needs to honestly ask is whether or not it still believes in the possibilities of actually getting rid of capitalism. This is not a rhetorical question or a meaningless ideological litmus test. There is simply no subjective basis for claims to socialist politics and unity if the struggles that take place continue to be directed into a strategic cul-de-sac whereby, once a certain critical political 'mass presence' has been achieved, the strategic focus becomes beating the capitalists at their own game and on a 'playing field' tailored by – and for – them (for example, policy reforms, contesting elections, and so on). Just like the national liberation movements of the past, stated 'tactics' become, whether intentionally or not, the strategy, and any accompanying organisational form merely reflects the demands of this strategic choice.

On the other hand, the last several decades of left politics in South Africa and globally have also shown quite clearly that the strategic sureties of a classical vanguardism have failed, precisely because the presumed class consciousness to which such a politics strives has proven to be historically fundamentally flawed. For those in need of confirmation, we only have to look at the consistent crisis of socialism, of the working-class movement, that is now almost a century old. The present crisis of the South African left is much more than simply a question of the late twentieth-century 'collapse of communism'. At its core it has to do with preconceived and prefigured notions of the 'working class' itself and a parallel mode of strategic thinking that fetishises a stagist conceptualisation of an ever-expanding productive base as the prerequisite for any fundamental change in sociopolitical relations beyond capitalism. In South Africa (as elsewhere), attempts to merely reconstruct the historically determined forms of vanguards – whether through accessing state power or through independent class struggle – have led, and will continue to lead, straight into political and organisational sectarianism and ideological absolutism.

In South Africa over the last several years, then, most of the left has tended to gravitate towards an issue-based anti-politics (often strategically conceptualised as a struggle for 'revolutionary reforms') or to seek refuge in the arms of a classical vanguardist (and often entryist) politics. More recently, the concept of the 'commons', which eschews any specific political and/or organisational form or direction, has also entered the scene, albeit mostly through theoretical interventions by left intellectuals. Despite verbal gymnastics to the contrary, left organisational forms and the resultant politics flowing from them have continued to be predominantly conceived as and cast in terms of a 'mass' versus 'vanguard' framework. More specifically, the strategic 'debate' emanating from these approaches has tended to revolve around the possible formation of a 'workers' party' (usually perceived as being born out of the womb of a formal COSATU/SACP break from the present ANC-led Alliance) and, to a lesser extent, the efficacy of politically independent grassroots/community struggles entering the realm of electoral politics as a means to contest the party dominance of the ANC and the capitalist policies of the present South African state.

The problem here is that an unnecessary strategic dichotomy has – whether intentionally or not – been erected between anti-capitalist mass action and the need for an organisational form to give political expression to such struggles. Historically, the South African left has adopted a strategic framework that has assumed the sociopolitical character of these struggles (and, thus, the 'consciousness' of those doing the struggling) as the basis for a politically predetermined organisational form. The all-too-evident result has been a marked failure to capture the political imagination of those most oppressed under capitalism and thus to generally limit consequent struggle to narrowly defined understandings of production and micro material-related sociopolitical relations.

A WAY FORWARD?

We are now in an 'epoch' in South Africa, and in many other places globally, in which the struggles of the broad working class are increasingly – and necessarily – framed by an anti-capitalist spirit, if not content. What is imperative, though, is for those who consider themselves socialist not only to catalyse such struggles through practical involvement and varying forms of political or ideological impetus, but to win the idea politically that what is desperately needed (indeed, demanded) is the organisational recognition and expression of such struggles as socialist. Meeting this challenge provides a potential means for overcoming the strategic 'divide' between and forging a practical unity among left forces and moving beyond what has become a somewhat stale and misdirected 'debate' in South Africa around a 'workers' party'.[28]

What is important in this regard is how the left understands the political character and organisational sustainability of the present ANC–COSATU–SACP Alliance and, thus, the best strategic approach to moving left politics and anti-capitalist struggle forward. For many years now it has been clear that the Alliance 'ties that bind' have weakened progressively. The very basis, historically, for the maintenance of a sustainable political alliance between unions and (ostensibly progressive) political parties that hold state power is the parallel maintenance of both a politically malleable union leadership and expanding benefits for a meaningful threshold of unionised workers. In the case of South Africa, on the first count, while such union leadership certainly remains alive and kicking, the objective realities of neoliberal capitalism for unionised workers continue to act as a powerful antidote to the dominance of comprador leadership. On the second count, the gains of all but the most highly paid unionised workers (in relation to their direct productive context) are being seriously offset by the combined erosive effects of the state's capitalist-friendly policies and the more-general crisis of capitalism on workers' (and their families – nuclear and extended) basic socioeconomic existence, that is, their total 'social' existence.

Nonetheless, unionism is ingrained, politics is not. What is therefore called for is a strategy that essentially forces unionised workers to respond politically to intensifying mass struggles from the very communities of which they are also part. As long as the struggles that are presently driven by the 'new' left remain in the political shadows – in terms of their political militancy, their social reach, and their potential to cause serious breaches in support for a capitalist-friendly ANC and the state it controls – unionised workers will feel little pressure to translate their own dissatisfaction with the political 'delivery' of the ANC-led Alliance into serious consideration of left political and organisational alternatives. What is needed, therefore, is the (re-)politicisation of unionised workers through the parallel socialist politicisation and organisation of these struggles. Here, then, is the nexus of a political strategy that can potentially achieve what endless ideological debates, union congress resolutions, limited industrial action and demonstrations, and the prefigured formation of another political party can never achieve, that is, a clear socialist strategy and the practical unity in action of broad working-class forces.

What makes absolute strategic sense in relation to COSATU in particular and organised workers more generally is for left intellectuals and activists to focus political debate and catalyse practical class struggles at the very 'point' where the political connection of workers to the ANC and the state is at its weakest and most vulnerable. Unlike the position that has been taken by many on the left outside the Alliance, this should not be understood simply to mean that the key political task is to call for and hasten a formal COSATU/SACP break from the ANC in order to form a 'workers' party'. This approach plays right into the hands of the capitalists in the ANC, allowing them to successfully use the organisational appeal of historic liberation movement loyalties and the political appeal of an unfinished 'National Democratic Revolution'. It also mistakes political form for class content grounded in and arising from sustained mass – and implicitly anti-capitalist – struggles, not simply that of organised (and predominantly industrial) workers.

A more meaningful strategic approach can begin to lay the political and organisational groundwork for a new kind of left politics. It can do so by strategically linking – ideologically and organisation-ally – the ongoing struggles of various layers of the 'masses' (in urban and/or rural poor communities, and so on) with the struggles of organised workers and, in so doing, exposing the political and strategic sterility of an approach that seeks to 'transform' capitalism and an ANC that has embedded and championed it within South Africa's post-apartheid political economy. This can be a major step forward to a real and meaningful left unity (as opposed to the present state of false unity based on spurious claims to a declassed, common 'National Democratic Revolution') both among and between organised workers and those struggling at the grassroots level.

With reference to such a potential unity, the left must also jettison what has been a very narrowly defined understanding of, and thus strategic approach to, who constitutes a 'worker'. Workers are not confined to those who have formal employment (or, more specifically, who belong to a union), but include the millions of those who have worked in the 'formal' capitalist economy (whether as industrial and/or agricultural workers) and continue to work in the 'informal' survival economy (often erroneously classified as 'unemployed', as if recognition of their work depends on 'formal' measurement). To this must also be added the hundreds of thousands of 'domestic' workers – not in the sense simply of those working for predominately white South African households, but all those – mainly woman – who are just as much workers (reproducing labour, and so on), but who are not politically and organisationally treated as such.

There must also be put forward the absolute necessity of a strategic link between the revolutionary potential of these combined struggles (that is, not predetermined, prefigured organisational forms that seek to capture that potential) and the forging of an organisational form that can directly (organically, so to speak) represent the political possibilities of extending ground-level struggles into the popular propagation of socialist demands on a broader, societal level. The more immediate 'struggle' thus requires engaging in a battle of ideas, not merely through intellectual endeavour, but through exposing the inherent weaknesses of existing forms of 'left' political organisation (and this includes trade unionism) to act as the fulcrum for a renewed and relevant left politics.

In more overt programmatic terms, the basis for such a strategic approach should not be centred primarily on the need to provide electoral opposition, although this must always remain a tactical option to further expose the limitations of capitalist 'democracy' and politics. The point of charting a new left strategy is not simply to oppose the ANC on the electoral terrain that it now occupies in a still-dominant but increasingly shaky position. Rather, it is to stake out that political and organisational terrain that the ANC continues to ignore and take for granted – that is, the mass of the *broad* working class in both urban and rural areas – as the grounding for a new organisational form with an explicitly socialist politics that has the potential to both unify practical left struggles and contest existing class power on its own terms.

For the left in South Africa to move out of its present crisis will require a politically qualitative and organisationally quantitative advancement of the very real struggles of the broad working class, but not predominantly in the intellectual and organisational capabilities of select individuals or in 'capturing the heart and soul' of the ANC. The advance can be extended by taking the idea of new forms of left political organisation directly into the heat of the practical struggles taking place (which are only going to get more intense). In this way, the possibility arises that through their own self-activity, combined with certain degrees of intellectual and activist 'push', organised workers and those in social movements and community organisations can prepare the ground for what can be a truly meaningful path to political and ideological independence. In other words, the objective conditions themselves are umbilically linked to the subjective will (and capacity) to sustain and intensify contemporary mass-based anti-capitalist struggle.[29]

Any serious left cannot but reject the philosophical, material and class basis for the capitalist political economy being pursued by the ANC-run state. The main task is not to force the ANC to review what it is that it has fully committed itself to, although the struggle for practical reforms that impact positively on the daily lives of the majority must always form part of the tactical arsenal of a meaningful left. It is the strategic responsibility of those who constitute that left to work towards a political alternative that emanates from and is grounded in the ongoing and linked struggles of the mass of organised workers and poor against the impact and consequences of capitalist neoliberalism and against those who manage and control the institutional and systemic means for its continuation. Not to undertake this task is to condemn class struggle and left politics in South Africa to the realm of cyclical mitigation and crisis.

NOTES

1. Here, the 'left' refers to any political and social force/organisation (inclusive of individuals) that professes adherence to an anti-capitalist ideology. Beyond this admittedly very broad definition, there is an array of strategic, tactical, organisational and more specifically ideological differences among the 'left', whether in South Africa or anywhere else across the globe.

2. The word 'socialist' is used to describe in broad analytical and strategic terms the vision and struggles of left forces in which those oppressed under capitalism (predominantly defined by class position) embrace a collective and democratic endeavour and consciousness as a means to wrest political, economic and social power from capital and then to transform that power into the forging of a society free from all forms of economic exploitation and social alienation.

3. Numerous studies and reports conducted over the last several years confirm this state of affairs. For example, see Vusi Gumede, 'Poverty, inequality and human development in a post-apartheid South Africa', paper presented at the conference on Overcoming Inequality and Structural Poverty in South Africa: Towards Inclusive Growth and Development, Johannesburg, 2010; Ashley Westaway, 'Rural poverty in South Africa: Legacy of apartheid or consequence of contemporary segregationism?', paper presented at the conference on Overcoming Inequality and Structural Poverty in South Africa: Towards Inclusive Growth and Development, Johannesburg, 2010; United Nations Development Programme, *Human Development Report 2009: Overcoming Barriers: Human Mobility and Development*, New York: Palgrave Macmillan, 2009; South African Cities Network, *State of the Cities Report 2006*, 2006, www.sacities.net/knowledge/research/publications/395-socr2006; University of South Africa, *Projection of Future Economic and Sociopolitical Trends in South Africa up to 2025*, Research Report No. 351, Pretoria: Bureau of Market Research, 2004; United Nations Development Programme, *South Africa Human Development Report: The Challenge of Sustainable Development in South Africa: Unlocking People's Creativity*, London: Oxford University Press, 2003; Department of Social Development, *Transforming the Present, Protecting the Future: Report of the Committee of Inquiry into a Comprehensive System of Social Security for South Africa*, Pretoria: DoSD, 2002.

4. See Dale T. McKinley, 'South Africa's third local government elections and the institutionalisation of "low-intensity" neo-liberal democracy', in Jeanette Minnie (ed.), *Outside the Ballot Box: Preconditions for Elections in Southern Africa 2005/6*, Johannesburg: Media Institute of Southern Africa, 2007, pp. 149–63.

5. The positive 'achievements' of the new social movements and community organisations should, however, be noted. Over the last ten years or so these have included placing mass struggles back onto the political and organisational 'agenda' of the left, which has involved a partial reclamation of the history and principles of the liberation struggle; providing critical opposition to both the ideas and practice of the neoliberal policies of the ANC government and contributing to a deepening of the class and ideological divisions with the ANC-led Alliance; and helping to create a renewed social, political, and moral consciousness and solidarity around the most basic needs of life, both domestically and internationally.

6. These are admittedly harsh charges to make but that does not make them any less real or appropriate. Sizeable portions of this chapter are precisely about how such characteristics have been put into practice (both within the 'traditional' and 'new' lefts), about the very particular ways in which crucial aspects of the left's political and organisational practice is inherently bound up with such egoism, such sectarianism, and so on. For a specific 'case study' of the presence and impact of such characteristics in a post-apartheid social movement, see 'A brief history of the Anti-Privatisation Forum', in Dale T. McKinley, *Transition's Child: The Anti-Privatisation Forum (APF)*, Johannesburg, South African History Archive, 2012. The entire report on the APF can be accessed at: www.saha.org. za/apf/transitions_child_the_anti_privatisation_forum_apf_2.htm.

7. Throughout the late 1980s and first two years of the 1990s, the ANC had consistently kept to it's 'line' that, once in power, it would nationalise key sectors of the economy, set about a radical redistribution of land and wealth, and ensure that the black working class became the main 'driver'/controller of a 'people's' state dedicated to popular/participatory democracy. The ANC's adoption in 1994 of the social-democratic Reconstruction and Development Programme (RDP) as its electoral platform served to further fuel such expectations. For a detailed exposition of the 'fundamentals' of the RDP, see, National Institute for Economic Policy, 'From RDP to GEAR', Research Paper Series, Johannesburg: NIEP, 1996.

8. Richard Ballard, Adam Habib and Imraan Valodia, 'Social movements in South Africa: Promoting crisis or creating stability?', in Vishnu Padayachee (ed.), *The Development Decade? Economic and Social Change in South Africa 1994–2004*, Cape Town, HSRC Press, 2006, p. 397.

9. See Dale T. McKinley, *The ANC and the Liberation Struggle: A Critical Political Biography*, London: Pluto Press, 1997.

10. Ballard et al., 'Social movements in South Africa', p. 397.

11. Stephen Greenberg and Nhlanhla Ndlovu, 'Civil society relationships', in *Development Update*, Vol. 5, No. 2 (2004), pp. 32–3.

12. For an overview since 1994 of the varying contents and consequences flowing from this reality, see Dale T. McKinley, 'The Congress of South African Trade Unions and the Tripartite Alliance since 1994', in Tom Bramble and Franco Barchiesi (eds), *Rethinking the Labour Movement in the 'New' South Africa*, Aldershot: Ashgate, 2003, pp. 43–61.

13. Such arguments have been vigorously proffered by successive leaders of both COSATU and the SACP ever since the early 1990s. While references are far too numerous to list here, most of the key documents/speeches that have been made public over the last ten years or so can be found on the respective websites of the two organisations: www.cosatu.org.za and www.sacp.org.za.

14. This acceptance has not been without its vocal critics within both COSATU and the SACP. For a detailed treatment of debate and opposition within the Alliance over the first few years of the post-1994 period, see Dale T. McKinley, 'Democracy, power and patronage: Debate and opposition within the ANC and Tripartite Alliance since 1994', in Roger Southall (ed.), *Opposition and Democracy in South Africa*, London: Frank Cass, 2001, pp. 183–206.

15. Wilson Johwa, 'ANC admits party racked by bribery, vote-buying', *Business Day*, 5 August 2010.

16. The 'construction' of this 'left political game' is not something that simply appeared after the 1994 democratic breakthrough but has a historic basis in

the construction and sustenance of the ANC-led Alliance itself. For a detailed critical treatment of this history, see Chapters 2 and 6 in Dale T. McKinley, *The ANC and the Liberation Struggle: A Critical Political Biography*, London: Pluto Press, 1997, pp. 25–40 and 103–27.

17. In 1945 the then ANC president, Dr A. B. Xuma, stated: 'it is of less importance to us whether capitalism is smashed or not. It is of greater importance to us that while capitalism exists, we must fight and struggle to get our full share and benefit from the system.' Cited in Robert Fine and Denis Davis, *Beyond Apartheid: Labour and Liberation in South Africa*, Johannesburg: Ravan Press, 1990, p. 52.

18. COSATU, 'Address by the general secretary to the Civil Society Conference', Johannesburg, 27 October 2010.

19. See David McDonald, *The Bell Tolls for Thee: Cost Recovery, Cut offs, and the Affordability of Municipal Services in South Africa: Special Report of the Municipal Services Project*, 2000, www.queensu.ca/msp/.

20. See David McDonald and Laïla Smith, 'Privatizing Cape Town', Occasional Papers, No. 7, Johannesburg: Municipal Services Project, 2003. See also Edward Cottle, 'The failure of sanitation and water delivery and the cholera outbreak', *Development Update*, Vol. 4, No. 1 (2003).

21. Some of the main/key movements and organisations born out of this period include the Concerned Citizens Forum in Durban (which no longer exists, but which spawned numerous community organisations that remain active); the Anti-Privatisation Forum in Johannesburg (one of South Africa's most enduring social movements for over ten years, but which has weakened considerably since 2010); the Landless People's Movement (a national movement that went through a divisive 'split' with its original NGO partner – the National Land Committee – and has since weakened, but remains active in some rural and peri-urban areas); Jubilee South Africa (a national movement centred around debt, reparations and social justice struggles/issues, but which also experienced a split in its ranks in 2005/06 that has since resulted in the existence of both Jubilee South Africa and a new formation – Umzabalazo we Jubilee); the Anti-Eviction Campaign based in Cape Town; and Abahlali base Mjondolo (a movement of shack dwellers mainly in/around Durban, which has begun to link up to other shack dweller organisations in other parts of the country)

22. There are many examples of this over the last several years, with the latest being COSATU's (alongside the Treatment Action Campaign (TAC)) and the SACP's public attacks on the 2010 campaign of road blockades around housing issues led by Abahlali (Western Cape). COSATU/TAC called for left forces to 'reject Abahlali's campaign of violence and chaos' while the SACP labelled Abahlali's actions as 'anarchy and reactionary'.

23. The most public expressions of the ANC's evident contempt for the new movements and their struggles was its statement in 2002 accusing them of being 'ultra left ... waging a counter-revolutionary struggle against the ANC and our democratic government' and of siding with the 'bourgeoisie and its supporters'. See ANC, 'Contribution to the NEC/NWC response to the Cronin interviews on the issue of neo-liberalism', internal ANC paper by the Political Education Unit, September 2002. President Mbeki waded in soon thereafter by claiming publicly that 'this ultra-left works to implant itself within our ranks ... it hopes to capture control of our movement and transform it into an instrument for the realisation of its objectives'. See Thabo Mbeki, 'Statement

of the president of the ANC, Thabo Mbeki, at the ANC Policy Conference', Kempton Park, 20 September, 2002, www.anc.org.za/docs. Since the World Summit on Sustainable Development in 2002, hundreds of community and social movement activists have been arrested and jailed, many injured and several tortured. See, for example, Dale T. McKinley and Ahmed Veriava, *Arresting Dissent: State Repression and Post-apartheid Social Movements*, Johannesburg: Centre for the Study of Violence and Reconciliation, 2005; Freedom of Expression Institute, 'FXI welcomes commencement of trial in Landless People's Movement torture case', press statement, 24 August 2005. In most cases, it has been a combination of the state's coercive forces alongside local/provincial ANC leaders/structures that have been at the forefront of the violent attacks.

24. For a more detailed exposition of this argument as applied earlier on in the development of the 'new' social movements, see John Apollis, 'The political significance of August 31st', *Khanya*, No. 2 (December 2002), pp. 5–9.

25. The two 'big events' referred to are the 2001 World Conference against Racism held in Durban and the 2002 World Summit on Sustainable Development (WSSD) held in Johannesburg. At both of these events, the new movements 'emerged' publicly in collective numbers and strength – especially at the WSSD, where a march of up to 25,000 people (eclipsing by a substantial margin a parallel march by the Alliance left) signalled the 'arrival' of the new movements as a potential challenge to the 'traditional left'. For an extended critical analysis of the WSSD and the role of the ANC state's attempts to repress opposition to it, see Patrick Bond, 'The Word Summit on Sustainable Development: Critiques from the left', paper presented to the University of Pretoria Department of Sociology, 18 July 2002.

26. Dale McKinley, 'South Africa's social conservatism: A real and present danger', South African Civil Society Information Service, March 2010, http://sacsis.org.za/site/article/440.1.

27. Dale T. McKinley, 'Xenophobia and nationalism: Exposing the South African state for what it is', *Khanya*, Special Edition No. 19 (July 2008), pp. 22–4.

28. More recently, some independent left academics, activists and community organisations/social movements have come together to form the Democratic Left Front in an attempt to forge a more inclusive, 'red-green' and national-level left force. While this initiative must be welcomed, it remains far too early to assess whether or not it will simply reproduce the same prefigured/vanguardist and electorally located politics or become a harbinger for the kind of strategic reorientation needed to usher in a new 'left' politics.

29. These and other arguments are contained in a paper I presented to the 2008 COSATU National Political Education School entitled 'Towards a socialist strategy and left unity in South Africa'.

3
Voice, Political Mobilisation and Repression under Jacob Zuma

Jane Duncan

INTRODUCTION: THE LISTENING PRESIDENT

In their study on social movements, Donatella della Porta and Mario Diani advance the theoretical proposition that the greater the number of points of access to a decision-making system, the more open the system is, and the more open political and social movements are to moderating their actions and using institutional channels.[1] The extent to which a system is open or closed has been a central concern of political opportunity or political process perspectives,[2] as these contextual factors may create opportunities for or set limits on the ability of these movements to make and win demands.[3] According to Sidney Tarrow, the components of the political opportunity structure include the degree of access to political institutions, the degree of stability or instability in political alignments, the availability and strategic posture of potential allies, and the extent of political conflict among and within the elite.[4] McAdam has gone further and identifies the following factors as being crucial to the conception of political opportunities: increasing popular access to the system, the existence of divisions within the elite, the availability of elite allies and diminishing state repression.[5]

Open systems also adopt more tolerant attitudes towards dissent, including the regulation and policing of protest. In this regard, della Porta notes changes in protest policing since the 1960s, with policing styles shifting away from enforcement of the law to keeping the peace, and from 'crowd control' to 'crowd management'.[6] More tolerant forms of policing, he argues, allows antagonists to engage in bargaining, which in turn encourages institutionalisation, as bargaining locks them into agreed courses of action. However, he also cautions that a more open system does not necessarily make for greater responsiveness to movement demands, as open systems are open to all, including movement opponents. With the advent of democracy in South Africa, policing, including the policing of protests, was in theory brought into line with international policing standards.

However, during the Thabo Mbeki administration, there were signs of some of these democratic advances being reversed. This administration stands accused of centralising power and reacting with great hostility towards those whom Mbeki considered to be his political enemies. Independent social movements were subject to covert and overt forms of repression, with the prohibition of gatherings, coupled with police violence against protesters, becoming more apparent.[7] The coming to power of President Jacob Zuma in 2009 promised to usher in a more open system, particularly for workers, the underemployed and the unemployed who had been marginalised by Mbeki's '1996 class project'.[8] Certainly, early in Zuma's presidency, there were signs that his administration was serious about creating more points of access to the system, thereby de-escalating conflicts around public participation and service delivery questions, many of which had spilled over into protests. The shift in power in the African National Congress (ANC) also supposedly opened up more political space for policy debates that did not exist previously – and for greater influence by the ANC's Tripartite Alliance partners, the Congress of South African Trade Unions (COSATU) and the South African Communist Party (SACP), although Adam Habib maintains that the tent-pole of the Mbeki administration – economic policy – was unlikely to change.[9]

The Mbeki administration also stands accused of having marginalised the ANC's other Alliance partners and even subordinating the party to the government.[10] Since Zuma's ascent to power at the ANC's 2007 Polokwane conference, official SACP documents have been at pains to project Polokwane as a major step forward for revolutionary forces in the Alliance, in that it supposedly opened up spaces for a radicalisation of the National Democratic Revolution (NDR) and a reinstatement of the ANC's control over government.[11]

Has the Zuma administration lived up to its original promise by ushering in a political opportunity structure that is more conducive to popular participation than it was under Mbeki? This chapter uses a series of case studies to explore this question, including the struggles against the unilateral reincorporation of municipalities into other provinces (in which members of the SACP played a prominent role), an examination of the Zuma administration's approach to dissent in the South African National Defence Force

(SANDF), and dissent in the build-up to and in relation to the 2010 FIFA World Cup.

ANTI-INCORPORATION STRUGGLES AND THE STATE OF DISSENT IN THE ALLIANCE

The event that put the episode of contention around the unilateral reincorporation of municipalities into motion occurred in 2005, when Parliament passed legislation to abolish cross-border municipalities by adjusting provincial boundaries to incorporate the affected areas into a single province. According to the Ministry of Justice, cross-border municipalities performed sub-optimally, mainly because different provincial laws applied for similar functions.[12] This move met with significant opposition in some municipalities, notably Khutsong (located in the Merafong City local municipality, Gauteng, but incorporated into the North-West Province), Matatiele[13] (located in KwaZulu-Natal, but relocated to the Eastern Cape) and Moutse (located in Mpumalanga, but relocated to Limpopo). Other townships hit by demarcation disputes include Siyathemba (in Balfour), which fell into Gauteng, but now falls into Mpumalanga; and Baga Mothibi, which fell into the Northern Cape, but now falls into the North-West. In all these areas, significant numbers of residents wanted to be returned to their original provinces.

Many residents considered the unilateral incorporation of the affected municipalities into different provinces to be the ultimate insult in a democracy, as decisions about their location that had profound implications for their ability to access government and services were simply imposed on them; small wonder that Trevor Ngwane has termed these unilateral reincorporations 'a kind of forced removal by pencil'.[14] The reasons for the resistance to these imposed changes were similar in all these areas, namely, unhappiness with levels of service delivery in the provinces into which the areas were relocated and concerns about the distances involved in accessing provincial services from these provinces. Residents also complained about the government's failure to consult with them over its decision to relocate the affected municipalities.[15] The SACP and its youth wing, the Young Communist League, played a key role in these struggles.[16]

The mass resistance to incorporation in Khutsong was fierce and included a local government election boycott, school boycotts and the barricading of streets, and at times the struggle became violent, shops were looted and official buildings burnt down. Protesters also burnt their ANC membership cards and T-shirts bearing Mbeki's picture.[17] After this long and bitter struggle, the ANC eventually conceded to residents' demands and returned the area to Gauteng Province.

Significantly, the ANC did not concede Matatiele and Moutse, although views-testing exercises were conducted in both areas, and according to the SACP secretary in Moutse, Seun Mogotji, and COSATU and SACP member Zamecibo Mjobe, the majority of those who voted favoured reincorporation back into their original provinces.[18] Mothiba Ramphisa, the chairperson of the Moutse Dermarcation Forum, also suggested that the ANC's lack of seriousness on the Moutse question was because 'Khutsong was burning more than Moutse and Matatiele'; furthermore, the areas are rural, while Khutsong is more urbanised, and the ANC's decision betrayed an urban bias.[19] Mjobe and Mogotji alleged that local politicians and businesspeople had developed vested interests in remaining in their new provinces, leading to pressure on the ANC leadership to let the status quo remain: according to Mogotji, 'the politics of the moment is the politics of the stomach, not the politics of principle'.[20]

The ability of protesters to trigger a search for new policy is also an indicator of the openness and responsiveness of the political opportunity structure.[21] The demarcation struggles triggered a search for policy alternatives by the ANC under Zuma, as the shift in power in the ANC created political opportunities for a reconsideration of the matter. Shortly before the 2009 national elections the government engaged in consultations with affected communities and a cabinet statement at the time noted that further consultation was needed to make a final decision on the matter.[22]

Zuma's ascent to power also impacted on relationships between protesters and the police in some of the affected areas. According to Mjobe:

Before [Polokwane] they [the Eastern Cape police] were harassing people, and as they were beating ordinary people like hawkers, so the police took sides, but as we continued with our struggle, our mass actions were never violent up to the present moment. The police do understand. They were sent to harass … and intimidate people so that they will be less visible in these actions, but we have been making follow-up on incidents where people have been beaten and killed. In 2006 to 2008 there were sporadic occasions where ... police who have been planted to control borders were also harassing people in town and villages. We are now interrogating them ... and cases are fading away day by day. Police ... in this Zuma era do not feel the same the way that they did under Mbeki. The SACP and COSATU are in the Alliance, and the police are members of POPCRU [Police and Prisons Civil Rights Union], and are COSATU shop stewards. Zuma is a person who is regarded as having a class bias [towards the working class] and they [the Zuma administration] do this kind of education to them [the police].[23]

Mjobe felt that the Zuma administration has been more open and responsive on the demarcation disputes, which became evident when the 2007 Polokwane conference reopened the matter and directed the ANC to find a political solution to the disputes; this resolution has opened political spaces that did not exist during Mbeki's term of office. However, Mjobe expressed concern at the amount of time being taken to release the results of the views-testing exercise, noting that 'people are asking, is this another Zimbabwe?'[24]

In a more recent struggle, the Baga Mothibi community has also chosen the non-violent direct action route, combined with making submissions to formal structures like the Municipal Demarcation Board. SACP activist Masego Khumalo described this mode of resistance as the 'civilised route', which he felt was the most appropriate technique of protest for a 'listening government'.[25] Moutse's struggle has been waged in various ways using at various stages negotiating strategies, a Constitutional Court challenge and direct action (violent and non-violent). Unlike in the other areas, eleven SACP members in Moutse decided to run as independent candidates in the 2006 local government elections, including Mothiba Ramphisa, who mobilised the community to resist the reincorporation. At the time, the SACP's Limpopo branch threatened to terminate the membership of all who opted to stand as independent candidates, because their stance conflicted with the SACP's decision to support the ANC in the elections.[26]

The ANC won the ward that Ramphisa contested in 2006 (Ward 7 in Greater Groblersdal), and the next year the SACP in Moutse supported Mbeki's replacement by Zuma. But in a significant turnaround of sentiment on the part of the community in the by-election held in May 2010, Ramphisa ran against the ANC councillor and won the ward, indicating that the ANC was rapidly losing electoral support owing to its failure to resolve the Moutse situation. The ANC subsequently expelled Ramphisa as a member, sending him a letter of expulsion in June without even calling him to a disciplinary hearing. However, in spite of its earlier threats to expel independent candidates, the SACP has 'managed to close one eye and look with the other eye',[27] suggesting that the party had recognised that mass support for the anti-incorporation struggles had contributed significantly to its growth in support in the affected areas[28] and that it would be shooting itself in the foot by alienating this support.

The police's conduct in the Moutse struggle confirms the Matatiele experience that when the police are external to a community and its struggles, then the chances of them being manipulated politically are higher. The SACP in Moutse has alleged a spate of assaults, and cases of intimidation, harassment and wrongful arrests by the Limpopo police 'aimed at members of the community who hold different political views than those of police officials'.[29] SACP district secretary Seun Mogotji has been arrested several times for inciting public violence, but these cases have been dropped. He claims that he has been denied bail for no good reason. According to Mogotji, '[t]he police punish before they prosecute. This is becoming a police state. If the government must be criticised, they must be criticised within the framework of the government. Illiterate people are being brainwashed.'[30] Unlike Mjobe, Mogotji felt that the police had become even more authoritarian under the Zuma administration. He attributed this growing authoritarianism in the South African Police Service (SAPS) to the ANC Youth League backgrounds of Minister of Police Nathi Mthetwa and the then Deputy Minister of Police, Fikile Mbalula, and to the League's hostility to the SACP.[31] Ramphisa noted that the most violent police came from outside the Moutse area.[32]

For the SACP in Moutse, formal negotiations with the ANC have not yet yielded fruit. With respect to Balfour, the ANC responded speedily when the first protests, which turned violent, took place in 2009. Another wave of protests swept across Balfour in February 2010.[33] In the wake of the protests, Deputy Minister Malusi Gigaba held a series of meetings in Balfour to discuss the community's grievances, followed by a surprise visit by Zuma.[34] But the demarcation disputes still remain unresolved.

Since the ANC conceded Khutsong, the activists interviewed have adopted a tactical rather than a principled stance towards the use of violence if the Zuma administration does not accede to their demands. According to Khumalo:

Our route has been to follow procedure. We have never had any violence. People who get into a march and start to do these things [violent acts], we then call the police if they do these things, but in future we won't stop people from going this route. The government will listen only when tyres and councillors' houses are burnt. [They] have fooled us into believing that this is a government that listens. The civilised route has not worked. People only listen when we burn tyres.[35]

According to the SACP in Matatiele, many are bitter about the fact that the ANC has conceded Khutsong, where residents used violence to achieve their objectives, while Matatiele, which has used non-violent means, has been ignored. Mjobe stated, '[t]he nature of our struggle being non-violent is being taken advantage of. [The] people of Matatiele will have to choose whatever strategy we need to get our way. We are capable of being violent, but have decided to use the correct legal means.'[36] But more radical forms of direct action are not the only strategies being pursued. SACP activists in Moutse formed a political party, called the Mpumalanga Party, which fielded independent candidates during the 2011 local government elections. According to Ramphisa, party members were willing to risk dismissal from the party, because 'the movement must listen to the people'.[37]

Within the realm of contentious politics, McAdam et al. have drawn a distinction between contained contention and transgressive contention: the former refers to those cases of contention in which actors use well-established means of claim making, while the latter consists of episodic, public, collective interaction between claim makers and decision makers where innovative collective action is used, adopting means that are either unprecedented or forbidden in terms of the existing rules of engagement.[38] Khutsong, Matatiele and Moutse all attempted contained contention at first, using litigation to have the unilateral decision to incorporate the areas into different provinces reversed, but apart from an initial victory in the case of Matatiele, the Constitutional Court indicated its preference for a political solution to the problem, which has thrown the ball back into the court of political contention. However, a political solution has not yet been forthcoming. This has been a key factor in the escalation of protest action, and increasingly the activists leading these struggles have become sceptical about the possibility of non-violent protest action yielding the necessary results, signalling a shift in approach away from contained contention and towards transgressive contention. The Khutsong victory has raised expectations by protesters that their efforts will yield the desired results if the struggle is pursued 'by any means necessary', which in turn will encourage them to escalate their protests.[39]

What is clear from the above account is that these struggles are escalating and are nowhere near the top of their cycle. The communities affected by demarcation disputes are highly mobilised. Furthermore, protest action in the affected areas is being radicalised and a strong sense has developed that more conventional forms of protest do not work, but there is no evidence of a revolutionary break with ANC politics. However, one major variable is the SACP leadership's likely response to the growing tensions between the party's own grassroots constituency and the ANC. If the SACP does not bow to ANC pressure and put a lid on these struggles, then the activists may be emboldened to leave the SACP and part ways with the Alliance, which in turn could open up space for more independent socialist politics. The demarcation struggles give an insight into the complex world of inter-Alliance politics, and specifically whether spaces for dissent within the Alliance have widened or narrowed under the Zuma administration.

RISE OF THE BLANKET BAN ON PROTESTS

Gatherings in South Africa are regulated in terms of the Regulation of Gatherings Act, which requires groups of 16 or more people who wish to hold a public gathering to notify the relevant local authority of their intention to do so. While SAPS must be consulted about gatherings, final decision making rests with the local authority. Furthermore, it is also clear that prohibitions must be preceded by a procedure set out in the Act, which involves negotiations with the convenor on likely threats to public safety and disruption of vehicular traffic. There is no provision in the Act for a blanket ban on gatherings; each case must be taken on its individual merits.

Yet in spite of clear conditions under which the right to assembly, demonstration and picket can be limited and even suspended, under the Zuma administration evidence has emerged of blanket bans in the run-up to and during the FIFA World Cup, which was hosted by South Africa from 11 June to 11 July 2010. Before the event, the South African government was particularly concerned about its international image in the wake of xenophobic attacks, service delivery protests and ongoing reports about crime, which raised question marks about the country's stability.[40] These events precipitated government attempts to project an image of stability in the country by preventing protest action through a series of unlawful blanket bans on the right to protest.

The one incident that caused particular concern in spin-doctor circles as it was beamed across the globe, involved members of the South African National Defence Union (SANDU), which organises soldiers in the SANDF, who had notified the Pretoria City Council of their intention to march to the seat of government at the Union Buildings in Pretoria on 26 August 2009. The protesters intended to hand a memorandum to Zuma, who is also commander-in-chief of the armed forces, about working conditions in the military. Under apartheid, unions were banned in the military, but SANDU petitioned the Constitutional Court in 1999 to have the section of the Act that banned unions declared unconstitutional. It won the case, and with it recognition that military personnel have a right to organise into trade unions and engage in acts of public protest.[41] However, by March 2008 relations between the unions and the Department of Defence had broken down and morale among the majority of soldiers was reportedly very low.[42] By July 2008 SANDU's patience had reached breaking point and it threatened an armed siege of the military's headquarters if its demands were not met. This long history of frustration led to the march on the Union Buildings in August 2009.

The march was prohibited by the Pretoria metro police after it was initially approved, and an application by the union to the North Gauteng High Court to compel the SANDF to grant its members leave to attend the march was dismissed on the basis that the police's u-turn on authorisation made the SANDU application moot. It is important to note that the merits of the police's prohibition were not canvassed in the court proceedings, which was unfortunate because – according to the SANDU general secretary, Pikkie Greef – the grounds for prohibition were questionable.[43] According to the official version of events, the march turned violent when some protesters stormed the lawns of the Union Building by scaling the perimeter fence. These actions led to pitched battles between protesters and the police.[44] The government's reaction was swift. Minister of Defence Lindiwe Sisulu condemned the involvement of SANDF members in an illegal march and dismissed the soldiers thought to have taken part in the march, but the dismissal was later overturned on appeal.[45]

The union's version of events differs in significant ways from the official account, as it maintains that there was, in fact, no march.

Soldiers arrived in the morning assuming that the march was going ahead and were then told that it had been prohibited. As Greef attempted to inform the crowd, a protester threw a stone at the Casspir (an armoured vehicle used by police) on which he was standing, which triggered a violent reaction by the police. According to Greef, police then cornered some soldiers in an enclosure in the grounds of the Union Buildings and shot them at point-blank range with rubber bullets. The soldiers scaled the perimeter fence to escape; so they were not trying to climb into the Union Buildings grounds, but to climb out. The presidency then used the 'march' as a pretext to ban all marches to the Union Buildings, although it subsequently denied the existence of such ban.[46]

Further marches by military personnel were also banned, which implied that a de facto ban on marches by military personnel was in force.[47] In the aftermath of the Union Buildings protest, the ANC National Executive Committee took a decision that the military must be deunionised in the interests of national security, in spite of the 1999 Constitutional Court ruling, and it has also indicated that it may seek a constitutional amendment preventing the unionisation of the military.

Military personnel are not the only ones to have experienced a blanket ban on protests. In February and March 2010, protests erupted in Gauteng, especially in Orange Farm, south of Johannesburg; in Sebokeng and Sharpeville in the Vaal area; and in Mamelodi and Soshanguve in Tshwane. In Orange Farm, protesters burned tyres, pelted the police with stones and blocked the Golden Highway with rocks.[48] In Sebokeng, residents marched over poor service delivery, barricading roads and the railway line,[49] and similar incidents repeated themselves throughout Gauteng. In March, evidence surfaced of a blanket ban on marches in Gauteng. The Concerned Residents of Sharpeville notified the Emfuleni local municipality of its intention to stage a demonstration on 12 March 2010. In response, the chief of traffic and security responded: 'The MEC [member of the executive council] for Gauteng Community Safety, has instructed that no permission for marches in Gauteng should be granted until further notice. This instruction is given by the MEC due to the volatile situation in the townships.'[50] Then in April a march planned by the Public and Allied Workers' Union of South Africa in Vanderbijl Park for 5 May was banned. In spite of the fact that the Vaal was off the beaten track in relation to the World Cup, the banning took place in response to a directive sent on April 29 by the Sebokeng SAPS Cluster to the station commanders of all police stations in the cluster, which reads as follows: 'By the directive of the Sebokeng Cluster, Major General DS de Lange, you are hereby informed that no authorization must be given for marches until the end of the World Cup 2010.'[51] This directive was issued despite the fact that no provision exists in the Regulation of Gatherings Act for SAPS to usurp the decision-making powers of local authorities around gatherings and none exists for a blanket ban on gatherings.

Then in May more evidence emerged of a directive having been issued by SAPS to a number of municipalities not to allow marches for the duration of the 2010 World Cup. This ban came to light when a civil society march for quality public education, scheduled to take place on 10 June to Constitution Hill in Braamfontein, was banned.[52] In a telephonic survey of the municipalities hosting World Cup matches, most revealed that a blanket ban on gatherings was in force for the duration of the tournament. According to the Rustenberg municipality, 'gatherings are closed for the World Cup'. SAPS told the Mbombela municipality that it was not going to allow gatherings during the World Cup. The Cape Town City Council claimed that it continued to accept applications for marches, but indicated that it 'may be a problem' during the World Cup period. According to the Nelson Mandela Bay, Ethekwini and Mangaung municipalities, the police would not allow gatherings over the World Cup period. The Polokwane municipality indicated that it was unlikely to approve gatherings during the World Cup.[53] According to Johannesburg metro police, the police did not have the capacity to regulate marches and the World Cup simultaneously.

SAPS's attempt to usurp municipalities' decision making about gatherings implied that protest action over the World Cup period was seen as a national security threat rather than a traffic management concern. SAPS's usurpation of local authorities' role in relation to gatherings needs to be set in a larger context. There are signs that the Zuma administration is rethinking SAPS's identity and even its very role in society. In 2009 the then Deputy Minister of Police, Fikile Mbalula, said that he wanted the police transformed into a paramilitary force with military ranks and discipline, which effectively meant a reversion to an apartheid-era conceptualisation of the police, and the Minister of Police, Nathi Mthethwa, argued to cabinet that the reintroduction of military ranks would herald a return of discipline and 'command and control' aspects that 'flew out of the window' when the police demilitarised at the end of apartheid.[54] Then in April 2010 the government announced that it intended to introduce a military ranking system into the police and revert to the apartheid-era name of the South African Police Force, signalling a deeper intent to bring back the culture of military discipline that existed under apartheid. According to Minister Mthetwa, this shift was informed by a new seriousness in fighting crime and should be accompanied by changes in 'attitude, thinking and operational duties' on the part of the police. The shift was also accompanied by attempts to amend the Criminal Procedures Act to enhance the police's power to use lethal force when arresting suspected criminals. Cabinet approved these amendments in September 2010.[55]

This shift is dangerous, because it threatens to reverse some of the transformation gains where the police's role was reconceptualised as being an accessible service to the community rather than being enforcers of discipline, aloof from the community they claimed to serve.[56] The dangers of this approach have been pointed out by the COSATU-affiliated POPCRU, which claimed that it had not been consulted about the change. The union opposed the militarisation of the police on the grounds that it promotes the perception that the police are a military by another name. A military culture, it argued, fostered a policing culture where lower-ranking officers were required to follow orders blindly, even if the orders were not in the interests of the community they claimed to serve, which could quickly lead to a culture of brutalisation, whereas a culture of empathetic and locally rooted policing was much more appropriate.[57] The accounts of the anti-incorporation activists in Moutse, Matatiele and Baga Mothibi related earlier in this chapter point to the benefits of a locally rooted police force and the tendency towards brutality of those police not rooted in the communities they police. If the militarisation of the police fuels alienation from communities, then police brutality against activists could intensify too.

CONCLUSION: THE JANUS FACE OF THE ZUMA ADMINISTRATION

What is the democratic content of Jacob Zuma's rule? Has he distinguished himself from the Mbeki administration by creating more political opportunities for grievances to be heard and responded to? With respect to the anti-incorporation protests, a clear shift in the political opportunity structure has been created by the political conflict within the ruling elite and Zuma winning the upper hand. Under Mbeki's watch, a non-negotiable decision was imposed on the abolition of cross-border municipalities – one that the 'new' ANC has demonstrated willingness to review.

There is evidence of some police brutality in the anti-incorporation protests, but the most tolerant forms of policing occur when there is police knowledge about the conditions that have given rise to the protests and a dynamic variable in the political opportunity structure, because it concerns police perception of external reality.[58] In contrast, police who are not unionised or who are external to the communities they police appear to be more open to political manipulation by pro-incorporation elements in the ANC and also exhibit more violent behaviour.

However, there is no clear indication yet that these political opportunities are yielding fruit. As Eisinger points out, formal political structures may exist for wielding influence, but if the political system is not responsive to the demands made, then the structure cannot be said to be a fully open one.[59] While the Zuma administration is listening to protesters, there is no evidence yet that it is hearing what they have to say. Activists are starting to suspect that the newly created points of access to the decision-making system may be designed to deflect oppositional voices rather than consider their demands seriously.

The Zuma administration fares less well with regard to protecting the labour and civil rights of the military. In an eerie echo of the past, it has demonstrated the sort of repressive attitude that characterised the Mbeki administration towards protests in the Vaal and threatened protests during the 2010 World Cup. The Zuma administration seems to be even more intolerant of basic rights in the military than the Mbeki administration, leading to an escalation of conflict to the point where the military has become a pressure cooker of frustration waiting to blow. The ANC's intention to deunionise the military, coupled with grievances being deflected into a structure controlled by the minister, carries significant risks for the party. Repressive responses to protests on the part of the state can have one of two effects: they can discourage protest action or they can lead to an escalation of protest action. The latter is more likely to occur when attempts are made by the state to shut down legal avenues for protest),[60] resulting in 'injustice frames' developing around the actions of the state. The risk that the ANC faces in pursuing its intention to close down the few democratic spaces that exist in the military is instability – and possible mutiny – in the SANDF.

The Zuma administration is showing growing signs of an obsession with the need to protect national security, which suggests that the security cluster occupies a central place in the administration and that tight control of this cluster is a priority. A twin process appears to be taking place in the security cluster, where the police are militarised, while the military is subject to increasingly tight forms of control: both suggest a de-democratisation of the few democratic spaces that do exist in the security cluster and that are essential to check any attempts at overt political manipulation of this cluster. A combination of these factors increases the chances of the sorts of abuse of security apparatuses that occurred under Mbeki.[61]

How does one explain the paradox of a political administration characterised by a combination of increasing openness and growing repression? A recurring argument in political process theory is that a curvilinear relationship exists between protest and the political opportunity structure; that is, protest occurs when systems are moderately repressive, but still fairly open. This is because claimants are not strong enough to win their claims through more conventional means, but neither are they repressed to the point where they cannot make claims at all. Conversely, protest tapers off when systems become either more open or more closed.[62] Yet a polity that provides openness to one kind of participation may be closed to others.[63] Furthermore, protests are more likely to occur in a system that is opening up and becoming more responsive to demands, as protesters come to the realisation that the system may be vulnerable to challenge, but may become impatient with the pace of change. Put more precisely, moderately repressive political systems allow for the broad articulation of demands, but do not accede readily to them.[64]

Regan and Henderson argue that the extent of repression is determined by the nature of the threat the government is facing rather than the type of regime and that semi-democracies are more likely to face serious threats, especially if the threat is potentially destabilising. If the threat is not viewed in this way, repression is unlikely. Non-threatening demands are those that are channelled into the formal debate with relative ease. But generally, in semi-democracies, the institutional infrastructure is usually not sufficiently developed to effectively channel the demands of opposition into the political arena.[65] These arguments suggest that states that lie 'in the middle' of the democracy spectrum are more likely to experience protests, but they are more likely to experience repression too.

These theoretical insights are useful in explaining why the South African government responded with more openness towards the anti-incorporation struggles and yet with such hostility to the military's attempts to retain basic labour rights and democratic practices, and to the threat of protest during the World Cup: the Zuma administration's responses are shaped by the nature of the threat to its continued existence. While the anti-incorporation protests could be considered 'friendly fire', threats to the centralisation of power in the security cluster would strike at the heart of Zuma's power base, hence the need to institutionalise his administration's hegemony over this cluster. However, there is a strong possibility that the government will become a great deal less tolerant of the anti-incorporation struggles if the struggles escalate and demonstrators begin to compete for formal political power. Threats will amplify as the state is increasingly unable to cater for its citizens,[66] and as more people realise that Zuma's purported openness is not changing lives, protests may well escalate and the extent of the anger expressed in these protests may be in proportion to the degree of expectation that his 'regime change' created among ANC supporters. To the extent that these protests constitute a real threat to the current status quo, they may well experience the true repressive potential of Zuma's security cluster, and Mbeki's 'celebrated' intolerance may pale into insignificance.

NOTES

1. Donatella della Porta and Mario Diani, *Social Movements: An Introduction*, Oxford: Blackwell, 1999, p. 225.
2. For the purposes of this chapter, I use Kitshelt's definition of political opportunity structure as 'specific configurations of resources, institutional arrangements and historical precedents for social mobilisation, which facilitate the development of protest movements in some instances and constrain them in others'. See H. Kitshelt, 'Political opportunity structures and political protest: Anti-nucleur movements in four democracies', *British Journal of Political Studies*, No. 16 (1986), p. 58.
3. P. Eisinger, 'The conditions of protest behaviour in American cities', *American Political Science Review*, Vol. 67, No. 1 (1973), pp. 11–12; Kitshelt, 'Political opportunity structures'.
4. Sidney Tarrow in Donatella della Porta, 'The policing of protest', *African Studies*, Vol. 56, No. 1 (1997), p. 98.
5. D. McAdam, 'Political opportunities: Conceptual origins, current problems, future directions', in D. McAdam, S. Tarrow and C. Tilly, *Dynamics of Contention*, Cambridge: Cambridge University Press, 2001, pp. 23–40.
6. Della Porta, 'The policing of protest'; see also Della Porta and Diani, *Social Movements*; D. Meyer, 'The South African experience in dealing with communal violence', *African Security Review*, Vol. 8, No. 1 (1999); B. Omar, 'Crowd control: Can our public order police still deliver?', *SA Crime Quarterly*, No. 15 (March 2006), p. 8; B. Omar, *SAPS's Costly Restructuring: A Review of*

Public Order Policing Capacity, Institute for Security Studies Monograph, No. 138, Pretoria: ISS, October 2007.

7. Jane Duncan, 'Thabo Mbeki and dissent', in D. Glaser (ed.), *Thabo Mbeki's World*, Johannesburg: Wits University Press, 2010, pp. 105–27.

8. According to the general secretary of the SACP, Blade Nzimande, 'since 1996 (perhaps even prior to that) a particular **class project** has consolidated itself and has become dominant in our movement and the state, spreading its influence to other layers of society, including sections of the media. This class project is a combination of certain objective processes of class formation in a democratic South Africa, and of deliberate policy choices followed by the government and capital, especially since the adoption of GEAR [the Growth, Employment and Redistribution programme] in 1996. The central economic thrust of the class project has been to seek to restore capitalist profitability after the capitalist crises of the last 10 years of the apartheid era, as a basis for addressing the massive developmental challenges in our country.' See Blade Nzimande, 'The class question in consolidating the faultline in the National Democratic Revolution', *Umsebenzi Online*, Vol. 5, No. 57 (7 June 2006), p. 1, www.sacp.org.za/main.php?ID=1858 (accessed 2 November 2011).

9. Adam Habib, 'Is economic policy likely to change under Jacob Zuma?', Polity.org, www.polity.org.za/article/is-economic-policy-likely-to-change-under-jacob-zuma-2009-03-25, 25 March 2009 (accessed 4 November 2010); Adam Habib, 'Substantive uncertainty: South Africa's democracy becomes dynamic', *Pambazuka News*, 2009, www.pambazuka.org/en/category/features/55638/print (accessed 4 November 2010).

10. Duncan, 'Thabo Mbeki and dissent', pp. 108–10.

11. F. Tregenna and D. Masondo, 'Towards a new growth path', *African Communist* (September 2010), p. 1.

12. J. de Lange, 'The second reading: Constitution Twelfth Amendment Bill', National Assembly speech, 15 November 2005, www.justice.gov.za/m_speeches/sp2005/2005_11_15_secondreading.htm (accessed 4 November 2010).

13. It should be noted that members of the Matatiele community have disputed whether the municipality was in fact a cross-border municipality.

14. Trevor Ngwane, 'Ideologies, strategies and tactics of township protests', in B. Maharaj, P. Bond and A. Desai (eds), *Zuma's Own Goal: Losing South Africa's 'War on Poverty'*, Trenton: Africa World Press, 2010, p. 389.

15. J. Kirshner and C. Phokela, *Khutsong and Xenophobic Violence: Exploring the Case of the Dog that Didn't Bark*, research report commissioned by Atlantic Philanthropies, Johannesburg: Centre for Sociological Research, University of Johannesburg, 2010, p. 9.

16. Ibid., p. 10; S. Johnston and A. Bernstein, *Voices of Anger: Protest and Conflict in Two Municipalities*, Johannesburg: Centre for Development and Enterprise, 2007, p. 33.

17. Kirshner and Phokela, *Khutsong and Xenophobic Violence*, p. 8.

18. Telephone interviews with Seun Mogotji and Zamecibo Mjobe, 15 October and 21 October 2010, respectively.

19. Telephone interview with Mothiba Ramphisa, 20 October 2010. Ramphisa was a member of both the SACP and the ANC (see below), as well as being chairperson of the Moutse Dermarcation Forum, in which SACP members were active, but the forum was independent of the party and was a broad community front.

20. Interview with Mogotji.

21. Kitshelt, 'Political opportunity structures', p. 84.
22. J. Maseko, 'Transcript of post-cabinet briefing', 10 September 2009, www.gcis.gov.za/newsroom/releases/cabstate/2009/090909_transcript.htm (accessed 2 November 2011).
23. Interview with Mjobe.
24. Ibid.
25. Telephone interview with Masego Khumalo, 22 October 2010.
26. R. Tabane, 'Khutsong, my personal hell', *Mail & Guardian*, 24 February 2006, http://amadlandawonye.wikispaces.com/Khutsong,++Rapule+Tabane,+M+and+G,+plus+Mtshali,+Star (accessed 2 November 2011).
27. Interview with Ramphisa.
28. According to Ramphisa (ibid.), 'everyone has become a member of the SACP in the area'. Kirshner and Phokela cite a *Sunday Times* report claiming that Khutsong has the largest SACP branch in the country; see Kirshner and Phokela, *Khutsong and Xenophobic Violence*, p. 20.
29. Interview with Mogotji.
30. Ibid.
31. Ibid.
32. Ibid.; interview with Ramphisa.
33. South African Press Association, 'Zuma heckled in Balfour', 23 May 2010, www.politicsweb.co.za/politicsweb/view/politicsweb/en/page71627?oid=177544&sn=Detail (accessed 27 October 2010).
34. K. Keepile, 'The day the president came knocking', *Mail & Guardian*, 6 August 2009.
35. Interview with Khumalo.
36. Interview with Mjobe.
37. Interview with Ramphisa.
38. McAdam et al., *Dynamics of Contention*, p. 5.
39. What has been termed the 'value-expectancy model'; see S. Carey, 'Dynamic relationship between protest and repression', *Political Research Quarterly*, Vol. 59, No. 1 (March 2006), p. 3.
40. According to Municipal IQ, the peak year for protests was 2009, although the first half of 2010 saw more protests than in the whole of 2009, with Gauteng Province being the hardest hit. See Municipal IQ, 'Municipal IQ's updated protest hotspots', 13 April 2010, www.bvm.gov.za/bvmweb/images/News/1%20december%202010.pdf (accessed 2 November 2011).
41. L. Heinecken, 'Ban military unions, they're a threat to national security! So where to from here?', *Strategic Review for Southern Africa* (November 2009), http://findarticles.com/p/articles/mi_hb1402/is_2_31/ai_n55089500/ (accessed 3 November 2010).
42. Parliamentary Monitoring Group, 'South African National Defence Force Union grievances', minutes of the meeting of the Portfolio Committee on Defence and Military Veterans, 18 March 2008, www.pmg.org.za/report/20080318-south-african-national-defence-union-grievances (accessed 5 November 2010).
43. Telephone interview with Pikkie Greef, 27 October 2010.
44. *Mail & Guardian*, 'Soldiers' violent protest condemned', 27 August 2009, www.mg.co.za/article/2009-08-27-soldiers-violent-protest-condemned (accessed 27 August 2010).

45. J. Greef, 'Founding affidavit of Johannes George Greef, in the matter between SANDF Union and another and the Minister of Defence and others, 20 August 2009', pp. 15–16.

46. Equal Education, 'Presidency retracts ban on "protests" at Union Buildings', 2010, www.equaleducation.org.za/bday-march (accessed 28 October 2010).

47. Telephone interview with Charles Jacobs, South African Security Forces Union deputy president, 3 November 2010.

48. News24, 'Orange Farm protests continue', 23 February 2010, www.news24.com/printArticle.aspx?iframe&aid=7198309c-c141-44f9-8317-ec1eda996058&cid=1059 (accessed 28 October 2010).

49. Eyewitness News, 'Sebokeng residents take on local council', 1 March 2010, www.eyewitnessnews.co.za/articleprog.aspx?id=33680 (accessed 28 October 2010).

50. Letter from M. T. Mollo, chief: traffic and security, Emfuleni local municipality, to H. Mosesi, Concerned Residents of Sharpville, 11 March 2010.

51. Email from Major General D. S. de Lange to the station commanders of the Vanderbijlpark/Sebokeng/Evaton/Orange Farm/Ennerdale/Sharpeville/Boipatong/Barrage/Sebokeng Cluster on the authorisation of marches until the end of the FIFA World Cup, 29 April 2010.

52. D. MacFarlane and T. Harbour, 'Cops ban "education for all" march', *Mail & Guardian*, 28 May 2010, www.mg.co.za/article/2010-05-28-cops-ban-education-for-all-march (accessed 4 October 2010).

53. Author's conversations with the Metro police departments of the following municipalities: Mangaung, Polokwane, Nelson Mandela Bay, Cape Town, Mbombela, Rustenberg and eThekwini, 27–28 May 2010.

54. DefenceWeb 2009, 'Police to revert to military ranks from April', 26 February 2010, www.defenceweb.co.za/index.php?option=com_content&view=article&id=6889:222&catid=3:Civil%20Security&Itemid=113 (accessed 7 November 2010).

55. N. Bauer, 'Cabinet approves "shoot to kill" bill', AllAfrica.com, 16 September 2010, http://allafrica.com/stories/201009170380.html (accessed 6 November 2010).

56. J. Burger, 'Institutional schizophrenia and police militarisation', Institute for Security Studies, 2010, www.iss.co.za/iss_today.php?ID=1024 (accessed 5 November 2010); A. Faull and G. Newham, 'Has our police force gone full apartheid circle?', *The Star*, 10 April 2010.

57. POPCRU (Police and Prisons Civil Rights Union), 'Memorandum to the ANC on re-militarisation of SAPS', 30 April 2010, www.popcru.org.za/press%20statements_10_memorandum.html (accessed 4 November 2010).

58. Della Porta, 'The policing of protest', p. 116.

59. Eisinger, 'The conditions of protest behaviour', p. 21.

60. K. Opp and W. Roehl, 'Repression, micromobilization and political protest', *Social Forces*, Vol. 69, No. 2 (1990), pp. 521–47, particularly p. 527. For a detailed discussion on the police repression of protest activity in South Africa, see M. C. Dawson, 'Resistance and repression: Policing protest in post-apartheid South Africa', in J. Handmaker and R. Berkhout (eds), *Mobilising Social Justice in South Africa: Perspectives from Researchers and Practitioners*, The Hague: ISS and Hivos, 2010, pp. 101–36.

61. A. Butler, 'Zuma's appointments and the mills of rumour and distrust', *Business Day*, 3 August 2009.

62. Eisinger, 'The conditions of protest behaviour', pp. 11–12; D. Meyer, 'Protest and political opportunities', *Annual Review of Sociology*, Vol. 30 (2004), p. 128.

63. Meyer, 'Protest and political opportunities', p. 136.

64. Kitshelt, 'Political opportunity structures', p. 62.

65. P. Regan and E. Henderson, 'Democracy, threats and political repression in developing countries: Are democracies internally less violent?', *Third World Quarterly*, Vol. 23, No. 1 (February 2002), p. 124.

66. Ibid., p. 133.

4
Barricades, Ballots and Experimentation: Making Sense of the 2011 Local Government Elections with a Social Movement Lens

Peter Alexander

INTRODUCTION

This chapter addresses a paradox. On the one hand, South Africa probably has the highest level of ongoing urban revolt in the world. The country's police recorded an average of 2.0 'unrest-related gatherings' per day in the five years from 1 April 2004 to 31 March 2009, and 2.9 per day for the period from then until 5 March 2012.[1] Using the erection of barricades as an indicator, many of these events amount to local insurrections, and the movement as a whole can be described as a rebellion of the poor.[2] Moreover, between 2004 and 2011 it is quite possible that South Africa lost more days through strike action per capita than any other country. According to one source, the figure was 332 per 1,000 for 2005–09 – almost twice as many as Canada, which came second. In 2010 South Africa recorded more strike days than in any previous year, and the figure for 2011 was the fourth highest in its history.[3] This resistance is underpinned by the highest income inequality and worst unemployment of any major country. However, in local government elections held on 18 May 2011 across the country, the ruling African National Congress (ANC) won 61.0 per cent of the votes for ward councillors, a figure only slightly lower than in the previous municipal ballot held in 2006 and fairly similar to every election since the end of apartheid.[4] Given that the rebellion has targeted local councils, which are overwhelmingly controlled by the ANC, the figure is all the more remarkable.

Literature on the relationship between social movements and elections is sparse, a point made by Doug McAdam and Sidney

Tarrow. Whilst, as they say, social movement studies have been interested mainly in 'the more disruptive forms of contention', electoral analysts focus on the performance of established parties, paying little attention to social movement interventions.[5] This chapter addresses our paradox and touches this lacuna by reflecting on aspects of the 2011 election. In an assessment of the same conundrum, Susan Booysen argued that the electorate 'appears to believe that "voting helps and protest works"', adding: 'voters vent their anger, engaging *their* ANC through protest and then see their way clear to remain electorally loyal'.[6] There is much to be said for this conclusion. For some voters and at a certain level of abstraction it must be right, for how else can we explain the ANC's continuing dominance? But the protesters are not necessarily the ones doing the voting. From a social movement studies perspective – one concerned with longer-term political change and strategic problems facing movement actors – one should investigate minorities as well as the electorate in general. In practice, there are different reasons for backing the ANC and different ways of not doing so, and an analysis that is limited to votes cast for different parties will exaggerate the extent to which the government enjoys popular support.

This chapter uses 'social movement' in both its senses: as social movement organisations and as a broad movement from below. The largest social movement organisation is the Congress of South African Trade Unions (COSATU) and unrest includes workers' strikes, but I have said less about these, partly because they are covered in the chapter by Claire Ceruti and partly because at the level of local government it is community organisations and the rebellion of the poor that matter. In brief, I seek to show that the rebellion and labour unrest contribute to and provide evidence of the ANC's hegemony crumbling at the edges, with this creating space for new left politics. The party's support among young people is particularly fragile and it is proposed that, partly through experience of unrest, people are beginning to experiment with political alternatives.

THE ROAD TO 2011

The 1994 election was a turning point, marking the end of the old apartheid order. But political transformation, already under way before the election, led to a decline in social movement organisation. Many battles had been won, foreign donors withdrew funds from non-governmental organisations, cadres moved into government or the private sector, and the South African National

Civics Organisation (SANCO) joined the ANC-led Alliance. The honeymoon period did not last long. COSATU opposed GEAR (Growth, Employment and Reconstruction), the government's neoliberal economic policy announced in 1996, and by the end of the 1990s surveys undertaken by the Human Sciences Research Council recorded growing unhappiness with the government. In 2000 the Treatment Action Campaign, the first of a new generation of social movements, turned its ire against the government, and the Anti-Privatisation Forum (APF), the most prominent coordinating body for militant community organisations, was formed in the same year.

From 2004 there was a shift in the character of community struggles. Trevor Ngwane, formerly chair of the APF, observed: 'the new community protests are unlike those of the social movements, which tended to be single-issue based and largely peaceful. They involve the whole community around its own set of grievances and demands.'[7] Lack of service delivery – including electricity, water, sewerage, garbage disposal, roads and houses – has been the main issue. But this led rapidly to complaints about unresponsive and/or corrupt councillors and officials, and sometimes to claims of police brutality. Other important concerns have been around jobs and 'demarcation' (that is, insistence that a municipality or part of the municipality be placed under a different province). The extensive repertoire of contention deployed in the protests has been considered elsewhere.[8] At least 24 protesters were killed by police or security guards between 2004 and 2011, and we have received reports of three places where torture occurred.[9]

The number of people participating in a protest has ranged from fewer than 100 to 10,000 and more.[10] Inequality is reflected in the rebellion through the location of protests, most of which emerge from the poorer parts of urban areas, especially badly serviced informal settlements. As with many of the new social movements, most participants are jobless, and in a survey conducted in a workshop with protest leaders we found that 14 protests were led by unemployed people compared to five cases where the leaders were a mixture of the unemployed and employed.[11] Levels of unemployment are strongly associated with age. In terms of the official rate, which excludes discouraged job-seekers, in the first quarter 2012 51.8 per cent of the 15–24-year-old labour force was unemployed, compared with an overall figure of 25.2 per cent.[12] From photographs and interviews, it is clear that 'youth' – from school students to those in their early thirties – constitute the core of the fighters at the centre of the protests.

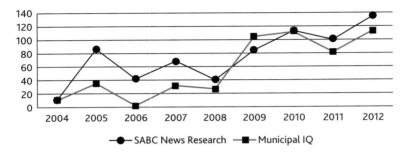

Figure 4.1   Number of service delivery protests recorded by SABC News Research and Municipal IQ, 2004–12

Notes: The first protest in 2004 was in August. The totals for 2012 only cover the period until end of July. SABC News Research records 'all service delivery protests' and Municipal IQ data is for 'major service delivery protests'.[13]

Fluctuations in the tempo of rebellion of the poor are reflected in Figure 4.1. The graph is based on data for 'service delivery' protests, thus excluding protests about other issues. Also it is dependent on media reports. Despite limitations, it provides a useful approximation of the ebb and flow of community protests. Because of its unrivalled electoral dominance, the ANC's elective congress held at Polokwane in December 2007 effectively determined who would become South Africa's next president. The outcome was strongly influenced by the unrest, with Thabo Mbeki replaced as president by Jacob Zuma, who was perceived to be the champion of workers and the poor.[14] After the general election held in May 2009, the intensity of the rebellion reached a peak. One explanation for the upturn is that people used protests to communicate with Zuma, who they felt would listen to their complaints. However, in Balfour there was an insurrection in July 2009, followed by another in February 2010, suggesting that people expected action as well as a sympathetic ear. There were doubtless other reasons for the escalation including, one assumes, the loss of nearly 1 million jobs in the first nine months of 2009.[15]

There was nothing exceptional about the number of protests preceding the 2011 elections, but they included large uprisings in Ermelo, Ficksburg (where TV cameras filmed the police killing Andries Tatane, a community leader) and Zandspruit and Thembehlile, two informal settlements close to Johannesburg. Before and after the election a number of protests were linked to abuse of the ANC's nomination procedures (on which more later). Immediately after the election there was a new upsurge, including very militant action close to Johannesburg, at Noordgesig (a 'coloured' area), Chiawelo in Soweto, and yet again in Zandspruit and Thembehlile. At the time of writing (7 June 2012) the pace of events was quickening. There had been more protests by the middle of 2012 than in the whole of 2010, the previous peak year (see Figure 4.1). Moreover, protests were occurring in rural as well as urban areas, the range of issues being raised was widening (to include such things as taxi fares and the location of a university), and damage to property was occurring in town centres as well as townships.

THE 2011 MUNICIPAL ELECTIONS

The 2011 municipal elections were hotly contested, with the Democratic Alliance (DA) – the main opposition party – arguing that efficient administration and lack of corruption had distinguished its municipalities from those governed by the ANC. The most memorable event was the so called 'toilet war', when the ANC exposed the DA for providing township toilets that lacked surrounding structures (thus leaving them fully open to public gaze), and the DA responded by revealing that the same had happened in an ANC municipality. The headline results of the elections showed the ANC winning handsomely, albeit with smaller majorities. It secured 61.0 per cent of the total ward councillor vote, compared to 64.1 per cent in 2006. The DA obtained 23.8 per cent, a considerable advance on the 16.2 per cent it had won in 2006.[16] The Inkatha Freedom Party (IFP), having suffered a major split, obtained only 3.6 per cent, compared to 7.5 per cent in 2006, with the breakaway organisation, the National Freedom Party (NFP), winning 2.5 per cent. The only other party to win more than 1 per cent of the total ward councillor vote was the Congress of the People (COPE), formed by dissident ANC members following Zuma's election as president and deeply divided at the time of the elections, which secured 2.1 per cent. Despite the DA's improved position, its base is restricted to ethnic minorities and, to a lesser extent, well-heeled Africans, mostly living in the suburbs. We can agree with the views that 'its pro-market ideology seems unlikely to appeal to constituencies which provide a foundation for radical social movements' and 'electoral outcomes will continue to be determined by what happens among the ANC's historic constituencies'.[17]

There are a number of reasons why the ANC's electoral success was paralleled by public protest. Firstly, local government is not uniformly bad and services have generally improved since the end of apartheid. However, progress in one area can generate a sense of injustice among its neighbours, and where protests produce victories this can have a knock-on effect. Secondly, there is considerable loyalty to the 'party of Mandela', especially among older voters.[18] One factor that goes some way to explaining this is that, with the end of apartheid, black pensions were raised to the same level as those paid to whites – a very significant reform. However, a large proportion of poor households are dependent on pensions and this, combined with rising prices, places considerable burdens on the elderly, who have been very visible in the new social movements. Thirdly, while unemployment and inequality have increased since 1994, average real wages have improved, bringing real benefits for many workers.[19] On the other hand, profits and directors' pay have increased more rapidly, an issue often raised by strikers.

Fourthly, one attraction of the ANC is the possibility it provides for gaining jobs and access to tenders. At the most obvious level, councillors are well paid compared to the overwhelming majority of township residents. In 2011 their remuneration ranged from R13,243 (about $1,820) for part-timers in the poorest municipalities to R60,266 (about $8,278) per month for full-timers in the wealthiest.[20] Even the lowest rate was about eleven times the value of a pension, set at R1,140 (about $160) for 2011. This kind of contrast helps explain why councillor positions are so highly prized, especially among the unemployed. Even at the lowest levels, councillors become socially distanced from their constituents and some move house, perhaps to a site outside their township. The ANC's new nomination procedures provided scope to remove unpopular councillors, and while it may have had this effect in some places, in others it backfired. The amended process, adopted in the wake of the Polokwane conference, required ANC branches to present four potential candidates to a mass meeting where they could be quizzed, enabling a community to indicate its preference.[21] However, the final choice was left to the district (an intermediate structure between the branch and the province) and some of these ignored popular sentiment, often leading to protests, some violent.[22] Three weeks before the election, Zuma announced that after the ballot it would be possible to remove councillors who had been selected incorrectly. After the elections there were further protests around the ensuing enquiries. In the most dramatic of these, the

ANC's offices in Pietermaritzburg were destroyed by activists, who threatened to make the city ungovernable and forced the new deputy mayor to resign.[23]

Fifthly, in most areas, the only serious alternative to the ANC, the DA, was still widely seen by black voters as a 'white' party. Even if voters were contemptuous of their own councillors and highly critical of Zuma, popular leaders such as Zwelinzima Vavi, general secretary of COSATU, and Julius Malema, president of the ANC Youth League, were campaigning for the ANC. With COSATU, the South African Communist Party (SACP) and SANCO still part of the ANC-led Alliance, there is no significant left alternative in elections. The other side of this coin is that discontent is channelled into the party, fuelling internal divisions. As Polokwane highlighted, the votes that decide the leadership of the country occur within its structures. It is difficult to imagine the ANC not winning the next general election; the issue is 'which ANC?' Differences of class interest, patronage and conflicts of personality have weakened Zuma's standing, creating uncertainty about the future of Malema as an individual expelled from the ANC. But the Youth League as an organisation is still campaigning for nationalisation of mines and land and it wants Zuma removed as president. Meanwhile, Vavi's close ally, Irvin Jim, general secretary of the National Union of Metal Workers, now the country's second largest union, has reiterated his union's support for nationalisation *without compensation*, adding: 'You have to be a moron of a special type to fail to grasp [that] … it is impossible to grow a democratic South Africa on the capitalist and apartheid economy.'[24]

ALTERNATIVES FOR REBELS

Turning now to alternatives for those involved in the rebellion or sympathetic to it, the most significant is a decision not to vote, particularly in local elections. Disturbingly for the ANC, this response is especially widespread among young people. The votes given above for the different parties were percentages of the *valid* votes. But only 57.6 per cent of the registered voters cast a ballot.[25] For election analysts the story nearly always stops there, but the social movement analyst needs to dig deeper. The key issue is that barely 75 per cent of the voting-age population (18 and above) registered to vote, so the real turnout was about 43 per cent, with the ANC's vote just 26 per cent of the voting-age population.[26] In a representative survey of potential voters undertaken for the

Independent Electoral Commission (IEC), only 44 per said they were satisfied 'with the way democracy is working in South Africa' (down from a high point of 63 per cent in 2004).[27] Among 18–19-year-olds, the proportion who registered was roughly 23 per cent, and even among 20–29-year-olds it was still only about 58 per cent.[28] From conversations with students, fieldworkers and township residents, there is clearly widespread cynicism among young people. While many are politically passive (at least for now), this is the generation that has been prominent in community revolts. So the ANC's hold on politics is more tenuous than it might seem, and the assumption that people participate in protests and then vote for the ANC needs to be challenged.

Some communities considered adopting a militant form of not voting – the electoral boycott. This was the case in Ermelo, where an uprising had followed the ANC's decision to impose an unpopular candidate.[29] One resident of the town told a fieldworker:

> even the youth ... are saying they are not going to vote; rather they will organise a bash [party] and drink alcohol. They said they will open the bash where people will be voting just to disturb them because there is nothing they gain after voting.[30]

Similarly, the 'community of Zandspuit' rejected the ANC candidate because she had not been chosen by the community, adding: 'If, and that's a big "if", she won the elections we don't want her here in Zandspruit ... we don't even want the IEC voting stations here in Zandspruit.'[31] In practice, leaders of the Ermelo revolt decided not to picket polling stations, since, although this might have been effective, it would also have provoked violence (perhaps youth against seniors, and almost certainly police against protesters). The upshot was that the older generation turned out to vote as normal. In Zandspruit, following Zuma's intervention three weeks before the election, the community agreed to lift its threatened boycott, and most voters backed the ANC.[32]

Another tactic was the spoiling of ballot papers. According to the IEC, the total number of spoilt votes amounted to 1.7 per cent of the total votes cast. However, there was considerable variation from one ward to another, suggesting the existence of local campaigns. Our workshop survey confirmed that this was the case. In a large majority of wards, the spoilt papers could be counted in tens and thus were probably errors or individual protests. However, in some wards, there were hundreds of spoilt papers, indicating some kind of collective action, and in Ward 83205015 in Bushbuckridge, Mpumalanga, the spoilt papers (2,290) outnumbered the valid papers (2,082).[33]

A further response to disenchantment with the ANC, at least locally, was to back an independent candidate. While independents were not necessarily former ANC voters, this is assumed to have been true in most cases. One factor driving this movement was the ANC's refusal to back nominees acclaimed by pre-election community meetings. In 2011 there was an increase in the number of independents to 774 (from 663 in 2006), with 38 of them winning election as ward councillors (compared to 34 in 2006).[34] Overall, independents' total ward councillor vote declined slightly from 2.7 per cent in 2006 to 2.3 per cent, but this still represented more votes than the number secured by COPE. In some areas independents constituted something approaching an alternative party. For instance, in Emfuleni municipality, Gauteng, 16 independents, who declared themselves 'loyal and disciplined members of the African National Congress', published a document calling for 'participatory democracy' and a 'society driven by generosity, caring and sharing'.[35] In Ermelo, the decision to mount a boycott had been precipitated by the IEC's disqualification of independent candidates put forward in the wake of the insurrection.[36]

Some community activists did form new parties, albeit local in scope.[37] The most successful was the Mpumalanga Party (MP), formed in March 2011 to advance the cause of re-demarcating the Moutse area so that it fell under Mpumalanga rather than Limpopo. One of the party's candidates complained: 'The visit [to Moutse] by the president surprised me ... After we had so many uprisings and protests, he only came for votes ... what he is telling us is that the votes are much more important than us.' He recalled a gradual transfer in the community's loyalty, moving firstly from the ANC to boycotting an election, then to standing as independents (in 2006), and then back to voting ANC (in 2009) after it had promised support and, finally, following disappointment, the new party was formed.[38] The process of learning from experience and adopting more radical alternatives is reminiscent of what Leon Trotsky called 'a method of successive approximations'.[39] The MP won twelve seats in Elias Motsoaledi and a further three in Greater Marble Hall, coming second in both municipalities.[40]

Another of the new parties was the Balfour-based Socialist Civic Movement (SCM), formed in January 2011. Emerging from insurrections in 2009 and 2010, it advanced the community's main demands, including the re-demarcation of the Dipaleseng municipality into Gauteng, and three days before the election it held a peaceful 'right to work' march to the local gold mine that mobilised 2,000 young people. Its leadership included a former Pan Africanist Congress (PAC) councillor and the more-radical youth involved in leading the uprising. Demanding a 'society of equals' and 'socialism in our life time', and adopting red as its colour, the SCM appealed to a wider audience than the PAC, one that included disillusioned members of the ANC.[41] On election day we surveyed 665 voters exiting voting stations in the three wards covering Siyathemba township, where the protests took place. Of these, the average age of ANC voters was 44, while that of SCM voters was 36, and the age gap would doubtless have been greater had a higher proportion of young people registered to vote.[42] This again suggests that the ANC is likely to have long-term problems as its membership matures. The SCM won two of the twelve council seats, and in August 2011, according to its publicity secretary, it was still going strong, with activists in four neighbouring towns showing an interest in joining.[43]

A third party to have grown out of the social movements was Operation Khanyisa Movement (OKM). This was formed in 2006 by eight APF affiliates, including the Soweto Electricity Crisis Committee (SECC), its strongest unit, and the Thembelihle Crisis Committee (TCC), which led the uprisings in that settlement.[44] The APF as an organisation refused to support the OKM; largely, it was said, because the centralised nature of a party conflicted with the decentralised character of the Forum. As Marcelle Dawson notes, division of opinion within the APF reflected a wider international debate about whether social movements should enter the electoral arena.[45] The OKM is overtly anti-capitalist and fights for a workers' government, free services, renewable energy and international working-class solidarity. It also takes a strong stance on the critical issue of accountability. All candidates publicly sign a 'pledge' that commits them to seeking mandates from, and agreeing to right of recall by, the community they represent, and also to handing their salaries to the OKM, which then pays them enough for basic needs.[46] The OKM won a single seat in the Johannesburg City Council, repeating this feat in 2011.

Also, on the far left, there is a new national formation, the Democratic Left Front (DLF), which draws together, among others, two prominent former members of the SACP; well-known activists like Trevor Ngwane; well-known academics like Martin Legassick

and Jackie Cock; the group associated with the International
Socialist Tendency; people who have a background in the Fourth
International; a few anarcho-syndicalists; and some green activists.
The DLF was launched at a conference held in January 2011, which
was attended by around 200 people, about 90 per cent of whom were
black, most of them from sympathetic community organisations.
In the recent elections, rather than nominating its own candidates,
it backed those of organisations such as the MP, SCM and OKM.
Importantly, the DLF provides the possibility of bringing together
individuals from different communities and of linking them with
workers, students and intellectuals.[47]

Thus far we have looked at matters largely from an electoral
perspective, but before concluding we should reverse the lens. Let
us begin with organisations associated with the biggest battles of
2011. In Ermelo, the Msukaligwa Community Committee backed
a boycott, but organised sports and other activities to reduce
the chances of violence outside voting stations. In Ficksburg, the
Meqheleng Concerned Citizens took the view that people should
vote for whoever they wanted. The Noordgesig and Surrounding
Unified Civic Organisation was formed after the election, but
some of its leaders had been involved in the politically agnostic
Soweto Concerned Residents and it is likely that the DA was the
most popular party in Noordgesig. In Zandspuit, the community,
including the SANCO branch, generally backed a boycott, but there
was some support for voting ANC on the understanding that the
local councillor could be removed after the election. In Thembelihle,
the TCC was affiliated to the OKM. In Chiawelo, where the protest
was organised by the SECC together with the Landless People's
Movement and the local community, the OKM had been supported
since its inception. As for other areas, Moutse established its own
party, and something similar happened in Bushbuckridge, where
the Residents' Association, formed just prior to the election, won
seven seats, coming second in the 74-member council. In Balfour,
some of the leaders from the Dipaleseng Youth Forum, which led
the 2009 revolt, backed independents and others helped establish
the SCM.[48]

Among these major protest sites, there is not a single case of the
protest leadership actively backing the ANC in the election (with
the partial exception of Zandspruit). Yet, apart from Noordgesig,
the conflicts occurred in areas where the ANC has historically been
dominant and it is reasonable to assume that most of the leaders had
previously identified with the party (although there were already

oppositional currents in some areas). Thus, the thesis that people protest against ANC councils but return to the fold in elections, oversimplifies a layered and fluid reality. At least in those areas where there have been major protests, people – youth in particular – are breaking with the ANC and exploring alternatives.

CONCLUSION

While electoral analysis gives width to social movement studies, pressing it to consider political problems, social movement analysis gives depth to electoral studies, obliging it to observe phenomena of little immediate consequence, but considerable portent. The stance adopted here has been to treat an election as a vantage point, as one might regard a strike or an insurrection. That is, one looks to see what has happened, but also pokes around for clues that help explain *why* it happened. At first glance, it does appear that the ANC is impregnable, with its 'children' stomping their feet, yet remaining in the family home. But today's ANC is different to the one that overthrew apartheid. Especially at Polokwane, community and trade union struggles left their mark, but so too have self-aggrandisement and factionalism, with the result that the ANC is now deeply divided and incapable of commanding unbridled loyalty in its urban heartland. This barely registers in formal election analysis, which focuses on votes cast and ignores those that are not. It can be detected, however, in three forms: widespread detachment from establishment politics, separation between ANC politicians and community leadership, and experimentation with alternative political solutions. Importantly, young people – the youth – are detaching, separating and experimenting to a greater degree than the old, and a generational divide is apparent.

Electoral politics undoubtedly pose problems for social movements, with support for a party threatening the unity required to win immediate battles. But 'non-politics' is also a problem, because it inhibits the replacement of politicians blocking changes that people demand. The balance is resolved in different ways. In Ficksburg, high tension, urgent practical problems and an inability to field alternative candidates mitigated against a political stance. In Balfour, the insurrectionary moment had passed and politics was a means of sustaining the struggle. As the limitations of local uprisings become apparent the trend is likely to move in the direction of politics. There is another consideration – what has been termed 'scale shift'; that is, the reframing necessary to unite similar conflicts in different places.[49] This does not necessarily require a political organisation – as shown by the development of local trade unions into national organisations – but in South Africa today it is probable that it will, if only because the two questions most likely to provide a basis for new frames – unemployment and corruption – both require political solutions. The trajectory of popular struggles, then, is towards politicisation, albeit a contested politicisation.

For a period in the late 1970s and early 1980s the most dynamic oppositional movement in South Africa was the 'non-political' Federation of South African Trade Unions (FOSATU). But when the struggle picked up pace, raising increasing numbers of political problems, FOSATU's 'workerist' ideology was found wanting, and the 'populism' associated with the ANC and its internal allies came to prevail. In the present period, it is likely that 'non-political'[50] social movements will be eclipsed. But what kind of politics will come to the fore? We can offer three scenarios: (1) Vavi breaks decisively from the ANC mainstream, drawing much of the SACP with him, and appeals for workers and the poor to unite in action. He has already begun to frame discourse around corruption (thus undermining both Malema and Zuma) and has frequently raised the spectre of unemployment. But it is likely that too many union leaders are wedded to the ANC and too many workers have benefited from union militancy for him to risk splitting COSATU; (2) Malema and the Youth League break decisively from the ANC mainstream, calling on the poor, specifically unemployed youth, to rise up. Malema's fiery personality certainly has much appeal, as does the League's framing of debate around nationalisation. However, Malema's expulsion may have been a decisive blow and he and his colleagues are too intimately tied to wealthy power brokers within the ANC to carry through on their threats; and (3) a dynamic DLF converges with insipient township politics to create a force that is sufficiently weighty to break apart the ANC. The new movement would be unencumbered by links to the ANC and would reflect the aspirations of grassroots fighters. But such a formation would lack resources and is unlikely to have significant support among workers. So, in the immediate future, it is probable that the ANC centre around Zuma will survive, but continue to decay. This in turn would produce more disaffection and allow opportunities for a hybrid of the scenarios to develop, possibly drawing together elements of COSATU and community organisations into a genuinely anti-capitalist structure. However, South Africa is becoming increasingly unstable and combustible, and its politics are difficult to predict. What we can say with reasonable confidence is that massive inequality and unemployment will persist, producing resistance and disaffection, and the youth in particular will continue to experiment with new political solutions.

NOTES

1. Peter Alexander, 'Protests and Police Statistics', *Weekly Mail & Guardian*, 13 April. The Minister of Police informed Parliament that from 2007/08 to 2008/09 the most common reason for 'conducting crowd management (unrest) gatherings' was related to service delivery issues, and there is no reason for thinking that the pattern has changed. In addition, many of the 'crowd management (peaceful) gatherings' would also have been about service delivery. Over the almost eight years covered by these statistics there were 97,970 'peaceful' gatherings and 6,814 'unrest' gatherings.
2. Peter Alexander, 'Rebellion of the poor: South Africa's service delivery protests – a preliminary analysis', *Review of African Political Economy*, Vol. 37, No. 123 (2010).
3. Mike Schussler and data from economists.co.za, quoted in Rene Vollgraaff, 'SA strike rate highest in the world', *Sunday Times*, 7 August 2011, *Business Times Supplement*, p. 4; Andrew Levy Employment Publications, 'Workdays lost to the economy', email communications from Jackie Kelly, most recently 7 June 2012. I am much obliged to Kelly, whose data show the four top years for strike days as follows: 2010 – 14.6 million; 2007 – 12.9 million; 1987 – 9.0 million; 2011 – 6.2 million. See also John Brand, 'Lessons from the 2011 Strike Season – The Role of Labour Law', presentation to SASLAW Seminar, 23 February 2012; and European Foundation for the Improvement of Living and Working Conditions, *Developments in Industrial Action 2005–2009*, downloaded from www.eurofound.europa.eu on 5 March 2012. The International Labour Organisation's (ILO) data for 2004–08 puts South Africa at the top of the league for 'days not worked per thousand employees'. However, many countries are absent from this series, either completely or for particular years. It records Argentina as having a higher average figure than South Africa for 2006–08.
4. IEC (Independent Electoral Commission), *Results Summary, Local Government Elections 2011*, 2011, www.elections.org.za. At the local level, 50 per cent of councillors are elected on a first-past-the-post basis and represent a specific ward, and the remainder represent a party and are elected by proportional representation. Technical details are available on the IEC website, www. elections.org.za. All figures given here are for ward councillor votes unless otherwise stated.
5. Doug McAdam and Sidney Tarrow, 'Ballots and barricades: On the reciprocal relationship between elections and social movements', *Perspectives on Politics*, Vol. 8, No. 2 (2010), pp. 529, 532–3.
6. Susan Booysen, 'With the ballot and the brick: The politics of attaining service delivery', *Progress in Development Studies*, Vol. 7, No. 1 (2007), pp. 26, 31; Susan Booysen, 'The "ballot and the brick" – enduring under duress', in Susan Booysen (ed.), *Local Elections in South Africa: Parties, People, Politics*, Bloemfontein: Sun Press, 2012, p. 296.
7. Trevor Ngwane, 'We, the protesters', *Amandla*, No. 14 (2010).

8.   Alexander, 'Rebellion of the poor'; Karl von Holdt et al., *The Smoke that Calls: Insurgent Citizenship, Collective Violence and the Struggle for a Place in the New South Africa*, Johannesburg: Centre for the Study of Violence and Reconciliation and Society Work and Development Institute, 2011, www.swopinstitute.org.za.

9.   Richard Pithouse, 'Debate-list-bounces', listserv, 2 May 2011, updated from Wikipedia entry on *Protest in South Africa*, with two deaths that occurred in Piet Retief added.

10. The higher figures are for Middelburg in 2010 (SABC News Research), and Ficksburg in 2011 (personal interview with leaders).

11. Workshop delegate survey administered at the Academic and Activist Workshop on Protest, Elections and Emerging Politics organised by the South African Research Chair in Social Change, University of Johannesburg, 18 June 2011.

12. Stats SA (Statistics South Africa), *Quarterly Labour Force Survey, Quarter 1, 2012*, Pretoria: Stats SA, 2011, pp. 29–30.

13. I am grateful to Ronesh Dhawraj from SABC News Research and Kevin Allan from Municipal IQ for access to their data.

14. Roger Southall and Edward Webster, 'Unions and parties in South Africa: COSATU and the ANC in the wake of Polokwane', in Bjorn Beckman, Sakhela Buhlungu and Lloyd Sachikonye (eds), *Trade Unions and Party Politics: Labour Movements in Africa*, Cape Town: HSRC Press, 2010, pp. 131–66.

15. Von Holdt et al., *The Smoke that Calls*; Peter Alexander and Peter Pfaffe, 'South Africa's rebellion of the poor: Balfour and relationships to the means of protest', paper presented at the Academic and Activist Workshop on Protests, Elections and Emerging Politics, University of Johannesburg, 18 June 2011; Stats SA, *Quarterly Labour Force Statistics*, Pretoria: Stats SA (compare numbers employed, which decline to 12.9 million in 2009 Quarter 3).

16. Here and elsewhere, election statistics come from IEC, *Results Summary 2006* and *Results Summary 2011*. The DA's vote increased partly because it had been joined by the Independent Democratic Party, which secured 2.1 per cent of the vote in 2006.

17. The first quote is from Neil Southern and Roger Southall, 'Dancing like a monkey: The Democratic Alliance and opposition politics in South Africa', in John Daniel et al. (eds), *New African Review 2: New Paths, Old Compromises*, Johannesburg: Wits University Press, 2011, p. 81; and the second is from John Daniel and Roger Southall, 'The Zuma presidency: The politics of paralysis', in the same book, p. 27. The DA's level of support would, though, be improved by a merger with a party whose support is mainly black; that is, COPE, the IFP or the NFP.

18. A common comment outside voting stations in Balfour, where I was conducting fieldwork on election day.

19. CDE (Centre for Development and Enterprise), *A Fresh Look at Unemployment: A Conversation among Experts*, Johannesburg: CDE, 2011, p. 17.

20. Republic of South Africa, 'Government notice: Determination of upper limits of salaries', 18 December 2010. The rate for executive mayors was higher still – R80,355 per month (about $11,038).

21. Independent candidates in Emfuleni Municipality, 'Statement: Together we thrive in taking back democracy to the people', in 'Memoranda and other documents produced by participants', Workshop on Protests, Elections and Emerging Politics, 18 June 2011.

22. These have been termed 'candidate revolts'. Susan Booysen, *The African National Congress and the Regeneration of Political Power*, Johannesburg: Wits University Press, 2011, pp. 150–3.

23. Sam Mkokeli, 'Zuma offers shock deal on disputed ANC lists', *Business Day*, 29 April 2011; News24, reports, 12 June 2011 and 21 June 2011, www.news24. com/news24/SouthAfrica/Politics (accessed 16 August 2011).

24. S'tembiso Msomi, 'Nationalise everything! Says Numsa's Irvin Jim', *Business Live*, 2 June 2012, downloaded from www.businesslive.co.za on 7 June 2012.

25. Justin Sylvester and Sithembile Mbete, 'The 2011 LGE: Separating the reality from the spin', unpublished paper for IDASA, Cape Town, 2011. This figure is actually higher than the 48.4 per cent recorded for 2006 and the 47.3 per cent recorded in 2000.

26. My calculations are similar to these provided by Collette Schulz Herzenberg, 'Trends in participation and party support in the 2011 municipal elections', in Susan Booysen (ed.), *Local Elections in South Africa: Parties, People, Politics*, Bloemfontein: Sun Press, 2012, p. 93.

27. HSRC (Human Science Research Council), *IEC Voter Participation Survey 2010/11: An Overview of Results*, Pretoria: HSRC Press, 2011, p. 15.

28. These statistics are estimates based on the following assumptions: (1) the population aged 18–19 is 2,042,837; (2) the population aged 20–29 is 9,498,551; (3) the total voting-age population is 31,641,878; (4) there are 471,878 registered voters aged 18–19; (5) there are 5,534,416 voters aged 20–29; (6) the total number of registered voters was 23,655,046; and (7) the ANC secured 8,143,541 ward councillor votes. Assumptions 1–3 are drawn from Stats SA, *Mid-year Population Estimates, 2011*, Pretoria: Stats SA, 2011, p. 9, with additional information from Ben Roberts, personal comment 17 August 2011 (thanks Ben). Assumptions 4–6 come from IEC, *Local Government Elections 2011: Information Brochure*, Pretoria: IEC, 2011, p. 69. Assumption 7 is from IEC, *Results Summary 2011*.

29. *City Press*, 24 April 2011, p. 4.

30. Interview with a resident of Emadamini conducted by Lufuno Gogoro, c. 8 May 2011.

31. 'Memorandum from Zandspruit community', 18 April 2011, in 'Memoranda and other documents'.

32. Booysen, '"The ballot and the brick"', p. 309.

33. IEC, 'Turnout and spoilt details, local government elections, 2011', 2011, www. elections.org.za (accessed November 2011).

34. Mcebisi Ndletyana, 'Municipal elections 2006: Protests, independent candidates and cross-border municipalities', in Sakhela Buhlungu et al. (eds), *State of the Nation: South Africa 2007*, Cape Town: HSRC Press, 2007, p. 96; *Independent*, 'Bread and butter issues win the day', 22 May 2011, pp. 8–9.

35. Independent candidates in Emfuleni Municipality, 'Statement'.

36. *City Press*, 24 April 2011, p. 4. Significantly, the IEC claimed that only a minority of signatures on the nomination papers were those of registered voters.

37. For the 2011 elections there were 121 registered parties (up from 97 in 2006).

38. Interview with Ali Maloba conducted by Lufuno Gogoro, May 2011.

39. Leon Trotsky, *History of the Russian Revolution*, London: Gollancz, 1965, p. 18. Thanks to Colin Barker for this quote.

40. Sylvester and Mbete, 'The 2011 LGE', p. 9.

41. *Siyabengana: Socialist Civic Movement Newsletter*, Vol. 1, Issue 1 (16 April 2011); SCM (Socialist Civic Movement), 'Join the SCM for the Right to Work March on 13th May', leaflet in author's possession; also interviews and notes from Siyathemba, Balfour, 13 and 16 May 2011.

42. Dipaleseng election survey carried out by the author, 16 May 2011.

43. Telephone interview with Lifu Nhlapo, 17 August 2011. The ANC went from having ten out of eleven councillors, to seven out of twelve. A former ANC independent won a position and the DA won two.

44. The organisation was named after Operation Khanyisa, the SECC's popular electricity reconnection campaign.

45. Marcelle C. Dawson, 'Social movements in contemporary South Africa: The Anti-Privatisation Forum and struggles around access to water in Johannesburg', Dphil. thesis, University of Oxford, 2008, pp. 260–70.

46. OKM (Operation Khanyisa Movement), 'OKM manifesto', 2011; OKM, 'Pledge', 2011. Thanks to Trevor Ngwane for these documents.

47. Various documents, including DLF, 'Press statement', 13 May 2011; *Phakamani*, 5 May 2011; discussions with members and participation in meetings.

48. Discussions with activists; *City Press*, 24 April 2011, p. 4; *Bushbuckridge News*, 7 June 2011.

49. Doug McAdam, Sidney Tarrow and Charles Tilly, *Dynamics of Contention*, Cambridge: Cambridge University Press, 2001, pp. 331–5.

50. This term is used here to refer to movements that abstain from political alignment.

5
Insurgent Citizenship, Class Formation and the Dual Nature of a Community Protest: A Case Study of 'Kungcatsha'[1]

Malose Langa and Karl von Holdt

INTRODUCTION

This chapter examines a case of community protest in a single town, which we call Kungcatsha,[2] which was rocked by two weeks of violent community protests in the second half of 2009. The protests started when a mass meeting of residents in the local stadium decided to call for a stay-away in protest against the town council's failure to explain to the community what had happened to a missing sum of R30 million (about $3.5 million). Violence flared up when the police were called in and attempted to disperse protesters with teargas and rubber bullets. Barricades of burning tyres were set up to prevent the police from entering the township. During the protest, a councillor's house, a community hall and a library were torched, and the council offices and a new community centre were partially destroyed.

We explore the dynamics of the protest movement and its relationship to internal contestations within the local African National Congress (ANC) and town council. In brief, we find that the protest movement in Kungcatsha has a dual nature, combining an internal power struggle in the local ANC with a mass movement of aggrieved township residents protesting against corruption, joblessness and the local town council's failure to provide municipal services. The protest leaders were active members of the ANC and its sister organisations, or of the South African Communist Party (SACP) with which it is in alliance. Once the protesters' demand for the 'dismissal' of the mayoral committee had been met, the crowds dispersed and the protest leadership were reabsorbed into the ANC, leaving no durable organisation to continue representing residents' interests. The protest movement itself was shaped by complex processes of class formation and class contestation within the local community and various sites of power, such as the ANC and the town council.

The protest movement, in other words, occupied a fluid space both inside and outside of the ANC. Both mainstream social movement theory and the left-wing activists in many of the South African social movements that emerged in opposition to the ANC government after the democratic transition tend to conceive of social movements as independent and durable organisations mobilised in opposition to the prevailing political authority – and in the case of South African movements such as the Anti-Privatisation Forum, stress the struggle for an alternative future to that presented by capitalism.[3] Some of the case studies of social movements in South Africa and other countries of the developing world suggest a more complex relationship among social movements, states and political parties. In place of the rigid boundaries between state and society presupposed in the former conceptions, Zuern finds a porous space in which a social movement may negotiate both alliances with and protests against a ruling political party.[4] Friedman and Mottiar explore the ways in which the Treatment Action Campaign (TAC) makes use of institutional strategies, negotiation and protest, and Heller argues that transformative political projects may be constituted by a combination of political action from above with social movement action from below.[5] Such distinctions pose important questions about the conception and place of 'social movements' and 'civil society' in post-apartheid South Africa, and perhaps in the global South more broadly.

It must also be noted that the subject of our study is a collective protest action rather than a social movement. The concept of social movement implies some degree of durable and more or less structured organisation that is able to engage in strategic action over time, in contrast to the more transitory and inchoate nature of a collective protest. There has been a rapid escalation in the latter kind of local protest action since 2009, sometimes with a somewhat greater, though usually still transitory, degree of organisation than in the Kungcatsha case. It can be argued that the escalation of this kind of protest is a distinguishing feature of the post-Mbeki period.[6] The trajectory of the protest movement in Kungcatsha provides a dramatic instance of the way in which the ANC remains the hegemonic political and social force at the local level, occupying both the political space structured by town-level politics and the broader social space beyond the political domain, and preventing the emergence of an autonomous civil society at the local level. Heller ascribes the withering away of social movements in post-apartheid South Africa to the attitudes and orientation of the ANC – namely, its commitment to centralised control and technocratic domination of the state and development, and the autocratic and insulating tendencies derived from its dominant-party status.[7] We take a different approach. By focusing on the internal dynamics of both protest and the local ANC we reveal the ways in which this domination over civil society is constructed from below by the agency of local elites and subalterns, rather than by instructions from above. Neither Heller nor any of the other South African studies referred to above place their analysis of social movements in the context of a close analysis of struggles within the ANC; nor do they explore the local dynamics of patronage politics, and the way this may shape the formation of social movements.

Thompson and Tapscott argue that social mobilisation in the global South tends to be oriented towards the attainment of socioeconomic rights and that such mobilisation has become the key dimension 'in the struggle to realise citizenship rights in the South'.[8] Our focus on the internal dynamics of the protest movement and its interactions with the ANC and the local state allows us to explore what conceptions of citizenship may be at play in the current explosion of popular activity. In pursuing this question, we draw on James Holston's work to argue that the protest movement constitutes a form of 'insurgent citizenship' for socioeconomic rights against the deprivations of 'differentiated citizenship',[9] but identify a darker side to insurgent citizenship constituted by xenophobic attacks, patriarchy, patronage networks and popular violence. Insurgent citizenship, as Holston argues, does not necessarily struggle only for a democratic expansion of socioeconomic rights, but may endeavour to reconstitute differentiation and the dynamics of inclusion and exclusion on a new basis.

The chapter concludes by arguing that community protest is shaped by processes of class formation through which a new elite emerges while an expanding class of the unemployed and the poor remains marginalised and excluded. These processes explain the dual nature of the protest movement, the instability and paralysis of the ANC and the way protest movements disappear, leaving no durable organisational legacy, when the protest leadership are reabsorbed back into the ANC.

It is important to note that this case study forms part of a wider study of collective violence in eight different research sites in South

Africa and that these dynamics are similar to those investigated in several of the other sites – to such an extent that we believe they can be described as broader trends, notwithstanding considerable local variation.[10] In Kungcatsha, in-depth interviews were conducted over a period of six months with 58 key informants, such as protest leaders, community leaders, the youth, local church leaders, union members, local councillors, and the mayor. Furthermore, the researchers spent time in taverns, on street corners, in parties and celebrations, and at by-elections observing interactions and engaging in informal discussions with some of the key informants. This methodology was useful to explore meanings, relationships, power dynamics and contestations within this town. Also given the sensitive nature of this research, it was important for the researchers to immerse themselves in the lives of the informants in order to gain their trust in talking about their roles in the protest.

GRIEVANCES

A central grievance of the protest movement concerned a sum of R30 million ($3.5 million) that was alleged to have been embezzled by councillors and municipal officials sometime before 2008. As one young protester explained: 'What made us fight is we wanted to know how it got lost, who ate it. Whoever ate it must be arrested. So we fought as the community.'[11]

But the anger about corruption was associated with other grievances. Young protesters complained about the declining state of recreational facilities such as parks, the soccer stadium, the swimming pool and the library; corrupt tenders that failed to deliver to the community; the shortage of houses and the lack of jobs; and nepotism in the allocation of what jobs the council was able to offer. According to them, the stadium was more like a grazing patch for cattle than a soccer ground, and the mayor had closed down the swimming pool. 'We can't even play soccer. That's why we have turned to drinking', a group of young men involved in the protests explained. There had been no progress or development in the town since the advent of democracy, they said, and even the amenities that residents had enjoyed as children, such as swings in parks, had disappeared.

Kungcatsha is the centre of a farming district, but also used to boast a sizeable textile industry. Both the Congress of South African Trade Unions and the local Democratic Alliance described how the major companies in town had closed their operations, leaving high levels of unemployment. Some of the protesters acknowledged their involvement in crime: 'We have nothing to do, that's why we get guns and carry out stick-ups', said one participant.

These grievances suggest the nature of differentiated citizenship as it is experienced by the residents of Kungcatsha: income poverty is exacerbated by the lack of amenities and housing. In contrast, the elite is able to display its wealth conspicuously in the form of cars, clothes and dwellings. Allegations of the embezzlement of public money serve as a lightning rod for popular frustration.

There is a gender dynamic to differentiated citizenship as well. Young men complained about the impact of poverty on their ability to play the role of young men in their community. For example, one of the male protesters angrily said 'I want to get married, but I cannot afford lobola[12] because I'm not working'; 'I hate that guy [a councillor]. He took my girlfriend. He has money and I don't have money. You can't find a girlfriend if you don't have money.'[13] Many young men talked about their inability to get married or support their wives and children. It was clear that poverty undermines their ability to achieve the ideals of what Connell terms 'hegemonic masculinity'.[14] Their sense of emasculation was further exacerbated by the insults of the mayor, a woman who had allegedly dismissed the protesters as 'unemployed, unwashed, dagga-smoking boys'.[15] Several informants, especially young men, asserted that this comment made the protesters angry. They were adamant that they could not be ruled by a woman, because women were poor leaders and stubborn.

PROTEST ORGANISERS

About six weeks before the protests, a group of young ANC Youth League activists started planning to mobilise the community with regard to the R30 million allegedly missing from the town council. We interviewed three leaders, including an executive member of the SACP and the Youth League (Mokoena), a trade unionist and ANC activist (Xaba) and an engineer (Mosoetsa)[16] who runs a small company in the area. These three leaders played a central role in mobilising the community. A forensic investigation had been instituted by the Mpumalanga provincial government in 2008, but the report was never made public or shared with the community. However, for reasons connected to infighting between the mayor and the speaker, the report was leaked, allegedly by the speaker, to members of the ANC Youth League. According to Mosoetsa: 'This was long overdue. We had been talking about service delivery since 2007. Comrades deployed in local government are failing us.'[17] Ironically, the forensic auditors reported that there was no evidence that the sum had ever existed or had gone missing, as the financial records were incomplete. Nonetheless, the group met regularly to build its campaign and plan protests against the mayor and the council, and then started calling public meetings.

At about the same time, the municipality introduced a credit control policy to get residents to pay for services and began cutting off the electricity supply to defaulters' houses. Two public meetings were held to discuss the municipality's new credit control policy. In these public meetings, the issue of the missing R30 million was also raised. On a Sunday in October, while the protest leadership were addressing a community meeting at the local stadium, the provincial member of the executive council (MEC) for local government paid a visit to the town, having heard that there was a danger of community protest. First, he visited the mayor and promised to assist in getting the municipality's affairs into order. Then he met with the protest leaders, who left the public meeting and went to a community hall to hold discussions with him. While they talked, the people in the stadium were getting restless. According to Mokoena: 'They felt we took too long. They marched to the hall to demand water and electricity.'[18] At this stage, the MEC went back to the mayor and instructed that the electricity should be restored. However, when he reported back to the people, who had by then returned to the stadium, '[t]hey felt they couldn't wait, and called for a stay-away and for barricades to be erected, but no burning'.[19]

But the violence started the same day, after the police were called in. The protest leaders placed the blame for this squarely at the door of the police. As one protest leader puts it: 'People would converge in public; the police would fire teargas. It made the people wild. Then the cops started shooting some and arresting others. That made people angry.'[20] As a result, the library, a community hall, a municipal office and the house of a senior councillor were burnt down. A man was shot dead while looting a shop behind the library. Some allege that this killing was done by the police and others that it was done by the Asian shopkeeper.

A week into the protests, 11,000 residents of Kungcatsha marched from the township into the town to present a memorandum to the council. Some protesters started to smash the windows of municipality offices and tried to set cars belonging to the council alight. The police fired at the crowd with rubber bullets, and protesters started looting street vendors' goods, throwing stones and missiles at the police, and barricading roads with stones and dustbins. After this episode, groups of youths took to erecting barricades across the regional road that bypasses the township, 'tolling' the road by demanding R20 ($2.40) from each motorist.

Violent clashes continued between young men and the police for about three weeks, with scores injured and others arrested for public violence. According to young men who had participated in the violence, it was the police conduct that angered them and persuaded them to demand that all councillors stand down. The protests ended when a team of senior ANC leaders arrived in the town and announced that the mayor and her mayoral committee had been 'dismissed'.

Protesters saw themselves using the destruction of property to communicate their grievances to those in authority beyond the town: 'Actually, when we fought, we were sending a message to the top, to Nelspruit [the provincial capital] that they must come and address our problems.'[21] Protesters made it clear to us that they saw collective violence as a means of forcing the powerful office bearers to acknowledge the dignity and legitimacy of the powerless after all else had failed.

Insurgent citizenship in the Kungcatsha protests was defined by its claim for work opportunities and housing, for an improvement in municipal services, and for the right to be heard and recognised. The repertoires of protest resembled those that were used in the struggle for full citizenship rights against the racially closed citizenship defined by apartheid, and the protesters in Kungcatsha explicitly claimed the rights of democracy and citizenship.

DIVISIONS IN THE ANC

The protest movement in Kungcatsha arose in the context of a deeply divided local ANC. The division between the mayor and the speaker of the council ran deep, to the extent that they no longer spoke to each other. According to several informants, it was the speaker who had leaked the report on the missing money to the protest organisers. According to members of a 'fraternal committee' of community elders who attempted to persuade the national head office of the ANC to intervene, the tension between mayor and speaker had paralysed the ANC at the local level, making it unable to respond to the protests.

The tension was not simply a personal matter. One of the protest organisers said that it was clear the speaker wanted to oust the mayor: 'He was planning that, once she is out, [he's] in as a mayor. He was using people, making promises: "I will give you tenders, jobs." Unfortunately for him, the anger was directed towards him in particular.'[22] In fact, the speaker's house was burnt down in the protests. The speaker in turn alleged that his house was burnt down by 'comrades [who] are positioning themselves for elections in 2011'.

The speaker was not the only councillor associated with the protests. Another was a man who in the 1980s had headed a local vigilante group sponsored by the apartheid security forces to disrupt and target the popular anti-apartheid movement. He was clearly a powerful figure in the community, because he became an independent councillor and then joined the ANC. He had played a part in generating discontent with the mayor, and a group of young protesters made clear their allegiance to him: 'He is the only councillor we won't harass. Some people said during the protests that we must also burn down his house. We said no. He is our guy. They won't touch him. There is nothing he should be punished for.'[23] But according to the mayor's bodyguard, it was this man and his former fellow-vigilantes who were the main problem in the ANC: 'They no longer had influence in the community, so they decided to join ANC. The goal was to take over the ANC, to take over government. People were dreaming of riches.'[24]

Although the protest leadership ultimately appeared not to be aligned with the two councillors, they were themselves members of the ANC and the ANC Youth League, and one was a member of the SACP. They represented a distinct grouping within the ANC that stood in opposition to the mayor and speaker and their allies. There was also a history of ANC Youth League mobilisation in protest against the leadership of the town council – we were told such protests had taken place in 2006, 2007 and 2008, and that the investigation into the missing money simply added ammunition to an ongoing campaign. Whether previous protests had been led by the same group as organised the 2009 protests is not clear, but other activists noted that some of the protest organisers, and in particular Mokoena,[25] had been very much 'part of the gang' running the council, profiting from tenders, until they had had a fallout of some sort. Mokoena himself, a member of both the ANC and the SACP, and one of the sharpest dressers in town, was unabashed about his ambitions:

I go into people's offices and demand something. I force my way in. I am a loyal and dedicated member of the ANC. I am not after positions. I am not an opportunist. I will defend the National Democratic Revolution. But I also believe I am entitled to a portion of the country's wealth.

It is clear from these interviews that the Kungcatsha town council and the ANC that dominates it form power centres around which local elites circle, seeking access to resources in the form primarily of salaried jobs and business tenders that enable self-enrichment and feed patronage networks. In other words, the ANC and the town council form sites of class formation, where a new black elite can access the resources that signify status and enable them to engage in petty accumulation. The opportunities for upward mobility are necessarily somewhat limited in a small town, especially one in which industry is in decline. The result is an intense competition within the elite for access to these opportunities and the power to dispense them to associates. Some, such as the former vigilante, are able to reinvent themselves in order to gain access to these opportunities. The cost of failure is high: the mayor, who had always lived in a Reconstruction and Development Programme house, was in the process of building a five-room double-storey home when she was deposed. It is unlikely she will be able to complete the building. The intensity of competition, the importance of the stakes and the consequences of failure may explain the instability of networks and alliances, and may also explain the high levels of violence that attend these struggles. The ANC constitutes the primary site for local class formation and the struggles it generates. This can be a brutal and vicious process. In Kungcatsha, the first mayor elected in 1995 was assassinated shortly after his election; the man chosen by the ANC to replace him was killed on the day of his nomination. A former mayor claims to have survived a number of attempts on his life. The recently deposed mayor, with the longest record of service at six years until she was ousted in the protests, survived 13 attempts on her life, according to her bodyguard. Violence appears to have become endemic in the internal struggles over council positions. The councillor whose house had been burnt down threatened revenge against those whom he believed were responsible. Another candidate during by-elections reported receiving thinly veiled threats like 'Is your house insured?'

The struggles within the elite played no small part in the mobilisation of protests against the town council. For some factions within the ANC, community protest provided an opportunity for engaging in struggle within the party to reconfigure power relations and gain access to council resources. Such dynamics are absent from the analyses of Heller and accounts of social movements in post-apartheid South Africa, and, we suggest, provide a fresh perspective on relations among social movements, civil society and the state.

PROTEST LEADERS AND THE MOBILISATION OF THE COMMUNITY

Among the protest leaders there were diverse motivations, with some regarding protest as an opportunity to oust their opponents in the town council and reconfigure power relations in the ANC so as to gain, or regain, positions of power and access to lucrative council business, while others appeared to be genuinely concerned to challenge corruption and incompetence. Protest leaders were mobilising popular anger, and there was a tension between the subaltern crowds who were protesting against corruption and for improved material conditions and services by attending mass meetings and marches, and engaging the police in street battles, and those in the leadership who were pursuing their own agendas. The subaltern crowds were well aware of these agendas. In the words of some of the protesters: 'It is not service delivery, but people are just fighting for tenders, but using the community to do so'; '[s]ome of the leaders were angry that they were no longer getting tenders and then they decided to mobilise the community against the municipality'.

This cynicism about the motivations of the leadership did not undermine popular mobilisation, however; as Mokoena said, 'I have never seen such a big march in the history of the township – everyone was there.' This shows that the protest movement was constructed through the agency of both the protest leaders – what Tilly calls 'political entrepreneurs'[26] – who use community members to fight their political battles, and the protesting crowds, who strategically use political entrepreneurs to present their grievances to relevant offices because of their access to local politics. The protest movement in Kungcatsha thus had a *dual character,* representing the struggle of an ANC faction to shift power relations and gain access to the opportunities and resources of the town council, and simultaneously a mobilisation by the poor over their grievances about corruption, local amenities, municipal services, housing and jobs. This dual character created a tension at the heart of the protest movement, shaped by contrasting processes of class formation – on the one hand, intense competition over access to positions within the rising elite, and on the other, the struggles of an expanding class of poor against their marginalisation from both wage income and the public goods represented by municipal amenities and services.

AFTERMATH

The aftermath of violent protest is as important for understanding the protests and the social forces that shape them as the origins and dynamics of the protests themselves. In Kungcatsha, after two weeks of violent protest during which the ANC resisted calls from the community to intervene, a high-profile ANC national team arrived and announced the 'recall' of the entire six-member mayoral executive. Three weeks after the ANC had announced the recall, three party members drawn from its proportional representation list were sworn in as replacements for the three proportional representation councillors who had been recalled. These new councillors had been among the organisers of the protests.

Three of the vacancies were for ward councillors, which required that by-elections be held. In terms of the law, a by-election needs to be held within 90 days, but this process in Kungcatsha took longer because there was a power struggle between candidates nominated by the protest leadership and candidates seen as representatives of the previous council. In the end, the protesters won and their preferred candidates (some of whom were leaders of the protests) were nominated to stand for the by-elections. On the day of the by-elections Mokoena told us: 'Today is like the 27th April 1994. The people of Kungcatsha are happy to come and vote for their leaders. This is the democracy that we fought for.' He continued:

Look there; look that side. It is early in the morning, but people are already queuing. This is massive, comrade. The people of Kungcatsha have come out in numbers to choose their leader ... The masses have spoken through their mass action last year and now they will exercise their democratic right to vote for their leader.

There was a massive voter turnout, and it seemed as if the protests had raised the political consciousness of the community. Some interviewees made reference to the Bill of Rights, including the right to protest and to receive services, such as access to clean water, housing, electricity, health and education. Overall, the elections were seen as a triumph for the protest leadership, because all their candidates won. 'The masses have spoken', said one. In many of the interviews, there was a sense of collectiveness, oneness, pride, excitement and happiness that the will of the people had prevailed. Interviewees drew on both human rights and democratic discourses to justify their violent protests against what they considered to be an incompetent and corrupt council: 'You see, the protest has paid off that we are now here voting for own people'; '[y]eah, we are happy to be voting for our own leaders'.[27]

However, the interviewees asserted that 'it is not guaranteed that violence would not happen again'.[28] Protesters hoped that the new leadership would fulfil all their election promises, but said they would resort to violence if it failed to do so. An important aspect to be noted here is that many community members (especially the youth) now felt that the use of violence was a solution to all their problems. One participant said: 'Violence is the language that this government knows. Look, we have been submitting memos, but nothing was done. We became violent and our problems were immediately resolved. It is clear that violence is a solution to all problems.'[29]

The protests were profoundly ambiguous, combining mobilisation by protest leadership, whose goal was to reconfigure power relations in the ANC and the council, with a mass movement galvanised by popular grievances such as lack of housing, water, jobs and so forth. Once the protests had achieved success with the disbanding of the mayoral committee, the crowds disappeared, re-emerging as queues of voters in the by-elections, while the leadership were reabsorbed into the ANC, where they engaged in fierce struggles to ensure their candidates were the ones who filled the vacant council positions. The protest movement, which had appeared so vibrant and broad based, rapidly disappeared, leaving no durable popular organisation that could occupy the space of civil society and continue representing the concerns and grievances of the poor and marginalised residents of the township. Put another way, the protest movement did not give rise to a social movement. Indeed, after the by-elections, a bitter struggle ensued among leaders of the protest movement as some were absorbed into the council while others were excluded. At the centre of this was the struggle for material resources and business opportunities in the council as the excluded protest leadership feel that they were used by those who succeeded in entering the council at the end of the community protest. One of the excluded leaders of the protest said: 'We are planning a second war against this council because like the previous council they are failing our people.'

The rapid class formation of the new elite and the fierce internal struggles this entails take place around and within the ANC as the dominant political organisation and the one that mediates relations between society and state. The result is a profoundly unstable ANC that at the same time exists in a state of profound paralysis. In the struggle for power and access to resources, networks and factions form, compete and reform.

Instability is reinforced by the duality between the ANC in government and its continued existence as a powerful force outside of government retaining some of its vibrancy as a liberation movement. This duality also plays into ambiguous government authority structures. While the mayor of Kungcatsha was senior to the speaker and the town manager at the local level, they outranked her politically in the ANC through their membership of higher structures. At the same time, it was rumoured that the mayor had been put in place and was protected by an MEC at the provincial level. The result was an organisation with multiple centres of power, paralysed by the interlocking nature of these centres of power and the accommodations and compromises between them, and by the struggles and alliances among different factions at different levels. The ambitions of the protest leadership, both before they gained access to the council and afterwards, exacerbated this instability and paralysed the local state even further, which in turn may reproduce or deepen the inequalities of differentiated citizenship, providing a stimulus for further insurgent citizenship mobilisation and reproducing cycles of violence in the town.

THE DARKER SIDE OF INSURGENT CITIZENSHIP

There is a tendency in the literature to adopt a fairly narrow focus on social movements as formal organisations with formally articulated demands directed towards the state, and on this basis assume that the conception of citizenship manifested by such organisations is a progressive and democratic one. Our research into the more inchoate and informal dynamics of protest movements and the 'crowds within crowds' suggests that the conceptions of citizenship finding expression through them are more ambiguous and contradictory, echoing the work of Holston.[30] We identify a darker side to insurgent citizenship, one that includes hostility to women, the assertion of patronage networks, xenophobia and the reproduction of cycles of violence.

In Kungcatsha, the mayor who was 'dismissed' was a woman. It is official ANC policy to increase the number of women in leadership positions in government structures. However, some of the young male protesters were adamant that they could not be ruled by a woman, because women made poor leaders, being incapable and 'stubborn'. The young men related angrily how the mayor had publicly dismissed them as 'unemployed, unwashed, dagga-smoking boys'[31] and so felt that her removal as mayor was justified.

Threats of violence were also directed at other women in leadership positions. For example, a woman councillor was unpopular with the protest leaders because of her association with some members of the previous council. Several informants, especially young males, expressed very sexist views in relation to her: '*Asibafuni abafazi*' ('we don't want women').[32]

Her daughter stated: 'Girls and women are scared to go to ANC meetings due to high levels of violence in some of the meetings.'[33] As argued above, differential citizenship is clearly shaped by differential experiences of gender, masculinity and power. In turn, violent repertoires associated with insurgent citizenship may reproduce new forms of differential citizenship, disempowering women from participating in political life.

Insurgent citizenship in this context provides an avenue for disempowered young men to reassert their power against elite women and men. Insurgent citizenship makes claims that expand the realm of democratic rights while at the same time reproducing gender oppression. In this case, insurgent citizenship attempts to overcome one form of differentiation while simultaneously entrenching another form – discrimination against women. This is not surprising, considering the way current forms of differential citizenship undermine the masculinity of young men by denying them the prospect of starting a family. Insurgent citizenship then constitutes – among other things – an assertion of masculinity in response.

The mobilisation of protest in Kungcatsha dramatised a claim to be heard as citizens and a rejection of corruption. Grievances regarding municipal amenities and services, jobs and housing, as well as the right to protest, expand the concept of citizenship to include social dimensions. However, the ambition of some of the protest leaders to themselves gain access to the town council and the opportunities it presents for self-enrichment carries the danger of undermining a notion of rights-based citizenship by strengthening the salience of patronage networks in relation to politics. Supporters packed ANC branch meetings to ensure that the candidates of the protest movement were elected as councillors. There is little doubt that such supporters would expect to be rewarded in some way, whether with projects, tenders or jobs.[34] Since the resources available to the town council cannot meet everyone's needs, beneficiaries are likely to be selected on the basis of loyalty.

What appears as a struggle for democratic rights and citizen participation may turn out, then, to produce its opposite: the subversion of democracy and the strengthening of practices of patronage and clientelism.

In Kungcatsha, shops owned by foreign nationals were burned and their goods were looted during the protest. These events were consistent with those in other of our case studies. Foreign nationals are evidently seen as easy targets due to their vulnerable and marginalised status. While insurgent citizenship lays claim to socioeconomic rights for South African citizens, in some cases it simultaneously deploys violence against foreign nationals in order to exclude them from access to rights and opportunities by enforcing the differentiation between citizens and non-citizens. Community protests are not the only form that insurgent citizenship takes. In the context of mass poverty and the struggle over livelihoods and resources, a struggle for new forms of differentiation that exclude groups seen as competitors – in this case, foreign nationals – may also emerge. This analysis reveals another darker side of insurgent citizenship.

CONCLUSION

The general tendency in studies of social movements in post-apartheid South Africa is to assume an optimistic view of the potential for such movements to expand citizenship rights, deepen democracy and struggle for a socialist future. Our study of collective action in Kungcatsha suggests a more ambiguous and fluid reality, in relation to both its organisational dynamics and the notion of 'citizenship' that found expression through it. Such protests appear to have become a distinguishing feature of the post-Mbeki period in South Africa, and so it is particularly important to investigate their internal dynamics and political significance. The most striking feature of the protest movement in the town was its dual nature. Factional struggles on the part of some protest leaders to shift power relations within the local ANC were combined with the struggles of the poor against corruption and for the provision of public goods. There was a tension at the heart of the movement between these two forces, with many among the protesters quite aware of the ambitions and interests of the leaders, but willing to make use of them to address their grievances to powerful authorities beyond the town, just as much as the leaders were making use of mass mobilisation to secure their own positions in the town council.

The dual character of the protest movement became particularly visible in the aftermath of the protest, when the national leadership of the ANC enforced the resignation of the mayoral committee, the crowds dispersed and the protest leadership were reabsorbed into the ANC, where they engaged in fierce battles to fill the newly vacated positions with their own candidates. Sections of the crowd then re-emerged as a newly recruited mass membership in some of the branches, where they supported the protest candidates, and then as voters in the queues on the day of the by-elections. The study demonstrates a fundamental ambiguity and fluidity in the trajectory of the protest movement and in the formation of political and civil society. While the residents of Kungcatsha were able to establish relatively autonomous public spaces and collective practices – public meetings, marches, the destruction of municipal buildings – these were simultaneously conceived of as struggles within the ANC, rather than struggles against it. The target was a particular set of councillors deemed to be arrogant, incompetent or corrupt, rather than the organisation itself. As soon as crowd actions had achieved a shift in the local ANC, the crowds on the streets became an assertive ANC rank and file in branch meetings, and then triumphant voters in the institutions of formal democracy. Militant protest leaders became ANC activists and then electoral candidates and town councillors. At the same time, the agency and autonomy of the protesters remained visible in the confident threats that they would return to the streets if their new representatives failed to honour their promises. These processes reveal an ambiguity in the way the local ANC dominates both the political terrain and the social terrain defined by civil society in Kungcatsha: while the ANC may occupy the terrain of civil society, residents and citizens are able to march, protest and confront the police from *within* the ANC, appropriating the ANC to articulate their own grievances. This suggests, perhaps, a new way to think about Zuern's findings regarding the porosity of boundaries between state and society in her study of the South African National Civics Organisation (SANCO). On the face of it this is also consistent with Heller's conclusions. But while his explanation emphasises the centralised, technocratic and autocratic character of an ANC that shoulders aside civil society and shuts down the space for democratic participation from below, our study reveals the ways in which both local elites and subaltern groups actively constitute the ANC as a network that fills most social spaces in the township, including the space of civil society.

These findings are consistent with those in other of our research sites, although with differing degrees of fluidity. Local histories may provide alternative social resources. In one case the protest leadership crystallised into a formal 'concerned citizens' committee, which dissolved soon after the protest movement had subsided. In another, an alternative political formation in the form of the Pan Africanist Congress provided a more durable structure outside the ANC. However, in all cases protest movements assumed a similar fluidity, moving in and out of political society, constituting public spaces of protest and collective action and then reconstituting these as political branch meetings or voters' queues.

The ANC, it seems, absorbs most things, and many things take place within it. It is the place where the local elite, activists, those with organisational ability, the talented and the ambitious congregate, both because it is the centre for accessing local opportunities and because of its linkages into broader regional and national networks. Likewise, subaltern groups mobilise within and through the ANC and its networks rather than locating themselves beyond it and organising autonomous associations. The struggle between subalterns and elites moves back and forth between the political terrain and public spaces beyond it, but its primary locus appears to be within political society rather than civil society – and it is therefore absorbed into political society rather than constituting a challenge from without.

This study suggests that class formation was a crucial dynamic shaping the trajectory of protest movement in Kungcatsha and the internal struggles within the local ANC, as in our other research sites. On the one hand, a new elite is rapidly emerging, focused on the resources and opportunities presented by the town council; on the other, the long-existing stratum of the poor and marginalised has been expanding as local industries in the town have closed operations. It is this process of class formation that explains the dual character of the protest movement, shaped by intense intra-factional contestation within the local and other levels of the ANC over entry into the elite, as well as by the struggle of the marginalised poor for access to incomes and public goods. The alliances forged in collective action seek to reconfigure power relations – both between different factions of the elite as well as between subalterns and the elite – within the ANC and the town council. Collective action mobilised by protest movements like this may serve to hold elites and political representatives accountable in some way to residents and citizens, and in this sense contribute to democratic deepening. However, its impact is limited. Firstly, the dual character of collective action is as likely to reproduce and strengthen patronage networks as it is to deepen democracy, since a web of obligations connects the new councillors to their associates and supporters. Secondly, protest movements organised in this way are episodic and fairly ephemeral moments of accountability. More durable, autonomous and structured social movements have enhanced strategic capabilities and the ability to more or less continuously hold public representatives to account, with an orientation towards concrete performance rather than personalities; the TAC provides a good example of this.[35] Such movements may have emerged here and there, but our research suggests that in general the current wave of protest is not producing them, and that breaking away from the tangled networks and relationships embedded in the ANC and its sister organisations will be extremely difficult. The role of popular agency from below in constituting the expanded political society described in this chapter provides insight into the continued dominance of the ANC over local civil society in the post-Mbeki era. Heller's research refers to the period from the late 1990s to the mid 2000s, when President Thabo Mbeki was able to consolidate centralised technocratic control over the ANC. Under President Jacob Zuma, centralised control has been shattered by open internal struggles among different factions; if centralised control was what narrowed the space for civil society, there would now be considerable potential for a flowering of autonomous associations. Instead, the contestation among factions for power and the mobilisation of popular discontent continues to take place through the ANC. As Partha Chatterjee suggests,[36] in the postcolonial world, political society and civil society may not obey the neat demarcations of Western theory.

This may be a reason why violence remains endemic in both intra-elite struggles and subaltern struggles for voice. Notwithstanding the democratic national constitution and institutions, single-party dominance means that neither intra-elite struggles nor subaltern challenges are decided at the ballot box. Nor are they decided through the democratic pressure provided by local social movements. Rather, these struggles are settled by the mobilisation of power within ANC networks – and violence is one way of shifting power relations.

The same dynamics explain why the local ANC is both paralysed and highly unstable as different factions are locked in struggle for control, and any substantial shift entails a change of personnel. As a further result, this instability and paralysis permeate the town council. The weakening of the council undermines its ability to provide the public goods demanded by the community, inviting further rounds of protest.

It cannot be said that all ANC cadres and every individual among the protest leadership were concerned only about their own interests and self-enrichment. Several appeared to be genuinely committed to ending corruption and improving the delivery of services and public goods; however, the ongoing cycle of poor performance by the council suggests structural impediments – not only the instability generated by the struggle over access to positions, but also the inadequacy of financial and technical resources in the face of the overwhelming poverty and unemployment of the township and the region. Thus, even where new councillors endeavour to improve performance, residents remain frustrated.

In line with Thompson and Tapscott's claims about social movements in the global South more generally, our research suggests that the protest movement in Kungcatsha constitutes a struggle for expanded socioeconomic citizenship. We draw on the concept of insurgent citizenship to explore the meaning of citizenship claims manifested by the protest movement. Community protests challenge the poverty, lack of rights and lack of voice of the poor by claiming rights to work and housing, basic services from the local municipality, an end to the misuse of public money, the accountability of politicians and officials, and the right to be heard. The democratic and human rights enshrined in the Constitution are used as reference points. This is the content of insurgent citizenship's challenge to differential citizenship.

However, we argue that its progressive and democratic dimension is bound up with a darker side, in the form of patriarchal prejudices, the reinforcing of practices of patronage, xenophobic attacks that accompany protest and the reproduction of repertoires of political violence. Such protest movements do not only represent an unambiguous struggle of the poor for democratic rights, but bear as well the weight of local power relations, prejudices and oppressive practices. Popular agency, in other words, may be mobilised by local demagogues and violent elites as much as by progressive forces. Popular protest carries the potential for diverse and contrasting future trajectories.

NOTES

1. The research for this chapter was conducted as part of a collaborative project on the dynamics of collective violence between SWOP and the Centre for the Study of Violence and Reconciliation, funded by the Royal Norwegian Embassy and the CS Mott Foundation.
2. 'Kungcatsha' is a pseudonym for this town in order to maintain the confidentiality of our informants, given the sensitive and controversial nature of the information they shared with us about corruption and power struggles in the town.
3. For mainstream theory, see Charles Tilly, 'Models and realities of popular collective action', *Social Research*, Vol. 52, No. 4 (1985); Sidney Tarrow, *Power in Movement: Social Movements, Collective Action and Politics*, Cambridge: Cambridge University Press, 1998; Alain Touraine, 'An introduction to the study of social movements', *Social Research*, Vol. 52, No. 4 (1985); for the Anti-Privatisation Forum, see Marcelle C. Dawson, 'Phansi privatisation! Phansi!: The Anti-Privatisation Forum and ideology in social movements', in William Beinart and Marcelle C. Dawson (eds), *Popular Politics and Resistance Movements in South Africa*, Johannesburg: Wits University Press, 2010. See also activists quoted in Steven Friedman and Shauna Mottiar, 'Seeking the high ground: the Treatment Action Campaign and the politics of morality', in Richard Ballard, Adam Habib and Imraan Valodia (eds), *Voices of Protest: Social Movements in Post-apartheid South Africa*, Scottsville: University of KwaZulu-Natal Press, 2006.
4. Elke Zuern, 'Elusive boundaries: SANCO, the ANC and the post-apartheid South African state', in Ballard et al., *Voices of Protest*.
5. Friedman and Mottiar, 'Seeking the high ground'; Patrick Heller, 'Moving the state: The politics of democratic decentralisation in Kerala, South Africa, and Porto Alegre', *Politics and Society*, Vol. 29, No. 1 (March 2001); and 'Democratic deepening in India and South Africa', in Isabel Hofmeyr and Michelle Williams (eds), *South Africa and India: Shaping the Global South*, Johannesburg: Wits University Press, 2011.
6. Peter Alexander, 'Rebellion of the poor: South Africa's service delivery protests – a preliminary analysis', *Review of South African Political Economy*, Vol. 37, No. 123 (2010); Municipal IQ, '2011 – a slower year than 2009 and 2010, but rising', press release 19 September 2011, www.municipaliq.co.za.
7. Heller, 'Moving the state'.
8. Lisa Thompson and Chris Tapscott, 'Introduction: Mobilisation and social movements in the South – the challenges of inclusive governance', in Lisa Thompson and Chris Tapscott (eds), *Citizenship and Social Movements: Perspectives from the Global South*, London and New York: Zed Books, 2010, p. 26.
9. James Holston, *Insurgent Citizenship: Disjunctions of Democracy and Modernity in Brazil*, Princeton: Princeton University Press, 2008, pp. 8–10.

10. Karl von Holdt et al., *The Smoke that Calls: Insurgent Citizenship, Collective Violence and the Struggle for a Place in the New South Africa: Seven Case Studies of Community Protests and Xenophobic Violence*, research report, Johannesburg: CSVR and SWOP, 2011.
11. Interview with ANC Youth League leader, 25 November 2009.
12. Bride price paid by a young man to his prospective wife's family.
13. Interview with a group of young males who participated in the protest, 26 November 2009.
14. R. Connell, *Masculinities*, Cambridge: Cambridge University Press, 1995.
15. Interview with a group of young males. It is alleged that the mayor made this comment in one of her public interviews.
16. These are pseudonyms to protect the identity of these informants.
17. Interview with one of the protest leaders, 29 November 2009.
18. Interview with ANC Youth League leader, 25 November 2009.
19. Ibid.
20. Interview with ANC leader, 1 December 2009.
21. Ibid.
22. Ibid.
23. Interview with a group of young males who participated in the protest, 26 November 2009.
24. Interview with the mayor's bodyguard, 27 November 2009.
25. This is a pseudonym to protect the identity of this informant.
26. Charles Tilly, *The Politics of Collective Violence*, Cambridge and New York: Cambridge University Press, 2003, p. 187.
27. Interview with a young voter, 27 April 2010.
28. Interviews with voters, 27 April 2010.
29. Interview with young male participant, 27 April 2010.
30. Holston, *Insurgent Citizenship*.
31. See note 15, above.
32. Group interview with young males, 26 April 2010.
33. Interview with the daughter of a female councillor, 26 April 2010.
34. Musawenkosi Malabela, 'The African National Congress (ANC) and local democracy: The role of the ANC branch in Manzini-Mbombela', MA research report, School of Social Sciences, University of the Witwatersrand, 2011.
35. Friedman and Mottiar, 'Seeking the high ground'.
36. Partha Chatterjee, *The Politics of the Governed: Reflections on Popular Politics in Most of the World*, New York: Columbia University Press, 2004.

6
Unfolding Contradictions in the 'Zuma Movement':[1] The Alliance in the Public Sector Strikes of 2007 and 2010

Claire Ceruti

Zuma ... have you forgotten those who put you there? ... we'll meet at the local elections.

(Teacher's placard during the 2010 strike (Figure 6.1))

Figure 6.1 'Have you forgotten those who put you there' (2010)
Source: Author.

INTRODUCTION

Trade union mobilisations seldom appear in writing about social movements, and it is seldom noticed that South Africa's second delivery movement, whose beginning is marked by riots in the

Western Cape in 2005, was a workplace movement as well as a township movement. These strikes transformed the face of government in that they contributed to challenging the president at the time, Thabo Mbeki, and his policies, but they were not transformative in the sense of fundamentally reshaping power, government policy or, indeed, the material position of the strikers.

This chapter explains how the potential power of the strikes was truncated, while maintaining that they could have gone further. In doing so, it crosses between academic and activist theorising. Activist theorising addresses 'different kinds of questions' from social sciences – questions that are geared towards 'strategic and tactical proposals: a complex proposition that links together a reading of the nature of the present situation ... with an action plan for the movement in the immediate future'.[2] These questions are not about developing general propositions from what actually happened (although general propositions may be illuminated), but about developing a picture of the potential in a particular situation *in order to change the outcome*. The 'what if ...?' element implied here is addressed in this chapter by the strategic proposal that the strikes were a (missed) opportunity for social movement activists who were critical of the ruling party to build links with the union movement, despite its ties to the ruling party, thus strengthening both.

Because we cannot assess a non-event (such as the failure of social movement activists to link to the strikes), the chapter focuses instead on what did happen, concentrating on the internal dynamics of the two public sector strikes under consideration. Detailed descriptions of the strikes bring to the fore two kinds of evidence to support the strategic proposal above. Firstly, I will highlight two levels of contradiction that pushed various actors into confrontation with one another, despite their alliance with one another and sometimes despite their intentions. Here I show that the African National Congress (ANC)-led Alliance generally manages these tensions, but can at other times exacerbate them because it serves different purposes for different collective actors. Secondly, I highlight the 'molecular change' in strikers' ideas over time, which arose when they were confronted by these contradictions. I have borrowed and adapted this concept from Gramsci to suggest that small changes in ideas may accumulate almost invisibly among a mass of people, becoming visible abruptly, if at all, under particularly pressing circumstances.[3] Here I show that strikers' attitudes to the government started off as ambiguous and hardened from one strike to the other, with their statements sounding more like the language of social movement activists.

I conclude by considering a different level of transformative power – the level of strikers' worldviews. Conflicted views do not always solidify into a transformation of ideas. Here I show how molecular change was shaped by the strategic and tactical decisions of the strikers, union leaders, other activists and government officials.

The discussion begins with analyses of the Alliance in activist and academic theorising about the strikes. Thereafter I detail the political context of the strikes and discuss each strike in turn.

THE OTHER DELIVERY MOVEMENT

Strike days in South Africa rose from a low point in 2004 to reach record highs in 2007 and 2010, owing to massive public sector strikes in those years (Figure 6.2).

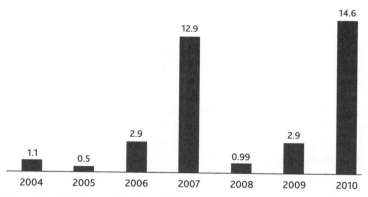

Figure 6.2   Absolute number of strike days in South Africa, 2004–10 (millions)

Note: The absolute number of strike days is calculated by multiplying the number of people on strike by the number of strike days.

Source: Andrew Levy Employment.

Both strikes were intensely politicised. The 2007 strike was one of a wave of strikes, protests and upheavals that Jacob Zuma rode to power. The second strike in 2010 was an early test of Zuma's government, and therefore a test of the unions' hopes for that government. Three-year wage bargaining agreements mean the rhythm of strikes differs from the rhythm of delivery protests (Figure 6.3), but the shared political context shows in the timing of the revival, the dip in 2008 during the interregnum between

Zuma being voted president of the ANC and assuming the role of the country's president, and the rise in protests and strikes under the reconstituted ANC.

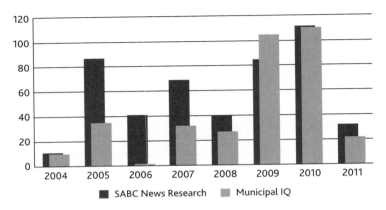

Figure 6.3 Number of delivery protests in South Africa, 2004–11

Note: The 2011 figures include the periods until May (SABC) and April (Municipal IQ).

Source: SABC News Research and Municipal IQ, in Peter Alexander and Peter Pfaffe, 'South Africa's rebellion of the poor: Balfour and the relationship to means of protest', paper presented at the South African Research Chair in Social Change Workshop on Concept and Evidence, University of Johannesburg, 2–4 July, 2011.

Many academics and activists missed or dismissed the rising number of strike days because left scholars had been busy *de*romanticising unions in post-apartheid South Africa. The social movement unionism of the 1980s,[4] where unions were embedded in a broad movement concerned with issues beyond the workplace, was overtaken by a kind of social policy unionism. Hein Marais notes that the strategy of shaping

> the economic and socio-economic terms of the transition at the top ... confirmed COSATU's commitment to a corporatist route (that would centre on social pacts between it, the state and business) and an overall pursuit of strategic compromises. It also cemented COSATU's political alignment with the ANC.[5]

Scholarship about the ANC-led Alliance began to centre on how it worked to dissipate militancy, despite the insults of Thabo Mbeki's home-grown Thatcherite programme,[6] leading Devan Pillay to argue that 'a working class revival' is 'highly unlikely at this stage' either within or outside the alliance.[7]

The first wave of new social movements,[8] such as the Anti-Privatisation Forum (APF), was greatly influenced by a similar analysis in our strategic approach to the strikes. When the APF was formed in 2001, COSATU was embattled in the alliance under Mbeki. Eager to prove its loyalty, it quickly distanced itself from the new forum's militant response to electricity cut-offs (see the chapters by Ngwane and McKinley in this volume). This experience, plus the fact that COSATU remained allied to the government responsible for the cut-offs, provided fertile ground for the emergence of South Africa's new social movements. Movement intellectuals such as Oupa Lehurule argued at the time that energies should be focused on the township protester, who was 'free from the ideological baggage' carried by COSATU members who were engaging in 'merely procedural' strikes.[9]

The analyses above work for explaining how the Alliance has diffused militancy, but they are weak at predicting where the mechanism could fail. It is only from some distance that the conclusion of the public sector strikes can be imagined as the smooth extrusion of an ideological bond to the Alliance. This chapter shows that other possibilities were foreshadowed in the strikes in that they complicated strikers' views of government and therefore, potentially, their attitudes to the theory of the Alliance. Rick Fantasia points out that strikes involving the rank and file may be 'processes [that] can be seen as relatively independent of the previously existing ideas and beliefs of individual participants'.[10] Barker and Cox continue:

> Most participants are not expecting the scale and the nature of the conflict they encounter. Their inherited knowledge is useful but does not tell them what is to be done in the specific circumstances … rather they have to argue about this, fumble their way forward, listen to different proposals.[11]

The chapter shows that the general operation of the Alliance to constrain militant protest was subtly subverted in the public sector strikes, with betrayed faith in the Alliance contributing to a heightened sense of militancy. Two sets of tensions in the Alliance contributed to volatile consciousness among strikers. The obvious tension was between the government and the striking unions. but the strikes also revealed that the union leaders faced different pressures to the strikers, a point often overlooked when COSATU is analysed only as an amalgamated whole. In the first strike, the marginalisation of the union leaders from the Alliance meshed with the discontent of members. This strike challenged the actually existing practice of the Alliance (by challenging the Mbeki presidency's prerogatives over other components of the Alliance and, indeed, his right to be president) without articulating a theoretical challenge to the Alliance (such as considering alternatives to it). That movement transformed the face of the presidency by replacing Mbeki with Zuma and thereby appeared to restore the channels for policy battles. In the second strike, the union leaders approached the restoration of the Alliance as the restoration of collective bargaining at a political level, but the strikers' expectations were raised – and their subsequent disappointment deepened – by the same reconstitution.

As a general proposition (in terms of academic theorising), the chapter shows that the differences in position among union members, leaders and government remain muted in 'normal times', allowing scholars and activists to maintain homogenised views of mass organisations. However, in confrontational movements, especially when participants are taking some risk and the stakes are therefore high, such differences may be magnified.

My main sources are direct and occasionally participant observation of the strikes in Johannesburg and Soweto in 2007 and 2010, repeat interviews with a cohort of strikers (most, but not all, conducted by myself), photos and footage of placards and songs at particular protests and picketing at certain sites, my notes about television news during the strike, and informal conversations. I also used news reports and documents circulated by the unions, the ANC and the South African Communist Party (SACP).

THE CONTEXT: HOW ZUMA BECAME ENTANGLED WITH THE DELIVERY MOVEMENT

This section illustrates that, although conflict between Mbeki and the unions was inevitable, the idea that Zuma was the best alternative was not. Friction inside the Alliance was already high by the time of the 2007 strike. Thabo Mbeki was then president. His arrogance within the ANC and his willingness to alienate trade union leaders in defence of a neoliberal path became legendary.[12] The cost to the working class – the ANC's biggest constituency – had been enormous. By the government's own conservative figures, at least a quarter of people of working age were unemployed. Using the expanded definition, the figure rises to 40 per cent. A survey by Naledi, the research arm of COSATU, 'found that between 1998 and 2002 workers' share of national income dropped from 50 percent to less than 45 percent. By contrast, company profits rose from just less than 27 percent to 32 percent.'[13]

As frustrations with Mbeki's style grew, the strategic decisions involved even in procedural strikes took on a more volatile quality. Unions were feeling the impact of the jobs crisis and wage restraints. Many had lost thousands of members to unemployment and casualisation,[14] increasing the burden on some of the employed. Union officials had to face the weakening of the unions that employed them and also the growing sense of embarrassment at being snubbed repeatedly by Mbeki.

The delivery protests – in response to early campaigning ahead of the 2006 local government elections – couched demands for basic services in terms of broken promises, accountability and democracy. These precipitated a crisis within the ANC. The 2005 ANC national general congress revolted against Mbeki. Firstly, it threw out an Mbeki-backed proposal to reduce workplace rights for young employees. Secondly, it demanded a rethink of internal procedures to make the president more accountable to the organisation.[15]

A public spat occurred between Mbeki and Zwelinzima Vavi, COSATU's general secretary, over more-interventionist policies to create employment. Vavi and Mbeki had traded insults before, but this time the rift did not go into hiding at the first press report. On 27 June 2005 the turnout for one of several scheduled one-day strikes surprised everyone. About 2 million people supported the strike against job losses and about 30,000 crammed into the centre of Johannesburg. There the assembled marchers heard Vavi lambast Mbeki, thus sending a signal that it was acceptable to directly confront the president. Vavi also linked the battle between labour and capital to a battle within the cabinet: a few days earlier Mbeki had suspended the deputy president, Jacob Zuma, from the cabinet because he was facing charges of corruption connected to a government arms deal. Zuma had never shown any particular enthusiasm for workers' struggle, but he was from the old school that listened to the unions before ignoring their suggestions and came from a rural area rather than a posh university like Mbeki.[16] That same week, at a strike rally of municipal workers, Vavi said: 'Workers have little reason to celebrate the gains of democracy as the rich have become richer and the poor poorer', and warned that the strike was the first of many.[17] The anger was compounded when several company executives decided to give themselves enormous pay increases.[18] Retail executives rejected workers' demands for a 9 per cent pay rise, while, as the Naledi survey says,

Studies have shown that, between 2005 and 2006 alone, executive pay rose by as much as 34 percent. Research conducted by independent analysts, the Labour Research Service, and trade union Solidarity demonstrates that executives in South Africa enjoy the bulk of company wealth, while the gap between remuneration of CEOs and that of workers runs by a factor of over 50 to one. In other words, remuneration for the average CEO is more than 50 times that of the average worker in the country.[19]

This was like a declaration that Mbeki's economic turnaround was not for everyone. By 2006 – the year of three major strikes of security guards, cleaners and shop workers – Mbeki was proclaiming the success of neoliberal policies as South African economists announced an economic turnaround: productivity was steady, business confidence was up and several companies announced large profits.[20] However, if unionists were hoping for easy victories now that there was money to spare, they had underestimated capital's understanding of wage restraint as the key to bumping up profits. Capital tried to starve out the strikers, and the settlements ending these early strikes were neither clear defeats nor victories. However, interviews suggest that some strikers developed a sense of a great battle being unleashed, in which the strikes themselves were just the first shot. For example, a group of cleaners asserted that their 2006 strike did not win their demands, but was a victory in that they had stood up for their rights.[21]

By 2007 the shock waves were being felt at the ANC's congress and policy conference. Crucially, much of this debate was cast in terms of capital versus labour. So, for example, ANC strategist Joel Netshitenzhe defended a proposed economic policy document at the conference by saying that 'our revolution is multi-class' and should not become a 'hostage to narrow sectoral interests'. Vavi replied that 'as the majority, the working class cannot be dismissed as pursuing narrow sectoral interests'. The ANC Youth League also replied to the document, saying: 'We have the problem of capital and labour being treated as equal partners of the developmental state ... There is an absence of characterising monopoly capital as an enemy in the unfolding democratic revolution.'[22]

However, Vavi and the leaders of the SACP remained constrained by their political outlook. They would not look beyond the outcome of the battle within the ANC. At the twelfth SACP congress, Vavi argued as follows:

The ANC remains an important progressive formation for the working class. The challenge is how we consolidate, retain and deepen its progressive posture and working class leadership under the current conditions of intense contestation. As ANC members we need to defend the progressive strand in ANC policy and its continued bias towards the working class.[23]

He argued elsewhere for changing the 'current situation where the movement works ... like a rubber stamp and the alliance a crisis management body',[24] but placed Zuma as the great hope for workers – even though Zuma's comment that the public sector strike was damaging the country's image abroad placed him firmly in the camp of those who wanted, at best, to achieve a balance between labour and capital. The Zuma strategy answered the strikers' search for political solutions in a way that allowed the cracks in the Alliance to release pressure and restore its viability – but, as we shall see, stored up new pressures for the future.

STRIKE ONE (2007): 'WE PUT THEM WHERE THEY ARE AND LOOK HOW THEY TREAT US'

This section emphasises the contradictory and shifting attitudes to government that emerged in the 2007 strike. A song from the 2007 public sector strike captures the distance strikers felt from government: '*Baikentse badingwana*' – 'they are making themselves gods'. This was a strike over wages and working conditions that shaded easily into the growing discontent about government, because government was the employer. Elsewhere, I detail a meeting of health workers towards the end of the strike where the crowd cheered enthusiastically for a string of organisations – including the APF-affiliated Soweto Electricity Crisis Committee, previously cold-shouldered by COSATU – but fell silent when the ANC was mentioned. I had never witnessed such a thing before.[25]

The strike brought to the fore contradictory feelings about government. For example, one of my interviews was with a public servant who was also an SACP activist. Listening to the recording again, I was struck by how confident and articulate he sounded, and grudgingly admiring of how he was able to 'hijack' my questions to seamlessly put across his own 'propaganda'. But when he began to speak about the government, he groped for words and fumbled with concepts.[26] Frequently, strikers demonstrated two or three contradictory views of government within the same interview. For example, a hospital worker said:

> The government does not respect and does not care about its workers. During the strike it was threatening essential workers. The government does not care [for] and appreciate and love its workers ... government is part of the workers. The problem is it forgets where it came from ... We vote for the government; it is our government; workers cannot live or function without a government, [but] the government cannot function without workers – they need each other.[27]

And a clerk complained:

> Our government is the enemy. They returned R13,000 from my Department of Justice to the financial treasurer, and they don't want to give us money. So there is money; they don't want to pay ... The government must just take care of workers here in the ANC, please, because we are planning to go overseas.[28]

These attitudes moved beyond mere discontent. 'We put you where you are and look how you treat us' was a recurrent theme that appeared in two forms: both as a reminder of who voted for the current government and a reminder that the strikers carried out essential tasks without which even a minister gets no gravy. An amusing version of this theme played out around the health minister's liver transplant (see Figure 6.4). The implication, only half grasped, is that power lies below – an implication that subtly destabilised the existing practice of the Alliance.

Strikers' justifications for their wage demands were threaded through with themes that had emerged over the preceding years concerning inequality, hardship and lack of delivery. When articulated during a demonstration, especially to a recorder or a camera, they become appeals to a broader audience implicitly assumed to have some grounds for sympathy with the public workers. Such appeals are by their nature self-interested, but also require the strikers to put themselves in the shoes of a patient or a person waiting in a queue (such as the clerk explaining that the strike was also about understaffing).

A handful of strikers drew explicit links between their own situation and the delivery protests, such as a striker from Correctional Services: 'The government is selfish and capitalist; do not care about

Figure 6.4 'Bring back our liver' (2007)
Source: Author.

its workers. On the other hand, the service delivery is not improving, but it creates millionaires each year. It is busy creating millionaires out of taxpayers' money, but fails to eradicate the bucket system.'[29] And a hospital clerk said: 'I will join a strike in future; I see myself as a politician; I like politics; I like to talk about politics; even where I stay in township, I confronted a local councillor on delivery issues.'[30]

Strikers accommodated themselves to the end of the strike in two ways. One group mirrors the union negotiator's script: 'In bargaining, you have to give something in order to get something. In history, the workers never won everything, they compromise. Anyone who thinks workers can get whatever they want is a dreamer.'[31]

These workers were accommodating themselves to the partial defeat of the strike, using a form of accommodation that allows them to attribute the outcome to factors beyond their control. A second group of strikers came out of the strike still arguing the justice of their semi-lost cause. Some of those who believed the strike was lost immediately moved to a repetition of the reasons they should have got a 12 per cent increase, absolutely resisting the reality of the settlement. These often develop strategic explanations for its failure, such as, '[a]s the strike progressed, we felt powerless, because you cannot strike without an income', and '[t]he problem is that the government is greedy. This explains why it failed to give us 12 per cent. The minister used this strike to score points, showing her bosses that she is capable of dealing with workers.'[32]

Some strikers emerged from the strike feeling very bitter about the government. Typical comments included this from a teacher: 'The ANC government also does not support workers. Its role is to blame workers whenever they embark on strike'[33] and '[t]he government or the ANC are not part of us, but serve the interests of the few elites. This government care[s] about the elites, not poor workers.'[34] Another teacher summarised the strike as follows:

> This strike demonstrated that the government is not prepared to accelerate service delivery. When it came to power, we were told that there will be a better life for all and decent jobs for all. But it has failed to give workers at least 10 per cent and improve working conditions. This is not amazing, because in other areas, this government perform[s] badly as well. For example, [the] backlog in housing delivery. That is why there are service delivery protests.[35]

Even among those willing to accept the government 'back into the fold', there remained a demand for accountability:

> the government I have today is not the same government of yesterday, [the] reason being we don't fight, we negotiate. But [the strike] shows that before we get things we need to fight first, you see, and I think it was not our aim that when we take our government to power we are going to fight. I was thinking that we are going to negotiate with good faith – but we need to fight. I was thinking we are having a government that is going to listen to the people, not this government that want[s] us to listen. Then they must listen to us first.[36]

In summary, the strikers' experience produced a contradictory and shifting consciousness. The nature of the employer – government – meant that an ordinary sectoral trade union consciousness nevertheless poked a hole through which the public sector striker could not help glimpsing politics in relation to the strike. The strike created uncomfortable ambiguities about government for those strikers who believed the ruling party was on their side and sharpened the question of whether the ruling class should be listening or listened to.

However, the approach of the union leaders remained centred on negotiations, and their own ambiguity to government fell ultimately on the side of changing things from the inside – the Zuma solution. For strikers, there were two material limits on the strike. The first was the sacrifice of wages. A month of 'no work, no pay' just about offsets any increase you might get. Secondly, even while strikers had bitter complaints about the direction of negotiations, the militancy of the meeting described above was not matched by a strategic imagination to prosecute a short, sharp strike, such as building a public support campaign. This forced them to conform to the limits of collective bargaining.

During the strike, I encountered few spontaneous references to Zuma, even in response to questions like 'Who are the friends of your strike?' But if the strike was not succeeding, the Zuma solution removed the personal risk involved in a strike and tackled the problem of government disloyalty to workers without posing the more difficult question of the workers' loyalty to the ruling party. In the 2007 strike, strikers settled for much less than the 12 per cent they originally wanted, but the Polokwane conference, where Mbeki's leadership was to be challenged, was already on the horizon, enabling strikers to defer their hopes to the political kingdom. The potential of the strike to directly transform – or at least improve – strikers' lives was diverted into the hope of transforming the Alliance. The 2010 strike was to be in many senses a test of this strategy, reviving the opportunities missed in 2007.

STRIKE TWO: CAUGHT BETWEEN THE COMRADES AND THE COMRADES IN 2010

This section emphasises how the 2010 strike exposed the differences in how union leaders and members experienced and responded to conflict in the 'renewed' Alliance. A striker's placard – 'Comrades, stay together just like buttocks, when buttocks separate 7% (shit) comes out' (Figure 6.5) – brings out the sense in the 2010 strike that government was breaking the Alliance. Strikers retained a contradictory attitude to government, but criticism centred on the person of Zuma preceded the strike. The ANC-led Alliance was conceived in terms of accountability to the strikers.

At the same time, the 2010 strike was a classic case of containment, where COSATU intervened as both conflict manager and strikers' interlocutor in the collective bargaining process. It is the story of the contortions of union leaders caught between betraying their

Figure 6.5   'Comrades, stay together' (2010)
Source: Author.

comrades in government and betraying their members, as well as the strategic contradictions involved in attempting a more assertive role in the Alliance.

The 2010 strike, unlike that of 2007, was forced on union leaders by members, and was pushed on members when government negotiators hardened up. The behaviour of the three key collective actors in the strike was conditioned by the reconstitution of the Alliance that followed the ANC's December 2007 conference at Polokwane, where Jacob Zuma replaced Thabo Mbeki as president of the ANC and which explicitly promised to deal with public sector grievances.

Hassen believes that union negotiators were confident of cooperation with government, given that the public service minister, Richard Baloyi, had in 2009 agreed relatively easily to above-budget salary adjustments.[37] Added to this, they trusted that COSATU's support for Zuma at Polokwane would be reciprocated. That they did not expect to strike is confirmed by the fact, reported by several strikers, that the strike was 'called suddenly' after workers rejected the government's final offer.

Government negotiators dug in their heels early in negotiations. Gentle thinks this is partly because they knew the union leaders were reluctant to strike and knew that COSATU and leaders like Vavi, the COSATU general secretary, were on the defensive in the Alliance.[38] I would add to this that government negotiators did not want to encourage greater aspirations from anyone, given the resumption of the delivery protests and the fact that all sorts of people, including but not limited to ANC Youth League leader Julius Malema, now felt sufficiently confident to criticise the direction of the ANC in public. Finally, the huge expenditure on the FIFA World Cup, combined with the ongoing global financial crisis, would have encouraged the government to rein in spending. The government's belligerent response to the unions' demands was demonstrated in its provocative announcement of a final offer of just 7 per cent on 11 August, the day after the unions marched in Pretoria in a one-day warning strike. 'Final' meant that they would sign and unilaterally implement the offer in 21 days.

The third and most important group of actors, the strikers, was the surprise element. In 2007 public servants enthusiastically responded to the union's call to strike. By 2010 the strike appeared to members as the obvious response to the provocative 11 August final offer. What 'made the public sector workers very stubborn', as one striker put it?[39] One element was the entrenchment of a sense of inequality and maldistribution of government resources. When I asked strikers where the government should get money from for their wage demands, most referred to the expenditure on the World Cup and to the 'tenderpreneurs', that is, ANC members who use their positions to grow rich through government contracts. For the hospital cleaner who had to buy her own mop three times that year, the meaning of the World Cup was that there could be money for essentials if there was money for international parties (see Figure 6.6).

Figure 6.6   'Money for the World Cup' (2010)
Source: Author.

Alongside this went a sense of shock and betrayal. Strikers interviewed at the 10 August 'warning strike' shared with the 2007 strikers an ambiguous relation to government inherent in a sense of betrayal. A unionist said during the 2010 strike, 'I think government is taking advantage of the fact that we are the people who rallied around government'[40] and another striker complained: 'It is extremely unfair because we all fought for this freedom, which we deserve, all of us.'[41] Nevertheless, outright expectation preceded the strike. One person there complained: 'Zuma promised us a lot of things, but I see nothing – nothing has happened.'[42] Throughout the strike, placards like the one cautioning Zuma to 'remember Polokwane promises' were also unavoidable reminders that people once took down a leader (Mbeki) from where they had put him. More than one angry placard reminded the president that workers had been called to defend him in the past (see Figure 6.7).

Figure 6.7 'We were ready to bail you out' (2010)
Source: Author.

Many strikers started off with faith that Zuma would set the minister right when the matter was brought to his attention. Such faith was totally undermined a few days into the strike when Zuma asserted on national TV that the government could fire workers who did not return to work. A few had their faith briefly restored when Zuma ordered government negotiators back to the table late in the strike, but many more went home and made placards directed at Zuma – reminding him that a teacher 'wiped his funny nose', warning him not to bring home any more wives from his state visit to China, and wondering whether he could support five wives on a teacher's income. Songs like '*Uskebereshe*' ('slut') are not simply insulting, but imply that someone sells themselves to the highest bidder. The song thus implies a demand for accountability.[43] This was sung about both Zuma and Minister Baloyi.

The course of the strike was heavily influenced by the way that the restoration of the Alliance locked the union leaders back into the logic of collective bargaining with a political edge. They were influenced by strategic considerations related to the Alliance and social policy unionism.

Despite its key role in propelling Zuma to the presidency, by 2010 COSATU had seen little reward in terms of key policies such as banning labour brokers. Therefore, by the time of the strike, relations among the Alliance partners were a little strained. The COSATU Central Executive Committee produced a statement some weeks before the strike was on the cards, stating that 'the alliance is again dysfunctional', and lambasting 'predatory elites' in the ANC.[44] Zwelinzima Vavi, general secretary of COSATU, repeated these sentiments during a march twelve days into the strike (where he also announced that COSATU had filed the necessary notice for a general solidarity strike), leading a government spokesperson, Themba Maseko, to complain: 'We are beginning to see and hear too many statements that are taking the strike beyond labour relations. It worries us.'[45]

Vavi had backed Zuma expecting to change things *through* the Alliance, and in this strategy the next crucial step was getting the ANC to adopt elements of COSATU's growth document. This agenda could not afford for the strike to lose outright, but neither did it need an all-or-nothing showdown with those expected to consider the document sympathetically at the upcoming ANC National General Council meeting. The safest action from Vavi's strategic viewpoint may have been a short, sharp strike and a quick victory before tensions grew beyond repair. He therefore played a contradictory role, militant on the streets, but pragmatic mediator at the negotiating table. Behind the scenes, Vavi had worked hard first to avert a strike and then to settle the strike. He describes this role in a remarkably unselfconscious letter responding to South African

Democratic Teachers' Union (SADTU) accusations that he had sold its members out. He says that the negotiators were 'acutely aware [of] how difficult it was for government to move' and describes a number of attempts to reach a compromise on figures suggested by the public sector union officials, but apparently not caucused with their members.[46]

A key turning point in ending the strike came with the return of the parties to negotiations about twelve days into the strike. Within the logic of collective bargaining, the aim of a strike is to force the employer back to the bargaining table rather than to achieve specific demands. When Zuma ordered the parties back to negotiations, strikers were enormously hopeful and COSATU called off the general strike before anything had emerged from the new negotiations. The offer that came back, however, was just 0.5 per cent more. Strikers were furious, but also demoralised. Picket lines that had survived police attacks shrank after the new offer was announced on 1 September. Adding to the confusion, Vavi announced the offer on public radio and recommended that unions should accept it before they had taken it to their members. In a letter written after the strike to justify his role, Vavi describes his turning point in the negotiations as being when government negotiators received a call at 3 a.m. after which they 'folded their folders and went home'.[47] Vavi's reading is that they felt betrayed by their union comrades who had twice promised a compromise they thought they could sell to members, only to be told that the members had rejected it. The next morning, Vavi announced on public radio that it was impossible to win anything more and the strikers should accept the deal. This was an unsettling moment for strikers. Vavi's loyalties became unclear – was he representing strikers to the government, or vice versa?

Strikers I interviewed were otherwise ambiguous about the suspension of the strike. On the one hand, there was an element of relief – 'no work, no pay' was biting. Also, most of the strikers were concerned about the effect of the strike on patients and schoolchildren. This was a key weakness of the strike: firstly, strikers made no effort to build a community campaign this time (in 2007, rudimentary efforts were made in Soweto, when the unions were beginning their revolt against Mbeki and therefore more open to outside support). The lack of such a campaign left the strikers at the mercy of the press – which was virulently anti-strike – to form public perceptions of themselves, which ensured that they felt more and more isolated as the strike wore on. Further, strikers made no attempt to decide for themselves who should be an 'essential worker' in the face of the government's long-standing refusal to sign an agreement on that issue. Strikers could very well have set up their own committees to keep a skeleton staff going in hospitals, thus building public sympathy, but they did not.

On the other hand, everyone I spoke to was deeply dissatisfied with the deal and strikers tried to resist the end of the strike. The strike was suspended despite the fact that the settlement was rejected, sometimes unanimously, by all the hospitals in Gauteng and by most regions of SADTU, the COSATU-affiliated teachers' union. Once again, most strikers accepted something of the logic of collective bargaining, but were extremely unsettled about the top-down manner in which it was implemented. Most came across as bewildered, depressed and tired at the end of the strike. One felt after Vavi's intervention that they had become pawns in a game to advance political agendas.

However, despite rejecting the deal, the strikers had once again not built an alternative to Vavi's logic. Loss of pay was again a real problem by day 20 of the strike and the picket lines shrank after the return to negotiations yielded nothing. The strike was weakened by the fact that there was no meeting that brought together strikers from different sectors and unions with communities to strategise or to discuss the offers on the table. Officials and office bearers met across the union divide, but members did not, except occasionally during picketing. Gauteng teachers were resolutely against the suspension of the strike, but were unable to give courage to the dejected and confused groups of hospital workers contemplating the deal, nor to strategise together. This meant that the leadership of the National Education, Health and Allied Workers' Union – the COSATU health workers' union – could blame the non-COSATU unions for accepting the deal and leaving them stranded, in turn leaving SADTU, the teachers' union, high and dry.

As in the last strike, strikers were extremely militant, but lacked either a strategy to go beyond the leaders' focus on the negotiating table or a theoretical framework to justify this. The left outside the Alliance was invisible in the strike, while the left inside the Alliance was not independently organised. In the absence of such organisation to contextualise Vavi's bewildering behaviour in the strike, some strikers concluded that striking was a waste of time. A young teacher who struck for the first time in 2010 said that she could now understand those second-time strikers who 'just stayed at home and did their washing and their housework' during the strike.[48]

CONCLUSION

Taken together, the strikes illustrated the development of contradictions in the ANC-led Alliance, which were pushed explosively to the surface in the confrontational atmosphere of the strikes. The 2010 strike demonstrated that the elastic holding the grassroots to the Alliance had been stretched to new limits since 2007 by renewed expectations of Zuma – the means by which the Alliance was to have restored itself. The spike in strikes and protests was not unlike the 18 months after the 1994 elections, when people took confidence from the defeat of apartheid and the notion that 'our government' was in power. In the following decade, the concept of 'our own government' worked as a leash on dissent within the Alliance. In the 2007 and 2010 strikes, the concept increasingly acquired an edge of demand.

The potential transformative power of the strikes and the truncation of this power were illustrated by their contribution, in the first instance, to deposing Mbeki, and in the second instance by the Zuma government's over-reaction to COSATU's civil society conference, which took place shortly after the strike and to which the ANC had not been invited – because it was a political party, but the ANC took this as a deliberate attempt at marginalisation. Elsewhere, I write: 'For the Zuma group in the ANC, struggling for control of conflicting interests, the spectre of the 2010 public sector strike is the spectre of an alliance with a union leadership unable to control its own members.'[49] The government's new growth path also recognised the need to placate labour in its promises of job creation, but without making any concessions to COSATU's specific economic proposals. The subversion of the practice of the Alliance was not matched with a rethinking of the theory. However, this was not just the same story of restoration over and over again, illustrated by the mere fact that the Zuma government was struggling to contain protest and internal dissent early in its term.

In terms of activist theorising, opportunities to begin to bridge the divide between the social movements and the workplace movement developed in the strikes. Not only were attitudes to the ruling party conflicted, but the period from 2007 to 2010 saw the development of a broader identification beyond public sector workers that had been present, but rudimentary, in 2007 with respect to the delivery protests. In 2007 only a handful of strikers were unambiguous about these protests. In 2010 all strikers I asked were adamant that 'there was nothing wrong' with people taking to the streets for their rights. Strikers began to generalise from their own direct experience of government to sympathise with people often substantially poorer than and frequently physically distant from themselves.[50]

It is uncertain as yet what the long-term effect on strikers' attitudes has been. Conflicted attitudes do not necessarily lead to strategic re-evaluation:

> On the ground, the political residue of the strike is harder to discern... the danger here is that adaption to disappointment turns into demobilisation ... however a still restive residue was evident in the skirmishes which continued after the strike was over, between the militant Johannesburg Central region of the teachers' union and the department of education ... the possibilities of rifts between the government and Cosatu have not closed, [and] such stresses will continue to challenge orthodoxies about the alliance.[51]

As a general proposition regarding the volatility of strikers' ideas, we have seen that 'molecular change' opens the possibility for a phase shift (a permanent change of state), but this depends partly on the actual outcomes and the available interpretations for those outcomes. We cannot say what would have happened if social movement activists had linked to the strikes more systematically. We can say that there were plenty of opportunities for them to do so.

NOTES

1. Here and elsewhere in the chapter I am using 'movement' in a generic sense, rather than the technical senses now associated with social movement studies. Hence, by 'Zuma movement' I mean that broad grouping of people and organisations who came together around the common aim of replacing Thabo Mbeki with Jacob Zuma, including, but not limited to, the Congress of South African Trade Unions (COSATU) and certain of its affiliates. Similarly, when I later speak of the delivery movement, I mean a collection of protests loosely united by common demands for government to 'deliver' on its promises around basic services, housing and accountability to the electorate.
2. Colin Barker and Laurence Cox, '"What have the Romans ever done for us?" Academic and activist forms of movement theorizing', paper presented at the Alternative Futures and Popular Protest Eighth Annual Conference, Manchester Metropolitan University, Manchester, 2002, pp. 3–4.

3. Antonio Gramsci, *Selections from the Prison Notebooks of Antonio Gramsci*, New York: International, 1971.
4. Jeremy Baskin, *Striking Back: A History of Cosatu*, Brooklyn and London: Verso, 1991; Jeremy Seekings, *The UDF: A History of the United Democratic Front in South Africa, 1983–1991*, Cape Town: David Philip, 2000.
5. Hein Marais, *South Africa Pushed to the Limit: The Political Economy of Change*, London: Zed Books and Cape Town: UCT Press, 2011, p. 444; see also Adam Habib and Rupert Taylor, 'Parliamentary opposition and democratic consolidation in South Africa', *Review of African Political Economy*, Vol. 26, No. 80 (1 June 1999); A. Desai and A. Habib, 'COSATU and the democratic transition in South Africa: Drifting towards corporatism?', *Comparative Studies of South Asia, Africa and the Middle East*, Vol. 15, No. 1 (March 1995).
6. Adam Habib and Imraan Valodia, 'Reconstructing a social movement in an era of globalisation: A case study of COSATU', in Richard Ballard, Adam Habib and Imraan Valodia (eds), *Voices of Protest: Social Movements in Post-apartheid South Africa*, Scottsville: University of KwaZulu-Natal Press, 2006; Devan Pillay, 'Cosatu, alliances and working class politics', in Sakhela Buhlungu (ed.), *Trade Unions and Democracy: Cosatu Workers' Political Attitudes in South Africa*, Cape Town: HSRC Press, 2006; Roger Southall and Geoffrey Wood, 'COSATU, the ANC and the election: Whither the Alliance?', *Transformation*, Vol. 38 (1999).
7. Pillay, 'Cosatu, alliances and working class politics', p. 190.
8. See, for example, Dale McKinley and Prishani Naidoo, *Mobilising for Change: The Rise of the New Social Movements in South Africa*, Development Update Series, Johannesburg: Interfund, 2004; Ballard et al., *Voices of Protest*.
9. Oupa Lehulere, 'The new social movements, COSATU, and the "new UDF"', *Khanya*, No. 11 (2005), p. 29.
10. Rick Fantasia, 'From class consciousness to culture, action, and social organization', *Annual Review of Sociology*, Vol. 21 (1 January 1995), p. 218.
11. Barker and Cox, '"What have the Romans ever done for us?"', p. 13.
12. See, for example, Sakhela Buhlungu, Roger Southall and Edward Webster, 'Conclusion: Cosatu and the democratic transformation of South Africa', in Buhlungu, *Trade Unions and Democracy*, p. 223.
13. Matuma Letsoalo, 'Lost: 11 million days', *Mail & Guardian Online*, 6 July 2007, http://mg.co.za/article/2007-07-06-lost-11million-working-days (accessed 7 August 2011). See also the original report: Simon Kimani, *Surviving below the Margin: Recent Trends in Collective Bargaining and Wage Settlements*, Naledi, 2007, www.naledi.org.za/index.php?option=com_rokdownloads&view=file&Itemid=267&id=115:survivingbelow (accessed 23 November 2011).
14. Buhlungu, *Trade Unions and Democracy*, p. 7; Devan Pillay, 'Globalization and the informalization of labour: The case of South Africa', in Andreas Bieler, Ingemar Lindberg and Devan Pillay (eds), *Labour and the Challenges of Globalization: What Prospects for Transnational Solidarity?*, London: Pluto Press, 2008.
15. Author's notes from television news. See also Moshoeshoe Monare, 'Pipe or machinegun for ANC presidency?', *Independent Online*, 1 June 2006, www.iol.co.za/news/politics/pipe-or-machinegun-for-anc-presidency-1.279991; Moshoeshoe Monare, 'People power under threat – Sadtu', *Independent Online*, 24 August 2006, www.iol.co.za/news/politics/people-power-under-threat-sadtu-1.290814; COSATU, 'COSATU's response to Deputy President

Kgalema Motlanthe', press statement, 4 November 2011, www.cosatu.org.za/show.php?ID=5638; Karima Bown, 'ANC tries to juggle state–party tension', allAfrica.com, 12 December 2007, http://allafrica.com/stories/200712120392.html.

16. Buhlungu, *Trade Unions and Democracy*; C. Ceruti, 'African National Congress change in leadership: What really won it for Zuma?', *Review of African Political Economy*, Vol. 35, No. 115 (2008).

17. *Mail & Guardian*, 'Municipal strike is the first of many, says Cosatu', 27 July 2005.

18. *Mail & Guardian*, 'Mboweni: Most don't remember such low rates', 23 February 2005.

19. Letsoalo, 'Lost: 11 million days'.

20. Donwald Pressley, 'Mbeki lauds SA's story of hope', *Mail & Guardian*, 27 May 2005; Henri du Plessis, 'Thousands of shop workers prepare for strike', *Independent Online*, 20 July 2005, www.iol.co.za/news/south-africa/thousands-of-shop-workers-prepare-for-strike-1.248698.

21. Focus group discussion with eight cleaners, Johannesburg, 28 November 2007.

22. Rapule Tabane and Vicky Robinson, 'ANC to the left, to the left', *Mail & Guardian*, 22 June 2007, http://mg.co.za/article/2007-06-22-anc-to-the-left.

23. Zwelinzima Vavi, 'Address of the COSATU general secretary to the SACP 12th Congress', 13 July 2007, www.cosatu.org.za/show.php?ID=1437 (accessed 15 November 2011).

24. Zwelinzima Vavi, 'Speech of Cosatu general secretary to the 8th National Congress of NEHAWU', Tshwane, 26–29 June 2007, www.wftucentral.org/?p=830&language=en (accessed 15 November 2011).

25. Claire Ceruti, 'Striking against a politically explosive background: Hidden possibilities in the 2005–2007 South African strikes', paper presented at the How Class Works conference, SUNY, Stonybrook, 2010.

26. Interview with public servant, Pretoria, 25 May 2007.

27. Telephone interview with hospital worker conducted by Lawrence Ntuli, July 2007.

28. Interview with a Department of Justice secretary, Pretoria, 25 May 2007.

29. Telephone interview with a Correctional Services officer conducted by Lawrence Ntuli, July 2007.

30. Telephone interview with a hospital clerk conducted by Lawrence Ntuli, July 2007.

31. Telephone interview with 'Sifiso' conducted by Lawrence Ntuli, July 2007.

32. Telephone interview with a health clerk conducted by Lawrence Ntuli, July 2007.

33. Telephone interview with a nurse conducted by Lawrence Ntuli, July 2007.

34. Telephone interview with teacher A conducted by Lawrence Ntuli, July 2007.

35. Telephone interview with teacher B conducted by Lawrence Ntuli, July 2007.

36. Interview with a health worker and shop steward at Chris Hani Baragwanath Hospital, 28 July 2007.

37. Ebrahim-Khalil Hassen, 'Unsatisfactory strike outcome: Public service agreement', *South African Labour Bulletin*, Vol. 34, No. 5 (5 December 2010).

38. Leonard Gentle, 'South African strike: Political watershed?', *Pambazuka News*, 9 September 2010, www.pambazuka.org/en/category/features/66783 (accessed 15 November 2011).

39. Telephone interview with a female Soweto teacher, 2 September 2010.

40. From handwritten translation of interview conducted by Tabea Nong with striker A in Pretoria, 10 August 2010.

41. Interview with a National Education, Health and Allied Workers' Union member in Pretoria, 10 August 2010.

42. From handwritten translation of an interview conducted by Tabea Nong with striker B in Pretoria, 10 August 2010.

43. Thanks to Mosa Phadi and Nomancotsho Pakade for this insight.

44. COSATU, 'The Alliance at a crossroads – the battle against a predatory elite and political paralysis', political discussion paper, September 2010, www.cosatu. org.za/docs/discussion/2010/dis0903.pdf.

45. Linda Ensor, Wilson Johwa and Alistair Anderson, 'Minister meets labour in bid to calm strike tempers', *Business Day*, 27 August 2010, www.businessday. co.za/Articles/Content.aspx?id=119296.

46. Zwelinzima Vavi, 'Re: Sadtu leadership has sold out. Letter to SADTU Mthatha Branch chairperson', 17 September 2010.

47. Ibid.

48. Interview with 'Dorah', Johannesburg, 21 September 2010.

49. Claire Ceruti, 'The hidden element in the 2010 public-sector strike in South Africa', *Review of African Political Economy*, Vol. 38, No. 127 (2011), p. 156.

50. Peter Alexander, 'Rebellion of the poor: South Africa's service delivery protests – a preliminary analysis', *Review of African Political Economy*, Vol. 37, No. 123 (2010), p. 25.

51. Ceruti, 'The hidden element', p. 157.

7
Labour Strikes and Community Protests: Is There a Basis for Unity in Post-Apartheid South Africa?

Trevor Ngwane

INTRODUCTION

Globalisation has sometimes been understood as spawning new forms of struggle and new forms of organisations that are different from earlier forms.[1] The emergence of new movements and organisations in post-apartheid society has led to analyses that are in line with this general understanding; thus, organisations such as the Anti-Privatisation Forum (APF), the Treatment Action Committee (TAC), Jubilee South Africa, Abahlali baseMjondolo and others that emerged at the turn of the millennium have been labelled the 'new social movements'.[2] As Anciano (this volume) points out, the use of this term in South Africa differs from conceptualisations employed in new social movement theory, which emerged in Europe in the 1960s and 1970s. Studies of post-apartheid resistance politics tend to suggest a sharp distinction between 'community' or social movement struggles and those waged by organised labour.[3] There has been no serious scholarly attempt to identify and theorise the links between workplace and community-based struggles in post-apartheid South Africa. As far as political practice is concerned, some celebrate this separateness, while others bemoan it.[4] The question that arises is: what is the nature of the relationship between these two forms or sites of struggle and their corresponding organisational forms, namely, the new social movements and trade unions? The separation in the two forms of struggle also raises the question of whether unity between them is desirable and achievable in the first place.

This chapter explores instances in which social movement organisations and trade unions have supported and cooperated with each other in struggles during the post-apartheid era. The discussion begins with the story of the Anti-iGoli 2002 Forum, which was formed to unite municipal unions and community organisations in the struggle against the privatisation plans of the Johannesburg City Council in the year 2000. Later, these processes culminated in the formation of the APF, now understood as a new social movement that is entirely distinct from trade union in terms of organisational identity and the issues it organises around. The lessons from this earlier instance of cooperation between labour and community organisations are valuable for theory, strategy, and tactics in the struggle for economic and social justice in the future.

Before telling the story, it is necessary to make a few theoretical remarks, because theory provides a conceptual lens that can allow for a systematic and rigorous investigation. It also provides a critical basis for testing the validity and accuracy of our thinking and conclusions about an issue. We should, however, remember that 'no theory is half as important as practice', and it is necessary that 'we keep our heads, and do not let ourselves be carried away by intellectualist talk or abstract reasoning'.[5] My starting point is to assume the class struggle between capital and labour as the primary contradiction in capitalist society and, following on from this, to attribute historical agency to the working class, because it is this social group that produces wealth.[6] My analysis therefore starts off with working-class struggle itself – that is, the (objective) development of political relations between classes in society – and then proceeds to relate the (subjective) expression of class interests in the form of ideas, actions and organisations that arise in response to this struggle. The chapter focuses on the relationship of struggles at the workplace and in the community – where workers work and live. Trade unions, civics, political parties, new social movements, and so on, are viewed here as the various forms of organisation that workers – employed and unemployed – create in order to fight for their needs. In establishing the class dynamic behind the political choices that organisations and their leaders make, it is important to always observe the maxim: 'Human beings make history, but not in conditions of their own choosing.'[7]

From this theoretical foundation, the following observations can be made about the post-apartheid period. The main feature of the political relations between classes in the 'New South Africa' is a government that, despite having been put in power by the working class, is busy supervising the intensification of the exploitation of labour and the worsening of oppressive living conditions for this class. The rich are getting richer and the poor poorer. The response has been a marked and steady increase in working-class combativity in the form of strikes and community protests. The rise in popular action goes together with the birth of new organisations, the revitalisation of old ones and the decline of others. But action and organisation are disparate and fragmented. There is turmoil without a centre of authority; there is no sense of a united working-class movement fighting and moving forward together, albeit on many fronts. Instead, there is division among the struggles of organised labour, the new social movements and community protests.[8] The forces of the working class are marching and striking separately. There is also marked ideological and theoretical diversity that reflects and informs these divisions.

Different groups of workers have at different times stood at the forefront of the class struggle in this country; for example, unorganised employed workers (1973), students (1976) and unionised workers (1980s). In the past ten years or so, South Africa's new social movements, working-class communities, public sector workers and, more recently, private sector workers have each risen up in open resistance, although at different times. Limited research has been done on the specific factors that explain the nature and timing of each of these mass mobilisations beyond general conditions that affect the whole class such as the 2008–11 (and continuing) economic crisis, the rise in the cost of living and other economic pressures on the working class.[9] In each case, leadership and organisation are important factors in determining the nature of the response. Often the different approaches to building struggle and unity in action are often a result of different theoretical visions and the way in which these are implemented in actual policies, strategies and tactics employed by organisations. A close examination of the struggle against iGoli 2002 – a bold plan to privatise municipal services by the Johannesburg City Council – and of the organisation and action that it engendered reveals how the campaign was practically and theoretically approached by the different actors, as well as their consequences for working-class struggle. It also reveals the nature of the relationship between community and workplace struggles.

THE STRUGGLE AGAINST iGOLI 2002 AND WITS 2001

On 23 October 1999 the Anti-iGoli 2002 Forum discussed, among other things, a plan to go to communities to spread the word and extend the campaign against the privatisation plans of the African National Congress (ANC)-led Johannesburg City Council. This committee consisted of representatives from the South African Municipal Workers' Union (SAMWU) and the Independent Municipal and Allied Trade Union (IMATU),[10] the two major municipal unions, and representatives from community and student organisations. The meeting noted that the two unions had a march planned for the following Tuesday. Workers agreed to gather and march to hand over a memorandum of grievances to the first democratic mayor of Johannesburg, Councillor Isaac Mogase, the former Soweto Civic Association leader. Comrades present at the meeting committed to do everything possible to drum up support for the struggle of the trade unions against privatisation, because this government policy was an attack not just on municipal workers, but on the working class as a whole.

The march was a 'success', but its significance went beyond the numbers that were present. It represented a moment when there was unity of action between trade unions and working-class organisations operating outside the workplace against the ANC government as the protector of capitalist interests. It is noteworthy that the clashes originated in a context where workers faced the government as an employer – as a boss. The moment was, however, short-lived and the subsequent development of the working-class struggle was marked largely by a division between the trade unions and the new social movements, with the two sections of the working class fighting separately and sometimes at cross-purposes. The exception was the South African National Civic Organisation (SANCO) and TAC because of their allegiance to the ANC–South African Communist Party (SACP)–Congress of South African Trade Unions (COSATU) Alliance and the highly focused framing of the HIV/AIDS issue.[11] But some of the movements, such as the APF, have generally not had an easy relationship with COSATU. A study of what happened during this moment of unity of workplace and community struggles in the post-apartheid era might yield some useful theoretical and political lessons. We shall see below how the APF was born of the unity that was forged; we shall also see how that unity unravelled.

The meetings of the Anti-iGoli 2002 Forum were also attended by union and student representatives fighting against Wits 2001, a University of the Witwatersrand privatisation plan that saw 601 cleaning and gardening workers lose their jobs and some of them rehired as contract workers. The university struggle gave birth to the Wits 2001 Crisis Committee and it was the merger of this committee with the Anti-iGoli Forum that led to the formation of the APF. The decision to form the APF took place at a meeting held on the tenth floor of COSATU House on 6 July 2000. Mazibuko Jara, who was then chairperson of the SACP's Johannesburg branch, proposed at the meeting that the two committees should combine forces against privatisation in light of the impending Urban Futures Conference (jointly organised by Wits University and the Johannesburg City Council, the two institutions pushing their respective privatisation programmes). Prior to the meeting, Jara circulated a four-page letter inviting 'organizations and individuals to endorse and join this Broad Activists' Forum'.[12] The letter also included a proposed programme of action, which involved the disruption of some the sessions of the Urban Futures Conference, as well as a range of other activities that included meetings, pickets and marches to build the two struggles. The meeting adopted both the programme of action and the formation of the APF Broad Activist Forum.[13] The 'member' organisations active at the time of the latter's formation included, among others, COSATU; the Johannesburg Branch of the SACP; SANCO; SAMWU; IMATU; the National Education, Health and Allied Workers' Union (NEHAWU); the South African Democratic Teachers' Union; the Campaign Against Neoliberalism in Southern Africa; the Wits Student Representative Council (SRC); the Wits Postgraduate Association; Wits residence house committees; the Gauteng Hawkers' Association; the Workers' Organisation of South Africa; the Democratic Socialist Movement; the South African Graduates Development Association; Jubilee South Africa; and the Ecumenical Service for Socio-Economic Transformation.[14] Each grouping was assigned a specific task. For instance, two student comrades were responsible for coordinating media, SAMWU and IMATU had to lead their joint march, the Wits SRC was tasked with calling residence meetings, NEHAWU had to organise a picket at the Commission for Conciliation, Mediation and Arbitration when a case in which it was involved was being heard, and so on. The significance of this was that the programme involved everyone's participation and did not sideline any particular group or set of interests.

SAMWU and IMATU were at the forefront of the municipal struggle, while NEHAWU and the students played a critical role in the university struggle. The broad theoretical perspective was that the struggle for a living wage and for decent services affected the working class as a whole. For example, a few years earlier, in the course of its struggle against water privatisation in places like Nelspruit, SAMWU had developed a position demanding a minimum amount of 50 litres of water per person per day in addition to its 'workplace' demands.[15] Thus, organisations such as SANCO, on behalf of the various communities, were made to see the connections between municipal workers and their struggle. The churches opposed privatisation because, among other things, they claimed to have 'a prophetic duty to stand with our people as we together face the challenges of hunger and poverty'.[16] The socialist organisations, left intellectuals and others during the early days of the APF as a broad activist forum, adopted this position in the name of the struggle for socialism. It must, however, be pointed out that in addition to the important strikes by municipal workers, communities were increasingly taking organised action to defend themselves from the privatisation and cost-recovery attacks by the state and capital, which mostly took the form of water and electricity cut-offs, evictions and job losses. This explains the increasing combativity of the working class about five or six years into the democratic order.

The APF became a beehive of activity for organising opposition to privatisation, owing to the commitment of the individual activists who increasingly did the work of the new organisation. There was a great deal of interaction with the unions and some of the organisations listed above. But the campaign lost some steam as the unions made some compromises along the way and the government offered some concessions. Actions increasingly took the form not of thousands of workers striking, but of marches of a few hundred or small demonstrations that sometimes amounted to impressive media stunts. There must have been alarm bells and damage control action inside the Tripartite Alliance, because gradually its organs dropped out of the APF: the unions, SANCO, and later the South African Students' Congress (SASCO). The SACP's withdrawal was messy, because it expelled Dale McKinley, its Johannesburg secretary, partly as a result of his involvement in the Anti-iGoli campaign. I was also stripped of my position as ANC ward councillor for Pimville, Soweto, before the formation of the APF for speaking out against iGoli 2002. This must have provided grist for the mill for those demanding the withdrawal of Alliance support for the APF. The change in composition of the APF as a result of Alliance organisations leaving it coincided with the development of an APF identity and policy as a movement of struggle in a rapidly changing political situation.

The unions were reluctant to confront the ANC government aggressively. But the deeper ideological reason underpinning their reticence was that the union leadership blamed problems facing workers in the post-apartheid era on the 'legacy of apartheid' rather than on capitalism. The struggle against apartheid's legacy was real enough, but it could not be won through the ANC government's pursuit of a largely pro-capitalist economic programme. Its attacks as an employer on workers in the municipal and higher education struggles had little to do with the legacy of apartheid but placed the ANC squarely on the side of the ruling class. The SAMWU and IMATU leadership appeared to retreat from the initial position of laying the blame for privatisation on capitalism and on the ANC government as its protector. Instead, the preservation of the ANC-led Alliance over-rode this analysis. In effect, the unions' anti-privatisation struggle was increasingly being guided by a theory that decreed that the ANC government should not be confronted as the organiser of the attacks against the working class. This served to weaken the struggle. In other words, having placed their struggle on a platform that had the potential of winning real victories for its members and for the working class as a whole, the SAMWU and IMATU leaderships subsequently pulled away from the unity that they had built with community organisations because of the primacy of their loyalty to the ANC. Since apartheid and not capitalism was regarded as the system that workers had to change in order to improve their lives, the attendant political policy was class collaboration (with the ruling class) rather than an independent working-class politics. We shall see below how the same approach characterised the COSATU leadership's response to the rise of the new social movements. Moreover, the discussion considers the topical question of whether there has been any change in the way in which the union federation is approaching the recent and recurrent community protests.

POLITICAL DYNAMICS INSIDE THE APF

The decision to launch the APF as a 'broad activist forum' introduced an ambiguity in the composition of the organisation and in its decision-making processes, because among those who attended and assumed leadership positions were delegates representing their organisations together with individual activists representing – to use 1980s language and with all due respect – 'their own jackets'. One reason for this is that the APF started as a movement of struggle rather than as an organisation. In the early days, this situation allowed many left activists, unionists and students to build the APF into a vibrant 'home of struggle', sometimes without the approval of or a mandate from their organisations. But the APF's centre of gravity gradually shifted away from the initial forces that had formed it – namely labour, civic, church and student organisations – towards working-class communities actively fighting around municipal services. Increasingly, the APF was the home of defensive community struggles against service cut-offs, evictions and forced removals waged by newly formed community organisations whose struggles were against and outside the organisational control of the ANC-led Alliance. Being so new, the relative weakness of these organisations was compensated for by the leadership and support provided by left groups and individuals, and especially the APF activists, whose influence became significant in the new movement. This influence had an important impact on the emergent political character of the APF.

Some of the left leaders in the APF became enamoured with the ideas of 'autonomism' or 'anarcho-autonomism', a trendy ideological current in the international anti-globalisation movement at the time.[17] The influence of these ideas in international left circles has been associated with the failures of the socialist project in the twentieth century and the disillusion wrought by the triumph of neoliberalism in the world.[18] In South Africa, and with respect to the APF, the adoption of neoliberal policies by the ANC government, its reliance on the Alliance for its hegemony and the failure of the labour movement to come to the rescue of communities under siege from the government's cost-recovery policies and other neoliberal attacks provided fertile ground for these ideas to find some resonance beyond intellectual circles into working-class organisations. Autonomism is able to live side by side with socialism because they are both leftist systems of thought and the former tends to be flexible, eclectic and somewhat inconsistent theoretically and in terms of programme. But it is possible to identify some key aspects of this approach such as an emphasis on direct action and militancy; a principled opposition to political parties and state power;[19] hostility towards trade unions, in particular COSATU;[20] suspicion of all forms of organisation and leadership because of the 'iron law of oligarchy';[21] an overly critical attitude towards the history of working-class struggle;[22] the rejection of socialism; and so on. Some of these themes have been influential in the political practice and theoretical formulations of the new social movements, with some of them serving to drive the wedge between unions and community organisations even deeper.

At best, the formulations of autonomism accommodated spontaneous upsurges of struggle around day-to-day issues that the ANC-led Alliance ignored. The autonomist perspective promoted a proactive and affirmative response to a mood among working-class communities that was increasingly receptive to organised and militant opposition. Ordinary workers were looking at the APF and other new social movements as centres of authority and hope. The new social movements were also inspired by the development of an international movement of struggle against neoliberalism and the negative impacts of globalisation.[23] They acquired their political authority from ordinary working-class people protesting, fighting, turning to each other and using their collective strength to change history. But there was a tendency to believe that this authority resided in the movements themselves rather than in the working class as a whole.[24] In the APF, for example, I remember that the orientation to the labour movement was highly contested, with strike support taking place after long and often acrimonious debates.

The APF was a relatively small organisation when compared with the organisations that formed the Alliance, but its emphasis on militant action and self-organisation in the struggle against aspects of neoliberal policy were politically significant in a context where the confidence of the working class in its own power to change history had been systematically undermined. In general, the new social movements came with change, vitality and growth representing a break with past patterns of working-class struggle that were becoming obstacles to the forward movement. But viewed against the broader working class, which consists of millions, they were a minority. The best thing that could have happened was for the militancy of the new social movements to orient to the millions and thus become a bridge to connect with the working class as a whole. It now appears as if this did not happen; instead, militancy became a substitute for mass mobilisation and the action of the militants took the place of the millions, thus leaving them isolated and centres of their own political universe. This is what arguably happened in the APF, but not in a straightforward and consistent way, because its political and organisational foundations were in formation and there was much contestation, as shown in the example below. On the other hand, the trade unions' failure to embrace this militancy and their insistence on prioritising their status as allies of the ruling party had the result of keeping workplace and community struggles separate, that is, of keeping the working-class movement divided.

THE MAY DAY DEBATE INSIDE THE APF

Still unsure of how to relate to the unions, the APF had a long and heated debate on whether the organisation should join the COSATU celebration or hold its own May Day event in 2003. Open, democratic political debate, with full translation into workers' languages, is a tradition that was established early in APF meetings. After a while the 'broad activist forum' had changed into a delegates' meeting of representatives from community organisations affiliated to the APF, and the organisation had held its first annual general meeting in 2003. The May Day debate is illuminating because the exhaustive discussion suggested that even though APF members and leaders purported to share the same principles and political ideals, when faced with the same political situation they responded in different and contradictory ways. It should not be surprising that an organisation formed as a movement during a wave of struggle should, when the dust settles, be found to be politically undeveloped and based on ill-defined political principles. The 'legacy' that presented itself immediately to the APF leadership, and which they could have used to construct a firmer foundation for the organisation's politics, consisted largely of the brief unity in action of the unions, community and student organisations in the anti-privatisation struggle directed at the capitalist class and the ANC government as protector of those interests. Agreement was reached on the APF platform, which emphasised the struggle against privatisation and capitalism ('neoliberalism'). Later, the APF adopted socialism as its official vision. But the May Day debate revealed that despite the apparent agreement on a set of political principles and objectives, ill-defined and even contradictory political positions continued to exist. It can be argued that from its inception until about this point in its life a struggle had raged inside the APF that had failed to crystallise because of unclear political positions and theoretical principles or an inconsistent method of applying these as a guide to action. But the situation was all the time pushing towards political clarification, as the new social movements increasingly gained authority as representing and expressing some of the working-class action in communities. Decisive leadership requires political clarity; ad hoc and empiricist responses to events as they arose were not good enough.

In August 2002, about a year before the May Day debate, the APF was at the forefront of organising against a meeting of the international bourgeoisie and their political representatives at the World Summit on Sustainable Development, also known as the Rio+10 meeting. These efforts culminated in a 20,000-strong march from Alexandra to Sandton – a march many saw as an expression and affirmation of the political significance of the new social movements. However, the march did not include the unions. Instead there was rivalry and hostility that resulted in COSATU marching with the Tripartite Alliance in a counter-march that received less support. The exact same scenario of the two marches had played out during the course of the World Conference Against Racism held in Durban in September 2001. The point is that the May Day debate took place at a time when the autonomist position could be said to have been buttressed by the evidence of actual events whereby the social movements had recently out-mobilised the Alliance in two major marches. The lines were drawn with one side consisting of the autonomists and socialists who also believed that the APF should hold its own May Day celebration. This position was theorised along autonomist lines, although this may not be immediately apparent in these examples: the unions were part of the neoliberal state, the APF and the new social movements should be constructed as 'poles of attraction' to win the masses to socialist politics, and so on. The position in reality was an amalgam of the overlapping arguments put forward by the APF's autonomists, anarchists and socialists, and deployed in a kind of triangular pincer action. Voices from the communities described conditions on the ground, but they were at times dealt with by way of an empiricist method that sometimes could have unexpected power because of an abstract idealisation of the working class and the 'poor' by some debaters.[25] The other side in the debate included mainly socialists who argued that the struggle of the working class was a single struggle despite its different forms and that the APF should use May Day to connect with rank-and-file COSATU members rather than worry about the leadership, and so on. The matter was eventually put to the vote and the outcome favoured the autonomist grouping: the APF gathered its members at the Johannesburg City Hall for its own May Day celebration, while about a kilometre down the road COSATU celebrated Workers' Day at Mary Fitzgerald Square.

The APF pamphlet inviting workers to its May Day rally provides some insight into the theoretical vision and historical method that informed the movement's decision to hold its own event. After a brief reference to the historical origins of May Day in the United States and the birth of the modern trade union movement in South Africa in the 1973 Durban wave of spontaneous strikes, the pamphlet lauds the tradition of worker control and democracy that the unions developed and how they put socialism on the agenda.[26] It then describes the worsening living conditions of the working class, blaming the ANC government for this, and then attacks COSATU for holding a joint rally with the government. It then calls for COSATU militants and workers not to attend the COSATU rally, but rather that of the APF. It also calls on workers to fight against the politics of class collaboration inside COSATU and to join the APF. Whatever the merits of the politics espoused by this APF pamphlet, its political significance is that it was calling for workers to be divided on May Day and not to celebrate this day together. It also called on workers to choose between the APF and COSATU and made the broader claim that the APF was the bearer of the noble tradition of workers' control and democracy in South Africa. Not only is this claim untrue, but it is inconceivable that the workers' movement in South Africa – and anywhere else, for that matter – could seriously challenge capitalist power and transform society without the trade union movement and the broader working-class unity that this entails.

THE COSATU RESOLUTION ON SOCIAL MOVEMENTS

The COSATU position on the new social movements such as the APF is recorded in a resolution that was presented at its eighth congress in 2003. In the document, COSATU acknowledged that some of its members and affiliates were involved in the newly established movements and, although it did not write off the movements completely, it claimed that 'the emergence of social movements hostile to the alliance … is a wake up call to the Alliance'.[27] COSATU committed itself to 'strengthening and consolidating … the political centre' so that it – rather than the social movements – could take the lead in working class struggles.[28] COSATU resolved to work with like-minded organisations, including TAC, in order to 'bring them into our fold'.[29] However, it spelled out a range of criteria 'to determine which social movements [it] would work with'.[30] One of these criteria stated that the agenda of the movement should not 'aim to liquidate or undermine the Alliance partners'[31] and, as such, it ruled out the possibility of the union federation initiating talks with movements like the APF and the Anti-Eviction Campaign, for example, which had spoken out publicly against both the ANC and the Alliance. It is clear that the overall thrust of this resolution was not so much to build the developing struggle of the workers, as is stated in the first instance, but rather to construct a measuring stick and model that all social movements should measure up to and fit in with. The logic and vision of the exercise was the preservation of the Alliance and its hegemony over the working class. The focus was not on the dynamics of collective action and how its development could be facilitated, but rather on how workers in action measured up to a set standard mainly based on loyalty to the Alliance. This approach failed to come to grips with the dynamics of spontaneous class action, because the focus did not make this the priority. The preservation of the Alliance was – and continues to be – the prism that refracts the unionists' picture of working-class action. This detracts from the 'the key mission of uniting the working class, defending it and deepening democracy'.[32]

At a public lecture in 2010, Zwelinzima Vavi, the COSATU general secretary, alerted the audience to 'the single biggest threat to the realization of creating COSATU as a revolutionary and transformative trade union',[33] which he identified as the failure of workers to be active in community struggles 'even when the leaders such as myself try all the time to bridge the gap'.[34] He reminded the audience that COSATU was formed on the principle that workplace and community struggles cannot be divorced, because: 'It is the same struggle. The struggle for decent work cannot be fully realized unless it is seen to be the same struggle for a better life for all.'[35] However, instead of heeding Vavi's call, the labour movement has in general tended to narrow its focus on workplace issues rather than take up the issues that affect employed and unemployed workers in communities.[36] COSATU has sought to control the alliances it makes rather than following the trend whereby trade unions increasingly and successfully 'enter into an alliance with community and other civic organizations without being in control'.[37] It is also noteworthy that COSATU has not significantly supported the burgeoning community protest movement in South Africa – the so-called 'service delivery protests' – as part of building working-class counter-power to capital. Instead, it has used the popular protests for the sake of political machinations, in particular, to campaign for President Zuma against the incumbent at the time, Thabo Mbeki. The weakness of this approach is apparent today as COSATU leaders admit that they are divided over whether to support Zuma for a second term as president of the country.[38] Even when COSATU exercised its autonomy and called civil society organisations to discuss joint strategies to fight neoliberalism, it was severely reprimanded by the ANC in its guise as an Alliance partner for taking this step, which was characterised as betrayal.[39] In general, COSATU's search for solutions has tended to take it in all directions except towards building and being confident in working-class strength, unity, solidarity and power.

SOME LESSONS

In a pamphlet issued to mobilise for a march on 9 September 2004, SAMWU states its vision of what a municipality should be:

> Municipalities should be places to hear and act on community needs, especially working class and poor communities. Places to plan and mobilize resources to meet basic needs for water, electricity and other needs. Places that recognize and respect rank and file workers who produce and maintain these services, paid for with decent wages and conditions. Places where workers and communities control their future.[40]

The underlying assumption here is unity of interest and purpose between workers at work and at home. This theoretical vision can be extended to the public sector as a whole; the full potential of public sector strikes would be realised sooner with this vision informing practice. COSATU seems to have travelled full circle, with its leader reminding workers of its original position after more than a decade of prioritising the unity of the Alliance and support for the ANC government above the need to relate to the actual dynamic and rhythm of the working-class struggle. Some of the new social movements, such as the APF, developed an abstract and idealised conception of the working class that could not relate to the fact that workers who vote for the ANC are not the property of the ANC and can and do take action against the ANC government. For a while, community struggles allowed the unemployed and 'poorest of the poor' to be projected as the revolutionary subject, while organised workers were dismissed as the conservative 'labour aristocracy', but reality is disproving this.[41] In the examples above we see the different policies, choices, and decisions that leaders and organisations make in response to the objective unfolding of the class struggle and how these are conditioned by the theoretical understanding obtaining in the situation. Most recently, for example, COSATU leaders have been urging the unions to relate to the upsurge in community protests; however, this must be done in such a way that it 'strengthen[s] appreciation in the trade union movement and civil society of the centrality of the South Africa constitution as a mobilising instrument'.[42] The use of the Constitution should not detract from knowing the place where the real power of the workers lies, namely in its collective strength and its confidence in the power and use of that strength. The scathing and militant rhetoric against the 'predatory elite' by COSATU leaders is impressive, but it continues to coexist with support for a broader political policy that subordinates the working class to a class alliance that it does not lead. This unstable radicalism might reflect less the development of a revolutionary position than the upward pressure on COSATU leaders of the groundswell of opposition to the ANC government that the public sector strikes (see Ceruti, this volume) and the community protests (see Alexander, and Langa and von Holdt, this volume) reveal.

The APF was born of a mass movement of renewed struggle that united workplace and community action targeting the capitalist class and the government. But the lines between the different parts of the workers' movement were hardened instead of being challenged and reconsidered. Each section was left to move into struggle alone rather than in unity with the rest of the class. This served to reinforce the demobilisation and loss of confidence and hope that accompanied the transition from apartheid to the democratic order. SAMWU's initial approach was to make common cause with other working-class struggles on the grounds of the unity of class interest and the imperatives of the struggle to fight to win. Loyalty to the Tripartite Alliance and the ANC deviated from this political and theoretical orientation. The APF, born as a forum that united labour, community and student struggles, became one that largely organises the unemployed in communities. Its socialist theoretical vision was modified by the infusion of autonomist ideas, which led to an approving rather than disapproving attitude to the split between community and labour struggles, and the downplaying and sometimes repudiation of working-class traditions and history in favour of the 'new' politics.[43] We cannot blame autonomists for the commonsense tendency to portray unions as representing employed workers and the new social movements as representing the unemployed. But such a view is challenged by the actual history of the workers' struggle. Underlying these apparently distinct sites of this struggle is a structural unity and symbiosis that cries out for a political method that must have as its priority the bringing together in struggle of these two sections of the same army. In South Africa, there is a great need to theorise and grasp the rising anger among wider and wider sections of the population and the increasingly organised, collective and combative form it took in the 2010 public sector strike. Workers tested the power of the state and tasted their own power in the process. The contest put power on the agenda and raised deeper questions about the real political alternatives facing workers. What kind of government would have the power and the pluck to solve all the problems faced by workers at work and at home? Political philosophers have pondered these questions ad infinitum, but when the millions and millions of ordinary workers in motion contemplate them, major historical changes perchance loom on the horizon.

NOTES

1. See, for example, Rob Lambert and Eddie Webster, 'Global civil society and the new labour internationalism', in R. Taylor (ed.), *Creating a Better World: Interpreting Global Civil Society*, Cape Town: Kumarian Press, 2004.
2. See, for example, the seminal work on these movements: Richard Ballard, Adam Habib and Imraan Valodia (eds), *Voices of Protest: Social Movements in Post-apartheid South Africa*, Scottsville: University of KwaZulu-Natal Press, 2006.
3. See, for example, Oupa Lehulere, 'The new social movements, COSATU and the "new UDF"', *Khanya*, No. 11 (December, 2005).
4. For example, Lehulere (ibid.) views the fulcrum of struggle as has having shifted away from the unions, which are seen as part of a 'labour aristocracy', to the communities, who consist mostly of the poor. On the other hand, others call for the development of a working-class counter-movement that unites labour and community struggles; for example, Ebrahim Harvey, 'The commodification of water in Soweto and its implications for social justice', PhD thesis, University of the Witwatersrand, 2007.
5. Lenin, 'The trade unions, the present situation and Trotsky's mistakes', speech, 30 December 1920, www.marxists.org.
6. The assertion that the working class is the revolutionary subject is the foundation of socialist politics and was originally laid out by Karl Marx in his *Preface of a Contribution to the Critique of Political Economy*, 1859, www.marxists.org.
7. 'Men [sic] make their own history, but they do not make it as they please; they do not make it under self-selected circumstances, but under circumstances existing already, given and transmitted from the past', Karl Marx, *The 18th Brumaire of Louis Bonaparte*, 1852, p. 1, www.marxists.org.
8. In the literature, there is a distinction between the struggles waged by the new social movements and the more recent 'service delivery protests', that is, the protests waged by working-class communities that made their appearance around the year 2004 and that have peppered the political landscape ever since. See Peter Alexander, 'Rebellion of the poor: South Africa's service delivery protests – a preliminary analysis', *Review of African Political Economy*, Vol. 37, No. 123 (2010). Meanwhile, the new social movement organisations have

experienced a decline in activity with some, such as the Landless People's Movement, disappearing or becoming moribund.

9. See the chapters by Langa and von Holdt, Alexander, and Ceruti in this volume.

10. SAMWU is a Congress of South African Trade Unions affiliate; IMATU is a Federation of Unions of South Africa affiliate.

11. Steven Friedman and Shauna Mottiar, 'Seeking the high ground: The Treatment Action Campaign and the politics of morality'; and Elke Zuern, 'Elusive boundaries: SANCO, the ANC and the post-apartheid South African state'; both in Ballard et al., *Voices of Protest*.

12. Letter from Mazibuko K. Jara, 'Join the Johannesburg Anti-Privatisation activists' forum linking struggles against Igoli 2002 and Wits 2001', 3 July 2000; copy in author's possession.

13. Ibid.

14. Johannesburg Anti-Privatisation Forum, 'Your involvement in Urban Futures is being used to legitimize retrenchments and privatization!', pamphlet, n.d.

15. Patrick Bond, *Unsustainable South Africa: Environment, Development and Social Protest*, Pietermaritzburg: University of Natal Press, 2003.

16. ESSET (Ecumenical Service for Socio-Economic Transformation), 'Churches concerned about iGoli 2002', pamphlet, n.d.

17. Alex Callinicos, 'Toni Negri in perspective', *International Socialism*, Vol. 92 (2001).

18. Colin Barker and Laurence Cox, '"What have the Romans ever done for us?" Academic and activist forms of movement theorizing', paper presented at the Alternative Futures and Popular Protest Eighth Annual Conference, Manchester Metropolitan University, Manchester, 2002.

19. John Holloway, *Change the World Without Taking Power*, London: Pluto Press, 2002.

20. Lehulere, 'The new social movements'.

21. Rebecca Pointer, 'Questioning the representation of South Africa's "new social movements": A case study of the Mandela Park Anti-Eviction Campaign (MPAEC)', mimeo, 2004.

22. Franco Barchiesi, *Classes, Multitudes and the Politics of Community Movements in Post-apartheid South Africa*, Research Report, No. 20, Durban: Centre for Civil Society Research Report, 2004.

23. Alex Callinicos, *An Anti-capitalist Manifesto*, London: Polity Press, 2003; Donatella della Porta, *The Global Justice Movement: Cross-national and Transnational Perspectives*, New York: Paradigm, 2006; Notes from Nowhere, *We Are Everywhere: The Irresistible Rise of Global Anti-capitalism*, London: Verso, 2003.

24. See Lehulere, 'The new social movements'.

25. I cannot provide names of comrades who argued these positions because I have not consulted the official record of the discussions, but I plan to do this in a future publication on the history of the APF, for which I am currently collecting material.

26. APF, 'Celebrate May Day: Celebrate 30 years of class struggle after the Durban strikes', pamphlet, April 2003.

27. COSATU, 'On emerging social movements', Resolution No. 3, *Resolutions of the 8th National Congress, 2003*, www.cosatu.org.za (accessed 29 October 2010).

28. Ibid.

29. Ibid.
30. Ibid.
31. Ibid.
32. Ibid.
33. Zwelinzima Vavi, 'SA still moving in apartheid direction', Irene Grootboom memorial lecture, Site B Hall, Khayelitsha, Cape Town, 18 October 2010.
34. Ibid.
35. Ibid.
36. Sakhela Buhlungu, *A Paradox of Victory: COSATU and the Democratic Transformation in South Africa*, Scottsville: University of KwaZulu-Natal Press, 2010.
37. Hilary Wainwright, 'Transformative resistance: The role of labour and trade unions', in D. McDonald and G. Ruiters (eds), *Alternatives to Privatization: Public Options for Essential Services in the Global South*, New York: Routledge, 2012, p. 19.
38. Matuma Letsoalo, 'COSATU comes clean on internal divisions', *Mail & Guardian*, 25 November 25–1 December 2011.
39. COSATU, 'Declaration of the Civil Society Conference held on 27–28 October 2010, Boksburg', Politicsweb, 28 October 2010, www.politicsweb.co.za/ (accessed 13 November 2010).
40. SAMWU, 'Mobilise and unite against privatization, casual jobs & pre-paid meters', pamphlet, September 2004.
41. See, for example, Heinrich Böhmke, 'The branding of social movements', *Dispositions*, Vol. 1 (2010); Luke Sinwell, 'Defensive social movements need to engage with politics', *Labour Bulletin*, Vol. 34, No. 1 (2010).
42. Vavi, 'SA still moving in apartheid direction'.
43. Nigel Gibson (ed.), *Social Movements and the Quest for a New Humanism in Post-apartheid South Africa*, Trenton: Africa World Press, 2006, p. 33.

8
Agents of Change? Reflecting on the Impact of Social Movements in Post-Apartheid South Africa

Fiona Anciano

EARLIER ANALYSES OF 'NEW' SOCIAL MOVEMENTS[1]

Scholars of democracy, both in South Africa and internationally, broadly celebrated the arrival of post-apartheid social movements, placing fairly high hopes on their role in the South African political landscape. A rich literature emerged written by both academics and activists looking at the composition, aims, leadership and impact of these movements. This chapter will use four key themes arising from this writing to assess the impact of social movements a decade after their emergence.

The first – and perhaps most dominant – theme was that of social movements challenging the hegemony of the African National Congress (ANC) and the state and, in so doing, creating a new political landscape. It was argued that social movements 'have implicitly launched a fundamental challenge to the hegemonic political and socioeconomic discourse that defines the prevailing status quo'.[2] The growth of social movements was seen to redefine the terrain of political identity and solidarity.[3] Indeed, seasoned activist Trevor Ngwane explains that movements 'have to fight the state, destroy it and replace it with a workers' state'.[4] This perspective was balanced by the view that new movements may want to challenge existing power relations, but do not always cast this as a political revolutionary project.[5] Allied to the idea of challenging hegemony was the view that movements would concomitantly generate state responsiveness. Authors argued that social movements contributed to the restoration of political plurality by creating substantive uncertainty, which in turn kept politicians on their toes, making them responsive in particular to the country's most marginalised citizenry.[6] Others argued that '[s]ocial movements have grown into a potent and decisive force in shaping the political agenda and strategies of the state'.[7]

A second theme encompassed the view that social movements had explicit and progressive economic and political agendas. A key argument was that such movements were established with the political aim of mobilising the poor to contest the implementation of neoliberal social policies; many movements were deliberately founded on the principle of the redistribution of scarce resources in favour of marginalised communities.[8] Where movements *did* focus on identity issues, these were actually driven by socioeconomic concerns. One view of the explicit political project of the movements argues that 'the bulk of the new social movements represent those who still believe in … the possibility of a non-capitalist future' and are 'resisting global neo-liberalism and forging an ideological and organisational alternative to the capitalist ANC'.[9] Authors note that although the majority of movements have explicit political agendas, political projects can be taken in different directions, for example, rights-based oppositions versus counter-hegemonic opposition. This contrasts fundamental transformation, on the one hand, with deepened claims to citizenship within existing structures, on the other.[10]

Thirdly, academic and activist writers held the view that social movements had the potential to generate mass mobilisation and support, through both individual movements and through building networks. There was a strong sense that the validity and strength of the movements lay in their real and potential mass support base; 'community movements' were distinguished by 'mass mobilisation' as their prime source of social sanction.[11] Reinforcing this notion was the outcome of the 2002 World Summit on Sustainable Development (WSSD). Two marches took place from Alexandra township to Sandton, Johannesburg's key financial and commercial centre. The march organised and supported by social movements attracted about 25,000 supporters, while the ANC-backed march had fewer than 5,000.[12]

The idea of building mass-based organisations correlated closely to that of linking like-minded social movements together to form even larger sources of mobilisation and pressure: 'the existence of a range of struggles, even if not coordinated in a national liberation movement, can result in a "chain of equivalence" that confronts and transforms relations with dominant powers'.[13] Others argued that the movements were starting to create new networks and make horizontal connections and linkages without coordinating structures and resources from non-governmental organisations (NGOs) and left activists.[14]

The final theme put forward by authors was the notion that social movements were agents of democracy and that organisations had the 'moral high ground', particularly in light of influencing democratic change: 'Civil society (and the state as well) is *made* democratic by the existence of social movements attempting to extend the notion of "rights" to the socio-economic sphere.'[15] Ballard et al. argued that social movements were the 'new voice of the masses' there 'to complete the unfinished business of democracy'.[16] The new movements represented the voices of the poor and marginalised and were able to apply pressure on government to pay greater attention to these groups. Indeed, 'even the more militant movements that engage in technically illegal activities … use the language of rights to invest their activities with a sense that they are endorsed by a higher code of "good"'.[17] For long-time activist Dale McKinley, the activities of social movements would result in an increasing number of people experiencing and practising meaningful democracy.[18]

How have social movements fared in relation to these four themes? The following sections will address these issues through close analysis of the Soweto Electricity Crisis Committee (SECC) and Sikhula Sonke. These movements have been chosen for analysis because they represent different ideologies (socialism versus rights-based), strategies (direct action versus negotiation), locations (urban versus rural), and approaches to the ANC-government and democracy.

THE SECC AND SIKHULA SONKE

Small opportunities are often the beginning of great enterprises.[19]

It was the embracing of small opportunities by a local group of activists that led to the formation of the SECC in May 2000. In 1999 the national electricity provider, Eskom, changed the electricity pricing structure in Soweto, resulting in a rise in electricity prices of nearly 47 per cent in one year.[20] Township residents spontaneously began forming small groups to fight this price rise.[21] At the same time a group of activists leading the Campaign against Neoliberalism in South Africa were looking for ways to spread anti-neoliberal ideas in Soweto. They realised they needed an 'issue' to attach to their campaign and thus focused on the electricity crisis facing Sowetans. They called a Soweto-wide mass workshop and invited other groups in the township to participate. This united smaller groups into a formal movement, named the Soweto Electricity Crisis Committee.[22]

Sikhula Sonke (meaning 'We Grow Together' in isiXhosa) emerged in 2002 in a very different context to the SECC. It is a rural-based organisation in the Western Cape that defines itself as a 'women-led social movement trade union' that deals with livelihood challenges faced by farm women.[23] In many respects it developed organically out of the needs of farm workers, but it was also invented, in the face of necessity, by the NGO Women on Farms. Although Sikhula Sonke was not initially conceived as a trade union, the movement soon evolved in this direction, because one of the most pressing problems facing wine and fruit farm workers was limited access to effective union representation.[24] Sikhula Sonke's objectives stretch beyond those of a traditional trade union, addressing all issues that affect women and their children.[25] It aims to 'craft an organisational model that will not only challenge the unfair labour practices applied to women farm workers, but also to address the social and economic development needs of women who live and work on farms'.[26] Sikhula Sonke is thus neither a traditional trade union nor a conventional social movement, but a unique hybrid of both.

CHALLENGING HEGEMONY

There is little doubt that many social movements such as the SECC have clear ideological agendas and in this sense conform closely to earlier writings arguing that social movements challenge hegemonic political and socioeconomic discourse. The SECC leadership initially strongly promoted the idea of socialism as the ideology of the movement.[27] It followed the view that 'the working class must control and have access to all goods and services and the means to produce these'.[28] Several years later this strong focus on a counter-hegemonic political project has waned to some degree, and today fewer in the movement talk passionately of overthrowing the hegemonic state or implementing an uncompromised socialist programme.[29] Sikhula Sonke, on the other hand, does not have a clear political ideology governing its work, thus it is not its explicit intention to shape the political agenda of the state. Much of its focus is on day-to-day trade union issues; in this respect it challenges the entrenched patterns of subordination on fruit and wine farms rather than hegemonic political discourses. However, in tackling workers' rights and social concerns on farms, it has in practice – albeit it to a limited extent – engaged with and challenged the state.

In challenging hegemony through generating state responsiveness, the SECC and Sikhula Sonke, like many other social movements, have had notable – albeit sporadic – victories. For the SECC, the most significant of these is related to Operation Khanyisa (meaning 'to light'), a campaign focused on providing access to electricity for all by illegally reconnecting homes to the electricity grid in Soweto. The SECC's mobilisation of sections of the community in Soweto around electricity provision, its widespread reconnections and its success in generating media attention resulted in Eskom (South Africa's main supplier of electricity) announcing a moratorium on cut-offs and offering an amnesty on arrears.[30] As Papadakis explains, '[w]ithout the key mobilization of, massive rent boycott by, and pressure coming from the SECC, Eskom and the government might have probably never accepted to write-off such large amounts of electricity debts to the benefit of the poor township residents'.[31] More recently, the work of the SECC has again compelled Eskom to stop cut-offs. By applying pressure from below through direct action, the SECC compelled the parastatal to change its technology: Eskom responded to SECC action by installing 'green boxes', which are essentially electricity meters that cannot be bypassed. In defiance of Eskom's response, the SECC organiser noted 'Eskom know we will reconnect'.[32] These meters were initially installed in one area of Soweto, but with the support of the SECC, other communities, such as Orlando, have fought the installation of new meters and to date Eskom has had no success in installing meters more widely in Soweto.[33]

In terms of creating uncertainty and facilitating higher levels of accountability, the SECC explain: 'We are the watchdogs for the residents of Soweto ... We put pressure on the state to deliver for working class residents.'[34] Certainly, in the early days of SECC activism, ANC councillors and local officials were very aware of – and wary of – the SECC's activities.[35] Johannesburg City Council's speaker explained that there had been discussions around why these movements were surfacing and whether there was a problem with the ANC's work.[36] In this regard, the SECC has been instrumental in keeping the debate about service delivery active. One official respondent noted: 'They are actually beneficial. What they do is make sure that those who are the leaders in council should exercise better leadership around how council governs.'[37] The SECC have also been an effective watchdog in regard to the process of policy implementation. Johannesburg Water explains: 'The SECC have not had much effect on policy, but they have changed the operational side in terms of the quality of work we do … It [the SECC's activities] has made us a lot more rigorous in our approach to make sure we do provide a quality service.'[38] One example of this more 'rigorous' approach is the employment of community facilitators who went to every household to explain the facts about the implications of a pre-paid meter.[39] In this way, the SECC compelled additional communication – albeit in one direction – between service deliverers and those they serve.

A further way in which the SECC has attempted to challenge the political landscape is by forming a political party and contesting local government elections. The SECC formed the Operation Khanyisa Movement (OKM) with the intention of 'making people aware of how oppressed they are',[40] and 'exposing bourgeois democracy' and 'the capitalist class agenda of the ANC government'.[41] In 2006, under the OKM banner, the organisation, although unable to gain a ward seat, won a proportional representation seat in the Johannesburg City Council. It contested the 2011 elections and again won one proportional representation seat. It recognises that its impact within the council is limited, but wants to 'bring a socialist voice into the bourgeois chamber'.[42] It also believes that having a city councillor will increase knowledge of the movement in the region and its support base will grow.[43] The decision to form the OKM was not universally supported. The umbrella body to which SECC belongs, namely the Anti-Privatisation Forum (APF), and its affiliates were unable to reach an agreement about what line to take on electoral politics. This arguably weakened the APF substantially.[44]

In challenging hegemony through generating state responsiveness, Sikhula Sonke too has had success. As part of a collective effort, it was able to win the first ever moratorium on farm dweller evictions. To fight against evictions in the Jonkershoek Valley near Stellenbosch in the Western Cape Province, which houses almost 80 farm-worker families, local farm workers formed the Jonkershoek Crisis Committee. This committee, with extensive assistance from Sikhula Sonke and other sympathetic partners such as the Congress of South African Trade Unions (COSATU), held marches and generated substantial media coverage. As a result of this ongoing action, key decision makers placed a moratorium on evictions in Jonkershoek and signed a memorandum agreeing that land tenure policy for farm workers is inadequate and needed to be reviewed. Indeed, the provincial Ministry of Agriculture felt that the process of dialogue and constructive engagement may well be the first of its kind in agricultural communities and could serve as a blueprint for other provinces.[45] Sikhula Sonke was also somewhat successful in its sectoral determination campaign, getting the Employment Condition Commission, which establishes minimum wages for farm workers, to scrap the two-tier system prescribing different minimum wages for rural and urban areas.[46] Moreover, the organisation has also been successful in holding government departments to account in instances where it has presented individual cases involving working conditions or wages to the Department of Labour, or cases involving social grants to the Department of Social Welfare.

Sikhula Sonke does not actively attempt to 'alter the political landscape', yet through its alliances with other civil society organisations, such as COSATU, it has at times generated substantive uncertainty in a localised setting. Sikhula Sonke has also effectively used the media to generate responsiveness from political leaders, such as in the Jonkershoek case. In 2007 the Department of Agriculture acknowledged that Sikhula Sonke exposes irregularities and to some extent functions as its 'eyes and ears on the ground'.[47] Similarly, the district mayor's office accepted that Sikhula Sonke's general secretary 'speaks her mind ... she is listened to and in this way they [Sikhula Sonke] are effective in voicing farm women workers' issues'.[48]

Although the SECC and Sikhula Sonke have generated some state responsiveness and taken a step in the direction of creating substantive uncertainty, they have neither fundamentally challenged the political status quo nor had a long-term impact in terms of challenging hegemonic socioeconomic discourses. For, example, the SECC's activities may have encouraged Johannesburg Water to explain to residents the reasons behind the installation of pre-paid water meters, but this is not a victory in the context of wanting to eliminate meters altogether. It must be recognised, however, that few policy decisions explicitly result from the actions of one group. For example, the government's free basic water and electricity policy may have been a response to action launched by the SECC and the APF; however, one cannot make a direct linear association between these variables, given the myriad other factors that led to the implementation of this national policy. Similarly, Sikhula Sonke has yet to have success in its long-term plan of improving land access and ownership for farm workers. This is partly because it is very difficult for any single organisation to influence government policy, but also because the majority of its programmes are targeted at employers and their members rather than at amending government policy. Its campaigns are reactive and primarily inward focused, looking to either strengthen the union or improve the lives and working conditions of its members on an individual or a farm-by-farm basis.

As a former leader of a social movement explains, the SECC has 'not managed to fundamentally change the orientation of government'. The movements may have 'cushioned the rough edges of liberal policies and forced government to readjust'[49] on some policies, but this impact has been limited. There are several reasons why movements have had only marginal success in changing government policy and challenging the hegemony of the ANC. The following sections will address these concerns, primary among which is the difficulty of mobilising large numbers of supporters.

ECONOMIC AND POLITICAL AGENDAS

The SECC conforms to much of the earlier writings about social movements, particularly with regard to its leadership's support of explicit economic and political agendas. The leadership's economic agenda promotes the idea of independent mass mobilisation of the poor to contest neoliberalism and capitalism. It wants to 'bring the bourgeoisie and working class onto an equal economic level', with a long-term view of all citizens having employment, housing, improved health services, free education, water and electricity.[50] In terms of a political agenda, the leadership of the SECC has, as with its economic views, a clear sense of purpose: 'We have identified the enemy as the ANC government.'[51] It wants to present an ideological alternative to the ANC and believes in fundamental transformation through counter-hegemonic opposition. Although no longer ongoing, in its earlier days, as part of its political agenda the leadership offered regular political training courses for members. It has also furthered its political project via the OKM.

Sikhula Sonke, too, supports mass mobilisation of the poor and marginalised. Its leaders, however, have not expressed an explicit desire to overthrow neoliberalism or capitalism. It is clearly a workers' movement, wanting to improve the livelihood of the working class, but it does this through working with capitalist structures rather than trying to overthrow them. Its 'economic agenda' functions predominantly on a small scale, farm by farm, or even individual by individual. To a very limited extent, Sikhula Sonke has tried to bring about economic reform at the national and international levels; however, its leaders do not follow a long-term ideological or anti-neoliberal project. Similarly, Sikhula Sonke does not follow a clear political agenda. Although the organisation does have a positive relationship with the ANC, some Sikhula Sonke leaders are sceptical of political party competition: 'Politics is about dirty fighting when there are elections. It is just about getting votes and then those who voted for you are treated as nothing.'[52] Sikhula Sonke's work may indirectly contribute towards strengthening a progressive economic and political agenda, but it cannot be said that the movement sees its work as an 'ideological and organisational alternative to the capitalist ANC'.[53]

For both the SECC and Sikhula Sonke, their economic and political agendas (whether explicit or not) are not necessarily followed by the majority of the movements' members. Drawing from short interviews with members of the SECC, it appears that the overwhelming factor behind joining the movement is to obtain assistance with service delivery issues, in many cases specifically to have their electricity supply reconnected or their water meter bypassed. When asked why they joined the organisation, members said things such as: 'The SECC has helped me not to pay electricity bills'; 'I was trying to help my mum find a way to pay for electricity'; 'If you have a problem with your electricity, you go to the SECC. They will reconnect you.'[54] Other members have joined because they see the SECC as an effective community group that can improve conditions in the township. Indeed, some members who initially joined for help with water and electricity concerns have stayed active in the organisation because they are convinced of the link between local service concerns and the broader ideological change that the movement's leaders advocate. However, a large proportion of SECC supporters did not join the movement because they believe in socialism or because they want to drive other forms of economic or political reform. They joined to find help in sustaining a livelihood and mitigating the harshest effects of government policies. In this sense, members see the SECC as a conduit to free services and an advice office rather than a movement that will generate broader economic reform. The ideology and principles of the SECC leadership may in practice seem far removed from the everyday realities of Sowetans.

As with the SECC, the majority of Sikhula Sonke's members join because of personal or livelihood challenges facing them as individuals rather than because of a commitment to any wider economic or political agenda. Many of the original members started working with the Women of Farms project in the 1990s because this NGO encouraged the idea that 'women are important' and 'everyone should respect each other'.[55] Experiences of subordination and powerlessness extend beyond gender relations in the farm-worker community. Male interviewees joined Sikhula Sonke because 'we had no one standing up for us whenever we had problems' and 'the union can help us to be treated fairly by the farmer, according to the law'.[56] This need to 'have someone on your side' is compounded by existing relations of paternalism on farms where workers are unable to effectively voice their concerns on an equal footing with employers. The history of paternalism has resulted in farm workers seldom being treated with respect or equality by employers.[57]

The ineffectual actions of other trade unions in the sector also led to a rise in membership, as did the broad focus of its work beyond traditional trade union activities. Sikhula Sonke can help with 'the conditions we live in on the farm', 'alcoholism problems', 'evictions' or 'getting an ID'.[58] It is thus apparent that for many members, being a part of Sikhula Sonke is seen as a way of gaining some personal power, be it as a woman or as a worker, but it is seldom an avenue for expressing an explicit broader ideological agenda. Thus, contrary to the suggestion in earlier writings, the promotion of explicit economic and political agendas was not a priority for many social movements, even those whose leadership claimed such an agenda to be paramount. Sikhula Sonke, for example, is an organisation primarily focused on protecting and enriching individual livelihoods and alleviating workplace concerns. More significant, however, is that the supporters of many movements, including those belonging to Sikhula Sonke and the SECC, struggle to identify with leaders' broader ambitions. Sinwell makes this point when he argues that the radical tactics of some social movements should be seen as reactions to the exclusion of the poor, which is brought about by neoliberal policies, rather than an attempt to seek an alternative to neoliberalism itself.[59] Thus, members of social movements more often than not look to their movements to help mitigate the harsh effects of government policy rather than to follow a broader ideological, anti-hegemonic agenda. The same concern is true of some members' approach to political projects. In many cases, members do not want to fundamentally challenge the ANC or its policy framework; they want improved livelihoods within the historical political framework they feel emotionally wedded to. The inherent danger of this reality is that movements may struggle to achieve their long-term goals and thus feel demoralised by a protracted pace of economic transformation.

Ultimately, movements are currently too small – as the section below demonstrates – and are supported by too few members with radical alternative political or economic views to generate a revolution that could significantly alter the economic policies of the state. For now, it is more likely that economic transformation, which encompasses improved access to opportunities to earn a living, will come through incremental reform.

BUILDING AND LINKING A MASS BASE

Have movements mobilised mass support and built effective networks? It is difficult to specify their actual membership numbers because by their nature they ebb and flow. Furthermore, mass support does not only equate to numbers of individuals verifiably active at one specific point, but can also include wider non-active community backing. In May 2005 the SECC had 7,652 members listed on its database, decreasing in 2011 to an estimated support of 6,000.[60] It is perhaps at the branch level where the true nature and size of *active* membership is most evident. In 2005 the SECC operated 37 branches across the township; however, in 2011 this had decreased to twelve functioning branches.[61] Attendance at branch meetings varies widely from a minimum of about ten participants up to about 70.[62] Taking into consideration branch attendance, observed support of marches and protests, and voter support for the OKM, a realistic estimate of the number of active SECC members may be around 2,000 people.[63] To put this figure into perspective, it might be worth adding that Soweto is the most populous black urban residential area in the country, with about 1.3 million inhabitants.[64] Even counting those who do not vote, the SECC has at best attained less than 0.2 per cent of the active support of this community. Yet, more broadly, many Sowetans have at times participated in SECC meetings, even though they do not consider themselves to be supporters of the movement. For example, an investigation on pre-paid electricity meters in Soweto in 2004 revealed that 8.6 per cent of respondents had attended SECC meetings.[65] The SECC is also part of the APF, which has approximately 30 affiliates in four regions in Gauteng. According to the APF secretary, support for these affiliates is in the region of 20,000 people.[66] Thus, the SECC has broader support than its membership numbers suggest, indicating that the movement is a legitimate organisation; yet this support does not go far enough towards constituting a mass base capable of achieving the SECC's goal of 'generating a revolution'. And indeed, over the years, its active support has waned.

Sikhula Sonke's membership is easier to quantify since, as a trade union, members are required to formally register. In 2011 the union had about 5,000 members drawn from over 200 different farms in ten geographic locations in the Western Cape, a significant increase from its 3,500 members in 2007.[67] It must be said that geographical constraints, including large distances between farms and a relative lack of central hubs, make recruiting and organising farm workers difficult, and Sikhula Sonke has some level of support beyond registered members. The organisation assists both workers and 'non-workers'. Certainly, the organisation is well known in the communities in which it works. As with the SECC, however, it is difficult to argue that Sikhula Sonke is generating mass mobilisation. As one commentator notes: 'It is possible to consider that they are movements that do not have a mass base, but a mass orientation.'[68]

The discussion above raises two questions: why have these movements struggled to mobilise mass support and why has Sikhula Sonke been more successful than the SECC at generating and sustaining support? In terms of the first question, a key reason espoused by the movements themselves is a lack of resources, both financial and human. The SECC organiser notes that 'funding would help with mobilisation and getting more support; people need help with the costs of attending a meeting and other activities'.[69] McKinley (this volume) stresses that without 'committed activists to mobilise resources' and 'support and sustain organisation in communities', the movements will continue to struggle to generate mass action. Linked to this concern is the reality that potential supporters may want help to fix immediate livelihood problems, but in practice, movement organisers have limited resources to be able to deal with these concerns. Furthermore, generating mass support has to involve younger generations, or movements will not be sustained. However, in societies where running the household is historically the responsibly of the older generation, few young people see an immediate need to fight for better service delivery and thus challenge government and ANC policies. This limits the achievement of meaningful transformation for poor communities. The movements thus face the challenge of engaging and attracting sustainable support from the youth (see Alexander, this volume).

Some scholars argue that movements struggle to build a mass base because they are led by a small 'vanguard cadre' whose members are in turn disconnected from the reality of the communities they try to support.[70] In a trenchant critique of social movements, a former leader of the South African NGO coalition argued that some social movements are 'largely led by intellectuals who were not rooted in the conditions of people ... They are led from without by white intellectuals with some black support and leadership. In reality they are NGOs rather than real social movements.'[71] Although members may not identify with leaders' ideological views, it is clear that movements such as the SECC and Sikhula Sonke are not run by a (white) vanguard elite with no connection to a mass base. Both movements have rooted membership with functioning local-level branches. It is true that both organisations have at times been led by dynamic and charismatic leaders who play an essential role in mobilising support for and publicising the aims of their movements. However, these leaders have demonstrably focused on developing deeper layers of leadership by empowering and training a second tier. They also encourage members to drive decision making, ensuring that members have ample opportunity to effectively express their interests. That both organisations are composed of multiple separate branches encourages the cultivation of local leaders and broader participation in the movements. For many members, movement activity is not ad hoc, but rather part of a culture of participation and engagement.

Insight into why Sikhula Sonke has grown and the SECC has not can shed further light on the dynamics behind movement mobilisation. Firstly, Sikhula Sonke has at the top of its programme agenda the recruitment of new members. In practice, mobilisation comes before all other activities. Secondly, Sikhula Sonke has made a concerted effort to recruit younger members, whereas the SECC states that many of its original members are now too old to participate.[72] Furthermore, as a fully staffed trade union, Sikhula Sonke is also more equipped than the SECC to meet the individual livelihood needs of its members. Finally, in contrast to the more-mainstream Sikhula Sonke, the SECC's technically illegal activities and strong anti-ANC stance may alienate some members of the community.

With regard to the issue of networking, both Sikhula Sonke and the SECC have made great strides in forming alliances and engaging with like-minded organisations. The SECC's ideology places it squarely on the left spectrum of South African politics and thus it has good relations with many left-leaning civil society groups. Sikhula Sonke also embraces the idea of networking and values learning from other organisations. However, it can be argued that over time the movements' relationships have not resulted in a 'chain of equivalence' that 'transforms relations with dominant powers'.[73] There are several reasons for this. Firstly, neither the SECC nor Sikhula Sonke have effectively tapped into or linked up with other mass community protests,[74] particularly those that swept the country after the 2009 elections.[75] Several social movement leaders have noted that established civil society organisations were seldom the organising forces behind community protests.[76] Evidence has shown that although organisations such as crisis committees or concerned residents' groups were facilitating the protests, they tended to be small and sporadically formed and not linked to any project or organisation beyond their own community.[77] Some commentators have suggested that the instigators of the protests 'have nothing' and 'have been marginalised'; they are 'beyond COSATU and beyond social movements'.[78] For one activist, those who are most marginalised constitute the bedrock of an unofficial movement, but the agitators behind the wave of community protests are not linked to any of the established social movements: 'They are part of thousands of protests, but do not link ... there is no ideological coherence. ... Incidences [*sic*] of civil society unrest have not found expression through known forms of organisations, such as social movements.'[79]

A second concern limiting the ability of social movements to build mass mobilisation is the lack of unity among organisations of the 'left', including social movements, other left-leaning NGOs and the South African Communist Party (SACP). SECC founder Trevor Ngwane highlights these strategic battles:

> Disagreements in the left are often based on different ideological viewpoints ... Bickering in the left is an expression of the politics of individual leaders ... It is important that a united front starts to stay together, even if we disagree behind the scenes.[80]

Although Ngwane describes a fragmented social movement sector, he does note that different personal ideologies are not always divisive. Overall, however, for Ngwane there has been a demoralisation of the left, 'because they have lost confidence in the power of the working class ... and the left [in the form of the SACP] is divorced from the masses'[81] (see also Ngwane, this volume). Another activist agrees with this view, explaining that 'progressive civil society on the left is locked in silos, with no conscious effort to build a common campaign'.[82] Others argue that after the successes of the WSSD march in 2002, the 'independent movement' has been 'chaotic, self-destructive, problematic and infiltrated' and that 'there is a problem with civil society and social movements really uniting so that there can be a strong force against government'.[83] Although it is too soon to tell, this dissociation may change with the advent of the Democratic Left Front in early 2011.

An earlier attempt to bring the different movements together in a unified force proved unsuccessful. The Social Movements Indaba (SMI) represented social movements who felt they had similar political aims, meeting from 2002 on a regular basis. The annual SMI meetings indicated a move towards encompassing political projects that, if successful, could pose a more sustained and substantial threat to government policies than previously posed by individual movements. From 2006, however, the SMI began to atrophy because there was apparent division about who did in practice and should in principle control it.[84]

In concluding this section, it must be recognised that the movements have yet to establish a large, consistent, mass base of support that is able to challenge the hegemonic status quo. Due to divisions in the 'left' and inadequate connections with wider community protests, the strength of some movements has been curtailed. Nonetheless, Sikhula Sonke and the SECC have continued to maintain consistent operations for a decade, and this in itself is a great achievement for any social movement.

MORAL-BASED AGENTS OF DEMOCRACY

Have social movements as moral agents strengthened South African democracy? In both case studies, it can be argued that they have done so.[85] Firstly, both the SECC and Sikhula Sonke create channels of articulation for the poor and marginalised and, in so doing, widen opportunities for participation between elections. The defining feature of SECC membership is that most members are unemployed or poor. Sikhula Sonke too undoubtedly represents the poor and marginalised. Although its paid-up members are employed, they earn very low wages. A government report explains that 'agricultural workers are worse off than those in every other sector of the economy'.[86] Farm workers, too, are marginalised in terms of their citizenship rights, experiencing, for example, 'great difficulties in accessing social services', which heightens their vulnerability and exposes them to 'human rights violations and abuse'.[87] Within the category of farm workers, women and non-permanent workers are further marginalised.

Secondly, the movements strengthen civil and political liberties through creating *representative* and *legitimate* channels for the articulation of interests. Both movements legitimately represent a citizen base – albeit a small one – and do so through internally democratic cultures, consolidating democratic decision making and internal accountability. Through their empowerment of branches and the frequent opportunities for participation in movement organisation and decision making, the movements are to a large extent functioning as 'schools of democracy'.[88] It must, however, be noted that their democratic culture is not unproblematic: the inexperience and inactivity of some of Sikhula Sonke's local committees means that members' participation is limited. With respect to the SECC, Soweto Concerned Residents split from the movement, pointing to potential weaknesses in the SECC and reducing its effectiveness as a unified channel for the articulation of interests.

Thirdly, as discussed above, the movements have had some impact in improving government accountability and – albeit to a lesser extent – generating some government responsiveness. In strengthening democracy, civil society needs not only to monitor government actions, but also ensure that government responds to the preferences of its citizens.[89] The SECC, more so than Sikhula Sonke, pays close attention to government policies, service delivery and the actions of political actors. Through its various electricity, water and housing campaigns, the SECC challenges not only what it perceives to be policy failures, but also the processes employed in policy making. The SECC is thus a vocal watchdog, monitoring and highlighting government shortcomings.

Although Sikhula Sonke focuses on non-state actors, paying more attention to union matters than government policy, it too is an effective watchdog in that it monitors labour and social security issues such as minimum wages and farm dweller evictions. The SECC and Sikhula Sonke are also both very effective in knowledge and information sharing. They use other civil society organisations and their own internal capacity to generate alternative sources of information to those provided by the government. This information is then distributed, either verbally or through pamphlets, to their membership and potentially beyond. This activity not only monitors government accountability, but also strengthens civil and political liberties and, by improving awareness of their rights, empowers citizens. Both organisations may be good watchdogs, but neither Sikhula Sonke's nor the SECC's successes have directly translated into sustained positive policy changes. Although these movements have had only a limited effect on government responsiveness, their strong performance in monitoring government actions results in an overall strengthening of accountability and a deepening of democracy.

Fourthly, these organisations have acted as agents of democracy where they have engaged with or, indeed, contested political institutions. In so doing, they potentially strengthen institutions, thus helping them to constrain executive power, and widen opportunities for participation in political processes. Sikhula Sonke in particular has engaged consistently with state institutions such as the Human Rights Commission and the Commission for Conciliation, Mediation and Arbitration (CCMA). Its use of government commissions, labour centres and the courts is highly beneficial for its members. Many state institutions and government structures are legally required to listen to citizens' views and communicate information in return. For Sikhula Sonke members, this often has the immediate effect of improving working conditions and delivering economic benefits at the micro level. It also directly increases participation in legal and policy processes. Engaging with state institutions also empowers members, and farm workers are turned from subjects of their bosses into citizens of the state, able to exercise their rights.

Although less active in this arena than Sikhula Sonke, the SECC has engaged with state institutions, including the Constitutional Court, by challenging the limited state provision of free basic water. Although ultimately unsuccessful, in this instance the court battle held the potential not only to strengthen political institutionalisation, but also to appreciably minimise poverty on a national level. Other strategies, such as the SECC's contestation of local government elections, have also impacted on political institutionalisation. In forming a political party, the SECC has offered both a democratic alternative to voters in Soweto and increased engagement with and participation in the political system. Utilising and at times contesting state institutions strengthens state bodies, which are then better able to constrain executive power where necessary.

Moreover, it can be argued that these movements have successfully promoted a rights-based discourse and, in so doing, empowered their members. Sikhula Sonke in particular has fostered greater gender, work-based and racial equality for what is one of the most socially and politically marginalised communities in South Africa. In providing training for farm workers in labour rights, developing women leaders, and helping workers to engage with employers as social equals, Sikhula Sonke potentially reduces poverty and directly empowers citizens. The SECC too consistently informs its members of their socioeconomic rights and encourages members to express opinions. The focus on socioeconomic rights as a key part of democracy signals that social movements are pushing for a substantive democracy that strives towards the 'broader ideal of democracy as liberation' rather than a liberal or electoral democracy that emphasises 'formal procedures'.[90] Thus, the activities of these organisations develop citizenship skills that can be used to deepen participatory democracy. The efforts of both movements in relation to honing citizenship skills and promoting social equality are significant in the broader struggle against oppression and injustice. Fostering empowered citizens is important as it helps to create a 'balance of power'. This in turn can be used to ensure that existing power holders do not capture public spaces for deliberation.[91] Where participatory decision making does occur, it is thus more likely to be democratic and reflective of all voices.

CONCLUSION

Social movements have undoubtedly had a significant impact on the South African political landscape over the past decade. As Habib notes, '[o]rganisations that were most influential post 2001/02 were not the organisations that were participating through state structures but ... those involved in contentious politics'.[92] Although social movements have had small successes and some influence on making the state more socially accountable, they have not fulfilled the prediction of earlier writers that they would fundamentally challenge the hegemony of the ANC. Indeed, the ANC – although its support declined from 69.69 per cent to 65.9 per cent – actually received 772,497 *more* votes in 2009 than in 2004.[93] Where ANC votes were lost in the 2011 municipal elections, these were to parties on the 'right' of the ANC.

Why has this been the case? Firstly, as discussed in the second theme above, many social movement members do not join an organisation because of conscious ideological beliefs; instead, they are looking for help to improve their livelihoods and mitigate the harsh effects of government policy. Thus, even where movement leaders have explicit political and economic agendas, they may struggle to engage their members in broader ideological, anti-hegemonic battles. This is linked to the second concern, namely that movements have had limited success in building and linking mass bases. Constraints in mobilising mass support hinder the ability of movements to effectively challenge the political and economic status quo. To have a greater impact on hegemonic discourses, movements need to tap into society's wider discontent, as demonstrated by social protests; link more effectively; and use the democratic space they have created to generate greater state responsiveness.

Social movements have, however, met the predictions of earlier analysts where they act as moral agents of democracy. In particular, they offer channels of representation to the poor and thereby widen opportunities for participation between elections, and they create empowered citizens who are better able to demand their socioeconomic rights and engage in participatory democracy. Where social movements have deepened democracy, they have contributed to the social transformation of South African society. However, it is economic transformation that is the country's principal concern and arguably this is where movements face their biggest challenge.

NOTES

1. In South African writing, the term 'new' refers to movements surfacing post-1999, which is different to European 'new social movement' theory.
2. Richard Ballard, Adam Habib and Imraan Valodia, 'Social movements in South Africa: Promoting crisis or creating stability?', in V. Padayachee (ed.), *The Development Decade? Economic and Social Change in South Africa, 1994–2004*, Cape Town: HSRC Press, 2006, p. 403.
3. Nigel Gibson (ed.), *Challenging Hegemony: Social Movements and the Quest for a New Humanism in Post-apartheid South Africa*, Trenton: Africa World Press, 2006, p. 6.
4. Trevor Ngwane, 'The Anti-Privatisation Forum (APF)', *South African Labour Bulletin*, Vol. 27, No. 3 (2003), p. 32.
5. Ran Greenstein, 'Civil society, social movements and power in South Africa', unpublished paper presented at a Rand Afrikaans University sociology seminar, 2003.
6. Richard Ballard, Adam Habib and Imraan Valodia, *Voices of Protest: Social Movements in Post-apartheid South Africa*, Scottsville: University of KwaZulu-Natal Press, 2006, p. 415.
7. Franco Barchiesi, *Classes, Multitudes and the Politics of Community Movements in Post-apartheid South Africa*, CCS Research Report, No. 20, Durban: Centre for Civil Society, 2004, pp. 3–4.
8. Tshepo Madlingozi, 'Post-apartheid social movements and the quest for the elusive "New" South Africa', *Journal of Law and Society*, Vol. 34, No. 1 (2007), pp. 76–97; Ballard et al., *Voices of Protest*.
9. Dale McKinley, 'Democracy and social movements in South Africa', in Padayachee, *The Development Decade?*, pp. 418–19.
10. Ballard et al., *Voices of Protest*, p. 400.

11. Ashwin Desai, *We Are the Poors: Community Struggles in Post-apartheid South Africa,* New York: Monthly Review Press, 2002.

12. McKinley, 'Democracy and social movements'.

13. Ballard et al., *Voices of Protest,* p. 403.

14. Gibson, *Challenging Hegemony,* p. 9.

15. Ibid., p. 5.

16. Ballard et al., *Voices of Protest,* p. 413.

17. Ibid., p. 402.

18. McKinley, 'Democracy and social movements'.

19. Demosthenes (384–322 BC).

20. Maj Fiil-Flynn, *The Electricity Crisis in Soweto*, Johannesburg: Municipal Services Project, 2001.

21. Interviews with Trevor Ngwane, Anti-Privatisation Forum and SECC, Soweto, Johannesburg and Durban, 17 March 2004–25 June 2009.

22. Peter Alexander, 'Anti-globalisation movements, identity and leadership: Trevor Ngwane and the Soweto Electricity Crisis Committee', unpublished paper presented at the South African Sociological Association Conference, Durban, 2006.

23. Interviews with Wendy Pekeur, general secretary, Sikhula Sonke, Stellenbosch, February–May 2007; Sikhula Sonke, 'Profile', unpublished document, Stellenbosch, 2006.

24. Interview with Sara Claasen, president, Sikhula Sonke, Stellenbosch, 19 April 2007.

25. Interview with Evelien Ockers, organiser, Sikhula Sonke, Stellenbosch, 19 April 2007.

26. Sikhula Sonke, 'Profile'.

27. Interviews with Bongani Lubisi, SECC organiser, Soweto, March–May 2005.

28. SECC, 'The struggle for affordable electricity for all', unpublished document, n.d.

29. SECC forum meeting, Soweto, 28 June 2011; interview with Zodwa Madiba, SECC organiser, Soweto, 4 July 2011.

30. Jeff Radebe, 'Speech by minister of public enterprises', Workshop on Service Delivery Framework, Gauteng, 2001.

31. Konstantinos Papadakis, *Civil Society, Participatory Governance and Decent Work Objectives: The Case of South Africa*, Geneva: International Institute for Labour Studies, 2006, p. 72.

32. Interview with Madiba.

33. Ibid.

34. Interviews with Lubisi.

35. See Comrade Tankiso, 'Beyond dreadlocks and demagogy', *Umrabulo* (June 2003).

36. Interview with Nandi Mayethula-Khoza, speaker, Johannesburg City Council, Johannesburg, April 2005.

37. Interview with Masego Sheburi, public petitions official, Office of the Speaker, Johannesburg, April 2005.

38. Interview with Lesego Lebuso, divisional manager for new services, Johannesburg Water, Johannesburg, April 2005.

39. Ibid.

40. SECC forum meeting, Soweto, 9 March 2005.

41. SECC Political Committee, 'Ideas on the SA local government election 2006', unpublished document, 2004.

42. Siphiwe Segodi, 'Thembelihle Crisis Committee contesting elections through Operation Khanyisa Movement', 2011, http://tinyurl.com/3u2w46x (accessed 9 August 2011).

43. Interview with Executive Committee member B, SECC, Soweto, 23 May 2006.

44. Marcelle C. Dawson, 'Social movements in contemporary South Africa: The Anti-Privatisation Forum and struggles around access to water in Johannesburg', DPhil. thesis, University of Oxford, 2008.

45. Ministry of Agriculture, Western Cape, 'Statement by Cobus Dowry, minister of agriculture Western Cape: Road forward for Jonkershoek', unpublished document, 2006.

46. Department of Labour, 'Farm workers' minimum wage increases 2007/8', 2 March 2007, www.labour.gov.za (accessed June 2007).

47. Interview with Alie van Jaarsveld, spokesperson, Western Cape Ministry of Agriculture, Cape Town, 30 April 2007.

48. Interview with Clarence Johnson, Cape Winelands district mayor, Stellenbosch, 8 May 2007; interview with Gwebs Qonde, Cape Winelands deputy municipal manager, Stellenbosch, 8 May 2007.

49. Interview with John Appolis, Anti-Privatisation Forum, Johannesburg, May 2005. Subsequent to this interview, the government shifted economic focus towards a developmental state, but the influence of social movements in this shift is difficult to trace.

50. Interview with administrator, SECC, Soweto, 5 May 2005; interview with Madiba.

51. Interview with Ngwane.

52. Interview with Ida Jacobs, organiser, Sikhula Sonke, Stellenbosch, 8 May 2007.

53. McKinley, 'Democracy and social movements', pp. 418–19.

54. Interviews with branch members from Dube, Soweto, 4 July 2011; SECC Senaone branch meeting, Soweto, 17 March 2005; SECC Rockville branch meeting, Soweto, 10 March 2005; SECC Noordgesig mass meeting, Soweto, 7 April 2005.

55. Interview with Estelle Coetzee, organiser, Sikhula Sonke, Stellenbosch, 8 May 2007.

56. Interview with Sikhula Sonke member and CCMA case applicant; interview with farm worker A, De Klapmuts Farm, Western Cape, 25 April 2007.

57. Employer–employee relations do differ from farm to farm and there are examples of good practice on some farms, although these are in the minority.

58. Interviews with Sikhula Sonke members from farms in the Cape Winelands, Western Cape, March–May 2007.

59. Luke Sinwell, 'Is "another world" really possible? Re-examining counter-hegemonic forces in post-apartheid South Africa', *Review of African Political Economy*, Vol. 38, No. 127 (2011).

60. Interviews with Lubisi and Madiba.

61. Interview with Virginia Setshedi, SECC, Johannesburg, 10 March 2004; interviews with Lubisi and Madiba.

62. SECC Dube branch meeting; SECC Senaone branch meeting; SECC Rockville branch meeting; SECC Noordgesig mass meeting.

63. The protests observed were: March to Protea Magistrates Court, Soweto, April 2005; demonstration at Moroka Police Station to hand over a memorandum,

Soweto, April 2005; Anti-War Coalition Solidarity March, Johannesburg, 19 March 2005.

64. City of Johannesburg, 'Context', n.d., http://www.joburg-archive.co.za/2008/sdf/soweto/soweto_statusquo_context.pdf (accessed 3 August 2011).

65. Michael Nefale, *A Survey on Attitudes to Prepaid Electricity Meters in Soweto*, Johannesburg: Centre for Applied Legal Studies, 2004.

66. Telephone interview with Kgothatso Mola, APF secretary, 9 November 2011.

67. Telephone interview with Sandra Hendricks, administrator, Sikhula Sonke, 7 July 2011.

68. Josep María Antentas, 'Resistance to neoliberalism', *IV Online Magazine*, IV380 (July–August 2006), www.internationalviewpoint.org/spip.php?article1088 (accessed 15 July 2011).

69. Interview with Madiba.

70. For discussion, see Madlingozi, 'Post-apartheid social movements' and Ballard et al., *Voices of Protest*, p. 408.

71. Interview with Abie Ditlake, director, SADC NGO Council, Harare, 4 August 2009.

72. Interview with Madiba.

73. Ballard et al., *Voices of Protest*, p. 403.

74. See Alexander's contribution in this volume.

75. From May 2009 a large number of protests occurred in all parts of South Africa. Protests centred on a range of concerns, including service delivery problems, labour conditions and wage negotiation strikes.

76. Comments made at the Global Governance Learning Network meeting, 2009.

77. Comments by Luke Sinwell, Centre for Sociological Research, at a Global Governance Learning Network presentation, Johannesburg, 2009.

78. Interview with Russell Ally, Ford Foundation, Johannesburg, 17 August 2009.

79. Interview with Leonard Gentle, director, International Labour Research and Information Group, Cape Town, 4 June 2009.

80. Interview with Ngwane.

81. Ibid.

82. Interview with Mazibuko Jara, ALARM, Cape Town, 3 June 2009.

83. Focus group with community activists, Centre for Civil Society, Durban, 22 June 2009.

84. See Shannon Walsh, '"Uncomfortable collaborations": Contesting constructions of the "poor" in South Africa', *Review of African Political Economy*, Vol. 35, No. 116 (2008), p. 261.

85. For more detail, see Fiona White, 'Strengthening democracy? The role of social movements as agents of civil society in post-apartheid South Africa', PhD thesis, University of London, 2008.

86. Crystal Prince, 'Conditions on farms: A draft paper', Unit for Social Research, Western Cape Department of Social Services and Poverty Alleviation, 2004, p. 3.

87. Ibid.

88. Alexis de Tocqueville in Ricardo Blaug and John Schwarzmantel, *Democracy: A Reader*, Edinburgh: Edinburgh University Press, 1988, p. 477.

89. Charles Tilly, 'When do (and don't) social movements promote democratization?', in Pedro Ibarra (ed.), *Social Movements and Democracy*, New York: Palgrave Macmillan, 2003.

90. E. Zuern, *The Politics of Necessity: Community Organizing and Democracy in South Africa*, Madison: University of Wisconsin Press, 2011, p. 169.
91. John Gaventa, 'Triumph, deficit or contestation? Deepening the "deepening democracy" debate', IDS Working Paper, No. 264, Brighton: Institute of Development Studies, 2006, p. 19.
92. Interview with Adam Habib, deputy vice-chancellor, University of Johannesburg, 14 September 2009.
93. Fiona White, '2009 elections', *South African Labour Bulletin*, Vol. 33, No. 3 (2009).

9
Resisting Privatisation: Exploring Contradictory Consciousness and Activism in the Anti-Privatisation Forum

Carin Runciman

INTRODUCTION

It has been over a decade since South Africa's so-called 'new social movements' began to emerge in opposition to the neoliberal turn of the African National Congress (ANC)-led government, and the Anti-Privatisation Forum (APF) has been one significant organisation through which both local and national anti-neoliberal struggles have oriented themselves. While much has been written about the APF and other similar movement organisations, as Sinwell has noted, much of this scholarship has avoided critically engaging with the internal dynamics and grassroots politics of the movement.[1] Drawing from eleven months of ethnographic fieldwork with the APF and a number of its affiliates, in this chapter I provide an insight into the often contradictory realities of social movement activism through developing a Gramscian perspective of resistance. Utilising the concept of the 'social movement community', I analyse the relationship among the APF, its affiliates and the wider community and demonstrate that the APF and its wider social movement community consists of a continuum of participants who may accept, reinterpret or reject a movement's message. I explore some of the ways in which the APF's politics is reinterpreted by its constituency and how in turn this affects the content of grassroots mobilisation. Rather than seeing such inconsistency as simply illustrative of a weak or incoherent movement, I argue that such challenges represent the very heart of the meaning work that the movement engages in. Finally, I provide a brief analysis of the political praxis of two

APF affiliates to illustrate the differing ways in which take up the individual challenges they face.

THEORISING RESISTANCE

Analysts of social movements are often concerned with questions of what makes social change possible. Marxist scholar Antonio Gramsci's theory of hegemony both analyses how the ruling classes produce and reproduce their dominant positions within society and suggests how such powers may be challenged. Developed from Lenin's work, Gramsci's theory of hegemony explores the ways in which structural relations are maintained and secured by the dominant classes both politically and ideologically through processes of coercion and consent. Gramsci's intellectual concerns centre around an analysis of political power and representation, the relations between the dominant and subaltern classes, and 'the cultural and ideological forms in which social antagonisms are fought out, regulated and dissipated'.[2] For Gramsci, all social relations involve the asymmetric distribution of power, and how power is distributed informs the lived experiences of subaltern groups who live in subordination to hegemonic forms of power. The maintenance of hegemony is a continuous project because the dominant classes can only maintain their position through continual maintenance of their dominant political and ideological position involving a dialectical relationship between the dominant and subaltern classes and hegemonic and counter-hegemonic forces.

Embryonic forms of counter-hegemonic consciousness emerge from the contradictions of the lived experiences of the subaltern under hegemonic relations of domination.[3] The forms of counter-hegemonic consciousness that may emerge are therefore entangled within these contradictions, which may entrench forces of hegemony while challenging others, leading to fragmented forms of resistance across a diffuse range of identities and interests. Conflict and tension therefore exist not only between movements and the wider political environment, but also within movements themselves. In order to consolidate and build upon these embryonic forms of consciousness, Gramsci argues, organic intellectuals must work to synthesise the diverse interests of challenging groups to build ideologies that will cement and lend coherence to political action. Such challenges are built from critiquing existing social, political and economic arrangements, and how such critiques are constructed will be dependent on the various social forces that are brought together in counter-hegemonic struggles, which may or not be class based in nature. Therefore, the ideologies formed from counter-hegemonic challenges are not necessarily logical and linear in their progression, but are bound to the contested social forces of society. Social movements thus work towards disorganising consent and organising dissent through critiquing the commonsense view of the world in order to allow people to begin to build what Gramsci called 'good sense'.[4] Gramsci's analysis of how counter-hegemonic consciousness emerges advances traditional Marxist understandings of 'false consciousness' and the theorisation of a unified class subject.[5] Throughout the rest of this chapter I shall demonstrate how Gramsci's theorisation of how oppositional counter-hegemonic consciousness emerges provides invaluable insight in analysing the broad continuum of participants that make up the APF.

THE APF'S SOCIAL MOVEMENT COMMUNITY

The APF was formed in July 2000, emerging from three related campaign groups: the Anti-iGoli 2002 committee, the Wits 2001 committee and grassroots community-based organisations such as the Soweto Electricity Crisis Committee (SECC).[6] From its birth in 2000 the APF has grown from having two community-based affiliates to a high of nearly 30 between 2006 and 2008, declining to around 20 during 2009–10. The APF also contains some political groups, for example Socialist Group and Keep Left, as well as independent activists. Primarily forged out of struggles against the privatisation and corporatisation of the City of Johannesburg, the APF attempts to 'collectivise knowledge and experiences and develop common positions and campaigns/struggles'[7] in an attempt to build and consolidate a critical anti-capitalist, anti-privatisation and anti-neoliberal challenge to the ANC's current development framework.

The APF can be best understood as providing a central node in an inter- and intra-movement network that weaves together a web of activists and community-based organisations (CBOs). This web constructs an organisation that is divided into a core of activists who occupy positions within some aspect of the formal structures of the APF and a larger periphery group who remain largely outside the formal organisation. Within this web, affiliate leaders provide a crucial link between the grassroots base of the organisation and the formal structures of the APF and its elected leadership. As 'bridge leaders', affiliate leaders play a key role in politicising the private issues of the community and linking 'the formal movement organisation's message and the day-to-day realities of potential constituents'[8] and therefore perform critical work as organic intellectuals within the movement.

However, as founding member Dale McKinley explains, communities that affiliate to the APF are not necessarily or primarily drawn to it because of the politics it advances:

> there was no other organisation which was available for a lot of people. SANCO [South African National Civics Organisation] was pretty much out of the picture, but by this stage I think people had realised clearly the ANC itself was not the place; in fact, they were the ones that were doing this ... they'd heard about the APF ... [and] oftentimes if there's a struggle in a particular community ... they almost immediately after a particular point look for others who are doing the same thing or who can provide some resources or support or who can bring together in some solidarity, and the very fact that the APF is the only ... social movement of its kind ... [and it] draws people to it, inevitably. Even if they might not know much about the APF or they might not know its politics or its history, it's the fact that it's there and it represents a potential home or a potential place where they can join with others.[9]

As Wolford suggests, often analyses of social movement participation stress the intentionality and rationale that lead people to join social movements. This assumes, she argues, 'a market-place of ideas and decision-making that invokes Liberal economic theory: believing in agency has come to mean believing in intentionality ... *someone* is making decisions with access to perfect information and in a competitive political market'.[10] However, as McKinley suggests, often many CBOs have been drawn to the APF because its independence from political parties provides much-needed support to struggling communities who have few alternatives allies.

The network of activists and communities that the APF weaves poses significant challenges to traditional social movement theory, which tends to be dominated by analysis derived from North America and Western Europe. Analysts frequently discuss social movements as if they are empirically unitary actors working towards a set of coherent and agreed goals. However, as Melucci argues, any sense of unity within a movement is often the 'the result rather than a point of departure; otherwise one must assume that there is a sort of deep "mind" of the movement, instead of considering it as a system of social relationships'.[11] However, organisations like the APF, with diffuse and federate structures, create movements that are multi-layered and require analysis that in the case of the APF situates it and its affiliates within the wider communities of which they are a part.

Stoecker suggests that social movement organisations (SMOs) that have their base within community organisations are inherently shaped by the geographical specificity, localised membership, resources and issue potential of this base and that these particular dynamics must inform our analysis of such organisations. Through his work with neighbourhood associations in Minneapolis, Stoecker develops the concept of a social movement community to provide a useful analytical lens through which to view such movements. He argues that these four spheres in which activism occur are analytically distinct, but related to one another: the social movement community, the social movement, the SMO and the individual.[12]

For an organisation like the APF, its relation to the communities in which its affiliates have their base structures the direction and content of its mobilisation. The wider community provides a backstage area in which social interactions and personal bonds forged in the course of daily life often become essential to successful mobilisation. Activists are then able to draw on and establish cultural rituals, personal commitments and collective memories to mobilise the community. However, as Stoecker highlights, 'the community is a place people have not usually chosen for political reasons, and it contains both activists and non-activists networked to each other, thus making political unity problematic'.[13]

For Stoecker, the lack of political unity distinguishes the social movement community from the social movement. A social movement consists of people who broadly orientate themselves toward the movement's aims and participate in its demonstrations. However, as Stoecker highlights, those who identify themselves as part of a movement and participate within its demonstrations are often not involved with the organisation that is coordinating or leading an action. This, he argues, is because they identify themselves 'with the goals and strategies of the action, not necessarily with the organisation'.[14] The implications of this are that movement membership is often unstable as people drift in and out of the movement.

SMOs are distinguished from the other levels of the social movement community by their formal organisation, stable membership and sense of collective identity. Stoecker notes that SMOs are likely to consist of a much smaller number than the movement itself due to the need for 'greater commitment of time, risk and energy'.[15] Uniting a range of activists, SMOs like the APF play a crucial role in linking the day-to-day realities of the wider network of the social movement community with the political message of the SMO. As one APF activist explained:

> In the community, we are dealing with specific community issues, but in the APF, a whole load of issues ... are now broader now. They will tell you about the GEAR [the government's Growth, Employment and Redistribution policy], they will tell you about ASGISA [the government's Accelerated and Shared Growth Initiative for South Africa] and that's where I was growing. Because if APF was not formed, I was not sure if I was going to be very clear in terms of politics ... So automatically, whatever we were learning from them we were able to translate it in the community to show them in the community how are we trusting GEAR, how does GEAR affect us, because people were not even understanding GEAR or ASGISA; they are just interested in seeing the issue of service delivery happen, but we managed to conscientise them and give them direction.[16]

In translating the political message of the APF into ways that connect with the day-to-day experiences of the wider social movement community, the core cadreship or 'bridge leadership'[17] perform the work of organic intellectuals through attempting to build 'good sense' within the wider movement. Indeed, one of the APF's key organisational goals has been to propagate political responses to the private troubles of ordinary people and to build a movement and cadreship 'that could go beyond just issue-based opposition to a particular privatisation'.[18]

However, as McKinley argues, communities that affiliate to the APF are not necessarily drawn to it because of its political orientation. The broad network of the APF's social movement community draws together a wide continuum of activists who interpret, adopt or even reject the movement's message. Rather than illustrative of a weak or incoherent movement, I argue that such contradictions are illustrative of the dialectic relations through which oppositional counter-hegemonic consciousness is formed that often entrenches forms of hegemonic dominance while challenging others. However, as Wolford argues, analysts of social movements 'tend to study the ideal members, the coherent messages, and the brightest media stars. We do not focus on the ambivalent or half-hearted members.'[19] In the following section, I explore some of the ways in which APF activists understand the APF or its affiliates as a political entity and the relationship of this to the APF's socialist orientation, and provide an analysis of the contested ways in which the struggle against privatisation is understood internally within the movement.

LOCATING POLITICAL CONSCIOUSNESS WITHIN THE APF

An exploration of the internal dynamics of a social movement throws up many puzzling contradictions. Such movements are conventionally understood as political entities. However, throughout the course of my fieldwork, activists, whether in interviews or at community meetings, would frequently identify themselves as non-political actors. In a survey conducted at the 2010 APF annual general meeting involving 14 affiliates, eleven identified their organisations as non-political, two as political and one was unsure.[20] For those who identified the APF as non-political, this was associated with its political independence from mainstream political parties and its ability to forge alternative 'free' public spaces outside of institutionalised democracy:

> I think there was [sic] a number of things that appealed to me [about] the APF. I think one thing is that it is a community-based organisation and if it is community based it is not supporting any ideologies of any political party, so everyone is welcome.[21]

For Dale McKinley, whether activists within the APF consider the organisation to be political or non-political was largely a conceptual issue:

> I think it's much more the conceptual aspect of it, but yeah, it's very understandable that people would have ... almost an aversion [to a political allegiance], precisely because of their experience with political parties. They've been betrayed; they've been sold out ... [a]ll the community organisations were within the ANC and within the liberation movement for the most part with [a] few exceptions ... and they were completely disappointed, and that's why they've moved into another form and they've moved into resistance, so it's very, very understandable that they would make the association between politics and a political party.[22]

While McKinley interprets whether the APF sees itself as a political or a non-political organisation as largely a conceptual discussion, for other activists, this conceptual issue has deeper roots and consequences:

> [They] say they are non-political. Basically, they are trying to avoid confronting the ANC ... That's why I say they are trying to duck, they are trying to evade the ANC, but they don't say we are evading the ANC. They don't say that we are running away from the challenges of questioning our members. They say we are non-political, we don't want to discuss any political party in our meeting. So people discuss everything, but inside they are ANC. So when Zuma comes, the working class believe there is a real ANC, but you know where the real ANC is? It's in their hearts. It's nowhere in reality, and then Zuma makes them think there's the real ANC and in five years they'll say no, Zuma is not the real ANC and they will look again.[23]

As a former APF chairperson reflected, a major challenge – particularly with the grassroots constituency of the APF – was 'the comrades who were sympathetic to the ANC'[24] and although many activists are vocal in their opposition to the ANC's development framework, attitudes towards the ANC remain far more ambiguous. For many activists, the role of social movements is to act as a 'watchdog' on the ANC and direct it onto the 'right' track either by reverting back to the Reconstruction and Development Programme policy or by pursuing the goals laid out in the Freedom Charter.[25] Therefore, although social movements have been able to contest some of the legitimacy of the ANC's development framework, the party continues for many to represent the spearhead of potential transformative politics, thus demonstrating the entangled nature through which counter-hegemonic consciousness emerges.

Although the APF has adopted socialism as its political platform, what socialism means as a political and ideological orientation was interpreted, reinterpreted and in some cases even rejected across the organisation. In a focus group with people who rejected socialism as a political goal, it was rejected partly because they associated socialism with the economic and social collapse of neighbouring Zimbabwe. For others, they rejected socialism because they recognised that without global economic change it would be very difficult for South Africa to be a socialist country in isolation.[26] For those that did not support the APF's socialist orientation, explanations of what socialism means were often closely associated with the African philosophy of *ubuntu*, whereby one's humanity is realised through one's relations to others:

> Socialism was called *ubuntu* and it was not owned by anybody. There was no division there that some people follow this person – you follow Karl Marx, you follow Trotsky, you follow whoever. It was just a communal thing among us African people that we have to help one another, that we have to be there for one another, that it was wrong to eat while others are starving. So when we looked at it we saw this was socialism too.[27]

In reinterpreting socialism as a form of *ubuntu*, the activists within the APF were adopting the political messages of the APF, but also reinterpreting it in ways that fitted their 'commonsense' view of the world, which often associated socialism with idealised forms of traditional communal living:

> Because if we remember those days of our ... grannies, they were living ... the socialist life because they could; you could go to next door and give you a sugar or tea or if they've got enough food they share around their friends. Those people are saying even if you are from another country, they take you, or from another culture, but so long as you are staying together they take you as if you are one family; they share everything that they've got.[28]

Similarly, another activist argued that 'Africans have their own way of defining socialism. That's why I said, before the settlers came into the country and took the land, we were equally sharing things; that is our own socialism.'[29] The association of *ubuntu*, traditional forms of communal living and socialism bring together different philosophical and political beliefs and an entanglement of progressive and traditional ideologies, resulting in a form of socialist politics that, on the one hand, is socially progressive, but, on the other, may also entrench a number inequalities, particularly around issues of gender.

For McKinley, the unevenness in the political understanding and interpretation of socialism was reflective of the process through which socialism was adopted as the APF's political platform. As he recalls, the drive to adopt socialism as the APF's political platform had come from certain sections of the organisation, particularly from political groups, and was therefore not a process that was predominantly driven through an 'organic process where people understand [and] ... own that process ... they begin to say "yes, that's what we're looking for, that's the kind of society we want", and they understand what that means, and that takes time'.[30] This was a view shared by fellow founding member John Appolis:

> I was one of the people who did not support the idea that the APF must adopt socialism, not because I'm not a socialist – I believe in socialism – it's because I thought it was premature if the activists, the militants and the constituency doesn't [sic] have a kind of understanding of the issue of socialism. You know, there are a whole lot of things about socialism and how socialism relates to the day-to-day struggles, the organisation building, the kind of organisation you build, the kind of struggles you engage with, where you take up issues and engage, the internal democracy – all of that has got to do with socialism.[31]

For both McKinley and Appolis, the process of adopting a political standpoint circumvented a more organic process through which the political identity of the APF could be forged more organically through a process of struggle. As Appolis has argued elsewhere, the adoption of the loosely defined socialist platform is characteristic of the continuing legacy of the 'old left' in South Africa, which continues to play a significant role within the new social movements. While this has had a number of benefits, particularly organisation-ally, the downside for Appolis is that 'the new generation of activists has not yet crafted out "a new politics" for movements. It has not yet put its own peculiar imprint on the political and ideological discourses of our movements, and indeed of South Africa.'[32]

Fantasia argues that the value of ethnographic movements is that they often expose the 'discontinuities and paradoxes' of consciousness that emerge within a movement.[33] As I have demonstrated above, the APF, through uniting a diverse constituency, has often struggled to construct a unified approach to its struggles and campaigns. Indeed, at times it was clear that often APF activists were unclear as to the nature of privatisation and the various forms in which it occurs. In a planning meeting in November 2009 the four regions of the APF met to draft a programme of demands for an upcoming week of action. One of the regions advocated the demand that the government should make more tenders available to local people and particularly to young people. Those present at the meeting did not question the consistency of this demand with the APF's political identity until another region advocated the counter-demand that the government should stop the programme of privatisation and that municipalities should resume responsibility for all services that had been privatised. In conflict here were two very different inter-pretations of what privatisation is, its effects in society and how it may best be remedied -- what Benford would call a diagnostic and prognostic framing dispute.[34] This conflict was resolved through a debate that encouraged those present to consider the ways in which tendering represents an aspect of privatisation and its effects in society and thus allowed those present to possibly gain a greater understanding of the nature of privatisation.

In this section, I have attempted to demonstrate the diversity and discontinuity among the APF's constituency. As I have shown, the APF contains a continuum of participants who possess a range of understandings about the nature of the organisation and its politics. Earlier I argued that 'bridge leadership' plays an integral role in connecting the political message of the APF to the grassroots base of the organisation. In the final section of this chapter I briefly consider how the uneven, contradictory consciousness of the APF shapes the mobilisation activities of two APF affiliates; Soweto Concerned Residents (SCR) and the Schubart and Kruger Park Residents' Committee (SKPRC). In comparing these two affiliates, I argue that the differing skills and experiences of the 'bridge leadership' shape the forms of mobilisation that occur in these spaces.

TRANSLATING CONSCIOUSNESS IN APF AFFILIATES

SCR formed in 2005 after splitting from the SECC. Like SECC, SCR has a structure of branches across approximately 15 areas of Soweto, predominantly within Orlando East, Meadowlands and Dobsonville. Branch meetings provide a space in which local residents can come together to discuss issues of concern both to individuals and the community at large, generally regarding issues of housing, water and electricity. Branch meetings can consist of an average attendance of anywhere between 20 and 70 residents, predominantly female pensioners. These meetings provide a forum in which residents can communicate grievances to the leadership and for the leadership to communicate messages from the (largely male) SCR executive leadership and the APF.

The SCR executive is made up largely of male activists who mostly have experience not only in the struggle against apartheid, while many have been involved with the APF in some form from its early days. Therefore, in coordinating its mobilisation activities, SCR is able to draw on a wealth of political and organisational experience. This translates into the SCR framing it demands and political platform in anti-capitalist and anti-neoliberal terms. In April 2010 SCR organised a march to the Eskom (the main supplier of electricity in South Africa) offices in Braamfontein in protest against the continued rollout of pre-paid electricity meters. In the memorandum handed to Eskom staff, SCR argue:

> The residents of Soweto and the organisation namely Soweto [C]oncerned [R]esidents/APF hereby wish to bring this matter to the attention of the world at large. Eskom together with NERSA [National Energy Regulator of South Africa] sanctioned by the ANC led government is forcibly installing pre-paid electricity meters in the entire black township in our country ... This move is more profit based and in complete disregard to our constitutional right to electricity [which] is a basic human right and not a pre-paid human right ... All our South African government[s]. The old apartheid ones and new democratic ones have accepted and operated the global capitalistic system. The capitalistic system can never change for the better. It is based on the exploitation and oppression of people on super profits from cheap labour. The system produces wealth for a minority and intense poverty and hardship for the majority. This is its track record throughout its history[:] billions of people who are unemployed and have no money. Are just abandoned ... to live in hunger, poverty, disease and war.[35]

While the core cadre of the SCR executive, who drafted memorandums such as the one above, had developed a fairly coherent oppositional consciousness, the members of the executive were also aware that this was not something shared by the majority of people who attended the organisation's meetings.[36] In a series of focus groups conducted within one branch of SCR, the primary reason for attending meetings that emerged through the discussions was that SCR provided residents with forms of assistance and support that they could not access elsewhere. Often these forms of support went beyond the work of opposing evictions in the community and took on an important dimension of emotionally caring for the community. It was commonplace for constituents to request the assistance of the branch during SCR branch meetings to mediate family matters or disputes between neighbours. The role that SCR activists have in attempting to mediate in such matters played an important role in forging affective bonds within the community, which, as Goodwin and his colleagues argue, can often be used to generate widespread mobilisation and support and subsequently orientate the organisation to more overtly political gains.[37] However, it was clear that for the vast majority of participants, SCR's political orientation was secondary to the wider support network that the organisation provided. In an attempt to bridge this gap, the SCR executive regularly arranged for members of the leadership to visit different structures in order to help politicise the issues of the community through delivering 'mini lectures' that linked immediate issues to the wider politics of the movement. As resource mobilisation theorists such as Edwards and McCarthy argue, resources, both material and non-material, are vital to mobilisation.[38] SCR activists have benefited from being able to draw from a range of political and organisational experiences within their ranks that has allowed them not only to challenge evictions and disconnections, but also to politicise these issues in order to transform them from the seemingly private troubles of individuals and move them into the political and public realm. While the political orientation of SCR is not evenly spread throughout the organisation, through its activities, SCR attempts to implant an anti-capitalist critique within the wider social movement community through its mobilisation activities, which open up spaces in which there is potential for a more coherent oppositional consciousness to be forged. As Maddison and Scalmer argue, 'the process of campaigning is itself educative. The hurly-burly of activism is a kind of schooling. The instinctive grasping of the radical opens up new kinds of knowledge – about politics.'[39]

In comparison to SCR, the core cadreship within the SKPRC executive was younger, between 25 and 40, and consisted of individuals without the same degree of organisational and political experience. The residents of Schubart Park faced a mass eviction from the high-rise complex located within the Tshwane central business district, which was originally built in the 1970s as low-cost housing for white residents. The complex provides underground parking, a shopping precinct, a community hall, and recreational facilities that include a swimming pool and tennis courts. Today the complex is home to social groups from across both South Africa and neighbouring countries, making it a distinctive social space within post-apartheid South Africa. According to residents, the complex was well maintained until the mid 2000s, when little by little it fell into disrepair. The lifts in the 21-storey blocks do not work, the recreational facilities are unsafe and the complex is plagued with a series of leaks that often cause water shortages, while other infrastructural problems cause power outages. Various residents' committees and members of the ward committee have through the years attempted to engage the authorities on the maintenance of the complexes, without success. In 2008, then Tshwane mayor, Gwen Ramokgopa, announced that there was to be a multi-million rand redevelopment of the complex, the scale of which would require all residents to leave. The threats and attempts to evict the residents reinvigorated the residents' attempts to organise, particularly after an attempt to evict residents in July 2008 tragically led to a fire in one of the blocks, Kruger Park, that led to the deaths of five people and the block being destroyed.

The current residents' committee is made up of a formally elected executive that is assisted by a wider group of largely male activists between the ages of 25 and 40, most of whom have little prior organisational or political experience. The executive meets at least once a week, but often executive meetings are held three times a week in order to meet the challenges of living in Schubart Park. Mass meetings are held with the community once a week that draw an attendance of anywhere between 100 and 500 residents. Meetings usually involve the executive providing feedback from the series of meetings the committee has had with the City of Tshwane authorities and their legal representatives at Lawyers for Human Rights, and updates on campaigns to help maintain the complex.

The struggle to maintain the complex in a liveable condition takes up the majority of the residents committee's energies. On an almost daily basis, the committee would be directing activities in terms of repairing or maintaining one aspect of the complex. In community meetings, such activities were embedded within a narrative that sought to reclaim Schubart Park from the City of Tshwane authorities and reclaim the identity of Tshwane itself, for example, during meetings the executive would frequently communicate that 'Schubart Park belongs to us, and the City of Tshwane belongs to us'.[40] By embedding the struggle to maintain the complex within a narrative that claims the identity of both the City of Tshwane and Schubart Park for the residents, the idea that the fate of the complex lay within the hands of the residents rather than the authorities was created and reinforced. Such narratives played a powerful part in motivating the cleaning campaigns and other activities undertaken that sought to maintain the complex, which were an important part of the day-to-day struggle at Schubart Park. However, they also served to isolate the struggles of the community from a wider critique of the political and economic system. Problems with infrastructure were attributed to a lack of funding and mal-administration, without questioning the wider meaning of this.

Although the SKPRC was an APF affiliate, its relation to the 'mother body' was weak. As a more recent affiliate of the APF, the SKPRC had not had the opportunity to engage with the APF over a sufficiently prolonged period of time that would have enabled the executive to build the same base of political and organisational knowledge as within SCR. The opportunities to build this knowledge base within the organisation were further curtailed by the fact that many of those on the executive were employed and therefore unable to participate in the majority of the APF's activities. In making a comparative analysis of SCR and the SKPRC, I have demonstrated that the differing skills, and organisational and political experiences of their members play an important role in shaping mobilisation.

CONCLUSION

In this chapter, I have argued that social movements are not unified and coherent actors, and that beyond the political rhetoric of any movement there will be a diversity of political standpoints. Using Gramsci's theory of counter-hegemonic consciousness, I have argued that such diversity is illustrative of the contested and fractional way in which counter-hegemonic challenges emerge through a coalition of forces. In analysing the ways in which APF activists interpret, reinterpret or even reject the APF's politics, I have attempted to provide a critical engagement with the messy and often contradictory realities of the internal dynamics of APF politics.

NOTES

1. Luke Sinwell, 'Is "another world" really possible? Re-examining counter-hegemonic forces in post-apartheid South Africa', *Review of African Political Economy*, Vol. 38, No. 127 (March 2011).
2. David Forgacs, *A Gramsci Reader*, London: Lawrence and Wishart, 1988, p. 189.
3. Kate Crehan, *Gramsci: Culture and Anthropology*, London: Pluto Press, 2002, pp. 115–22.
4. Roger Simon, *Gramsci's Political Thought: An Introduction*, London: Lawrence and Wishart, 1982.
5. Stuart Hall, 'Gramsci's relevance for the study of race and ethnicity', *Journal of Communication Inquiry*, Vol. 10 (June 1986).

6. For more detail on the emergence of the APF, see S. Buhlungu, 'Upstarts or bearers of tradition? The Anti-Privatisation Forum of Gauteng', in Richard Ballard, Adam Habib and Imraan Valodia (eds), *Voices of Protest: Social Movements in Post-Apartheid South Africa*, Scottsville: University of KwaZulu-Natal Press, 2006.

7. APF, 'Background to the formation & activities of the APF', undated internal document.

8. Belinda Robnett, *How Long? How Long? African-American Women in the Struggle for Civil Rights*, Oxford: Oxford University Press, 1996, p. 92.

9. Interview with Dale McKinley, February 2010.

10. Wendy Wolford, *This Land is Ours Now: Social Mobilization and the Meanings of Land*, London: Duke University Press, 2010, pp. 17–18; original emphasis.

11. Alberto Melucci, 'The symbolic challenge of contemporary movements', *Social Research*, Vol. 52, No. 4 (Winter 1985), p. 793.

12. Randy Stoecker, 'Community, movement, organization: The problem of identity convergence in collective action', *Sociological Quarterly*, Vol. 36, No. 1 (Winter 1995).

13. Ibid., p. 112.

14. Ibid.

15. Ibid., p. 113.

16. Interview with male APF sub-committee coordinator, November 2009.

17. Belinda Robnett, *How Long? How Long? African-American Women in the Struggle for Civil Rights*, Oxford: Oxford University Press, 1996, p. 92.

18. Interview with McKinley.

19. Wolford, *This Land is Ours Now*, p. 11.

20. Survey conducted by author, April 2010.

21. Interview with male APF part-time organiser, October 2009.

22. Interview with McKinley.

23. Interview with Trevor Ngwane, November 2009.

24. Interview with former APF chairperson, February 2010.

25. Author's field notes.

26. Focus group with female APF activists, May 2010.

27. Interview with male APF office bearer, May 2010.

28. Interview with female Soweto Concerned Residents activists, March 2010.

29. Focus group, APF housing sub-committee coordinator, June 2010.

30. Interview with McKinley.

31. Interview with John Appolis, May 2010.

32. John Appolis, 'South African social movements: Where are we now?', *Khanya*, No. 5 (April 2004), p. 39.

33. Rick Fantasia, *Cultures of Solidarity: Consciousness, Action and Contemporary American Workers*, Berkeley: University of California Press, 1989, p. 5.

34. R. Benford, 'Frame disputes with the Nuclear Disarmament Movement', *Social Forces*, Vol. 71, No. 3 (1993), p. 678.

35. SCR, 'Soweto Concerned Residents: A march against the basic human rights violation', memorandum delivered to Eskom Braamfontein, 18 April 2010.

36. Author's field notes.

37. Jeff Goodwin, Jaems M. Jasper and Francesca Polletta, 'Emotional dimensions of social movements', in David A. Snow, Sarag A. Soule and Hanspeter Kriesi (eds), *The Blackwell Companion to Social Movements*, Oxford: Blackwell, pp. 418–21.

38. Bob Edwards and John D. McCarthy, 'Resources and social movement mobilisation', in Snow et al., *The Blackwell Companion to Social Movements*, p. 116.

39. Sarah Maddison and Sean Scalmer, *Activist Wisdom: Practical Knowledge and Creative Tension in Social Movements*, Sydney: University of New South Wales, 2006, p. 49.

40. Author's field notes.

10

The Challenge of Ecological Transformation in Post-Apartheid South Africa: The Re-emergence of an Environmental Justice Movement[1]

Jacklyn Cock

INTRODUCTION

The ecological crisis, particularly climate change, is having devastating social and economic impacts, including water scarcity, crop failures and rising food prices. Those worst affected are the poor and powerless, who are least responsible for the carbon emissions that cause climate change. The response of the post-apartheid state is that the system can continue to expand by creating a new 'green capitalism', bringing the efficiency of the market to bear on nature and its reproduction. This chapter addresses the question, do local environmental organisations present a challenge to this green capitalism?

Such a challenge is essential for transformation into a social order that is both just and sustainable. Ecological sustainability requires a just transition from the present dependence on fossil fuels to a low-carbon economy. This suggests an additional dimension to understandings of transformation, which emphasise social, political, and economic processes in the redistribution of power and resources. The themes of 'justice' and sustainability are strongly promoted by an embryonic environmental justice movement that may be re-emerging and building on its historical precursor, the Environmental Justice Networking Forum. Driven by the master frame of environmental justice and radicalised by activists from other forces such as the growing climate justice movement, it may have considerable potential for mass mobilisation, for linking environmental and labour struggles, and for demonstrating that the ecological crisis is caused by the expansionist logic of the capitalist system.

GREEN CAPITALISM

The two pillars on which green capitalism rests are technological innovation and expanding markets, while keeping the existing institutions of capitalism intact. More specifically, green capitalism involves the carbon-trading regime enshrined in the Kyoto Protocols; appeals to nature (and even the ecological crisis) as a marketing tool; developing largely untested clean-coal technology through carbon capture and storage, which involves installing equipment that captures carbon dioxide and other greenhouse gases and then storing the gas underground; the development of new sources of energy such as solar, nuclear and wind, thereby creating new markets; and the massive development of biofuels, which involves diverting land from food production.

The process is disguised by a heavy reliance on manipulative advertising – so-called 'greenwash' – to persuade us of the efficacy of these strategies. The main concern remains profitability and the awareness that shrinking natural resources could damage it and that 'green' measures such as energy efficiency could reduce costs, lessen risks and enhance companies' public images.

Underlying all these strategies is the broad process of commodification: the transformation of nature and all social relations into economic relations, subordinated to the logic of the market and the imperatives of profit. According to John Bellamy Foster, these visions amount to little more than 'a renewed strategy for profiting from planetary destruction'.[2]

This notion of green or sustainable capitalism is being subjected to growing criticism, rooted in the understanding that it is capital's logic of accumulation that is destroying the ecological conditions that sustain life.[3] As Wallis states, the environmental crisis 'is a crisis arising from and perpetuated by the rule of capital and hence incapable of resolution within the capitalist framework'.[4] This understanding is slowly percolating through to a nascent environmental justice movement in South Africa.

AN EMBRYONIC ENVIRONMENTAL JUSTICE MOVEMENT: THE VALUE OF FRAMING

At present there is no single, collective actor that constitutes the environmental movement in South Africa and no master 'frame' of environmentalism encoded in any blueprint. Some social movement scholars have emphasised the importance of framing in their analyses of the relative strength and success of movements.[5] Their framing perspective seeks to understand how activists construct meaning and put different elements together to ensure that 'one set of meanings rather than another is conveyed'.[6] Snow and Benford suggest that movement leaders and supporters 'frame, or assign meaning to and interpret relevant events and conditions in ways that are intended to mobilize potential adherents and constituents, or garner bystander support, and to demobilize antagonists'.[7] In the absence of a common frame, environmental struggles have no coherent centre and no tidy margins; they constitute an inchoate sum of multiple, diverse, uncoordinated, and fragmented struggles and organisations.

This fragmentation involves a fault line that divides the 'movement' into two main streams: those organised around the discourse of sustainable development and those organised around the discourse of environmental justice. Both of these are powerful discursive strategies, especially in relation to apartheid practices.

During the apartheid regime, environmentalism operated effectively as a conservation strategy that neglected social needs. The notion of environmental justice represents an important shift away from this traditional authoritarian concept of environmentalism, which was mainly concerned with the conservation of threatened plants, animals and wilderness areas, to include urban, health, labour and development issues.[8] The process of framing can thus be 'contentious', as it involves the generation of interpretive frames that not only differ from existing ones, but 'may also challenge them'.[9] The outcomes of the framing process are 'collective action frames',[10] which are regarded by Gamson as 'not merely aggregations of individual attitudes and perceptions but also the outcome of negotiating shared meaning'.[11] In the context of the environmental justice movement, a useful collective action frame would entail one that is built on the discourse of environmental justice and that provides a radical alternative both to the traditional view and to the dominant emphasis on sustainable development. It questions the market's ability to bring about social or environmental sustainability.

HISTORICAL PRECURSOR:
THE ENVIRONMENTAL JUSTICE NETWORKING FORUM

During the 1990s the Environmental Justice Networking Forum (EJNF) was the organisational expression of a coherent, comprehensive environmental justice movement in South Africa.

It was a nationwide umbrella alliance of over 400 participating organisations characterised by an ideological and social diversity. It described itself as a 'democratic network, a shared resource, a forum which seeks to advance the interrelatedness of social, economic, environmental and political issues to reverse and prevent environmental injustices affecting the poor and the working class'.[12] It aimed to achieve this through two broad interconnected programmes, namely environmental governance and community campaigns, which focused on mining and ecological debt, energy, food security, and waste.

The EJNF was initiated at a conference hosted by Earthlife Africa in 1992. From the outset there was a clear and strong commitment to transformation through an expanded conception of environmental justice that was directed towards meeting basic human needs. To signal a decisive break with the dominant, narrow, authoritarian conservationism, pioneer founder Chris Albertyn promoted a very inclusive understanding of the environment.

Over the ten years of its existence the EJNF changed a good deal. In its pioneering phase, from 1994 to 1998, the emphasis was on policy formulation in close collaboration with the state. After that the focus shifted to grassroots campaigning, its ideology became increasingly racialised, relations with the African National Congress (ANC) and the post-apartheid state became increasingly confrontational, and today it is moribund.

However, by naming the experiences of the poor and the marginalised, and drawing out from those experiences of the connections among power, development, rights, and social and environmental justice, the EJNF contributed to the reconfiguration of the discourse on environmentalism in South Africa.

EARTHLIFE AFRICA

As the initiator of the former environmental justice movement codified in the EJNF, Earthlife Africa continues to be a key node in the re-emerging environmental justice movement in South Africa. This movement is best described as a web-like universe made up of highly interconnected networks clustered around a few key nodes or hubs such as Groundwork, Climate Justice Now, the Environmental Monitoring Group, the South Durban Community Environmental Alliance (SDCEA) and Earthlife. It is characterised by a radical decentralisation of authority, with no governing body, official ideology or mandated leaders; minimal hierarchy; and horizontal and informal forms of organising.

Earthlife is not only a key node in this movement, it is both locally grounded and globally connected. It thus transcends the primary emphasis on localism that Albo has identified as a common weakness in ecology movements.[13] A specific Earthlife project, the Sustainable Energy and Climate Change Project (SECCP), illustrates this exceptional 'reach' that stretches up into global campaigns and down into grassroots communities. For example, in partnership with Groundwork and others in 2009, the SECCP played an important part in making connections among organisations in the Global North and South to mobilise opposition to the World Bank loan to build more coal-fired power stations. It demonstrated that the $3.75 billion loan to Eskom (the South African power generator) would increase the price of electricity for poor people and worsen South Africa's contribution to CO_2 emissions and climate change. An Earthlife/Groundwork briefing document was produced and within three months more than 200 organisations across the world were mobilised to endorse a critique of this loan.

Earthlife and the SECCP assisted the World Bank inspection panel in a tour of the areas surrounding the Medupi power station. This is one of the planned coal-fired power stations that will pump 25–30 megatonnes of CO_2 into the atmosphere annually, more than the output of 115 countries.[14] The organisation helped to bring together a coalition of residents, traditional leaders and farmers to oppose the development. The SECCP argued that 'this loan is not about poor people or jobs or even the climate', but will benefit vested interests.[15] They were accused by Public Enterprises Minister Barbara Hogan of being 'unpatriotic'. While it failed to block the loan, as Tristen Taylor, Earthlife policy officer, states, 'the campaign showed that environmental groups in South Africa have the international and domestic reach to seriously interfere with government plans'.[16]

This example demonstrates Earthlife's capacity to globalise local resistance. Doing so frequently involves linking four repertoires of action: capacity-building workshops with grassroots communities, targeted protest actions, policy interventions and research. All four repertoires were illustrated when in 2010 Earthlife launched a research report on a major polluter (in global terms), Sasol, which was done in partnership with Groundwork.[17] It was simultaneously released in both Johannesburg and at the United Nations Framework Convention on Climate Change (UNFCCC) negotiations at COP 16 in Cancun,[18] thus connecting the local and the global.

All four repertoires – especially Earthlife's research – bridge ecological and social justice issues in that they put the experiences, needs and rights of the poor, the excluded and the marginalised at the centre of their concerns. The research report, for example, has exposed how, in the name of sustainability and cost recovery, the introduction of technological tools such as pre-paid water and electricity meters has had devastating impacts on poor households. Earthlife community surveys have provided the evidence to argue for an increase in the amount of free electricity provided: an amount of 200 kW to all households in addition to a step-block tariff (that is, cross-subsidisation through a rising tariff with increasing electricity use).

In South Africa, the energy crisis has two aspects, environmental and social: firstly, current energy production is highly polluting and, secondly, it involves unequal access to the electricity grid. Ninety per cent of the country's electricity is generated through burning coal and South Africa is the largest emitter of greenhouse gases in Africa. Most of these emissions come from the energy sector and two companies in particular: Eskom's coal-fired power stations and Sasol – especially its Secunda coal-to-liquids plant.

At the same time, millions lack access to electricity either due to the lack of infrastructure or unaffordable pre-paid meters. They have to rely on dangerous paraffin stoves and candles, or the time-consuming collection of firewood. The outcome for some is shack fires that sweep through informal settlements in South Africa almost every weekend. These are fires in which the poorest of the poor lose all their possessions and sometimes even their lives. Justice demands the provision of basic energy for all; sustainability demands that energy is not only affordable, but clean and safe, which means renewable energy. With the highest potential for solar power in the world, research has demonstrated that this is viable in South Africa.[19]

This is the context in which the SECCP claims a contribution to a number of important victories, such as:

- the abandonment of the multi-billion rand pebble bed modular reactor;
- the abandonment of the aluminium smelter at Coega;
- making future World Bank funding for coal-fired electricity-generating plants less likely; and

- breaking the veil of secrecy around below-cost electricity pricing to multinationals such as BHP Billiton and Anglo-American.

While a small organisation in terms of membership, its capacity lies in its effective networking and collaborating around specific issues with organisations such as the Legal Resources Centre, the Greenhouse People's Environment Centre, the Federation for a Sustainable Environment, the Centre for Environmental Rights, the Wits Centre for Applied Legal Studies and Groundwork.

The organisation takes advantage of available political opportunity structures including engagement with the state in what Miraftab calls the 'invited spaces' of formal political structures and the 'invented spaces' of grassroots capacity building and campaigning.[20] Through frequent engagement with official policy processes, it has demonstrated how the post-apartheid state is mainly concerned with producing large-scale centralised power from coal and nuclear sources of energy rather than creating a sustainable long-term solution by investing massively in renewable energy, public transport and urban agriculture. In the process, the state is prioritising corporate interests.

Earthlife/SECCP has consistently pointed out that it is unclear how South Africa will reduce carbon emissions by 34 per cent by 2020 and by 43 per cent by 2025, as promised at the Copenhagen talks. In their submission on the National Climate Change Response Green Paper 2010, it is stressed that the Green Paper promotes two dangerous strategies – carbon trading and nuclear energy – and endorses an 'emission trajectory which allows for the belief that for the most part development and growth can continue as close to a business as usual scenario as possible'.[21] However, the critique fails to show how this paper fits into a green capitalist framework.

In his 2009 annual report on the SECCP, project coordinator at the time Tristen Taylor emphasised the importance of protests, connecting with grassroots communities and media coverage, but stressed that '[t]he SECCP sees itself as building a movement that works to pressure and change formal policy processes. This is the key, we believe, to changing South Africa's dirty development to green development.'[22] However, he describes the SECCP relationship with government as 'somewhat of a ferocious and non-compromising nature'.[23]

According to Taylor, in 2008 'an official from the government department of environmental affairs stood up before a group of environmentalists and NGO representatives and said: "Where is the environmental movement? Where are the placards? We can't change things without the pressure of citizens."' Taylor commented: 'The official's comments were spot on: South Africa's environmental organizations have not successfully stimulated popular resistance to ecological destruction, which is a necessary condition for change.'[24]

Change is necessary because the post-apartheid state is characterised by both policy incoherence and discrepancies between policy and practice. The constitutional mandate to ensure a clean and safe environment for all, linked to the commitment made at COP 15 at Copenhagen to reduce carbon emissions, should provide a clear direction. However, the Copenhagen commitments are weak, vague and conditional, and the commitment is undermined by the building of two new coal-fired power stations and 40 new coal mines in South Africa. Government policy favours carbon trading and is rooted in a green capitalism that involves technological innovation in expensive untested schemes like carbon capture and storage underground, as well as nuclear energy and expanding markets, while keeping existing institutions intact.

Three new political initiatives directed at transformation could radicalise Earthlife and mobilise a powerful environmental justice movement. There is some historical continuity here, because all three initiatives include individuals who were activists during the apartheid period.

I. THE EMERGENCE OF THE CLIMATE JUSTICE MOVEMENT

The climate justice movement has been steadily growing since the network Climate Justice Now (CJN) was formed in 2007 from different strands in the women's movement, environmental movements, and democratic popular movements from the Global South like Via Campesina and Jubilee South. It is an alternative to the global coalition of well-funded environmental foundations and NGOs that often lack democratic accountability.

Three themes in the CJN movement speak strongly to the South African reality. Firstly, there is a focus on 'climate justice', which is stressed in both global and local terms. Globally justice is a strong theme among activists who claim that a wide range of activities contribute to the ecological debt owed to countries in the Global South: the extraction of natural resource, unequal terms of trade, the degradation of land and soil in the production of export crops, the loss of biodiversity, and so on. Locally, it is demonstrated that it is the poor and powerless who are most negatively affected by pollution and resource depletion and will bear the brunt of climate change. CJN's focus includes confronting the root causes of climate change and amplifying the voices of those most directly affected, who are the least responsible for the carbon emissions that cause climate change.

Secondly, it is recognised that it is the expansionist logic of the capitalist system of production and consumption, driven by large multinational corporations, financial markets and captive governments, that is the cause of climate change, along with loss of biodiversity, water scarcity, the acidification of the oceans, and so on. CJN is marked by an anti-capitalist discourse. It explicitly rejects 'the false solutions based on market mechanisms such as the Clean Development Mechanism (CDM) and REDD [the UN Collaborative Programme on Reducing Emissions from Deforestation and Forest Degradation in Developing Countries]'.[25] In the CJN South Africa (CJNSA) statement and submission on the Integrated Resource Plan (IRP) 2010 it is stated: 'The IRP displays the continued power of the corporations at the centre of the minerals-energy complex to shape development to their own interests. For the people of South Africa and the environment, it is catastrophic.'[26]

In a different draft CJN position paper on a variety of issues, it is stated:

> Capitalism is not compatible with addressing climate change. It requires never ending economic growth for its survival. Growth has brought unprecedented wealth to the owners of capital, prosperity to the world's middle classes and untold misery to the majority of people particularly in the global South. Capitalism plunders the resources of the earth and of the people. It is the driving force behind ecological disruption on all scales from the local to the global. Climate change is the ultimate symptom of this renting of the earth system.[27]

Thirdly, CJN is driven by the recognition that global elites have to date failed to solve the environmental crisis through the United Nations Framework Convention on Climate Change (UNFCCC) process. There is no global binding agreement on limiting carbon emissions and one is unlikely to emerge from COP 17 in Durban.[28] This failure underlies the potential of this moment for global civil society to build transnational solidarity.

Earthlife Africa Johannesburg has become central to this climate justice movement. In 2006 it was the secretariat of the South African Climate Action Network and is now the CJN lead organisation in South Africa. Earthlife was crucial to a meeting in January 2011 when more than 80 environmental, social trade union, faith-based, community and climate justice organisations representing a broad spectrum of civil society attended a COP 17 planning conference in Durban. A coordinating committee of 17 mandated people representing a wide range of civil society organisations was formed and tasked with coordinating civil society initiatives round COP 17. The meeting included many different shades of green and has been described as 'fraught', with a major source of division being the issue of market-based solutions to climate change, particularly carbon trading. One participant described the fault line as 'deep political differences between liberal and socialist approaches'. There were elements of opportunism, with some organisations clearly stating that they 'want to get organisational gains from the COP 17 process'.[29]

One Earthlife official stated, 'COP 17 is not the end goal – it is a means of creating a stronger environmental movement'. Other groupings such as the World Wildlife Fund and Greenpeace disagree with some CJN principles, such as the opposition to carbon trading, and for this reason do not belong to the CFJN network. One participant reported that 'my main concern is how to keep politics out of it'.

Clearly, the variety of political positions among participants could subvert any unified action. One participant insisted that '[c]limate justice could unify a broad church, but this involves the danger of settling for the liberal agenda as the lowest common denominator'.

There are deep differences between many climate justice activists. Some locate climate change in the liberal discourse of human rights. Others understand the issue as a stark choice between 'green capitalism' and 'eco-socialism'. One participant mentioned the problems of 'anti-state and anti-ANC rhetoric which could alienate some'. Taylor believes that there is potential for unity if there is tolerance for political differences, and the campaign focuses around one simple idea: stop climate change now. Then the different organisations can take the idea in different political directions, he says.[30]

Several activists were informed by the politically splintered protests that marked Copenhagen in 2009 and Cancun in 2010. One participant is eager to 'avoid a Cancun-type situation where civil society was very split and the end result was that there were four separate spaces, none of which were well utilised'.

Kumi Naidoo, the director of Greenpeace, has emphasised the importance of unity:

> As the host of COP 17 the government of South Africa has a great opportunity to represent Africa who will be hardest hit by climate change. We must come together and speak with one voice … Having different marches at the World Summit on Sustainable Development meant we let South Africa down.[31]

Several analysts have stressed the unifying potential of the climate justice movement. According to Patrick Bond, 'the CJ organisations and networks offer great potential to fuse issue-specific progressive environmental and social activists, many of which have strong roots in oppressed communities'.[32]

Overall, the main fault line runs along ideological lines between those organisations with a reform agenda and those with a transformative one. All are working to mobilise civil society. All emphasise the need for change towards the goal of a low carbon economy, but differ on the scale of the change involved and the means of reaching it. Those organisations with a reform agenda accept market-based solutions such as carbon trading, place a heavy reliance on technologies such as carbon capture and storage, and view the UNFCCC process and the South African government's negotiating position in positive terms. These strategies are the object of intense criticism by those organisations with a transformative agenda, who stress that market-based solutions such as carbon trading are one way in which capital is attempting to appropriate the crisis and make climate change a site of capital accumulation. They are sceptical of expensive and untested technologies such as carbon capture and storage, and there is strong emphasis on the expansionist logic of the capitalist system as the cause of the climate crisis.

Provisional mapping of the climate change terrain would indicate a loose grouping around a few key nodes such as Earthlife Africa Johannesburg, which is now the lead organisation in South Africa of the international CJN alliance and which supports a transformative agenda. According to one informant, Earthlife Africa Johannesburg 'is hegemonic within the civil society initiative on the issue'.[33] Another key node in an alternative approach centres on the World Wildlife Fund, an international NGO that supports both carbon trading and the South African government's negotiating position in a reform agenda. The thrust of its policy is toward reforming or greening the present form of 'suicide capitalism'.

These lines of contention could limit unified action. However, it seems that the explicitly anti-capitalist discourse of the climate justice movement is percolating into the wider South African context. This could be strengthened by two new left political developments: the emergence of the Democratic Left Front and the labour movement's engagement with the issue.

II. NEW LEFT INITIATIVES

A concern for environmental issues is strong in the declaration that came out of the conference of the Democratic Left Front (DLF) in January 2011. This gathering included about 250 delegates, ranging from trade unionists from all the labour federations to a wide range of social movement activists. The conference resolved to 'join the growing movements for environmental and climate justice. COP 17 is in our sights.' The declaration states: 'We believe that our anti-capitalism must be green as well as red. Global capitalism threatens our world with disaster. If it is left to plunder the natural resources of our planet and pollute the atmosphere, the oceans and the soil life itself will be under grave threat.'[34]

Many DLF activists are committed to a new form of ethical, democratic and ecological socialism. This is not encoded in any blueprint, but is to be built 'from the bottom up'.[35] Monthly workshops on climate change demonstrate that the ecological crisis is caused by the expansionist logic of the capitalist system. A DLF press statement in February 2011 announced the resolution 'to work closely with the Climate Justice Now network and other organisations towards making COP 17 a focal point to expose the alignment of the South African government to green neo-liberal capitalism.'[36] This ideological thrust could promote the mobilisation of the labour movement.

III. THE MOBILISATION OF LABOUR

The labour movement in South Africa has traditionally neglected environmental issues in favour of jobs, as illustrated by the 'steel valley struggle'.[37] However, this is changing. The climate justice movement challenges the false dichotomy that portrays labour–environmental relations as a trade-off between jobs and the environment. As Kazis and Grossman write: 'Environmental protection not only creates jobs, it also saves jobs ... Forestry, tourism, agriculture and the growing leisure and outdoor recreation industries are all important sources of jobs which depend directly upon clear water, clean air, and wilderness for their continuation and growth.'[38] The job potential of 'green' alternatives such as renewable energies is emphasised.

Through mobilising labour, the climate justice movement could strengthen global unionism and revitalise trade unions both globally and locally. It is increasingly recognised that workers and their organisations are an indispensable force for a just transition to a low-carbon economy. As Jakopovich writes: 'Environmentalists are workers' obvious potential allies in their efforts to advance workplace health and safety, and also to tackle environmental concerns of working-class communities: for workers bear the brunt of environmental degradation and destruction, both in terms of health and quality of life issues.'[39]

The Confederation of South African Trade Unions (COSATU) has endorsed a climate jobs campaign structured around the notion that a 'just transition' to a low-carbon economy using renewable energy instead of coal will depend on workers. It is also stressed that climate jobs must be 'decent jobs' that promote equality and justice. Zwelinzima Vavi, the COSATU general secretary, speaking at the Madrid Dialogue – the 2011gathering of trade union leaders from around the world to discuss a new development paradigm – said: 'We will not support any form of capital accumulation that breeds inequalities – even if those forms of capital accumulation are "green".'[40] COSATU is starting to recognise climate change as a developmental and social issue. It resolved at its 2009 congress to increase its research capacity on climate change and at the Tenth National Congress made it clear that 'climate change is one of the greatest threats to our planet and our people'.[41]

The labour/civil society conference convened by COSATU in October 2010 included over 300 civil society organisations and resulted in a declaration that included some flashes of recognition of the ecological crisis. For example:

> we need to move towards sustainable energy, to migrate the economy from one based on a coal to a low carbon or possibly carbon free economy. The renewable energy sector will grow, needing different skills and different locations. We have to make

sure that we are in change of this process and do not become the objects of it.[42]

There are also references to 'eco-agriculture', a rejection of nuclear power, 'zero-waste' and 'green jobs'.

Within the discourse of climate change, the labour movement is beginning to explicitly challenge green capitalism. For example, a document endorsed by COSATU, the National Council of Trade Unions and the Federation of Unions of South Africa entitled 'Labour's initial response to the National Climate Change Response Green Paper 2010' states:

> We are convinced that any efforts to address the problems of Climate Change that does not fundamentally challenge the system of global capitalist is bound not only to fail, but to generate new, larger and more dangerous threats to human beings and our planet. Climate Change is caused by the global private profit system of capitalism. Tackling Greenhouse gas emissions is not just a technical or technological problem. It requires a fundamental economic and social transformation to substantially change current patterns of production and consumption.[43]

This kind of thinking could take labour beyond the 'real world historical options of green capitalism where economic growth is de-linked from emissions and environmental destruction generally', or 'A suicide capitalism scenario where fossil-fuel corporations and major industry, agriculture, transport and retail interests are successful in maintaining business as usual.'[44]

CONCLUSION

Globally, neoliberal capitalism is driving a key feature of capital's response to the ecological crisis: the commodification of nature. The immediate outcome is the deepening of both social and environmental injustice.

But poor people are not passive victims of this process. Some of the most active forms of new social activism in post-apartheid South Africa are focused on 'brown' or urban environmental issues. Despite almost two decades of democracy, the lack of basic services, particularly sewerage and sanitation for millions of urban South Africans, remains an urgent environmental justice problem that is generating resistance.

Current struggles around access to such services and to water and energy are intensifying, driven by a new kind of 'insurgent citizen'.[45] Much urban, collective action of marginalised groups in informal settlements does not only involve demands on the state to deliver substantial social citizenship in the form of access to adequate water and electricity, but includes insurgent actions such as illegal (and often dangerous) reconnections of the water and electricity supplies of households that have been cut off from the infrastructure, as well as land invasions and housing occupations.

Most of these mobilisations are localised, episodic and discontinuous. But while access to clean water and adequate sources of energy is not framed as an 'environmental issue', it could provide the ideological basis for unified collective action in an environmental justice movement. Justice demands that the needs of the 25 per cent of households who presently lack access to electricity be addressed; sustainability demands that it should take the form of clean, affordable, renewable energy. Framing access to energy issues in terms of environmental justice could capitalise on the current concern with climate change, as well as providing a bridge to the labour movement.

The ideology of environmental justice could provide a linking frame for the localised and scattered collective actions that are protesting against the lack of access to substantive citizenship in the form of water and energy. It could forge new collective identities, alliances, and coalitions, and link them to a global project of transformation that challenges green capitalism.

Earthlife Africa Johannesburg has an organisational significance in this process. It is strengthening people's understanding of environmental issues and their capacity for solidarity actions through linking engagement with the state with social mobilisation and protest. These actions have a transformative power. In its community workshops, research, protest actions, policy engagement and media work, it is strengthening the capacity of South Africans to resist both social and environmental injustice.

Implicit in its focus on the most vulnerable is a link between the discourses of sustainability and justice. It is challenging current notions of development that equate development with economic growth and demonstrating that development is accompanied by growing inequality both within states and globally.

The immediate challenge to the emerging environmental justice movement is threefold: to fold the mass-based episodic struggles around 'service delivery' into a coherent coordinated struggle; to mobilise the labour movement; and, finally, to demonstrate how the ecological crisis – and specifically climate change – contains both a threat and a challenge. The threat is that the crisis will continue to be appropriated by green capitalism. As Satgar writes, the UNFCCC negotiating process is 'increasingly being led by an agenda that favours utilizing the ecological crisis as a new outlet and fix for capital accumulation'.[46] But the crisis also presents the opportunity to demonstrate that the notion of a 'transition to a low carbon economy' contains the embryo of an alternative social order.

It is clear that the post-apartheid state is driven by vested interests. It perpetuates market-led economic growth models that benefit large corporations at the expense of job creation and the social needs of the majority. It will not drive ecological transformation and solve the problem of climate change that threatens us all. Neither will capitalism. As David Harvey writes, 'an ethical, non-exploitative and socially just capitalism that rebounds to the benefit of all is impossible. It contradicts the very nature of what capital is about.'[47] But it is possible that we are about to see a widespread and extensive recognition that the climate crisis is caused by the expansionist logic of the capitalist system and that this system has to be changed if human survival is to be secured.

An environmental justice movement could be emerging that is larger, deeper and more powerful than anything before. It could drive the 'eco-socialist political challenge (which) is to connect particular local struggles, generalize them and link them to a universal project of socio-ecological transformation, against the universalization of neoliberalism and capitalist markets as the regulators of nature and society'.[48]

NOTES

1. The research on which this chapter is based involved a review of relevant primary and secondary sources, interviews and informal conversations with key environmental activists, and observations from my participation in environmental struggles in South Africa for 40 years.
2. J. B. Foster, *The Ecological Revolution*, New York: Monthly Review Press, 2009, p. 1.
3. Ibid.; J. Kovel, *The Enemy of Nature*, London: Zed Books, 2002; L. Panitch and C. Leys (eds), *Coming to Terms with Nature: Socialist Register 2007*, London: Merlin Press, 2006.
4. V. Wallis, 'Beyond green capitalism', *Monthly Review* (February 2010), p. 32.
5. See, for example, R. D. Benford and D. A. Snow, 'Framing processes and social movements: an overview and assessment', *Annual Review of Sociology*, Vol. 26 (2000); D. A. Snow and R. D. Benford, 'Ideology, frame resonance,

and participant mobilization', *International Social Movement Research*, Vol. 1 (1988); D. A. Snow and R. D. Benford, 'Clarifying the relationship between framing and ideology', *Mobilization: An International Journal*, Vol. 5 (2000); D. A. Snow and R. D. Benford, 'Master frames and cycles of protest', in C. Mueller and A. Morris (eds), *Frontiers of Social Movement Theory*, New Haven: Yale University Press, 1992; D. A. Snow, 'Framing processes, ideology, and discursive fields', in D. A. Snow, S. Soule and H. Kriesi (eds), *The Blackwell Companion to Social Movements*, Oxford: Blackwell, 2004.

6. Snow, 'Framing processes', p. 384.
7. Snow and Benford, 'Ideology', p. 198.
8. J. Cock, 'Introduction', in J. Cock and E. Koch, *Going Green: People, Politics and the Environment in South Africa*, Cape Town: Oxford University Press, 1991.
9. Benford and Snow, 'Framing processes', p. 614.
10. Ibid.
11. W. A. Gamson, *Talking Politics*, New York: Cambridge University Press, 1992, p. 111.
12. Earthlife Africa, 'Mission statement', 1996, p. 1.
13. G. Albo, 'The limits of eco-socialism: Scale, strategy and socialism', in Panitch and Leys, *Coming to Terms with Nature*, p. 359.
14. P. Bond, 'South Africa prepares for "conference of polluters"', unpublished paper, 2011, p. 127.
15. F. Adam, T. Taylor and B. Peek, 'South Africa's US $3.75 billion world bank loan – developing poverty', *Amandla*, No. 14 (May/June 2010), p. 12.
16. Interview with Tristen Taylor, policy officer, Earthlife Africa Johannesburg, 7 October 2010.
17. F. Adam, *Sasol Profits from Poison*, Johannesburg: Earthlife Africa Johannesburg, 2010. Sasol's main activity is the conversion of coal to oil; in the process it produces huge amounts of greenhouse gases.
18. The 16th Conference of the Parties to the Kyoto Protocol.
19. R. Worthington and L. Tyrer, *50% by 2030: Renewable Energy in a Just Transition to Sustainable Energy Supply*, Johannesburg: World Wildlife Fund, 2010.
20. F. Miraftab, 'Feminist praxis, citizenship and informal politics', *International Feminist Journal of Politics*, Vol. 8, No. 2 (2006), p. 200.
21. Earthlife/SECCP, 'Labour's initial response to the National Climate Change Response Green Paper', unpublished document, p. 4.
22. T. Taylor, *Annual Report to the Johannesburg Branch of Earthlife Africa*, unpublished, 2 October 2010, p. 3.
23. Ibid.
24. Ibid.
25. CJN, 'Statement', 14 June 2011, p. 2.
26. CJNSA, 'Statement', July 2010.
27. CJN, unpublished position paper, August 2010, p. 5.
28. This chapter was written just before the Durban meeting.
29. The following points made by participants arose in informal discussions. Participants' identities are not disclosed for reasons of confidentiality.
30. Interview with Tristen Taylor, policy officer, Earthlife Africa Johannesburg, 12 March 2011.
31. Interview with Kumi Naidoo, director of Greenpeace, Uppsala, 13 April 2011.

32. Bond, 'South Africa prepares', p. 3.
33. Interview with Louise Oliver, World Wildlife Fund official, Johannesburg, 11 March 2011.
34. DLF, 'Declaration of the Democratic Left Front adopted by the First National Conference, Johannesburg, 20–23 January 2011', Johannesburg, 2011.
35. Ibid.
36. DLF, press statement, 20 February 2011.
37. Jacklyn Cock, 'Sustainable development or environmental justice? Questions for the South African labour movement from the Steel Valley struggle', *Labour, Capital and Society*, Vol. 40, No. 1 (2007), p. 42.
38. R. Kazis and R. Grossman, *Fear at Work: Job Blackmail, Labour and the Environment*, New York: Pilgrim Press, 1982, p. 35.
39. D. Jakopovich, 'Uniting to win: Labour–environmental alliances', *Capitalism, Nature, Socialism*, Vol. 20, No. 2 (June 2009), p. 75.
40. Z. Vavi, 'The Madrid Dialogue took off', *Sustainlabour*, 2011, p. 2, www.sustainlabour.org (accessed 18 April 2011).
41. Interview with Fundi Nzimande, Naledi researcher, Johannesburg, 3 September 2010.
42. 'Declaration of the Civil Society Conference, Boksburg, 27–28 October 2010.'
43. Earthlife/SECCP, 'Labour's initial response', p. 10.
44. S. Sweeney, 'How unions can help secure a binding global climate agreement in 2011', 4 March 2011, p. 9, www.sustainlabor.
45. J. Holston, *Insurgent Citizenship: Disjunctions of Democracy and Modernity in Brazil*, Princeton: Princeton University Press, 2008.
46. V. Satgar, 'The World Social Forum, and the battle for COP 17', *Pambazuka News*, 18 February 2011.
47. D. Harvey, *The Enigma of Capital*, New York: Oxford University Press, 2010, p. 239.
48. Albo, 'The limits of eco-socialism', p. 359.

11
'Tacticians in the Struggle for Change'? Exploring the Dynamics between Legal Organisations and Social Movements Engaged in Rights-Based Struggles in South Africa

Kate Tissington

INTRODUCTION

How do social movements in South Africa engage with legal mobilisation and rights-based approaches to social change?[1] And what kinds of relationships are formed between social movements and legal non-governmental organisations (NGOs) in the process? This chapter explores these questions and advocates for a pragmatic, utilitarian approach to the use of rights discourse and rights-based or legal approaches by poor people's movements and community-based organisation (CBOs) in South Africa. Drawing on the author's experiences as a researcher at the Socio-Economic Rights Institute of South Africa (SERI) – a socio-legal organisation providing an explicit platform for rights-based campaigns by social movements and CBOs – the chapter examines the tensions, trade-offs, understandings, benefits and problems that emerge from social movements engaging in rights-based struggles for social change. There is in fact a broad spectrum of highly nuanced and negotiated relationships between social movements and legal organisations, which form part of the iterative process of contestation linked to the lack of systemic transformation in South Africa. In lieu of viable political solutions to persistent socioeconomic problems, public protest and courts are being used as vehicles for recourse and remedy. Many of the new movements of the poor springing up throughout the country are eager to try out new tactics that include rights-based mobilisation and litigation.

At the same time, critiques of middle-class supporters of social movements and their alleged 'romanticisation' of movements have reverberated throughout the academy and leftist activist circles. These critiques have forced critical questioning of the integrity and usefulness of the relationships between sympathetic academics, lawyers, NGOs and social movements. While important, these critiques have mostly been unhelpful in their de facto dismissal of the gains of social movements and their allegations of the insidious role that middle-class supporters play in overstating these achievements. Undoubtedly, viewing poor people or poor people's movements as 'pure agents' or 'a fixed, virtuous subject' is equally unhelpful.[2] However, given the lack of participatory democracy and governance at the local level, and lack of significant change to the lives of poor people in South Africa, efforts by individuals, communities and social movements to mobilise around issues of concern should be encouraged and supported. This will inevitably entail the formation of complex and messy relationships that require ongoing reflection and interrogation on the part of both social movements, and those 'outside' groups or individuals that provide support in various forms.

When the latter are legal NGOs, there are added dimensions in that these organisations deal with the law and rights as 'currency', the legal system as 'terrain', and lawyers and judges as professional 'players'. The so-called 'turn to law' by CBOs and social movements has been met with both scepticism and hostility, and it appears this perception is due in part to the contentious and often misunderstood nature of the legal currency, terrain and players. For example, development NGOs and practitioners often find litigation too antagonistic towards government, or have had bad experiences with lawyers in the past. Academics often find litigation not radical enough in terms of their broader social change agenda. Leftist activists often tend to be frustrated at the lack of politics infused in cases, and a lack of resonance with broader social and political struggles. Social movements and communities often get frustrated with the process and protracted timelines of cases. A common thread in the criticism is a lack of contextualisation of cases, too high expectations of outcomes of litigation, and a lack of recognition of the dearth of alternatives (to using the law) available to communities. Indeed, much of the scepticism and hostility appears to be based on an unhelpful reliance on the 'myth of rights' as a point of reference and the winning of court cases as a sign of success. Briefly, the 'myth of rights' refers to the direct linking of litigation with social change outcomes. This concept will be discussed in more detail in the following section. It is a rather narrow lens, and this chapter aims to expand it, drawing on conceptual arguments as well as the author's first-hand experiences while working at SERI.

The first part of the chapter examines critiques of rights, law and social movements using these approaches to bring about socioeconomic change in South Africa, using the currency–terrain–players lens described above. The second part draws on experiences and lessons from the relationship between SERI and the Abahlali baseMjondolo Movement, a shack-dwellers' movement based in Durban, highlighting how the movement uses rights-based and legal approaches.

CRITIQUES OF RIGHTS-BASED/LEGAL APPROACHES TO SOCIAL CHANGE

Concurrent with the rise of social movements and popular dissent in South Africa is another project dedicated to transformation and its contestation – the constitutional project. South Africa is routinely praised internationally for having justiciable (legally enforceable) socioeconomic rights contained in its Constitution. These rights are given substance through a plethora of largely progressive socio-economic-related legislation and policy around housing development, the prevention of evictions, access to water and sanitation, labour protection, education, health care, freedom of expression, access to information, and so on. Despite these constitutional entitlements, material change has not occurred for millions of South Africans in the past 17 years. While potentially transformative law and policy exist, implementation has been slow or skewed, and those government departments and institutions mandated with delivery are often not functioning effectively or in a pro-poor manner.

It is no surprise that the liberation document of the African National Congress – the Freedom Charter – still resonates more with many South Africans than the Constitution does. For most, the latter is viewed as a document existing somewhere 'out there' containing abstract rights and providing a blueprint of an ideal society that has not been realised (or at least has not been realised for them).

Do we blame the Constitution or the constitutional project for failed transformation and simply discard the rights contained in it as worthless, or find ways to use them and make rights work for change? Are these positions necessarily mutually exclusive? Is the Constitution an end in itself (which has de facto already been realised by its existence) or a means to an end? Are the law and rights intractable false panaceas or potential tactical tools for poor people and social movements advocating for change? To answer the latter, while definitely no panacea, the 'judicial enforcement of socio-economic rights is one limited means of addressing their needs'.[3] Since 1996, a number of socioeconomic rights cases have reached the Constitutional Court, some rooted in social movement mobilisation and some not. There has been robust analysis of both the gains made as a result of socioeconomic rights litigation and the limits to this kind of engagement for marginalised groups.[4]

Rights and Law: How Much is the Currency Worth?

A central critique of rights (and rights-based approaches to social change) articulated by Critical Legal Studies scholars is that they are entrenched within the liberal framework and are 'formulated, interpreted, and enforced by institutions that are embedded in the political, social, and economic status quo', so can never be transformative in nature.[5] Daria Roithmayr argues that 'rights-based approaches to persistent inequality have proved both ineffective and counterproductive in dismantling persistent inequality'.[6] She posits a radical critique of human rights, which is that the entire rights project is flawed from the ground up in its design because, as it is framed, human rights discourse serves not to resist, but to legitimise neoliberalism.[7] Roithmayr argues that the 'legalisation of human rights dilutes them and robs them of any real power', rendering change all about 'consciousness raising and recognition rather than redistribution and reparation'.[8] She believes rights-based litigation and legal remedies are of limited use in dismantling persistent race and class inequality in South Africa. She argues rather for a 'sustained political conversation about the commons', which emphasises common interests and the key social networks that mediate social life.[9]

There is clearly a fundamental danger in 'uncritical acceptance of a purely legalised, rights-based approach/discourse to solving socio-economic injustice and inequality',[10] which entails a parallel acceptance of the institutional framework of a capitalist society and its democratic order. According to activist Dale McKinley, this would imply that rights-based struggle can only 'mitigate the injustice and inequality inherent in the capitalist relations but never move beyond this towards a revolutionary change in political, economic and social relations'.[11] This reading renders rights discourse and mobilisation not only ineffective in bringing about social change, but actually as a means to reinforce and entrench the status quo.

In his seminal book *The Politics of Rights*, Stuart Scheingold describes what he terms the 'myth of rights': the assumption that 'litigation can evoke a declaration of rights from courts; that it can be used to assure the realization of these rights; and finally, that realization is tantamount to meaningful change'.[12] The 'myth of rights' is thus 'premised on a direct linking of litigation, rights, and remedies with social change'.[13] Scheingold criticises this approach as 'overrating the progressive capacities of the law', and calls for a political approach to analysing the usefulness of litigation that attaches primary importance to the 'redistribution of power'.[14] He calls this approach the 'politics of rights', which scholars such as Michael McCann have elaborated on. Stuart Wilson argues that one of the aims of a politics of rights could be to develop what McCann has called a 'jurisprudence from below' in which constitutional rights are 'defined and internalised through an assessment of their meaning and import to a particular social struggle, by people directly engaged in that struggle'.[15] This is a very useful concept. Indeed, the translation of socioeconomic rights should not be a one-way, top-down process and there is an important role for litigants, activists and social movements in ensuring that 'conceptually empty socio-economic rights are awarded content "from the bottom up," so as to resonate with the experiences and needs of those for whom their effective vindication matters most'.[16]

In their recent article, Jackie Dugard and Malcolm Langford interrogate assumptions around public interest litigation and perceptions of the way in which legal practitioners and social movements should act strategically in order to advance social change in South Africa. They dismiss any kind of prescriptive, pseudo-scientific approach to analysing public-interest litigation impacts, calling for an 'expansive model … which explicitly draws the socio-political dimension into the frame'.[17] They argue that absent from the current analytical frame is an 'examination of the role of law as a politicising agent in the dialectical relationship between structures of power (whether social, political or socio-economic) and the agency of social actors'.[18] According to them, what is required is an 'explicit recognition of the less material role of law as a politicising – or enabling (destabilising) – agent' and a rethink of the win-or-lose binary in terms of which public-interest litigation is often viewed.[19] McCann and others have shown that rights-based campaigns can contribute to movement building by both generating internal solidarity and enlisting external support.[20]

What is needed, according to McKinley, is activism that 'combines a tactical legal approach with strategically defined grassroots struggles for more systemic change'.[21] Law can be a 'useful tool/medium to expose, defend and push back misuse, oppression and reaction'.[22] This tactical use of law in response to, and emanating from, practical struggle is promising. However, the law is undoubtedly a 'double-edged sword', and in South Africa, activists are mostly drawn in on highly unfavourable terms, forced to engage in defensive litigation around evictions, services cut-offs, arrests, and so on. While social movements and community leaders may be keen to engage in more proactive campaigns around issues of land, housing and basic services, community members daily face a never-ending barrage of evictions, demolitions and cut-offs. Time and energy often has to be deployed to the immediate needs of communities, particularly as communities provide legitimacy and support to community and social movement leaders.

The failure of social movements to make bigger gains in South Africa has been lamented by scholars such as Ashwin Desai and Luke Sinwell. Desai argues that while fights against evictions from shacks in court are important defensive battles, 'one can see how they do not advance a broader anti-capitalist struggle'.[23] Sinwell echoes this sentiment, stating that 'while defensive battles are clearly welcome and necessary, the demand to think, speak and act on behalf of oneself does not necessarily challenge the neoliberal status quo'.[24] These criticisms highlight a tendency of the frustrated left to criticise community-based movements because they are either unstrategic, not vanguardist enough or, at worse, counter-revolutionary. While current community struggles may not manifest in overtly revolutionary ways, as activists and academics would have them, they often have broader transformative potential which is not harnessed strategically, or at all.

Another criticism of social movements using the law is that success depends on establishing a personal entitlement, which could rely on distinguishing one's cause from others with similar claims. This is clearly problematic for collective action and solidarity among social movements, and would render rights-based claims by specific groups, communities or individuals divisive in terms of the struggle for systemic change. Linked to this is the criticism that legal or rights-based challenges demobilise the radical, counter-hegemonic articulation and action of social movements and can affect their ability to engage in 'extra-institutional actions' – for example, direct protest action or civil disobedience – or take time and resources away from other forms of mobilisation (because litigation is lengthy, expensive and intensive).[25] This criticism has been levelled against the Anti-Privatisation Forum in relation to the movement's involvement in the *Mazibuko* v. *Johannesburg Water* water rights case. In the wake of the disappointing Constitutional Court judgment, concerns were raised over the potential demobilisation of the movement by taking on such a lengthy case, the alleged role of lawyers in preventing civil disobedience during the course of litigation, and the fact that the case was lost in the Constitutional Court (although it was won in the lower courts).[26] No doubt, 'litigative tactics can impose a heavy burden on the process of political organisation'.[27] However, in the *Mazibuko* case it has been shown that the 'turn to law' was taken as a last resort when political tactics and civil disobedience had been quashed, and it did provide a new basis for ongoing mobilisation. According to McKinley, the *Mazibuko* case 'provided something to organise around; hope and recognition after having been fucked over by the police – it became the centre of mobilisation and reinvigorated the struggle, as well as catalysing political discussions and redefining strategy'.[28] It is this kind of politically conscious, strategic and pragmatic approach that should be infused into current debates and practice.

The Legal System: Navigating Harsh Terrain

For most people, the legal system is harsh and unforgiving terrain. It is laden with confusing jargon, procedures, time lines, etiquette, institutions, penalties, fees and gatekeepers. For an ordinary person (or, in legal jargon, a 'lay person'), this elitist system can be extremely alienating and can militate against access to justice for poor people and social movement activists who are drawn into the system on unfavourable terms, for example, resisting unlawful evictions and arrests after protests. Lack of access to justice for the poor remains a fundamental barrier to transforming the paper rights contained in the Constitution into the socioeconomic liberation for all people living in South Africa. As with education and health care in the country, where the rich can 'opt out' and pay for private hospitals and schools, the legal system is more easily navigable for those with money to buy the time of good lawyers. However, the ability of the majority of people to access affordable, high-quality legal representation, particularly in the specialised field of socioeconomic rights, is constrained by the limited number of already overburdened legal NGOs working in this field.[29]

While state legal representation – via Legal Aid South Africa – exists for those earning below a certain income threshold, it is mostly available for criminal cases and provides very little assistance for civil cases. Legal Aid lawyers are often overloaded, overstretched and inexperienced. Further, while there may be legal NGOs and pro bono departments within legal firms in cities, very little legal assistance is available for those living in rural areas and small towns. When local lawyers are available, they charge high fees for their services and are often not equipped to deal with the complexities of socioeconomic rights cases and the nuances of working with activists and marginalised communities. Even when pro bono lawyers are available, the cost of litigation and lengthy appeal processes affects their ability to direct their full attention to pro bono cases and to stay the course.

McKinley argues that 'we can have no illusions in the law/courts precisely because the institutional framework is not class-neutral and is designed (at the macro level) to benefit and protect the interests of the dominant classes'.[30] Indeed, litigation is often an extremely lengthy, resource-intensive and expensive process. Even legal organisations set up for the purpose of supporting social movements (generally internationally donor funded) have to deal with high demand for their services, and therefore pick cases that will have a broader public impact and set good precedent. The system is by no means fair or equitable, but it is nonetheless extremely powerful and can be useful if navigated strategically and pragmatically.

Judges and Lawyers: What if the Players aren't Game?

Whether drawn into the legal system on unfavourable terms or proactively pursuing litigation as a tactic for social change, social movements inevitably have to deal with lawyers and judges. These legal professionals are in most cases the intermediaries and interlocutors of justice. Engagement between litigants and judges is most often mediated through lawyers, both attorneys (who engage directly with 'clients') and advocates (who argue in court). These relationships are complex and require grooming and practice. There are rules not only for interactions between lawyers and their clients (individuals, communities and social movements), but also between attorneys and advocates, and between advocates and judges. This section will examine the role of judges and lawyers in more detail.

Judges

Two common arguments relating to the role of the judiciary in adjudicating socioeconomic rights revolve around legitimacy (what standing do judges have to make the kind of decisions they do?) and competence (are they well placed and capable of making these kind of decisions?). This section will focus on the latter argument around judicial competence.

In South Africa, the judiciary is expected to 'promote the values that underlie an open and democratic society based on human dignity, equality and freedom' and is required always to 'promote the spirit, purport and objects of the Bills of Rights'.[31] However, as an institution, the judiciary has been slow to adjust to its role as adjudicator of socioeconomic rights claims, particularly those brought by poor people. According to Dugard, 'the post-apartheid judiciary has collectively failed to act as an institutional voice for the poor ... the courts in South Africa have not adequately realised their potential to promote socio-economic transformation in the interests of materially-disadvantaged South Africans'.[32] Socioeconomic rights claims often have budgetary implications for the state; are perceived to interfere too heavily with the separation of powers between the judiciary, legislature and executive; and require some kind of analysis of the content of rights, as well as competing interests and potential trade-offs. The reality is that courts mostly rely on the state for the implementation of socio-economic-related decisions, are acutely aware of this dependence, and have arguably been timid and sometimes vague in the definition they have given to these rights.[33] The Constitutional Court, the highest court in South Africa, has often not grasped opportunities to pronounce on potentially transformative issues unless absolutely required, adopting an adjudication stance referred to as 'judicious avoidance'.[34]

Another barrier relates to the inevitable ideological viewpoints of individual judges and the impact of these on the way they engage with radical social movements as rights claimants appearing before them. There is a dearth of progressive and bold judges in South Africa, and the judiciary is characterised by lingering 'counter-transformative tendencies' that oppose social change.[35] This is particularly evident at magistrate and high court level, where magistrates and judges are often still influenced by legal formalism rather than embracing a constructive interpretation of the law in light of the values in the Constitution.

In terms of socioeconomic rights, the Constitutional Court has implicitly stated that it will not rule on 'minimum core' obligations of the state and applies the 'reasonableness test' to policy and legislation.[36] As Wilson and Dugard state, 'the Court has demonstrated itself immune to many ingenious attempts to get it to set normative standards towards which the state must strive in the progressive realisation of socio-economic rights'.[37] While the lower courts appear more willing to engage with and interpret socioeconomic rights appeals and craft workable remedies, the Constitutional Court is itself prone to romanticising 'the poor' and abdicating its responsibility when it comes to specific challenges to the state by poor people.

Indeed, the court appears to have fallen prey to the state's discourse of the 'deserving poor' versus the 'undeserving poor', and to struggle with equity issues that arise when poor claimants come before it and it is 'forced' to weigh these claims against the thousands of others not before it. David Bilchitz has argued that the Constitutional Court seems to have endorsed an 'equality of the graveyard' approach to socioeconomic rights.[38] This approach is neither necessary nor desirable, as the problem lies less with limited state resources or competing interests of poor communities and groups, and more with a discomfort on the part of judges to engage with issues of poverty, inequality and class.[39]

Regardless, socioeconomic rights litigation can still achieve some progressive impact, and while wary of giving content to rights, the Constitutional Court has shown its willingness to do this when dealing with a negative infringement or 'when requiring the state to take steps provided for in, or consistent with, its own policy, or when expanding on the content given to the right by applicable legislation'.[40] Wilson and Dugard argue that it may also be possible to 'use the content the Court has given to socio-economic rights in cases of negative infringement to give definition to future claims seeking to impose positive obligations on the state'.[41] Lower courts appear to be more predisposed to the latter, perhaps because they are able to take more risks with progressive rulings and remedies, given the safeguard of the appeal process. This said, many judges will not do this for fear of their rulings being overturned on appeal.

Lawyers

Lawyers and litigators are central to communicating the limits and potential of litigation, as well as assisting social movements to navigate the legal terrain and position rights claims before the court. According to Shah and Elsesser, conflicts between activists, organisers and social movements, on the one hand, and traditional legal services lawyers, on the other, are often attributed to differing political orientation, understandings of class, social change, and analyses of systemic inequality and oppression.[42] Rather than viewing lawyers as 'saviours or gatekeepers', they should be regarded as 'tacticians in the struggle for change' and, it is to be hoped, regard *themselves* in the same way. The attitudes and approaches of lawyers are critical. Shah and Elsesser raise a number of salient points about the role of lawyers in community and social movement struggles, including the need for:

- accountability, self-scrutiny and honest reflection around power dynamics between lawyers and communities;
- ensuring that rights are not mobilised in a purely individual-istic way, but focus on positive collective impact;
- ensuring the law is not viewed as a solution, but rather as a tactical tool;
- stressing that winning is not everything (and that often losing can be beneficial as part of a larger strategy); and
- recognising that lawyers (and legal cases) often take up a lot of space, and power can gravitate to lawyers to be vigilant about 'managing and passing along power'.[43]

As mentioned before, communities and social movements often have unreasonable expectations of what the law and courts can deliver. Often they approach lawyers as a last resort when all other tactics have failed to yield results, or they believe this to be the case. According to McCann and Silverstein, while 'cause lawyers' tend to privilege litigation, they are able to resist its lure and view litigation as 'one arrow in a quiver that includes, for example, leveraging the threat of litigation, lobbying, and under the right circumstances, political mobilization'.[44] Lawyers may be brought in by social movements or communities to assist as 'framers', or may be brought in afterwards to assist with an already developed legal strategy.[45]

In terms of the framing role, social movement or community lawyers need to ensure that any legal frames they offer do not come at the expense of more radical frames. They must adapt legal advice to the context of supporting social movement struggles – by providing information, choices, potential legal repercussions, recourse, and so on, and let movements decide what is best in terms of their broader strategy. Thus, lawyers must understand and respect broader political goals, and be open to using legal strategy to further these agendas, even when this may conflict with what is legally desirable or what is the most 'winnable' case. Sometimes a perceived 'losing case' can be taken to show up a farcical system and can in fact becomes a victory due to other circumstances. When Abahlali baseMjondolo proposed a legal challenge to the KwaZulu-Natal Elimination and Prevention of Re-emergence of Slums Act, there was hesitancy on the part of public-interest lawyers to take up the case. However, the social movement pushed this legal strategy and was eventually successful in the Constitutional Court, with broader impact and consequences (see the following section of this chapter).

Many of the marginalised individuals or poor communities that approach legal organisations are not members of a broader social movement mobilising and lobbying collectively around a social change agenda. In addition to providing direct assistance to individuals and communities, lawyers who are embedded in social justice struggles are able to play a networking role in this regard, linking up people to broader formations and providing broader context and legal education on issues faced on the ground.

Another criticism of lawyers working with poor people is the process of 'legal storytelling' that occurs between attorneys and litigants, attorneys and advocates, advocates and judges, judges and litigants, and so on.[46] Often, clients try to be pure and virtuous when they consult with lawyers, and while this kind of relationship is inevitable, it can often be detrimental to a case. Trust is critical. Lawyers need the truth, however messy, in order for litigation to be possible and, ultimately, successful. In some cases, lawyers need to balance their professional ethics with the reality that social movements (together with their members and leaders) are not perfectly formed, perfectly strategic or perfectly organised. Sometimes, they operate outside the law as a tactic or out of necessity, for example, illegally connecting water or electricity.

The attitude of lawyers is this regard is tantamount to 'success', which should be defined more broadly than simply the winning of a case. In practical terms, legal practitioners working with social movements on community-based struggles have to be prepared to consult outside of office hours and offices – for example, over weekends – with large groups of people in inner-city buildings or informal settlements. They must be able to listen, as well as communicate complex terms and concepts to community leaders and members. They must also be sensitive to the myriad challenges faced by leaders on the ground in the course of organising and mobilising. These challenges may be personal, organisational, economic, political, and so on. These realities are often outside the scope of the lawyer's mandate, but they can adversely affect litigation if not dealt with effectively. A traditional lawyer–client relationship is generally not possible, nor is it desirable; however, certain aspects of this relationship are quite useful in establishing the perimeters of engagement, and ensuring a professional and workable relationship between lawyer and community/CBO/social movement is built and sustained.

Social movement and community leaders who challenge the state and/or break ranks from traditional party political structures are often targeted, sometimes with overt intimidation and physical violence. Community and public-interest lawyers must be prepared to assist leaders and members where possible; however, lawyers and litigation are rendered effectively useless in local-level political tensions or disputes (which are often brought about as a direct result of legal mobilisation, litigation or development in an area). Strong organisation, communication and – sometimes – mediation on the ground are required in these situations. Community lawyers need to develop relationships with other individuals, organisations and networks that can assist in these situations, if they are unable to themselves.

UNPACKING THE PRAXIS:
THE ABAHLALI BASEMJONDOLO MOVEMENT

Abahlali baseMjondolo (AbM), a shack-dwellers' movement based in Durban, is arguably the most organised and powerful movement of poor people in post-apartheid South Africa. The movement began in 2005 after confrontation between shack dwellers and government officials over access to land, and the movement has grown extensively and mobilised successfully over the past six years.[47] AbM is also a founding member of a broader network of movements of the poor called the Poor People's Alliance, together with Abahlali baseMjondolo of the Western Cape, the Western Cape Anti-Eviction Campaign, the Landless People's Movement in Gauteng and the Rural Network of KwaZulu-Natal. The movement and its philosophy has taken shape organically over the years; however, AbM's fundamental tenet is that of a 'living politics' and the struggle for urban inclusion and a 'right to the city' for shack-dwellers in South Africa (which includes access to land, housing and services). The movement challenges a technocratic, top-down approach to development and promotes participatory democracy and in situ informal settlement upgrading.

SERI has formed a relationship with AbM and currently acts as the movement's lawyers, providing legal advice, litigation assistance and paralegal training to AbM community leaders. Legal assistance has been provided in illegal eviction cases, where shack dwellers are forcefully removed from land by the state, often relocated to far-flung transit camps, and in obtaining interdicts against the demolition of shacks. For AbM, it is small victories that motivate the movement, and while the movement may not be shouting down capitalism and the doors of the World Bank or the Minister of Finance, it has brought relief from eviction to many households, and a sense of dignity and hope to some of the most marginalised members of South African society (see Anciano, this volume, for more on this point).

AbM has a strong leadership and is very well organised and well resourced, which means that SERI's role as support partner is less complicated than with some of the other CBOs and communities the organisation works with. In terms of movements of the poor in South Africa, AbM is a welcome anomaly and a model for other movements and organisations. It has its own office with access to a computer, the internet, a library and other resources through its own efforts, as well as via sympathetic supporters and organisations (both local and international). However, the movement has a strict policy regarding its working with NGOs, stating that 'we are willing to work on areas of common concern with organisations that respect our autonomy but the fact is that there are very, very few NGOs that are willing to respect the autonomy of a poor people's movement'.[48] It has cut ties with a number of NGOs and networks in the past.

AbM has been the target of much of the criticism outlined in the previous section around the romanticisation of the movement by middle-class supporters, the use of rights-based discourse and a turn to law, and the enforcing of the status quo through conservative politics and demands on the state. In terms of the latter, Sinwell has argued that AbM's push for informal settlement upgrading 'essentially earns the right for the poor to remain in shacks and upgrade them'.[49] This attitude towards local struggles of communities to obtain security of tenure on well-located urban land – and to gain access to water, sanitation and electricity, as well as recognition as citizens of the city – misses the point. Challenging the state's approach to development, highlighting the inequalities in

South Africa's land and housing redistribution, and mobilising for something different is an important step towards challenging the status quo and the current economic system. It is only when local struggles around, for example, dignity, participation, governance, housing, and so on, are collectively linked to bigger challenges to state policy and programmes (litigation being one potential avenue) and to broader struggles for economic liberation for all, that real transformation in South Africa will take place.

SERI's defensive litigation eviction work with AbM has been the catalyst for SERI's involvement with other informal settlement communities throughout the country. This work includes applied research (documenting community struggles), popular education (holding rights and paralegal training workshops in informal settlements), advocacy (engaging with civil society networks and government officials, using the media, and so on) and litigation (resisting evictions and relocations, demanding access to services on well-located land, pushing for the upgrading of settlements in situ, and so on). The aim is to maximise collective pressure from below and to improve accountability and responsiveness of the state to citizens (and non-citizens). When engaging with communities and CBOs throughout the country, SERI often refers community leaders to AbM, and the movement acts a source of inspiration and tactics for other formations of the urban poor. The disempowerment and anger that marginalised communities in South Africa currently feel cannot be underestimated, although is evident from the community protests that have mushroomed across the country in the last few years. No social movement has been able to successfully harness this localised energy, and transform local struggles into a legitimate and recognised national campaign for social change. AbM, arguably, comes the closest to achieving this in the Western Cape and KwaZulu-Natal.

For AbM (as for SERI), using the law is regarded as a last resort. According to Sbu Zikode, founding president of AbM:

> the third tactic [after collective mobilisation and use of the media] we need to use is the law. We must use lawyers but we use lawyers last because we don't want it to happen that we lose the fact that *amandla awethu* [power is ours]; that we lose the fact that we can think; and that what made us poor is people like us.[50]

This approach is squarely in line with the pragmatic, political approach to law and rights outlined in the previous section of this chapter. Madlingozi writes that AbM has used 'courts as arenas of mobilisation and politicking', and every time they go to court they hold a mini-rally outside the courthouse.[51] The movement has developed a keen sense for using the media and organising public protests successfully. Madlingozi argues that although AbM

> consciously endeavours to engage rights-based strategies and adopt rights discourse in a way that does not lead to professionalization/NGOisation and depoliticisation, there is no doubt that human rights discourse has played a role in shaping the movement's collective frame, tactics and strategies.[52]

He further states that 'the mobilisation of the rights discourse is an important asset in Abahlali's attempt to build countervailing power'.[53] However, according to Zikode, while AbM tackles human rights issues, they are not human rights-*based* or can be called a human rights organisation. There is wariness around unhelpful labelling and essentialising of the movement. According to Zikode, 'being called rights-based depoliticises, like being called a charity. It avoids reality, which is that problems and solutions are political.'[54] This does not detract from the fact that AbM utilises rights as useful tools in the movement's struggles, and root many of their claims within the Constitution.

In 2008, SERI's director of litigation, Stuart Wilson, assisted AbM to bring the proactive constitutional challenge to the KwaZulu-Natal Slums Act. As mentioned above, this abstract review did not appear at the time to be winnable; however AbM – after having closely scrutinised the Act when it was a Bill and after it was enacted – understood the symbolic and substantive importance of challenging the legislation. The Constitutional Court victory in October 2009 affirmed AbM's interpretation of the Act, and ensured that a potentially repressive and constitutionally inconsistent piece of legislation is inoperable and will not be replicated in other provinces.[55]

AbM has a very strong internal democratic structure, which means that strategic decisions are taken within the movement, and then outside assistance and support is enlisted, if necessary. In-depth discussions around legal strategy are held between the movement's representatives and lawyers, and a mutually agreed course of action is taken back to movement before it is made final. There is a two-way process of engagement between the movement and the lawyers, and much of this interaction involves the lawyers hearing about lived realities, current struggles, and community needs and values. Wilson and Dugard refer to the importance of providing courts with an accurate account of the needs, purposes and values which must be served by socioeconomic rights, and argue that courts can and must develop a 'theory of these needs and purposes, by listening more closely to what poor litigants say in their papers about how the social context of poverty affects their access to socio-economic goods'.[56] Therefore 'legal practitioners, too, must be prepared to put time and effort into understanding these needs and experiences and to give voice to them in pleadings, affidavits and written argument'.[57] In SERI's experience, where debate and discussion around strategy does not occur, or where there is no democratic structure that can give instructions to lawyers or report back effectively to communities regarding a case, litigation is not as successful or impactful. Lawyers, particularly those representing communities or social movements, require organisation on the part of their 'clients'. AbM provides a model that can be replicated in other communities and with other CBOs, and which is very important to the success of litigation in both the narrow material sense, and the broader politicising sense.

However, AbM's attempts to organise outside party political structures to hold government accountable have – perhaps unsurprisingly, given the current context in South Africa – been met with hostility. In 2011, SERI concluded its involvement in a trial where twelve people affiliated to AbM were wrongly arrested and charged with public violence and murder, following armed attacks on AbM leaders and members at the Kennedy Road informal settlement in September 2009. All twelve accused – dubbed the 'Kennedy 12' – were acquitted of all charges in the Durban Regional Court, and it appears that the attacks – widely believed to have been punishment for AbM's criticism of state-sponsored unlawful evictions and challenge to the KwaZulu-Natal Slums Act – were orchestrated by the local branch of the ANC, with police complicity and most likely with provincial ANC endorsement.[58]

CONCLUSION

It is perhaps appropriate to end this chapter with mention of the Kennedy 12 acquittal, as it brings into sharp light the reality of contestation of transformation in South Africa at present. Other chapters in this book have dealt with the nature of the ANC and its attempts to maintain hegemonic power and resist all forms of opposition, including at local level. In South Africa, the Constitution, and law generally, is contested terrain that is constantly in flux and shaped by actors, albeit mostly those with power and access to resources and legal expertise. In this respect, the court is just another 'political venue', and rights are less 'established facts' than potentially useful 'political resources' that can be legitimately deployed in pursuit of a broader socioeconomic agenda.[59] AbM – and, indeed, all social movements, CBOs and communities representing poor people in South Africa – faces an uphill battle in holding government accountable, challenging the status quo and advocating for socioeconomic transformation for all. With many factors militating against them – unabating defensive litigation brought about by anti-poor policies, lack of financial resources, intimidatory local politics, organisational and leadership difficulties (including co-option), disillusioned and angry communities, corrupt officials, and so on – community and social movement leaders first and foremost require access to information and, secondly, legal advice and assistance when required.

Lawyers and those working in legal organisations have an important role to play in this regard, provided they have the required attitude and sensitivity when engaging with communities and social movements. They can offer a useful, and potentially powerful, political currency and platform to social movements and communities who are attempting to challenge state and private power in an effort to bring about social change, often at the local level. While the gains made in litigation may appear relatively small or non-existent, they should be examined with a broader lens. This lens should focus not only on material gains through court, but also on the less material role of rights and law as a politicising agent, and the potential for politicisation of this nature to act as a counterbalance to party and electoral politics that dominate the South African landscape at present. It is this politicisation which is an important step in a broader conversation about participatory democracy, social change and transformation in South Africa.

NOTES

1. Rights-based approaches or strategies for social change can include tactics like rights talk, legal mobilisation, litigation, and so on. Public-interest litigation is a particular type of litigation that is taken on behalf of a class of people, not just an individual or a community.
2. Shannon Walsh, '"Uncomfortable collaborations": Contesting constructions of the "poor" in South Africa', *Review of African Political Economy*, Vol. 35, No. 116 (2008), p. 255.

3. Stuart Wilson and Jackie Dugard, 'Constitutional jurisprudence: The first and second waves', in Malcolm Langford et al. (eds), *Socio-Economic Rights in South Africa: Symbols or Substance?*, Cambridge: Cambridge University Press, 2013.

4. See, for example, Langford et al., *Socio-economic Rights in South Africa*; Jeff Handmaker and Remko Berkhout (eds), *Mobilising Social Justice in South Africa: Perspectives from Researchers and Practitioners*, Pretoria: Pretoria University Law Press, 2010; Stuart Wilson and Jackie Dugard, 'Taking poverty seriously: The South African Constitutional Court and socio-economic rights', *Stellenbosch Law Review*, Vol. 22, Issue 3 (2011).

5. Marius Pieterse, 'Eating socio-economic rights: The usefulness of rights talk in alleviating social hardship revisited', *Human Rights Quarterly*, Vol. 29, No. 3 (2007), p. 797.

6. Daria Roithmayr, 'Transition towns: Using the commons to dismantle racial inequality', paper presented at a University of Southern California workshop, 15 October 2010, p. 2.

7. Daria Roithmayr quoted in Patrick Bond, 'Capitalism, the privatisation of basic social services and the implementation of socio-economic rights: Challenges and advocacy strategies for human rights and social justice actors, learning from the Johannesburg Water defeat', paper presented at the Southern Africa Socio-Economic Rights Camp, International Commission of Jurists, 31 August 2010, p. 1.

8. Ibid., p. 2.

9. Daria Roithmayr, 'Lessons from *Mazibuko*: Persistent inequality and the commons' *Constitutional Court Review*, Vol. 3 (2010), p. 319.

10. Dale McKinley, 'Brief notes for input to Khanya College Winter School workshop on Law and Organising', Johannesburg, 2 August 2010.

11. Ibid.

12. Stuart A. Scheingold, *The Politics of Rights: Lawyers, Public Policy and Political Change*, 2nd edn, Ann Arbor: University of Michigan Press, 2004, p. 5.

13. Ibid., p. 5.

14. Ibid., p. 6.

15. Stuart Wilson, 'Litigating housing rights in Johannesburg's inner city: 2004–2008', *South African Journal on Human Rights*, Vol. 27 (2011), p. 129. See also Michael W. McCann, *Rights at Work: Pay Equity Reform and the Politics of Legal Mobilization*, Chicago and London: University of Chicago Press, 1994.

16. Pieterse, 'Eating socio-economic rights', p. 829.

17. Jackie Dugard and Malcolm Langford, 'Art or science? Synthesising lessons from public interest litigation and the dangers of legal determinism', *South African Journal on Human Rights*, Vol. 27 (2011), p. 41.

18. Ibid., p. 55.

19. Ibid.

20. Scheingold, *The Politics of Rights*, p. xxxi.

21. McKinley, 'Brief notes'.

22. Ibid.

23. Ashwin Desai, 'Rejoinder: The propagandists, the professors & their poors', *Review of Radical Political Economy*, Vol. 35, No. 116 (2008), p. 95.

24. Luke Sinwell, 'Defensive social movement battles need to engage with politics', *South African Labour Bulletin*, Vol. 34, No. 1 (March/April 2010).

25. Tshepo Madlingozi, 'Post-apartheid social movements and the quest for the elusive "New" South Africa', *Journal of Law and Society*, Vol. 34, No. 1 (2007), p. 89.

26. Roithmayr, 'Lessons from *Mazibuko*', p. 327.

27. Scheingold, *The Politics of Rights*, p. 5.

28. Dale McKinley quoted in Jackie Dugard, 'Civic action and legal mobilisation: The Phiri water meters case', in Handmaker and Berkhout, *Mobilising Social Justice in South Africa*, p. 94.

29. A number of legal NGOs conduct socioeconomic rights litigation in South Africa, for example the Legal Resources Centre, Lawyers for Human Rights, SECTION27, Centre for Applied Legal Studies, Women's Legal Centre, Centre for Child Law and SERI. University legal aid clinics also provide free legal advice and litigation assistance, for example Wits Law Clinic, Stellenbosch University Law Clinic, and so on. Some private law firms have established dedicated pro bono departments that take on socioeconomic rights cases and work with poor communities and social movements. Also, ProBono.org – a legal clearing house – facilitates the provision of free legal services for the poor by volunteer private lawyers.

30. McKinley, 'Brief notes'.

31. Jackie Dugard, 'Courts and the poor in South Africa: A critique of systemic judicial failures to advance transformative justice', *South African Journal on Human Rights*, Vol. 24, No. 2 (2009), p. 214.

32. Ibid., p. 215. See also Gerald N. Rosenberg, *The Hollow Hope: Can Courts Bring about Social Change?*, 2nd edn, Chicago and London: University of Chicago Press, 2008.

33. Wilson, 'Litigating housing rights', pp. 128–9.

34. Dugard, 'Courts and the poor', p. 237.

35. Pieterse, 'Eating socio-economic rights', p. 797.

36. Sandra Liebenberg, *Socio-economic Rights: Adjudication under a Transformative Constitution*, Cape Town: Juta, 2010, pp. 163–83.

37. Wilson and Dugard, 'Constitutional jurisprudence'.

38. David Bilchitz, 'Is the Constitutional Court wasting away the rights of the poor? *Nokotyana v Ekurhuleni Metropolitan Municipality*', *South African Law Journal*, Vol. 127, Part 4 (2010), p. 603.

39. Wilson and Dugard, 'Taking poverty seriously', pp. 664–82.

40. Wilson and Dugard, 'Constitutional jurisprudence'.

41. Ibid.

42. Purvi Shah and Chuck Elsesser, 'Community lawyering', *Organizing Upgrade: Left Organizers Respond to the Changing Times* (1 June 2010), www.organizingupgrade.com/index.php/modules-menu/community-organizing/item/71-purvi-amp-chuck-community-lawyering (accessed 4 June 2012).

43. Ibid.

44. Michael McCann and Helena Silverstein quoted in Scheingold, *The Politics of Rights*, p. xxxviii.

45. Lynn Jones, 'The haves come out ahead: How cause lawyers frame the legal system for movements', in Austin Sarat and Stuart A. Scheingold (eds), *Cause Lawyers and Social Movements*, Stanford: Stanford University Press, 2006, p. 192.

46. Christopher P. Gilkerson, 'Poverty law narratives: The critical practice and theory of receiving and translating client stories', *Hastings Law Journal*, Vol. 43 (1991–92).

47. For a comprehensive historical overview of Abahlali baseMjondolo, see Tshepo Madlingozi, 'Post-Apartheid Social Movements and Legal Mobilisation', in Langford et al., *Socio-economic Rights in South Africa*.

48. Abahlali baseMjondolo, 'Once again the name of our movement is being abused by the NGOs', press statement (14 May 2010), www.abahlali.org/comment/reply/6702 (accessed 4 June 2012).

49. Sinwell, 'Defensive social movement battles'.

50. Tshepo Madlingozi, 'Human rights, power and civic action in developing societies: South African organisational study – Abahlali baseMjondolo', background paper for *Rights, Power and Civic Action (RIPOCA)*, Leeds University, 2011, p. 16.

51. Ibid.

52. Ibid., p. 21.

53. Ibid.

54. Interview with Sbu Zikode (25 April 2012), Durban, South Africa.

55. Niren Tolsi, 'Landmark judgment in favour of poor', *Mail & Guardian* (18 October 2009), www.mg.co.za/article/2009-10-18-landmark-judgment-in-favour-of-poor (accessed 4 June 2012).

56. Wilson and Dugard, 'Taking poverty seriously', p. 665.

57. Ibid., pp. 665–6.

58. Niren Tolsi, 'Kennedy Road 12 taste freedom', *Mail & Guardian* (29 July 2011), http://mg.co.za/article/2011-07-29-kennedy-road-12-taste-freedom/ (accessed 4 June 2012).

59. Shah and Elsesser, 'Community lawyering'.

12
How the Law Shapes and Structures Post-Apartheid Social Movements: Case Study of the Khulumani Support Group

Tshepo Madlingozi[1]

INTRODUCTION

One narrative of the past 'decade of dissent' concerns the role of the law in shaping, facilitating and disciplining post-apartheid social movements.[2] On the one hand, social movements have appealed to state law to frame their collective identities and grievances, to attract resources and public sympathy, to shield them from repression, and to extract concessions from the state. On the other hand, 'rights talk' and legal strategies have narrowed down the demands of movements, deradicalised some movements, and transformed 'comrades into victims' in need of the salvation of experts, non-governmental organisations (NGOs), lawyers and judges. The state has also used the law to increase the cost of mobilisation by banning marches, and arresting and prosecuting activists. To put it differently, post-apartheid legal norms, discourses, procedures and institutions have provided significant discursive and institutional political opportunities and threats that have structured the emergence of social movements, their trajectory and outcomes.

The aim of this chapter is to investigate the role of law in social movement activism. Using a case study of the Khulumani Support Group (Khulumani) – a social movement of victims and survivors of atrocities committed during apartheid – the chapter demonstrates the ways in which law functions as a resource *and* constraint for social movements. The author was Khulumani's national advocacy coordinator between 2005 and 2010. During this period, he interviewed Khulumani members and engaged in participant observations and discursive analysis of the movement's documents to carry out this research.

The next section provides a brief overview of the role of law in post-apartheid social movement activism. Its basic aim is to demonstrate that all social movements, both rights-based and 'counter-hegemonic', rely on 'rights talk' and legal tactics to pursue their objectives. This reliance has important consequences for their political orientation and outcomes. The third section provides an in-depth case study of Khulumani in order to make two claims: firstly, that Khulumani's adoption of the human rights discourse, and thus its vision of transformation, was necessitated by the political macro context it operates in and the particular nature of its constituents; and secondly, that even though Khulumani's reliance on the human rights discourse and legal tactics might be important factors in the state's ability to marginalise the movement, the human rights discourse and legal tactics have, however, not contributed to the disempowerment of Khulumani members.

FROM POWER DISCOURSE TO RIGHTS DISCOURSE

The shift from anti-apartheid social movement activism to post-apartheid social movement activism can be usefully understood as a shift from a power discourse to a rights discourse. 'People's power' was the ideological expression of the political practices of the United Democratic Front (UDF) and its affiliates during the mid 1980s.[3] Through street committees, street courts, defense committees, student representative councils and other alternative structures of governance, local and mass-based organisations came to be seen as 'organs of people's power'. For the UDF and its affiliates, 'organs of people's power' were the means by which power *itself* could be transformed, even before formal transfer of power happened via capture of the levers of the state.[4] The significance of 'people's power' thus goes beyond the fact that it enabled people to take control over their lives. In theory and in practice, it introduced, albeit unevenly, a new mode of politics based on accountable, mass-based democratic leadership.[5]

Moreover, the central demands of anti-apartheid activists were not simply about inclusion in institutional structures of decision making or the delivery of basic services; they rejected the whole political and economic system that underlined apartheid. Houston has therefore argued that the politics of UDF-aligned community movements conformed to Antonio Gramsci's notion of counter-hegemonic politics.[6] More significant for our purposes is the fact that the anti-apartheid lexicon of mass-based movements did not contain a discourse of human rights.[7] In this regard, reviewing the politics of the UDF and its affiliates, Seekings concludes that '[p]eople's power was ... unambiguously about power. A discourse of power had conclusively replaced [a] discourse of rights within the UDF'.[8] The embrace of the dominant rights discourse by some post-apartheid social movements has arguably resulted in a truncated transformative vision that is often limited to struggles for formal equality, to the assertion of the right to be invited into state-created institutions of participatory governance, to demands for the right to due process and to claims of the rights to basic services *within the limits of available resources*.[9]

Rights-based movements such as the National Coalition for Gay and Lesbian Equality (NCGLE) and the Treatment Action Campaign (TAC) have used rights discourse and legal strategies to catalyse their struggle, to secure funding, to mobilise their constituents, to build cross-class alliances, to win policy changes and to monitor the implementation of relevant policies.[10] While not dismissing the important policy gains that the NCGLE and TAC have made, some analysts argue that over-reliance on human rights discourse and legal strategies have weakened these two movements.[11] A focus on formal equality and institutional victories is seen as one of the reasons why the NCGLE was not able to grow gay activism beyond its base of white, male, middle-class membership, leading to its temporary collapse and inability to engage in political activities aimed at winning the war against homophobia in the court of public opinion. As far as TAC is concerned, critics charge that the movement's successful deployment of rights strategies has had a negative impact on the movement and its members. These analysts claim that TAC's reliance on human rights discourse and legal strategies has led to TAC's professionalisation/NGO-isation, the (over-)medicalisation of HIV/AIDS, and the disempowerment of those infected and affected by HIV/AIDS.[12]

Movements that claim to pursue a 'counter-hegemonic'/socialist agenda have also started increasingly to rely on 'rights talk' and legal tactics to achieve their objectives. Firstly, although the legal consciousness of movements such as Abahlali baseMjondolo, the Anti-Privatisation Forum and the Western Cape Anti-Eviction Committee is shaped by the supposed lack of faith in 'bourgeoisie discourses' and 'instruments of class rule', and a history of law being used to suppress their struggles,[13] these movements have found themselves having to resort to legal tactics to 'assist' their struggles when extra-institutional, extra-legal tactics have not succeeded.[14] Despite arguing that legal tactics are only engaged with to get a 'breather' from state repression and to 'shift the terrain of the struggle',[15] it would seem that the more movements suffer defeats in the extra-institutional realm, the more they come to value courtroom tactics.

Secondly, some 'counter-hegemonic' movements strategically deploy 'rights talk' to package their message in a language understood by the mainstream media and its middle-class readers. Such exposure could help build relationships with NGOs, lawyers, academics and other elites. Analysts have long recognised the role of 'rights talk' as a 'frame bridge' between poor, marginalised people and the general public and elites.[16] This elite support can bring with it resources that poor people's movements need to help sustain collective action. Elite support has, however, not been completely benign and has led to allegations of vanguardism, co-optation, paternalism and racism.[17] The following remark points to some of the dangers 'counter-hegemonic' movements encounter when they decide to engage legal tactics and seek elite intervention:

> It [litigation] has been a majorly demobilising thing and a factor that brings conservative ethos into the struggle of our people. And it is very loved by the white liberals because again it gives them power. They will prepare the papers, they will come up with lawyers, they will get money from the funders, they will control the media outlets. It takes power away from the people.[18]

As is clear from this overview, a legal mobilisation framework provides a useful approach to understanding the limitations and potential of social movements.[19] The following case study of the Khulumani Support Group demonstrates this.

THE KHULUMANI SUPPORT GROUP

Khulumani is the over-55,000-strong social movement of survivors of the human rights violations that occurred during apartheid. It was formed in 1995 in response to the setting up of the Truth and Reconciliation Commission (TRC). Beyond the TRC, the organisation campaigns for reparations, the combating of impunity, social reconciliation and social justice. In recent years the organisation has articulated its mission in the slogan 'transforming victims into active citizens'. Khulumani utilises a discourse of human rights to frame its collective identity, to mobilise its target constituency, to legitimise its demands and ultimately to contribute to the empowerment of its members to be active citizens. This research investigated the possibility of achieving this mission through the use of human rights discourse and legal tactics.

POLITICAL OPPORTUNITIES AND THREATS LEADING TO THE ESTABLISHMENT OF KHULUMANI

Khulumani is a product of both the institutional opportunity structures and the dominant discursive framework that made up the political context of South Africa's transition to constitutionalism. The political context of the 1990s was shaped to a large extent by the politics of transition and transitional justice discourses. The TRC was a key institution during this transitional process – and the main institutional opportunity structure responsible for the emergence of Khulumani.

The TRC was a product of the elite compromise between the apartheid government and the African National Congress (ANC). Victims of gross human rights abuses and popular organisations were not consulted about the shape that the process of 'dealing with the past' was to take. Victim groups decided to set up a movement of victims and survivors of apartheid in order to support each other's engagement with the TRC. The name Khulumani – isiZulu for 'speak out' – was chosen because victims decided that silence was not an option.

The TRC's Human Rights Violations Committee declared an applicant a 'victim' if in its opinion the applicant suffered *gross* violation of human rights; 16,837 individuals have been declared as such. As the TRC process was coming to an end, Khulumani argued that, as a result of a number of administrative and political flaws in the TRC process, many people who qualified to be identified as victims had been left out of the process. After the closure of the TRC, Khulumani made it its mission to highlight the commission's 'unfinished business'. The organisation has declared that its 'real goals' beyond the TRC are to want 'to end impunity, to ensure reconciliation and to create agency and not dependency'.[20]

FRAMING, RESOURCES, MEMBERSHIP AND TACTICS

A movement's framing process is never an independent, agentic process. Movement frames are shaped by the macropolitical context and counter-framing by the state and other adversaries.[21] With respect to Khulumani, the transitional justice context it grew out of and operates in shapes and limits its framing and vision of what transformation entails. It is therefore necessary to say a few things about 'transitional justice'.

Firstly, 'transitional justice' is a global project aimed at reconstructing Third World states in Western liberal democratic terms.[22] In terms of this project, 'post-conflict' societies are cajoled into adopting a series of institutions and processes associated with liberal democracy, including a supreme constitution that guarantees individual freedoms, the vertical and horizontal separation of state powers, and a free market economy. Secondly, the whole enterprise of transitional justice is 'overdominated by a narrow legalistic lens'.[23] McEvoy shows that one way in which legalism is discernible is a tendency towards an understanding of justice that is both state centric and top down.[24] Victims and local communities are therefore robbed of agency and are merely seen as either victims to be healed or perpetrators to be prosecuted. Thirdly, the dominant model of transitional justice, with its strong focus on healing and the building of a new human rights culture, facilitates a move from activist to victim.[25] In line with this model, those who suffered gross violations of human rights are divided into 'good victims' and 'bad victims'.[26]

'Good victims' are the 'realists' who are content with a moral victory and have accepted the terms of the new dispensation – in the South African case, a united, reconciled Rainbow Nation, for example. 'Bad victims' are the 'radicals' who reject the elite compromise and declare that genuine reconciliation is not possible until economic and political power has been redistributed. The liberal and dominant understanding of post-conflict transformation, the overly legalistic and top-down nature of transitional justice processes, and the quest to produce 'good victims' are all factors that provide a check on Khulumani's collective action frame and thus its conception of what transformation entails.

Another factor that affects Khulumani's framing process is a dominant state and media counter-frame that suggests that matters relating to past human rights violations were adequately dealt with by the TRC. Government officials have also adopted a strategy of vilifying the organisation, accusing it of not understanding what the struggle was about, turning victims into 'mercenaries',[27] reducing activists to 'beggars'[28] and acting like a 'surrogate government' in launching a lawsuit in the United States.[29] Khulumani thus finds itself having to constantly justify its existence and ongoing relevance.

This discourse also affects its ability to attract elite support and funding. As we shall see later, all these factors – a dominant state- and media-constructed counter-frame, resource constraints, and lack of elite support – impact on the movement's ability to come up with a 'radical frame' and to engage in disruptive collective action. Its decision to make human rights discourse its key 'organising principle' should also be understood against this background.

As far as membership is concerned, the majority of Khulumani members are 'currently older than 50 years, not married, without a matric qualification, unemployed and responsible for four or more dependents'.[30]

The Khulumani Apartheid and Reparation Database contains the names of just over 55,000 members. The movement has organised member groups in all provinces, varying between eight and 15 member groups per province. These groups meet weekly or monthly, depending on local conditions. Most of the movement's activities are carried out at the regional and local levels. A 'national contact centre' situated in Johannesburg coordinates the movement's work.

Turning to Khulumani's tactical repertoire, the most commonly used tactics involve non-disruptive protest marches, the submission of memorandums of demands, and the publication of newspaper articles and press statements. These tactics have not succeeded in extracting concessions from the state. In spite of this, members are ambivalent when asked whether Khulumani should be more 'militant'. This following response from a staff member indicates a preference for tactics of persuasion and negotiation over disruptive and violent forms of protest:

> I don't think it will help to go out onto the streets and damage property of government or businesses. What we can do is to organise peaceful marches to the Department of Justice or to Parliament or to the Union Buildings and hand in memorandums to challenge the government to meet with victims and hear their views, needs and requests.[31]

From the movement profile sketched earlier it should be understandable why members prefer these non-confrontational tactics: the lack of adequate external resources – moral and material – and the age, health status and survivalist existence of most of the movement's membership means that it can ill afford costs associated with arrests, bails and court trials. The movement's legal mobilisation is discussed in the next section.

Khulumani has stated that the human rights discourse is the 'organising principle' for its struggle, and that this discourse pervades and informs all its advocacy activities.[32] At a tactical level, it employs, among a range of other tactics outlined above, legal tactics to further its struggle. Because of strictures of space, the next two sub-sections focus only on two instances of litigation – one instituted in a foreign court and another launched in the local High Court.

Litigation against Multinational Companies

The case previously known as *Khulumani & Others* v. *Barclays Bank and Others* was instituted in New York in 2002 against several multinational companies that allegedly aided and abetted the apartheid regime. Khulumani has sought redress from the court by invoking the Alien Tort Claims Act of 1789, the only legislative measure that presently exists internationally that could potentially be used to hold multinational companies accountable for human rights violations committed in breach of international law. Khulumani alleges that defendant companies aided and abetted the apartheid regime in carrying out the crime of apartheid by supplying weapons, vehicles and information technology. Further, it alleges that foreign banks provided the foreign currency needed to facilitate these acts.

This lawsuit is a culmination of a long struggle for reparations by victims of apartheid atrocities. By the time the lawsuit was launched in 2002, victims had waited for four years for the government to announce its reparation policy. Between 1998 and 2002 Khulumani engaged in a range of activities in an attempt to persuade the state to pay reparations to victims. These included discussions with state officials, protest marches to Parliament and to state departments, stimulating public debates in the media and hosting the Reparations Indaba in 2001 in which government representatives participated. When these activities failed to persuade the state, Khulumani agreed to partner with Jubilee South Africa, a social movement that campaigns against odious debt, to bring a lawsuit against multinational companies that supported and benefitted from apartheid. In 2002 Khulumani and Jubilee hired a US-based lawyer, Michael Hausfeld, on a contingency basis to institute this lawsuit.[33]

A few months after the case was launched in New York, President Mbeki finally announced that final reparations in the form of one-off payments would be paid to TRC-identified victims.

Khulumani members and supporters draw a link between the institution of this international lawsuit and the sudden decision to announce a reparation scheme. This lawsuit has gone to the highest court in the United States, but is now back in the district court, where judgment is awaited on yet another appeal launched by the defendant companies.

How has this courtroom battle affected Khulumani's activism? Because of the technical nature of this lawsuit and the need to secure confidentiality in relation to plaintiff information and future strategies, Khulumani members are not directly involved in shaping specific legal strategies. Michael Hausfeld and Khulumani's local lawyer engage in regular teleconferences with Khulumani's national director to plan legal and political strategies and to respond to members' enquiries, while Hausfeld and his associates have also convened meetings with victims in South Africa. Staff members at the national contact centre receive regular briefings on the lawsuit to enable them to respond to telephone enquiries from members and to give updates when visiting branches. Indeed, 'the lawsuit update' is a constant agenda item at branch meetings. During these meetings, members engage in extensive discussions and debates about the lawsuit, ranging from how the movement should respond if any of the defendants propose a settlement to how compensation should be distributed. Khulumani members regularly organise collective activities around the lawsuit, including marches to local police stations, magistrate's court and Parliament to hand in memorandums calling on the state to withdraw the 'Maduna declaration'[34] and night vigils before a hearing. Therefore, although members do not participate directly in shaping this legal strategy, they use this case and the media attention it generates to make public and collective demands for reparation, restitution and social justice.

Activities surrounding the lawsuit help put, albeit fleetingly, the issues of the 'unfinished business' of the TRC on the national agenda. Every time there is a new development, the media cover Khulumani and its activities extensively.[35] The organisation has creatively leveraged this attention to comment not only on the lawsuit and issues related to reparations, but to link these issues to the questions of impunity for apartheid crimes and social injustice.[36] Therefore, despite the fact that the lawsuit has not yet resulted in any direct material benefits to Khulumani members,[37] the organisation leverages the symbolic benefits derived from this high-profile case to (re)activate its members, garner public support and remind the world about the 'unfinished business' of the TRC.[38]

Litigation against Apartheid Criminals

The second high-profile case Khulumani became involved in is a constitutional challenge to the National Prosecuting Authority's (NPA's) amended prosecution guidelines of 2005.[39] These guidelines were adopted in December 2005 with the aim of dealing with the 'prosecution of offences emanating from conflicts of the past and which were committed on or before 11 May 1994'.[40] Those who opposed the envisaged operation of the guidelines argued that they amounted to a re-run of the TRC amnesty process. This was because the criteria introduced by the amended guidelines were strikingly similar to those used by the TRC Amnesty Committee. Khulumani argued that the guidelines posed a threat to the process of reconciliation and served to perpetuate impunity.[41]

During key national events, Khulumani members went on protest marches and handed in memorandums calling for the withdrawal of the guidelines, all of which the state ignored. At Khulumani's 2006 Annual General Meeting, members took a resolution mandating the movement to be part of any litigation against the guidelines. In August 2007 Khulumani joined seven other applicants to challenge the guidelines in court. A public-interest litigation organisation represented the applicants in court. On 12 December 2008 the Pretoria High Court delivered a judgment setting aside the guidelines.

The remainder of this sub-section looks at the impact of this case on Khulumani. On the one hand, this tactic posed a challenge to the movement's internal democracy. Lawyers representing the applicants had emphasised that they were worried that victims may give contradictory opinions to the media and asked the author, then Khulumani's national advocacy coordinator and a non-practising lawyer, to be the sole spokesperson for Khulumani on this case. This request posed a significant challenge to the movement's ethos as a membership-based organisation that has set itself the goal of contributing to members becoming 'active citizens'. Further, the lawyers gave all the applicants a 22-page 'talking points' sheet from which applicant organisations were to structure their comments to the media so that 'we all sing from the same hymn sheet'.[42] This anecdote goes a long way in supporting critical scholars' arguments that the spectre of elitism and demobilisation looms large when social movements decide to engage in litigation. As other studies have shown, lawyers do not just represent movements; they at times become framers for the movement and, due to their social status and resources, assume a de facto leadership role in movement campaigns.[43]

On the other hand, the author observed that this litigation and the issues surrounding it energised the movement in ways not seen before. A few months before this litigation, under the auspices of the amended guidelines, the former Minister of Law and Order, Adriaan Vlok, and five associates were handed suspended sentences for the attempted murder of the former director general in the Presidency, Frank Chikane. This case led to the biggest mobilisation of Khulumani members the author had witnessed since joining the movement. Outside the court, hundreds of Khulumani members from different provinces – a rare phenomenon – came together in a vibrant protest march. For over four hours they sang anti-apartheid songs and demanded justice for apartheid victims. The high-profile nature of the case attracted dozens of local and international media reporters, resulting in the movement being profiled all over the world.[44] Having anticipated a large media presence, Khulumani also used the day to launch its Charter for Redress. This charter was compiled from participatory workshops with Khulumani members and contains a comprehensive list of demands and proposals for ensuring social justice for victims of apartheid. The public square where Khulumani members convened after the court case was turned into a mini political rally.

Khulumani members recall this event with pride and as something to look back on when needing motivation. It is therefore not surprising that when one member was asked what tactics the movement should adopt to persuade the government to respond to its demands, she responded: 'It would be good if Khulumani repeats what it did on 17 August [2007] when we went to [demonstrate outside] court. We showed everyone, including foreign countries, that Khulumani is alive and well ... After that demonstration we have this pride, courage and strength that we can make it!'[45]

In the remainder of this section I look at the impact of human rights discourse and legal tactics on members' political subjectivities. As should be clear from the above, Khulumani has adopted the human rights discourse as its main frame of reference and has engaged in legal tactics when others have failed. These approaches have not won the movement any significant victories at the policy level, however, and the state has ignored its demands and proposals relating to reparations, disappearances, the combating of impunity and sustainable reconciliation. Court victories are yet to translate into material victories at a policy level. As Khulumani's national director laments: 'We believe the problem is that government is sticking to an approach of minimalist engagement with Khulumani ... Government conducts its operations and makes decisions without consulting with organised groups of victims and survivors.'[46]

However, success at a policy level is not the only way to assess the effectiveness of a social movement. This especially applies to 'identity' movement campaigning for the rights of marginalised groups such as sexual minorities, non-nationals and, of course, victims of past human rights abuses. In respect of these movements, assessment must go beyond evaluation that begins and stops at the policy level, but must also look at how far the organisation has been able to afford members a sense of dignity and worth by belonging to a group and being able to express their moral outrage.[47]

Khulumani's mission is to contribute to the transformation of its members' political subjectivity from victimhood to active citizenship. In the past three years, culminating in the recently articulated mission of the organisation, the theme of 'empowerment' has featured prominently in Khulumani's narrative. Most interviewees also spoke of the sense of pride, dignity and empowerment in belonging to the movement, when previously they had felt neglected, marginalised and disempowered. Khulumani staff explain this sense of empowerment by asserting that in the movement, those who make a transition to become active citizens

are the ones who take the lead in organising meetings, counseling, participating in activities that promote human rights, organising memorials and participating in democracy enforcing activities such as information sharing, voting, protesting against the violation of rights, striving for financial independence etc. They empower those behind them who then rise to empower others.[48]

During the course of the past six years the author observed concrete acts of empowerment and active citizenship by members as a result of their involvement with Khulumani, including actively monitoring the performance of local governments through the application of the Promotion of Access to Information Act, taking part in community police forums, providing trauma counselling at local police stations, observing the 2009 national elections as accredited observers, offering support to victims of sexual abuse, conducting door-to-door visits to care for vulnerable children and their caretakers when they are ill, and organising and hosting community memorial events.[49] This demonstration of active citizenship and empowerment is remarkable when bearing in mind that fact that most Khulumani members are victims of horrendous and psychologically disempowering atrocities. Clearly, then, the adoption of a human rights frame by a social movement does not necessarily lead to the disempowerment of movement activists, as feared by critical scholars,[50] some of whom have overdetermined the constitutive power or ideological grip of legal norms, symbols and discourses.[51]

CONCLUSION

We do not need help from the government; we need our rights. It is our right to be recognised.[52]

This chapter has explored the role of law in post-apartheid social movement activism. It has shown that 'rights talk' and legal tactics have become an important part of political claim making and contestation in South Africa. Whether engaged with as a core strategy or just another tactic, post-apartheid movements rely on legal norms, discourses, and tactics to animate and justify their struggles and to seek concessions from the state. An important point made here is that reliance on the law shapes and structures the political orientation and outcomes of movement struggles, because the law is never just an instrument of state power or a resource for movements, but always plays a *constitutive* role in shaping understandings of the world, personal aspirations, political subjectivities and the terms of conflict.[53] The discursive move of translating desires and demands into rights claims might provide a normatively resonant frame leading to public sympathy and elite support, but it might also lower expectations, narrow down the cause of conflict, transmute desires and ultimately domesticate movements. This chapter used the case study of the Khulumani Support Group to evaluate the ways in which the law structures and shapes conceptions of 'resistance' and 'transformation' by post-apartheid social movements.

The chapter speculates that one of the key factors in the ability of the state to marginalise Khulumani is that it relies on the statist discourse of human rights and institutional tactics of law. At the same time, it shows that despite the fact that the movement has not succeeded in making an impact at a policy-making level, at meso and micro levels Khulumani is slowly succeeding in contributing to the empowerment of its members as active citizens. The conclusion from this chapter is that the adoption of a human rights discourse and the deployment of legal tactics do not (over)determine the political subjectivities of the rank and file of social movements. In this case, the ongoing mission to 'transform victims into active citizens' was not hindered by the adoption of these institutional discourses and tactics.

Lastly, two further implications can be gleaned from the case study of Khulumani. The first is that for analysts to make normative judgements as to whether a movement's conception of transformation is 'counter-hegemonic' or not, they need to pay close attention to the macropolitical context and the counter-framing processes movements have to contend with. Second, unless analysts are privy to ongoing political/cultural and interpersonal work taking place within movements, they should be cautious about using terms like 'deradicalised' and 'demobilised'.[54] As Khulumani's director points out, most poor people's movements carry out intra-movement activities of empowerment and transformation, quietly, away from the validation of researchers:

> As Khulumani we have been focusing on the long, hard road of equipping people with knowledge and competencies for not being used as cannon fodder for some organisation's agenda but towards the ability to express themselves coherently in ANC meetings, in public forums etc. This is truly transformative. This is what we do in Khulumani. I experience that there is evidence of greater emancipation when I witness Khulumani finding their own power and being able to present issues about the economy, for example on media discussions, or in interviews, or in public spaces away from the glare of academics.[55]

NOTES

1. The research for this chapter formed part of the author's sociology Master's dissertation carried out under the supervision of Professor Michael Neocosmos at the University of Pretoria. Professor Neocosmos's extensive written comments and conversations are gratefully acknowledged. This research would not have been possible without the encouragement and camaraderie of Dr Marjorie Jobson, Khulumani's national director, and the hundreds of Khulumani members who welcomed the author into their struggle. The author is currently a member of the Khulumani's board of directors.
2. The term 'social movement' here refers to collectives of marginalised actors who develop a collective identity; who put forward change-oriented goals; who possess some degree of organisation; and who engage in sustained, albeit episodic, extra-institutional collective action.

3. J. Seekings, *The UDF: A History of the United Democratic Front in South Africa 1983–1991*, Cape Town: David Philip, 2000; G. Houston, *The National Liberation Struggle in South Africa: A Case of the South African United Democratic Front 1983–1987*, Brookfield: Ashgate, 1999; M. Neocosmos, 'From people's politics to state politics: Aspects of national liberation in South Africa', in A. Olukoshi (ed.), *The Politics of Opposition in Contemporary Africa*, Uppsala: Nordic Africa Institute, 1998; T. Lodge and B. Nasson, *All Here and Now: Black Politics in South Africa in the 1980s*, Cape Town: David Philip, 1991.

4. R. Suttner, 'The UDF period and its meaning for contemporary South Africa', *Journal of Southern African Studies*, Vol. 30, No. 3 (2004).

5. G. Adler and J. Steinberg (eds), *From Comrades to Citizens: The South African Civics Movement*, New York: Macmillan, 2000.

6. Houston, *The National Liberation Struggle*, p. 2. On Gramsci's notion of counter-hegemony, see A. Gramsci, *Selections from the Prison Notebooks of Antonio Gramsci*, New York: International, 1971.

7. I. van Kessel, 'The United Democratic Front's legacy in South Africa: Mission accomplished or vision betrayed?', in S. Ellis and I. van Kessel (eds), *Movers and Shakers: Social Movement in Africa*, Leiden: Brill, 2009; S. Robins, *From Revolution to Rights in South Africa*, Pietermaritzburg: University of KwaZulu-Natal Press, 2008.

8. Seekings, *The UDF*, pp. 173, 292.

9. The South African Constitution of 1996 places an obligation on the state to 'progressively' realise the right of *access* to adequate housing and the right of *access* to health care, food, water, and social security 'within available resources' (sections 26(2) and 27(2), respectively). On the limited nature of post-apartheid social movement demands and politics, see L. Sinwell, 'Is "another world" possible? Re-examining counter-hegemonic forces in post-apartheid South Africa', *Review of African Political Economy*, Vol. 38, No. 127 (2011).

10. A. Currier, 'Decolonising the law: LGBT organising in Namibia and South Africa', in A. Sarat (ed.), *Studies in Law, Politics and Society*, Vol. 54 (2011); TAC, *Fighting for Our Lives: The History of the Treatment Action Campaign 1998–2010*, 2010, www.tac.org.za/community/files/10yearbook/index.html (accessed 1 August 2011); M. Heywood, 'South Africa's Treatment Action Campaign: Combining law and social mobilization to realize the right to health', *Journal of Human Rights Practice*, Vol. 1, No. 1 (2009); J. Cock, 'Engendering lesbian and gay rights in South Africa: The equality clause in the South African Constitution', *Women Studies International Forum*, Vol. 26, No. 1 (2003).

11. T. Dirsuweit, 'The problem of identities: The lesbian, gay, bisexual, transgender and intersex social movement in South Africa', in R. Ballard, A. Habib and I. Valodia (eds), *Voices of Protest: Social Movements in Post-apartheid South Africa*, Scottsville: University of KwaZulu-Natal Press, 2006; Cock, 'Engendering lesbian and gay rights'.

12. M. Neocosmos, *Civil Society, Citizenship and the Politics of the (Im)Possible: Rethinking Militancy in Africa Today*, 2007, http://abahlali.org/files/Neocosmos%202007%20citizenship%20and%20politics.pdf (accessed 1 August 2011); K. Johnson, 'Framing AIDS mobilization and human rights in post-apartheid South Africa', *Perspectives on Politics*, Vol. 4, No. 4 (2006).

13. D. McKinley and A. Veriava, *Arresting Dissent: State Repression and Post-Apartheid Social Movements*, Braamfontein: Centre for the Study of Violence and Reconciliation, 2005.

14. See, for example, A. Cassiem, *The Role of Law and its Ability to Protect Poor Families Facing Evictions in the Western Cape, 2005*, RASSP Research Report, Vol. 1, No. 6, Cape Town: University of the Western Cape, 2005; Coalition Against Water Privatisation and Anti-Privatisation Forum, *Lessons from the War against Prepaid Water Meters: The Struggle against Silent Disconnections Continues*, 2006, http://apf.org.za/IMG/pdf/Final_PPM_Research_Report_-_102006-2.pdf (accessed 1 August 2011); Abahlali baseMjondolo, 'Abahlali baseMjondolo takes the provincial government to court over the notorious Slums Act', press statement, 13 February 2008, http://abahlali.org/node/3335 (accessed 1 August 2011), Landless People's Movement, 'Celebrating our court victory, reflecting on our struggle', press statement, 12 November 2009, http://antieviction.org.za/2009/11/12/lpm-celebrating-our-court-victory-reflecting-on-our-struggle/ (accessed 1 August 2011).

15. Interview with Sibusiso Zikode, Durban, 15 August 2010; telephone interview with Dale McKinley, 13 October 2010.

16. D. NeJaime, 'Convincing elites, controlling elites', *Studies in Law, Politics and Society*, Vol. 54 (2011); S. Tarrow, *Power in Movement: Social Movements, Collective Action and Politics*, Cambridge: Cambridge University Press, 1998; Michael W. McCann, *Rights at Work: Pay Equity Reform and the Politics of Legal Mobilization*, Chicago: University of Chicago Press, 1994.

17. A. Alexander and A. Mngxitama, 'Race and resistance in post-apartheid South Africa', in S. Essof and D. Moshenberg (eds), *Searching for South Africa: The New Calculus of Dignity*, Tshwane: UNISA Press, 2011; H. Böhmke, 'The branding of social movements in South Africa', *Dispositions*, Vol. 1 (1 May 2010).

18. Interview with Andile Mngxitama, 2 November 2008.

19. For an in-depth analysis of the role and impact of legal mobilisation on social movements, see T. Madlingozi, 'Post-Apartheid social movements and legal mobilisation', in M. Langford et al. (eds), *Socio-economic Rights in South Africa: Symbols or Substance?*, Cambridge: Cambridge University Press, 2013. In that chapter, I tease out the context-specific and contingent factors that play a role in effective legal mobilisation – that is, legal mobilisation that does not lead to co-optation, demobilisation and deradicalisation – by comparing legal mobilisation by TAC and Abahlali.

20. Khulumani Support Group, *Khulumani! Speak Out!*, 2006.

21. D. Snow, 'Framing process, ideology and discursive fields', in D. Snow, S. Soule and H. Kriesi (eds), *The Blackwell Companion to Social Movements*, Malden: Blackwell, 2004; R. H. Williams, 'The cultural contexts of collective action: Constraints, opportunities, and the symbolic life of social movements', in Snow et al., *The Blackwell Companion to Social Movements*.

22. P. Lundy and M. McGovern, 'Whose justice? Rethinking transitional justice from the bottom up', *Journal of Law and Society*, Vol. 35, No. 2 (2008); R. Nagy, 'Transitional justice as a global project: Critical reflections', *Third World Quarterly*, Vol. 29, No. 2 (2008).

23. K. McEvoy, 'Beyond legalism: Towards a thicker understanding of transitional justice', *Journal of Law and Society*, Vol. 34, No. 4 (2007), p. 421.

24. Ibid.

25. T. Madlingozi, 'On transitional justice entrepreneurs and the production of victims', *Journal of Human Rights Practice*, Vol. 2, No. 1 (2010); R. Meister, 'Human rights and the politics of victimhood', *Ethics and International Affairs*, Vol. 16, No. 2 (2002).

26. T. Madlingozi, 'Good victims, bad victims: Apartheid beneficiaries, victims and the struggle for social justice', in W. le Roux and K. van Marle (eds), *Law, Memory and Apartheid: Ten Years after AZAPO v President of South Africa*, Pretoria: Pretoria University Law Press, 2007.

27. Former president Thabo Mbeki cited in T. Borer, 'A taxonomy of victims and perpetrators: Human rights and reconciliation in South Africa', *Human Rights Quarterly*, Vol. 25, No. 4 (2003), p. 1094.

28. Former minister of justice Dullah Omar cited in M. Fullard and N. Rousseau, 'An imperfect past: The Truth and Reconciliation Commission in transition', in J. Daniel, A. Habib and R. Southall (eds), *State of the Nation: South Africa 2003–2004*, Cape Town: HSRC Press, 2003, p. 87.

29. Penuell Maduna, 'Declaration to the United States New York District Court', 2003, www.khulumani.net/reparations/corporate/item/128-declaration-by-former-justice-minister-penuell-maduna-and-khulumanis-detailed-response.html (accessed on 18 November 2011).

30. Khulumani, *Speak Out!*

31. Interview with Freedom Ngubude, Braamfontein, 26 November 2007.

32. Khulumani, 'Organisational profile', 2007, p. 3, unpublished document on file with author.

33. Jubilee South Africa, 'Update on apartheid reparations campaign', 2002, p. 4, unpublished document on file with author.

34. The 'Maduna declaration' refers to an amicus brief – 'friend of court' submission – that former Minister of Justice Penuell Maduna submitted to the US court asking for the dismissal of the lawsuit; see Maduna, 'Declaration'.

35. A recent example is the media storm that was created after Khulumani exposed the fact that the late anti-apartheid activist and ANC veteran Kader Asmal had filed a brief supporting the defendant companies; see T. Madlingozi and M. Jobson, 'Asmal brief is befuddled', *Sowetan*, 18 January 2010.

36. An example of this was the movement's month-long Red Card campaign during the FIFA World Cup in June 2010; see the campaign blog, http://redcardcampaign.wordpress.com/ (accessed on 1 August 2011).

37. In February 2012 one of the defendants, General Motors, reached a settlement with plaintiffs. See Khulumani Support Group, 'Bankrupt General Motors agrees to settle in Apartheid lawsuit', press statement 28 February 2012, www.khulumani.net/khulumani/statements/item/620-breaking-news-bankrupt-general-motors-agrees-to-settle-in-apartheid-lawsuit.html (accessed 23 May 2012).

38. For a good analysis of material versus symbolic benefits of litigation, see McCann, *Rights at Work*.

39. NPA, *Prosecutions Policy and Directives Relating to the Prosecutions of Offences Emanating from Conflicts of the Past and which Were Committed on or before 11 May 1994*, Tshwane, 2005.

40. Ibid.

41. M. Jobson and T. Madlingozi, 'Reject NPA prosecutions guidelines', *Mail & Guardian*, 25 August 2007.

42. As stated to the author.

43. See A. Sarat and S. Scheingold (eds), *Cause Lawyers and Social Movements*, Stanford: Stanford University Press, 2006.
44. See, for example, *Guardian*, 18 August 2007; *Voice of America*, 17 August 2007.
45. Interview with Nesta Ndebele, Braamfontein, 22 November 2007.
46. Email from Marjorie Jobson, 20 August 2007.
47. See B. Klandermans, 'The demand and supply of participation: Social-psychological correlates of participation in social movements', in Snow et al., *The Blackwell Companion to Social Movements*, p. 361.
48. M. Jobson and Z. Mthetwa, 'The memorialisation of historical crimes: Constraints, possibilities and new directions: The case of the Sharpeville massacres between 1960 and 1992', 2009, unpublished document on file with author.
49. For more details, see Khulumani, 'Organisational profile'.
50. For examples of this important and necessary caution, see K. van Marle, 'Laughter, refusal, and friendship: Thoughts on a "jurisprudence of generosity"', *Stellenbosch Law Review*, No. 1, Vol. 18 (2007); W. Brown and J. Halley (eds), *Left Legalism/Left Critique*, Durham: Duke University Press, 2002; P. Gabel and D. Kennedy, 'Roll over Beethoven', *Standard Law Review*, Vol. 36, No. 1 (1984).
51. For critique of the tendency to over-determine the power of human rights discourse and legal strategies, see McCann, *Rights at Work*, chap. 8.
52. Interview with Nomarussia Bonase, 10 October 2009.
53. See also B. Fleury-Steiner and L. B. Nielsen, 'Introduction: A constitutive perspective of rights', in B. Fleury-Steiner and L. B. Nielsen (eds), *The New Civil Rights Research: A Constitutive Approach*, Aldershot: Ashgate, 2006.
54. See for example, Neocosmos, 'Civil society', p. 9, which argues that 'the overall effect then [of the TAC's success], has been the "liberalisation" of struggle, the ongoing contribution to a passive citizenry'. However, in *Fighting for Our Lives*, TAC highlights the many ways in which its members continue to be active citizens at the micro level through their involvement in treatment literacy programmes, support groups, and community-based campaigns against xenophobia, abuse of women and so forth.
55. Email from Marjorie Jobson, 6 September 2011.

13
Managing Crisis and Desire in South Africa

Shannon Walsh

INTRODUCTION

It has become difficult to deny that organised left resistance to capitalism in South Africa has significantly declined in the post-apartheid period. The wave of progressive social movements outside of the African National Congress (ANC)-led Alliance that many hung their hopes on through the 1990s and 2000s and that seemed to contest enclosures, the encroachment of capital into everyday life and the commodification of everything have largely dissolved.[1]

This is not to say that the streets of South Africa are quiet. Hardly: people continue to revolt in one way or another across the country. Yet it is difficult to understand these skirmishes as being akin to the articulated challenges to the dominant order that have previously characterised South Africa. As I argue below, there is a biopolitics at work in which the streets on fire signal tactical negotiations for basic services more than the arrival of politically coherent 'movements'. While the organised left continues to trumpet sites such as Balfour, Ficksburg, Thembelihle and other 'hot spots' where people take to the streets in battles with police, the reality is far more complex – both in a reading of the potential of such 'revolutionary subjectivities' and in understanding this moment in the expansion of empire that manages both crisis and desire.[2]

The issue is a fundamental one. If we misunderstand what we are fighting against, how can we fight? If the goal is to positively change the world in which we live and to do so with those we feel an affinity, then at the very least we must understand the changing nature of our adversary. If we neglect the micro scales of power within the post-apartheid moment and the effects that privatised, neoliberal state policies around basic services have had on resistance, we miss both the eruption of new dimensions to the political landscape and the reasons why old political configurations have been hollowed out.

The contradictions are rich, yet they are almost continually homogenised and reduced to an opposition to neoliberalism by the left.[3] Something is missing in our analysis of the way that capitalism fundamentally *organises* and *manages* desire and crisis. You will find an outspoken critic of government policy toyi-toying on the streets for socialism, while simultaneously being a loyal ANC supporter interested in developing a small business, or buying designer shoes, or involved in damaging intolerance or abusive personal relationships.[4] These micro politics point towards a more complex reading of both capital and resistance.

Power exists not only on the economic terrain, but also in the social, personal and cultural spaces of our everyday lives, tearing into the ways in which resistance operates. Further, the glorification of the radical subjectivity of the poor in South Africa has become so beyond reproach that the waves of xenophobic attacks in 2008, for example, that had some roots in community spaces valorised by progressive 'lefties' came as a shock to the cadre living outside of the townships or shack settlements, and have since for the most part been ignored. When taken into account, they are understood as co-option by right-wing elements, not as a failure to deal with the nitty-gritty of the *effects* and *mechanisms* of capitalism on our lives, on our ways of relating, on our dreams and desires.[5]

Others share my sense that what we have been doing leads us further from progressive goals. As Prishani Naidoo, an organiser active through this period, reflects, 'we have failed to acknowledge that many of our own values, beliefs and ways of interacting and engaging within (and as) social movements are produced by the very structures of capitalism that we claim to resist'.[6] Activism stretches us away from the concrete ability to *occupy* our collective and personal lives. With every rush towards where we think we see power, we re-enact this impossibility. The desert expands all around us, blooms within us.

The ongoing management *within* continual crisis leaves no room for the old oppositions we have grown comfortable with. There is not *a* proletariat, or *a* poor subject that acts as the repository for justice and truth, any more than there is a state that is not a function of empire, governing that is not biopolitical, nor a social movement that is not also, always, spectacle.

But to return to the ground, how does this operate in everyday life in South Africa? How is crisis being managed within social antagonisms? What have been the effects of the romanticisation of social movements in contributing to this radical spectacle and, I would argue, a 'radical chic' in academic spaces of knowledge production? How has the progressive left lost itself to the spectacle, almost without noticing, and why must its tired rituals be discarded?

In attempting to answer these questions, I'd first like to present a few propositions.

MANAGING CRISIS: NEOLIBERALISM, THE POLICE AND THE POOR

Proposition 1: Neoliberalism can be understood as a set of distinct economically liberal fiscal policies, but the current system of global capitalist relations is a far more complex set of apparatuses to control and manage desire and crisis, to nurture individualism, and to subdue revolt in this context of constant civil war. Multiple interlocutors are able to regulate these crises. Here, the inclination towards the courts, towards the smooth space of 'democratic' liberalism, finds perfect resonance (see Tissington, this volume). How this operates precisely in South Africa can be seen from a few examples – self-regulation of water usage, on the one hand, and African nationalism and/or xenophobia, on the other, which I discuss further below.

Proposition 2: Everywhere where there are eruptions and crisis, there will be management. This is the fundamental operation of biopolitics.[7] 'Nothing is more irrelevant to Empire than the question, "who controls what?" – provided, of course, that control has been established.'[8] 'The term 'biopolitics', as used by Foucault and others from the 1970s onwards, refers to the way in which the control and management of human life itself are at the core of contemporary politics. Biopolitics is not a new politics, nor does it announce a new radical subject.

Proposition 3: The South African left's fixation on the grand narratives of the revolutionary, humanist subjectivity of the poor ignores the techniques of power happening at the micro scale on a continual basis and their basis in bare life. These worn-out 'revolutionary' ideas are painfully wielded, clumsy contortions of an era long past. This fixation also ignores the ways in which the democratic idea is also an imperial idea, since 'the equivalence among forms-of-life can only be implemented *negatively*, by preventing, with all the means at its disposal, ethical differences from attaining in their play an intensity that makes them political'.[9] But given its monopoly on morality, the left marches on.

Its romance with a revolutionary subjectivity has allowed the left to further the status quo. It is a wedding with humanism that, no matter how radical, cannot conceive 'what is to be done' in terms other than the philanthropic. Along with international financiers, petty gangsters, venture capitalists, mercenaries, NGOs and the state, the left is yet one more manager of crisis.

* * *

At a lecture he gave at the University of KwaZulu-Natal, James Ferguson said that we should evict the use of 'neoliberalism' from our vocabulary and rather insist on saying precisely what we mean when we use the term. Are we talking about fiscal reform? – then which exactly? Is it the new world order, or cultural practices; and how is it either of these? We have become lazy, he cautioned, using a term that obscures as much as it reveals. Further, he writes,

> In thinking about the rapidly expanding literature on neoliberalism, I am struck by how much of the critical scholarship on topic arrives in the end at the very same conclusion – a conclusion that might be expressed in its simplest form as: 'neoliberalism is bad for poor and working people, therefore we must oppose it.' It is not that I disagree with this conclusion. On the contrary. But I sometimes wonder why I should bother to read one after another extended scholarly analysis only to reach, again and again, such an unsurprising conclusion.[10]

I return to Ferguson's comments because he is right that using such a basic notion of neoliberalism to describe the main issues at play in South Africa can often obscure the more diverse processes and techniques happening on multiple scales beyond the purely economic. Seeing the main enemy as neoliberalism gives force to the idea that a frontal attack is possible, based on particular structures within particular limits and contours, and thus makes it more difficult to see clearly the incessant processes of power at play, moment by moment, encounter by encounter, every day. 'Neoliberalism' describes only one set of techniques in a multiplicity of techniques that manage and control resistance and our lives. As Jodi Dean[11] outlines, the left ascribes too much power and unity to this catchall understanding of neoliberalism.

Given the dangers of creating too neat a story through an analysis of neoliberalism, it is absolutely the case that the financial and technical mechanisms used by the South African state have been critical in changing political subjectivity. Through economic liberalisation, the ANC and the South African business elite have adopted a whole set of neoliberal logics, including expanding individual property rights; privatising industry; and commodifying land, water, housing and electricity, to name a few. These changes brought with them changes in responses from the ground. In the first wave of resistance after 'liberation', there were direct contestations of the ANC's project, at a time when it was not popular to do so, and mass mobilisations that questioned the fundamental goals of the transition. I am thinking here of the early contestations around the shift from the Reconstruction and Development Plan to the overtly neoliberal Growth, Employment and Redistribution programme in 1996, and also the birth of the Anti-Privatisation Forum (APF), the Landless People's Movement and the Soweto Electricity Crisis Committee (SECC), and the mass mobilisations around the World Summit on Sustainable Development in August 2002 and against the war in Iraq in 2003. By 2003 the South African National Civic Organisation and the South African Non-governmental Organisation Coalition had their funding cut, as did other organisations with more-progressive agendas. I would include the Treatment Action Campaign (TAC) in both phases, as it was already using legal routes early on to win decisive battles, such as its court challenge to the Pharmaceutical Manufacturers Association in 2001, which pushed for the provisions of generic treatments for HIV and the anti-retroviral roll-out that followed in 2003. The TAC also nurtured an alliance with the ANC and leaned heavily on the courts, but TAC's slippage between global and local positioning was quite different in those early years from what we are seeing now. Of course, the desire to use the courts as a tactic to make strategic gains is crucial and cannot be discarded, but it must be understood in its own terms, as I discuss further below.

In the second wave, spanning perhaps 2003 to the present, there is evidence of a move from a sense of collective power as a counter-hegemonic force towards immediate bare-life issues and entitlement in community responses to local crises. Structural analysis and cohesion are lacking not because, as some would have it, the left has not been doing its educational role well enough,[12] but because of a fundamental misreading of the situation. This second wave also includes, but is not limited to, a shift away from the political realm towards the judiciary and executive. The turn to the judiciary – and to the technical norm – is yet another tool in the management of crisis under capital. It has increasingly been the approach in the last decade by wide-ranging social movements such as the TAC, the APF, and Abahlali baseMjondolo, which has had some depressing, but indicative, results. The failures and limitations of the possibilities for what (consumption) rights and judicial processes offer, specifically in relation to access to water in South Africa, are telling. In a sobering reassessment of court action, Bond et al. reflect on the 2009 Constitutional Court overturning of lower-court rulings in *Mazibuko* v. *Johannesburg Water* that had been widely celebrated by social movements in South Africa as securing the right to basic water provision.[13] The same kind of analysis could be done in looking at the legal battles against the KwaZulu-Natal Slums Act. The turn towards the courts as a space of struggle is crucial. As Ashwin Desai writes:

> Recently, we have seen a number of court cases involving social movements as applicants. Some cases have been won, some lost. There is of course nothing wrong with taking action – including in the courts – that might increase the rights of citizens, particularly the poor ... Whatever the case, an actual 'victory' in court is not my quibble ... It is the kind of reform that guts poor people's movements of the levels of social antagonism that *alone* has given them whatever social concessions have come their way from the state as a whole. It is based on the entirely misplaced and, indeed, intensely vain conception that a certain professional legal caste among us – can secure in the constitutional court meaningful precedent (and consequent compliance by the executive) that advance the struggle of the poor in a fundamental way. They can't. The system doesn't work that way. Jurisprudence is a smokescreen.[14]

During this phase there was also a shift away from ideological and political contestations towards a politics of bare life by movements themselves. I would argue that these changes in the way politics is enacted have also occurred in tandem with South Africa's integration into the core of the global neoliberal project, which could not have been entirely completed until the apartheid state was dismantled.[15] As Franco Barchesi contends, contrary to the United States or the United Kingdom, where [this] shift has been produced by the growing convergence at the top of mainstream political traditions (liberal and conservative, Tory and labour) towards a pragmatics of governance focused on the care (hence production) of individual aspiration and desire, in South Africa that outcome has been produced 'from below' by the social movements themselves, with the radical separation they produced between 'community' (seen as a pure, transparent, authentic expression of emancipative meanings) and the political (seen not so much as a realm of power, governance and domination, but as one of betrayed expectations for change that only the moral purity of the community could restore).[16]

These shifts make sense when we think about the very processes of global capitalism. For example, James Ferguson looks at the social meaning of production and accumulation and its often-specifically moral (or embedded) terms in African society.[17] Through neoliberalism – or 'scientific capitalism' – morality is turned into a technique, disembedded from the social, leaving individuals to fend for themselves in what he calls *demoralising economies*. We could draw this right back to the development of modern market economies, which went hand in hand with the development of the modern state. As Karl Polyani argues, in the free market the economy was disembedded from its function *within* the complex networks and attachments of social life.[18] Instead, human society was subordinate to the market. The market became the instrument – the *technique* – of organising social relations.

'The conditions of capitalism is that it first breaks the attachments with which a group finds its means to reproduce',[19] separating individuals from what makes them alive and what makes them human. Through this process of disembedding the social from the economic, individuals must fend for themselves, eking out their singular existence within the precise contours of capitalism.

We can also see this process of disembedding social relationships at work in social movements in South Africa over the last decade. For example, the highly visible struggles around water and electricity have had some significant evolutions. In the case of electricity, South Africa privatised the state-owned electricity provider Eskom in 1999, which led to massive electricity cut-offs for thousands. People began reconnecting themselves illegally in Soweto, and by 2001 the SECC launched Operation Khanyisa ('reconnect the power'), where volunteers would reconnect the power of those who had been cut off by Eskom.[20] Facing dangerous conditions, electrocution, persecution by the police and jail time, these volunteers turned the power back on for needy families.

As Ahmed Veriava and Prishani Naidoo have closely documented, the struggle to reconnect electricity through Operation Khanyisa put direct pressure on Eskom to change policy, 'ushering in a new form of payment rule, one in which individualised, commodified systems of service delivery are naturalised through techniques of self-government and individual saving and restraint',[21] as Eskom introduced pre-paid meters for electricity. In the newest wave of corporate management of resistance, in 2011 Eskom appropriated the name Operation Khanyisa to launch its own campaign, only this time Operation Khanyisa as used by Eskom was an effort to police the community and convince people to report on their neighbours for illegal electricity connections.[22]

At the same time as electricity was being privatised and then individualised through technological payment techniques, so was water. Again, social movements such as the APF, the Coalition Against Water Privatisation, the Phiri Concerned Residents Forum and other struggles erupted across the country, focusing on water cut-offs. Groups were reconnecting water for residents who had been cut off because of non-payment, but with the introduction of pre-paid meters, an internalised and individualised logic of payment set in. Individuals now had to pay *up front* for water, therefore 'the accumulation of debt would not be permitted, and the responsibility for securing access would become the individual paying customer's and no longer that of the state and/or private company'.[23]

These privatised and technical mechanisms used in relation to water and electricity, often in response to the resistance mounted by residents, have caused fractures between collective and individualist responses to the damages done by the market, establishing 'a new culture of payment brought forward by the companies'.[24] Prishani Naidoo discusses

> how municipal policy has mutated as community struggles have grown. The introduction of prepaid technology at the height of protests against water and electricity cut-offs in Johannesburg and the growth in illegal reconnections, is evidence of this. With cut-offs, one is punished for non-payment *after* receiving a service, whilst with the prepaid meter, you have to pay *before* you receive a service – you are cut off until you can pay. The prepaid meter also removes any responsibility for delivery from the state and

the private service provider, making the individual responsible for gaining access to basic services.[25]

As these examples outline so well, the crises that erupted through lack of access to basic services were technically managed – without rubber bullets – but with changes that made collective resistance less possible and that individualised to a far deeper level the relation of the single body to what it needs to reproduce itself – in this case, access to water.

Taking into account the *real* impacts and machinations of these struggles, the ever-increasing service delivery protests can be read into a schema in which negotiations of power are enacted through distinct, contained moments of crisis, to be managed and controlled by whatever means necessary. The politics of 'demand and recognition' falls squarely into such a schema, in which being heard and managed is often the end result.[26] While I am not arguing that this is a conscious move on the part of those struggling for basic necessities, I am arguing that the reduction of politics to that of bare life, to biopolitics, cannot be seen as a progressive tendency, but rather as the ever-deepening reach of capitalism.[27] 'The politics of necessity', or 'Fanonian humanism' as some have called it, is not a new politics at all; it is the death of politics.[28] It is evidence and enactment of empire:

> Unlike the modern State, Empire does not deny the existence of civil war – instead, it manages it. If it denied it, it would have to do without certain means it needs to steer, or contain, this same civil war. Wherever its networks are insufficiently intrusive, it will ally itself for as long as it takes with some local mafia or even some local guerrilla group, on the condition that these parties guarantee they will maintain order in the territory they have been assigned.[29]

Be it Eskom responding through technological innovation or semi-organised riots that bring small concessions case by case, larger political possibilities are evicted with each resolution of crisis. Given an understanding of the reduction of politics to bare life and its management, we must also recognise that this management is not necessarily the sole terrain of the state and the police. The police expand in all directions, are among us, and in many cases are us. These are crisis regulators of a new kind, continually looking for eruptions and continually dealing with them. In South Africa, the management of crisis is outsourced in many different forms – gangsterism, bribery, shacklords, tenderpreneurs, venture capitalists, xenophobic violence and African nationalism, among other things. As I saw in my own fieldwork the same radical collective acts of reconnecting electricity seen in Soweto are actually also found in other, less progressive forms in shack settlements across the country, where private individuals will illegally hook up your electricity for an exorbitant fee, or the electricity lords of a particular area will charge neighbours to hook into stolen electricity for sometimes four or five times the municipal rates. These are also the foot soldiers in the management of empire. They maintain the status quo, even in ugly conditions. African nationalism can also serve this function, as Hein Marais reminds us:

> One tried and trusted way of defusing uproar is to affirm and valorize bonds that can muffle discord, or channel it in diversionary, more manageable directions ... The bonding and disciplinary force of African nationalism remains the cardinal ideological turnkey of South Africa's transition ...
>
> There is a real danger of recourse to rousing affirmations of identity and entitlement, and to populist discourses of authenticity – who is 'really' South African, African or black, what is a man, and where do women fit into all this.[30]

While not meant to diffuse dissent, the same tactics are unwittingly used by the left, which also rouses 'identity and entitlement' and 'authenticity' as the nucleus of progressive politics. The tendency by the left to see the poor (or other 'authentic' revolutionary subjects) as a unified block reveals the ongoing humanist, existential liberalism that underpins its complicity with the dominant power structures of our times.[31]

It is a misreading of the processes of power to try to prop up the poor as a homogeneous subjectivity. The idea that what binds people together is their very poverty itself is something only the most rudimentary understanding of social dynamics and everyday practices of power – and of global capitalism – could support. While the proletariat at least held the factory floor and had their relationship to the means of production to unite themselves with others, the poor are given only their wretchedness as their common unifier. We become complicit by celebrating the dangerous fiction of the homogeneous 'community' of the shack settlement, racial grouping or class category,[32] ignoring the essential antagonisms that exist in these same categories. The real forces that tie people together erupt from practices that happen every day – forms of life that forge ties and build bonds between singularities:

> That is how the classical definition of politics spreads the desert: by abstracting humans from their worlds, by disconnecting them from the network of things, habits, words, fetishes, affects, places and solidarities that make up their world, their *sensible* world, and that gives them their specific substance ... Classic politics is the glorious stagecraft of bodies without worlds.[33]

In this continual process of crisis control, the burning tires strewn across the tarmac, and other random acts of arson and blockade are opening gestures beckoning towards the negotiating table, not, as they are often read, as the breaking point of control.[34] They signal an opening for negotiation, not an outright refusal. 'Let's talk', not 'We reject you'. They are further apparatuses used to contain and manage crisis:

> Often a central demand of protestors is for the President to meet with the community and hear their grievances first-hand. The assumption is that the ANC leadership, once alerted to the facts, will call the transgressors to book, and act promptly and fairly .... Paradoxically, a protest can also be a backhanded vote of confidence in the organisation – as long as the organisation takes up the grievances, and acts to resolve them.[35]

I would go further and say that it is *always* a vote of confidence, not so much in the ANC or the 'organisation' as such, but in this process of negotiating grievance. Should the 'revolt' get big enough to warrant compromise or concession in the hands of the leadership of the contending parties who hammer out possible deals, it will be a disposing of ideological stakes. As outlined above, it is here where the courts and judges enter as the negotiators par excellence of the (technical) norm.

A sweeping look at the main concerns in the second wave of mobilisations across the country to blockade roads, march on the city or express discontent shows that they mainly deal with the provision of basic services, housing, and corruption within the ANC and among local-level councillors. Some would like to have it otherwise, claiming that there are grander plots afoot, but it is unfortunately not the case, nor the substantive basis of demands that are being made. Rather, as I have tried to point to earlier, the 'service delivery protests' are elaborations of the full-scale enactment of biopolitics in South Africa – the negotiating of political value through the unit of bare life itself. It is power negotiation and management continually operating within a state of exception rather than the birth of any new radical political subject. The 'politics of necessity' is not a potentially revolutionary politics, as such; it is biopolitics exposed, in which bare life is the only possible political unit.

While I do not have the space to properly discuss this here, desire is also being managed, with the rise of aspirational and 'middle' classes becoming increasingly present in contemporary South Africa. The creative power of capitalism to capture and give immaterial *value* to our worlds is surely not lost on the politicians, who mobilise the language of aspiration to quiet public discontent and who operate within the spectacle of public relations and the magic of politics. Nor is it lost on industry, which transforms the ways in which the public relates to products and to business, even (and especially) if they are angry, disruptive consumers. Nor is this distinction lost on the police, who arrive everywhere, not to keep public order, but to manage disorder. Under these conditions, democracy becomes mere spectacle.

THE RISE OF RADICAL CHIC

As I have mentioned above, the South African left has a specific and important role in this spectacle. Elsewhere I have written about the uncomfortable collaborations forged as we try to form alliances across huge divisions of power, but in fact they are very often extremely comfortable.[36] Movements leverage support from academics, while academics offer up little of their actual privilege in return for further 'radical' status and by writing about deprivations and poverty. We do not have to share the struggle, pain and hardship, but we can write about it. Chapters get written like this one, conferences attended, articles published, and the poor end up with travel excursions to exotic places like New York, where they are lauded on platforms and there are workshops, jobs and training. Some even get degrees. Why did I think this was uncomfortable? That these collaborations had their own machinations was easier to ignore. I must agree with Jacques Rancière, who writes in the preface to *Proletarian Nights*:

If, for once, we let the thoughts of those who are not 'destined' to think unfold before us, we may come to recognize that the relationship between the order of the world and the desires of those subjected to it presents more complexity than is grasped by the discourses of the intelligentsia. Perhaps we shall gain a certain modesty in deploying grand words and expressing grand sentiments.[37]

Instead, what seems to be going on here (and elsewhere) is the rise of radical chic, obscuring more about the nature of this moment and people's resistance to it than it reveals about the function of power in the production of knowledge. 'Radical chic' was a term coined in an essay by Tom Wolfe in 1970 to describe 'the adoption and promotion of radical political causes by celebrities, socialites, and high society'. It was described as 'an exercise in double-tracking one's public image: on the one hand, defining oneself through committed allegiance to a radical cause, but on the other, vitally, demonstrating this allegiance because it is the fashionable, au courant way to be seen in moneyed, name-conscious Society'.[38] While this socialite aspect of radical chic still exists, it seems that a new radical chic is afoot within the academic left, conjuring the revolutionary subject from the shack-lands of South Africa and elsewhere. With often the best of intentions, academic radical chic promises social reward through proximity to desperation – or 'radical' subjectivities – without actually having any real intention to disrupt the status quo or hegemonic order. In the South African context, we can see the origins of some of these practices in what Helliker and Vale discuss around the usefulness of Marxism for radical whites:

> Faced with [the development of Black Consciousness], the appeal of Marxism for radical Whites was not simply on the basis of any objective truth and rationality, but rather, because it provided them with 'a comfortable discourse' – class over race – with which to 'interrogate structures of power' ... It permitted them to remain politically relevant as 'Whites' in South Africa; it was a 'self-preservation mechanism' ...[39]

Through a stranglehold on knowledge production, this academic radical chic dangerously obscures the real nature of struggles. It creates a systematic, if often unconscious, dismantling of resistance. Of course, it must be said that even a critique of radical chic profits from some of these same tendencies, and perhaps I am also guilty of this position. Yet the need to define such a particular radical subjectivity has been part of the reasons behind the faltering and flagging social movements in this last period. This is not to imply that this is the only factor, but it seems due time to look critically into the fundamentals of how political alliances are formed and elaborated. Radical chic has little regard for the complex encounters between politics and power, leaving out power struggles fundamental to the encounter between researchers, (often-) middle-class activists and the communities they support. It seems more important than ever to look critically at the romanticisation of social movements by intellectuals, especially within the academy, to uncover the ongoing separations between movement-relevant theory and the movements themselves. It seems that the contradictions at play have been easier to ignore or write about than to face and discuss. What critical analysis can offer should be exactly what academic contribution to social struggle should be: a process of conscientisation that cycles between action, critical reflection and re-engagement.

I point to these tendencies not just to critique for critique's sake, but to begin to offer insights into post-apartheid progressive politics and its failures, insisting that we look at the various reasons why this has been the case, such as relying on the emissaries of an academic radical chic rather than actually entering the terrain of struggle. Perhaps through auto-reflection we can create a new context of engagement and progressive politics.

BEYOND THE MANAGER

I began this chapter from the fundamental starting point that the social movements and broader radical political energy of the grassroots that seemed to carry forth through the transition in South Africa have come undone. In thinking this through, I have focused on the ways in which empire and its multiple apparatuses of control have come to manage crises and desire. I have argued that the neoliberal era contains far more than shifting economic policies, but has come to shape the way in which we see ourselves and the social fabric of our everyday lives. I have also argued that this change has been largely lost on the organised left, who are still looking to fixed 'radical' subjectivities as the nucleus of change, while in reality, these subjectivities are often caught up in the mechanisms of biopolitics, in which the unit of negotiation and management is bare life itself.

Asking these questions, looking for ways to assess the evident *lack*, comes from an urgency underwriting the moment we are in. We have known these weak political configurations for too long. We must abandon them. This means reinhabiting our worlds, which is to say, our forms of life. We are in continual civil war that spans more than the spatial territory of a state and is also nearer to yourself than you care to admit.[40] Recognising this may pave the way towards a new politics.

NOTES

1. Perhaps this change was in part the slow fade out of the anti-apartheid struggle, in which those progressives who had opposed the consolidation of power by the ANC through the 1980s, continued to resist, if only now dressed up in new slogans and T-shirts.

2. I am referring to empire as described in Tiqqun in which '[e]mpire does not confront us like a subject, facing us, but like an environment that is hostile to us'; Tiqqun, *Introduction to Civil War*, Los Angeles: Semiotext(e)/MIT Press, 2010, p. 171. This follows, though remains distinct from, the way Michael Hardt and Antonio Negri describe empire as the end of conflict between nation states and a move towards a global world order with a particular kind of conflict; M. Hardt and A. Negri, *Empire*, Cambridge, Mass.: Harvard University Press, 2001. I disagree with Hardt and Negri in their insistence that the nation state has entirely dissolved. Tiqqun does a better job at a nuanced understanding of empire in terms of the internal and external *hostile* environment.

3. Examples of a few authors who do this would include Patrick Bond, *Elite Transition: From Apartheid to Neoliberalism in South Africa*, London: Pluto Press, 2000; David Harvey, *A Brief History of Neoliberalism*, New York: Oxford University Press, 2005; Ashwin Desai, *We Are the Poors*, New York: Monthly Review Press, 2002; John S. Saul, *The Next Liberation Struggle: Capitalism, Socialism and Democracy in Southern Africa*, Durban: University of KwaZulu-Natal Press, 2005; Luke Sinwell, 'Is "another world" really possible? Re-examining counter-hegemonic forces in post-apartheid South Africa', *Review of African Political Economy*, Vol. 38, No. 127 (2011); Mike Davis, *Planet of Slums*, New York: Verso, 2007.

4. This is not so surprising. In movements in the global North I have been part of, the same thing is true. Wearing the black uniforms of monks and nuns of the movement, worn out after a long day of organising, we would get home and crack a beer and watch a sit-com, go shopping or return to an abusive home life.

5. Throughout the chapter I refer to 'us', 'we' or 'our' role. By this I mean the collection of activists and academics who feel committed to social change and who have been primarily operating within the tropes of traditional left politics. I include myself in this grouping.

6. Prishani Naidoo, 'Subaltern sexiness: From a politics of representation to a politics of difference', *African Studies*, Vol. 69, No. 3 (2010).

7. See Michel Foucault, 'Governmentality', in G. Burchell, C. Gordon and P. Miller (eds), *The Foucault Effect: Studies in Governmentality*, Chicago: University of

Chicago Press, 1991; *Power: Essential works of Foucault, 1954–1984*, ed. James D. Faubion, trans. Robert Hurley et al., New York: New Press, 2000. Giorgio Agamben, who further interrogated this crossing of politics into life (between *zoe* and *bios*), marks it as the critical event of modernity; Giorgio Agamben, 'Beyond human rights', in *Means without Ends: Notes on Politics*, Minneapolis: University of Minnesota Press, 1996; *Homo Sacer: Sovereign Power and Bare Life*, trans. D. Heller-Roazen, Stanford: Stanford University Press, 1998; *The State of Exception*, Chicago: University of Chicago Press, 2005. Other influential political and philosophical uses of biopolitics, bare life and biopower emerge in Hannah Arendt, *On Revolution*, New York: Viking Press, 1963; Maurizio Lazzarato, 'From biopower to biopolitics', trans. Ivan A. Ramirez, *Pli: The Warwick Journal of Philosophy*, Vol. 13 (n.d.), www.generation-online. org/c/fcbiopolitics.htm; Hardt and Negri, *Empire*; and Tiqqun, *Introduction to Civil War*. Detailed ethnographic accounts of biopolitics at work in everyday life and in diverse parts of the world can be seen in the work of Aihwa Ong, *Neoliberalism as Exception: Mutations in Citizenship and Sovereignty*, Durham: Duke University Press, 2006; Sandra Hyde, *Eating Spring Rice: The Cultural Politics of AIDS in Southwest China*, Berkeley: University of California Press, 2006; Vihn-Kim Ngyuen, 'Antiretroviral globalism, biopolitics and therapeutic citizenship', in Aihwa Ong (ed.), *Global Assemblages: Technology, Politics and Ethics as Anthropological Problems*, Malden: Blackwell, 2004; and Adriana Petryna, *Life Exposed: Biological Citizens after Chernobyl*, Princeton: Princeton University Press, 2002, to name a few.

8. Tiqqun, *Introduction to Civil War*.

9. Ibid., p. 122.

10. James Ferguson, 'The uses of neoliberalism', *Antipode*, Vol. 41, No. S1 (2009), p. 166.

11. Jodi Dean, *Democracy and Other Neoliberal Fantasies*, Durham and London: Duke University Press, 2009.

12. Patrick Bond, Ashwin Desai and Trevor Ngwane, 'Uneven and combined Marxism within South Africa's urban social movements: Transcending precarity in community, labour and environmental struggles', paper presented at the conference Beyond Precarious Labor: Rethinking Socialist Strategies, City University of New York Graduate Center, May 2011.

13. Ibid.

14. See Ashwin Desai, 'The state of the social movements', paper presented at the CCS/Wolpe lecture panel Social Justice Ideas in Civil Society Politics, Global and Local: A Colloquium of Scholar-activists', Centre for Civil Society, Durban, July 2010.

15. Merle Lipton has outlined some of the pressing historical arguments between liberals and revisionists and neo-Marxists around the role of capitalism in apartheid and their more-recent shared analysis; Merle Lipton, *Liberals, Marxists and Nationalists: Competing Interpretations of South African History*, New York: Palgrave Macmillan, 2008.

16. Franco Barchesi, personal communication, August 2011.

17. James Ferguson, *Global Shadows: Africa in the Neoliberal World Order*, Durham and London: Duke University Press, 2006.

18. Karl Polanyi, *The Great Transformation: The Political and Economic Origins of Our Time*, Boston: Beacon Press, 2001 [1944].

19. Invisible Committee, *Call*, self-published, 2007, p. 30.

20. Patrick Bond, 2002, 'Power to the people in South Africa: Operation Khanyisa! and the fight against electricity privatization', *Multinational Monitor*, Vol. 23 (January/February 2002), p. 1.

21. Ahmed Veriava and Prishani Naidoo, 'From local to global (and back again?): Anti-commodification struggles of the Soweto Electricity Crisis Committee', in David A. McDonald (ed.), *Electric Capitalism: Recolonising Africa on the Power Grid*, Cape Town: HSRC Press, 2009.

22. We might see in ANC Youth League president Julius Malema's nationalisation politi-speak the same kind of co-option and management of the real crises brewing among these elements in the country in 2011.

23. Coalition Against Water Privatisation and Anti-Privatisation Forum, *Lessons from the War against Prepaid Meters: The Struggle against Disconnections Continues*, Johannesburg: Anti-Privatisation Forum, 2006, p. 4, http://apf.org.za/IMG/pdf/Final_PPM_Research_Report_-_102006-2.pdf (accessed 1 August 2011).

24. Veriava and Naidoo, 'From local to global', p. 328.

25. Prishani Naidoo, 'Struggles around the commodification of daily life in South Africa', *Review of African Political Economy*, Vol. 34, No. 111 (2007).

26. See, for example, Richard J. F. Day's critique of such politics of demand and recognition in *Gramsci is Dead: Anarchist Currents in the Newest Social Movements*, London: Pluto Press, 2005.

27. As Jessica Harris reports, '[m]embers from all three organizations were adamant that their identities exclude race and politics'; Jessica Harris, 'Towards a movement of the poors? A survey of Durban activists' views on struggle, unity, and the future', unpublished paper written for the School for Development Studies, University of KwaZulu-Natal, Durban, as part of the School for International Training South Africa, www.abahlali.org/node/848#attachments. Harris reports that one activist asserted that 'all that matters is poor people's basic, practical problems – the politics of the poor' (interview with Church Land Programme, an NGO affiliated with Abahlali, 22 November 2006). Another affirmed, '[w]e don't talk about politics. We talk about people's needs' (interview with Abahlali member, 22 November 2006).

28. Jacques Rancière describes politics as follows: 'As far as *arche* [Greek: "to begin", "to lead", "sovereignty", "domination"] is concerned, as with everything else, the conventional logic has it that there is a particular disposition to act that is exercised upon a particular disposition to "be acted upon." Thus the logic of *arche* presupposes a determinate superiority exercised upon an equally determinate inferiority. In order for there to be a political subject(ivity), and thus for there to be politics, there must be a rupture in this logic.' Further: 'Politics is a specific rupture in the logic of *arche*. It does not simply presuppose the rupture of the "normal" distribution of positions between the one who exercises power and the one subject to it. It also requires a rupture in the idea that there are disposition "proper" to such classification.' Jacques Rancière, 'Ten theses on politics', in Steven Corcoran (ed. and trans.), *Dissensus: On Politics and Aesthetics*, London and New York: Continuum International, 2010, p. 3.

29. Tiqqun, *Introduction to Civil War*, p. 148.

30. Hein Marais, *South Africa Pushed to the Limit: The Political Economy of Change*, London and Cape Town: Zed Books and UCT Press, 2011, p. 417.

31. It is a very similar tendency that can be seen through NGO-isation and the development industry binding aid to the very structures of capitalism itself, or the

'anti-politics machine' as it is referred to by James Ferguson in *The Anti-Politics Machine: 'Development,' Depoliticization, and Bureaucratic Power in Lesotho*, Minneapolis and London: University of Minnesota Press, 2000.

32. For further critique on the danger of romanticising community, see Miranda Joseph, *Against the Romance of Community*, Minneapolis and London: University of Minnesota Press, 2002.

33. Invisible Committee, *Call*, p. 18.

34. The point could well be made that this is not entirely new to South African political machinations. One could even look to the Durban bus boycotts in the 1950s and the ways in which strike-like tactics have long been a way of fighting for concessions from the state beyond the workplace.

35. Marais, *South Africa Pushed to the Limit*, p. 377.

36. Shannon Walsh, 'Uncomfortable collaborations: Contesting constructions of the poor in South Africa', *Review of African Political Economy*, Vol. 116 (2008).

37. Jacques Rancière, *Proletarian Nights*, trans. Noel Parker, Radical Philosophy series, Vol. 31, 1982, p. 250, www.scribd.com/doc/65081569/Ranciere-Preface-to-The-Nights-of-Labour-1981.

38. Tom Wolfe, 'Radical chic', in *Radical Chic & Mau-Mauing the Flak Catchers*, New York: Farrar, Straus and Giroux, 1970, p. 37.

39. Kirk Helliker and Peter Vale, 'Fanon's curse: Re-imagining Marxism in South Africa's age of retreat', paper presented at the Twelfth Annual Conference of the International Association of Critical Realism, Rio de Janeiro, July 2009.

40. 'War, because in each singular play between forms-of-life, the possibility of a fierce confrontation – the possibility of violence – can *never* be discounted. Civil, because the confrontation between forms-of-life is not like that between States – a coincidence between a population and a territory – but like the confrontation between parties, in the sense this word had before the advent of the modern State. And because we must be precise from now on, we should say that forms-of-life confront one another as *partisan war machines*.' Tiqqun, *Introduction to Civil War*, p. 33.

14
Transforming Contestation: Some Closing Words

Luke Sinwell and Marcelle C. Dawson

This collection of essays has sought to reflect on the state of social movements in South Africa today. Taken as a whole, the book studies twenty-first-century popular resistance in South Africa against the backdrop of the range of struggles comprising the Global Justice Movement, including the resistance efforts elsewhere on the African continent. Many of the social movements of the post-apartheid era emerged at a time when – in academic circles – the elitist nature of the transition to democracy became more apparent.[1] Of course, within marginalised communities, the effects of limited socioeconomic reform had already been felt quite sharply not long after the euphoria of the transition from apartheid died down. Globally, the resistance against neoliberalism provided a further impetus for the emergence of the kinds of movements that were mentioned briefly in the introduction and explored at length by Ballard et al.[2] Amidst claims that the African National Congress's (ANC's) honeymoon was over, those who were disillusioned by the limited reforms that the ruling party had to offer experimented with other kinds of social expressions that were beginning to question the dominant political narrative. Many pinned their hopes on the social movements that emerged out of bread-and-butter struggles, which were, in many ways, a continuation of the struggles under apartheid.

Ballard et al., in their well-received collection, *Voices of Protest: Social Movements in Post-Apartheid South Africa*, provided rich and detailed accounts of the organised movements that began to make their mark. This collection was based on the first wave of resistance between 1999 and 2006, most of which was 'directed against government policy on distributional issues'.[3] There seemed to be a general assumption that movements were challenging the ANC, but the nuanced account of movements by Ballard et al. had already begun to suggest that they were not necessarily providing a counter-hegemonic alternative.

Today, more than ten years after the emergence of these movements, when many of them, as this book suggests, are indeed in decline, we are able to reflect not only on their shortcomings, but also on the shifting terrain of popular resistance and the implications thereof for democracy in South Africa. The range of chapters in this book reflects quite clearly the contested nature of transformation. In this concluding chapter, we attempt to understand movements in relation to other political actors including trade unions, the state and political parties. In the South African context these three entities have tended to be understood as separate and distinct from movements. We argue that the ways in which movements navigate this terrain has a significant impact on their political trajectory. In the final section of this chapter, we unpack lessons that have been learned from earlier movements and suggest that contestation will need to be transformed if it is to provide a counter-hegemonic alternative to the ruling ANC. Furthermore, we propose that an anti-capitalist national umbrella organisation is necessary at this current conjuncture. In this regard we offer a brief, but critical, assessment of the efforts of the Democratic Left Front (DLF).

SOCIAL MOVEMENTS, POLITICAL PARTIES, LABOUR AND THE STATE

As the institutionalized center for the legitimate monopoly on the means of violence, the state is the ultimate arbiter for the allocation of socially valued goods. The state is therefore simultaneously target, sponsor, and antagonist for social movements as well as the organizer of the political system and the arbiter of victory. As organizer of the political system, the state shapes the relationships between social movements and the institutionalized interest representation system ... Social movements that aim to alter social institutions and practices have to come into contact with the state, if only to consolidate their claims.[4]

This excerpt by Jenkins and Klandermans drives home the importance of including the state in analyses of social movements. Such an analysis should concern itself with political opportunities and how these impact on the emergence and nature of social movements, but also with the ways in which social movements impact on the state. The nature of social movement demands is central to understanding this relationship, as is the actual outcome of their actions.[5] Also important are the effects of social movement activism on the political representative system and the incorporation (or not) of social movement proposals into public policy. Several of the chapters in this book – although not claiming specifically to provide an analysis of state-social movement relations – touch on these issues. One of the key political developments in the period 2000–10 was Jacob Zuma's rise to party leader at the ANC's Polokwane conference in 2007, the ousting of Thabo Mbeki in 2008 and the election of Zuma as the country's president in 2009. Zuma rose to power partly on the ticket that he – in comparison to the aloof Mbeki – was a 'listening president' (see Duncan's chapter, this volume, for a critique). This had a knock-on effect on many of the social movements. As McKinley notes,

> [T]here was little doubt that at the community level the left-populist rhetoric of Zuma – combined with the previously intense opposition to the Mbeki regime – created both short-term confusion and a variegated 'turn' away from independent movement-community politics and struggle towards institutionalised party politics and a creeping (Zuma-inspired) social conservatism.[6]

However, it was not long before people began to realise that the Zuma administration was no more in favour of pro-poor policies than Mbeki's government was. Although the widespread community protests across the country were not regarded as a direct threat to state security, there were violent police crackdowns on protest. Duncan (this volume) suggests that as people become increasingly aware that the Zuma administration is doing very little to change people's lives, popular resistance efforts are likely be scaled up to the point where they do in fact represent a serious threat to the status quo, in which case movement activists are likely to experience the full might of Zuma's security cluster. This kind of mobilisation will bring movement activists into a highly confrontational relationship with the state; one that has the potential to fundamentally shift the balance of power.

Understandably, given the structural circumstances in which they have emerged, social movements have not yet managed to substantially transform the socioeconomic status quo, but they have certainly made important gains that have helped to mitigate the dire conditions faced by marginalised communities. In the areas of service delivery, health care and housing, for example, it would be negligent to deny that the resistance efforts of community activists have influenced government decision making. Achievements such as the writing off of payment arrears by Eskom (the country's electricity provider), reductions in water and electricity cut-offs and evictions, the provision of treatment to people with HIV/AIDS, undoubtedly have been influenced by the efforts of the social movements. Moreover, popular resistance against municipal re-demarcation has been successful in some communities. While these gains are often credited to the government, and to the ANC in particular, they should rather be interpreted as a victory for democracy from below.

It can be argued, however, that state concessions weaken popular struggle. For instance, resistance in Khutsong died down once residents won the battle to remain in Gauteng province. The Treatment Action Campaign (TAC) has achieved impressive gains, including a court victory to have anti-retroviral treatment provided through the public health system. This remarkable achievement has saved millions of lives and has, in many instances, prevented mother-to-child transmission of the virus. However, the TAC is arguably a victim of its own success in that – although still active – it functions more like a well-funded non-governmental organisation than a politicised, contentious social movement. From its inception the TAC's intention was not to oppose and attempt to alter the capitalist system. For Mark Heywood, founding member of the TAC, '[e]xtensive and lasting reform is possible within the boundaries of capitalism and the current state'.[7] Moreover, the TAC – unlike some of South Africa's other social movements – has also enjoyed a favourable relationship with the ruling alliance, and with the Congress of South African Trade Unions (COSATU) in particular. Although such a relationship can be quite fruitful, in the case of the TAC its reformist demands – although honourable – have been limited as far as social transformation is concerned. Other movements have had different experiences with the ruling alliance and it is necessary, at this juncture, to consider this issue briefly as part of a broader discussion on the relationship between social movements and political parties and between movements and unions.

Bénit-Gbaffou and Piper question whether social movements (and other civil society organisations) are able to 'bargain with political parties to access certain public goods, or influence certain local urban policies'.[8] Indeed, local branches of the South African Communist Party have been implicated in the re-demarcation struggles in Khutsong[9] and in housing struggles in Alexandra,[10] and the Democratic Alliance (DA) has enjoyed the support of township residents in Protea South (Soweto) based on the belief that it would deliver on demands for housing, water and electricity. Sinwell has documented a case of a member of the Landless People's Movement (LPM) joining the DA and standing for election in the 2011 local government polls. Based on a case study of Anti-Privatisation Forum (APF) activists in Soweto, Matlala and Bénit-Gbaffou highlight an apparent contradiction in the relationship between social movements and political parties.[11] Several of the respondents in this study claimed that, despite the failures of the ANC – experienced at the community level as a lack of service delivery, housing, access to health care, and so on – they would continue to vote for the ruling party in elections. Some authors have suggested that the two-pronged strategy is effective and that it does not hamper ANC loyalty.[12] Others, however, have proposed a more nuanced analysis of this paradox. For example, read together, the chapters by Alexander and by Langa and von Holdt (this volume) highlight the contradictory nature of loyalty to the ANC and show that allegiance to the ruling party is dynamic. Moreover, Matlala and Bénit-Gbaffou contend that community activists distinguish between the ANC today and 'the "real" ANC of the past'[13] and they suggest that although protesters are disgruntled by the party in its current form and by its lack of delivery, they remain loyal to 'the "spirit" of the (anti-apartheid) struggle'.[14] Taking a different line, Alexander (this volume) argues that while the some of the electorate may very well engage in protest action to get the government's attention, not all demonstrators take part in the elections. He investigates why people are *not* voting and provides insight into alternative ways of making social change, which tells us more about the relationship between protest and political parties than an analysis of election results alone. Some of the alternatives include electoral abstention or boycotts, spoiling one's vote or forming local political parties, which some communities have done with varying success.

While debates on the relationship between social movements and political parties may resonate elsewhere in the world, the relationship between social movements and organised labour is somewhat of an anomaly in South Africa. COSATU's membership to the ruling alliance has placed it in a rather invidious position in relation to social movements that oppose the ANC. In the first phase of post-apartheid movement formation (late 1990s) debates ensued about whether or not COSATU would split from the ANC, which would have made it easier for the movements to lobby the trade union federation, thereby shifting the balance of power. This was not to be and, during the first decade of dissent – notwith-standing a few exceptions such as the South African Municipal Workers' Union and to a lesser extent the National Education, Health and Allied Workers' Union – COSATU-affiliated unions have demonstrated their loyalty to the ANC and have distanced themselves from the more radical social movements. Although there have been attempts over the years by the social movements to reach out to COSATU-affiliated unions, the uneasy relationship between the two, as Ceruti (this volume) points out, made it difficult for the movements to throw their weight behind the public sector strikes in 2007 and 2010. In the current period, in a context of a divided ANC, talk of a split in the alliance is again abounding in certain circles.[15] Although it is unlikely that such a split will happen in the foreseeable future, the last decade of social movement activism has revealed that organised labour is a serious contender in the battle for a more equitable society. Closer linkages between community and workplace struggles are crucial for progressive socioeconomic and political transformation in twenty-first-century South Africa. In the section below, we look at the potential of these relationships through the lens of a national anti-capitalist alternative.

BUILDING A NATIONAL ANTI-CAPITALIST ALTERNATIVE IN SOUTH AFRICA

As indicated in the introduction to this volume, the theme of contesting transformation enables an approach that addresses both the perspective of academics studying social movements and resistance and that of the activists who are directly involved in popular mobilisation. Taken together, because of the various political positions of the authors and their positionality within, or outside of movements, the collection does not provide a homogeneous account of ordinary citizen's contestation over political power in South Africa. Some chapters illustrate and critique the 'regeneration of power'[16] by the ruling ANC (see Langa and von Holdt, McKinley, Duncan, and Walsh), while others look at the strategies and tactics of various movements and their potential to challenge the status quo (Cock, Runciman, White, and Alexander). Still others suggest that we should evaluate the transformative politics of movements based on their own definitions (Tissington and Madlingozi) while some authors call for an overtly anti-capitalist political organisation that brings together community struggles and workers (Ceruti and Ngwane).

Referring to activist-intellectual Trevor Ngwane, founder of the Soweto Electricity Crisis Committee, leader of the APF and now actively involved in the Gauteng and National DLF, Ballard et al. questioned whether or not a transformative politics was possible without a long-term coherent socialist or anti-capitalist programme.[17] Citing the work of Greenstein (2003), who draws on the work of Laclau and Mouffe, they point out that, 'movements do not imagine that the only way to oppose state power is to seek to overthrow it'[18] and that we should not 'reduce the definition of counter-hegemonic to state capture'.[19]

We start from the assumption that those umbrella social movements like the APF, Abahlali baseMjondolo, the Anti-Eviction Campaign and the LPM, which had a critical place in the political landscape in South Africa, are now in decline. The current state of affairs in movement politics can partly be explained by Tarrow's notion of 'cycles of protest'[20] which suggests that movements experience high points and downturns in their struggles. Those that are rooted in broader struggles, or that have a national profile, may have a stronger chance of surviving setbacks in mobilisation, while highly localised movements, which tend to be narrowly focused on a single set of issues are more susceptible to co-optation by the state.

The DLF has come to the fore in the wake of the downturn in movement mobilisation. The DLF regards itself as 'a new, united and democratic mass movement of the oppressed and exploited that builds a counter-power to the power of capital, the market, the investors, the black bourgeoisie, the state functionaries and other social layers that the capitalist state in South Africa rests upon'.[21] The DLF has drawn on the strengths of its predecessors but aims to overcome some of their shortcomings. Its starting point has been to work from a master frame, or master narrative of anti-capitalism.[22] A recent pamphlet developed out of a national DLF committee meeting in June 2012 reflected this sentiment:

> South Africa is in crisis. Unemployment stands at an all-time high forcing many of us into extreme poverty, and giving rise to thousands of protests for basic necessities. Many others are homeless, landless, and without basic services. This is all because of capitalism. Capitalism means profits for a few, and misery for many. Capitalism threatens our world with disaster. If it is left to plunder the natural resources of our planet and pollute the atmosphere, the oceans and our soil, life itself will be under grave threat.[23]

The DLF has successfully developed a coherent set of anti-capitalist ideas that stands in sharp contrast to the dominant political parties and also to big business. It is also committed to building alternatives from below through people's power and popular struggles. While the DLF has been relatively successful at relating to the struggles of community-based organisations, having provincial structures in eight of the nine provinces in South Africa, it has not been able to embed itself fully into community-based structures. Furthermore, like the some of its predecessors, it has been less effective at building relationships with unionised workers – although, at least in its public projections – it has committed itself to doing so.

It remains to be seen whether or not the DLF will be able to shift localised campaigns in communities to a national campaign that simultaneously builds the capacity of local struggles, connects with the struggles of organised workers and begins to challenge aspects of the ANC's neoliberal programme. The DLF national committee's recent decision to have its next national conference held in a township (previously its meetings were held at universities across South Africa and it was criticised for being elitist), arguably signals a shift away from a common perception that the DLF is a bourgeois organisation and suggests instead that the organisation is rooted in the struggles of communities, and perhaps eventually workplaces. However, it is too early at this stage to plot the direction the DLF.

Leadership is a critical factor in determining the political trajectory of any movement. As Ballard et al. point out:

> Despite the fact that some social movement activists may be reluctant to acknowledge the centrality of leadership and a vanguard cadre we would be remiss if we did not recognise that none of these movements would be what they are without their leadership and vanguard cadre and the resources these individuals were able to broker from a variety of institutional settings.[24]

However, as Walsh (this volume) points out, academics and other so-called outsiders may have a negative impact on struggles since they do not necessarily have a genuine commitment to challenging the status quo. The DLF would perhaps do well to take heed of some of the issues raised by Walsh. One of the key criticisms of the earlier movements was that they were too dependent on the resources of outsiders. While it may have been necessary for these earlier movements to rely on such resources in light of the fact that their support base was largely unemployed, it also set up a situation where people began to expect handouts in exchange for attendance at political education and other public meetings held by that organisation. The ability of movements primarily made up of the unemployed to finance themselves remains a key challenge.

Earlier efforts at building local and national movements are commendable and as we move into a new period of popular resistance, we need to revive the idea of building an umbrella national social movement organisation. As various chapters in this volume have highlighted, it is indeed important to take very seriously transformation from the perspective of movement activists themselves, but we maintain that this should not be an end in itself. Any new organisation that emerges with a proclaimed alternative to the ruling ANC should have a shared understanding, or 'master frame', which makes clear that capitalism is to blame for the problems that have been visited upon the vast majority and our planet.

NOTES

1. Patrick Bond, *Elite Transition: Globalisation and the Rise of Economic Fundamentalism in South Africa*. London: Pluto Press; Pietermaritzburg: University of Natal Press, 2000.
2. Richard Ballard, Adam Habib, Imraan Valodia and Elke Zuern (eds), *Voices of Protest: Social Movements in Post-Apartheid South Africa*, Durban: University of KwaZulu-Natal Press, 2006.
3. Ibid., p. 399.
4. J. Craig Jenkins and Bert Klandermans (eds), *The Politics of Social Protest: Comparative Perspectives on States and Social Movements*, Minneapolis: University of Minnesota Press, 1995, p. 2.
5. Ibid., p. 3.
6. Dale McKinley. 'Transition's child: A brief history of the Anti-Privatisation Forum', in *Transition's Child: The Anti-Privatisation Forum (APF)*, Braamfontein: SAHA, 2012, p. 17.
7. Mark Heywood, 'Social movements: Challenging the state', paper prepared for the Harold Wolpe Memorial Seminar, presented at The Edge Institute, 4 May, www.the-edge.org.za/seminars.htm, 2005, pp. 3–4.
8. Claire Bénit-Gbaffou and Laurence Piper, 'Party politics, the poor and the city', *Geoforum*, Vol. 43, No. 2 (2012), p. 173.
9. Joshua Kirshner and Comfort Phokela, *Khutsong and Xenophobic Violence: Exploring the Case of the Dog that Didn't Bark*, research report commissioned by Atlantic Philanthropies, Johannesburg: Centre for Sociological Research, University of Johannesburg, 2010, p. 9.
10. Luke Sinwell, 'Transformative left-wing parties and grassroots organizations: Unpacking the politics of "top-down" and "bottom-up" development', *Geoforum*, Vol. 43, No. 2 (2012).

11. Boitumelo Matlala and Claire Bénit-Gbaffou, 'Against Ourselves – Local activists and the management of contradicting political loyalties', *Geoforum*, Vol. 43, No. 2 (2012).

12. Susan Booysen, 'With the ballot and the brick: The politics of attaining service delivery', *Progress in Development Studies*, Vol. 7, No. 1 (2007); Susan Booysen, 'The "ballot and the brick" – enduring under duress', in Susan Booysen (ed.), *Local Elections in South Africa: Parties, People, Politics*, Bloemfontein: Sun Press, 2012.

13. Matlala and Bénit-Gbaffou, 'Against Ourselves', p. 207.

14. Ibid., p. 216.

15. DLF National Committee Meeting, 9–11 June 2012, Johannesburg.

16. Susan Booysen, *The African National Congress and the Regeneration of Political Power*, Johannesburg: Wits University Press, 2011.

17. Ballard et al., *Voices of Protest*, pp. 402–3.

18. Ibid., p. 403.

19. Ibid., p. 405.

20. Sidney Tarrow, *Collective Politics and Reform: Collective Action, Social Movements, and Cycles of Protest*, New York: Cornell University Press, 1991.

21. DLF, 'Declaration of the Democratic Left Front', Article 53, 24 January 2011, http://democraticleft.za.net.

22. David A. Snow and Robert D. Benford, 'Ideology, frame resonance, and participant mobilization', *International Social Movement Research*, Vol. 1 (1998), pp. 197–217; Robert D. Benford and David A. Snow, 'Framing processes and social movements: An overview and assessment', *Annual Review of Sociology*, Vol. 26 (2000), pp. 611–39; see also Jacklyn Cock in this volume.

23. DLF, 'Another South Africa and World is Possible', First Democratic Left Conference Report, 20–23 January 2011, University of the Witwatersrand, Johannesburg, p. 2.

24. Ballard et al., *Voices of Protest*, p. 407.

Bibliography

Abahlali baseMjondolo, 'Abahlali baseMjondolo takes the provincial government to court over the notorious Slums Act', press statement, 13 February 2008, http://abahlali.org/node/3335 (accessed 1 August 2011).

Adam, F., *Sasol Profits from Poison*, Johannesburg: Earthlife Africa Johannesburg, 2010.

——, T. Taylor and B. Peek, 'South Africa's US $3.75 billion world bank loan – developing poverty', *Amandla*, No.14 (May/June 2010).

Adler, G. and J. Steinberg (eds), *From Comrades to Citizens: The South African Civics Movement*, New York: Macmillan, 2000.

Agamben, Giorgio, 'Beyond human rights', in *Means without Ends: Notes on Politics*, Minneapolis: University of Minnesota Press, 1996.

——, *Homo Sacer: Sovereign Power and Bare Life*, trans. D. Heller-Roazen, Stanford: Stanford University Press, 1998.

——, *The State of Exception*, Chicago: University of Chicago Press, 2005.

Albo, G., 'The limits of eco-socialism: Scale, strategy and socialism', in L. Panitch and C. Leys (eds), *Coming to Terms with Nature: Socialist Register 2007*, London: Merlin Press, 2006.

Alexander, A. and A. Mngxitama, 'Race and resistance in post-apartheid South Africa', in S. Essof and D. Moshenberg (eds), *Searching for South Africa: The New Calculus of Dignity*, Tshwane: UNISA Press, 2011.

Alexander, Peter, 'Anti-globalisation movements, identity and leadership: Trevor Ngwane and the Soweto Electricity Crisis Committee', unpublished paper presented at the South African Sociological Association Conference, Durban, 2006.

——, 'Rebellion of the poor: South Africa's service delivery protests – a preliminary analysis', *Review of African Political Economy*, Vol. 37, No. 123 (2010).

—— and Peter Pfaffe, 'South Africa's rebellion of the poor: Balfour and relationships to the means of protest', paper presented at the Workshop on Protests, Elections and Emerging Politics, University of Johannesburg, 18 June 2011.

—— and Peter Pfaffe, 'South Africa's rebellion of the poor: Balfour and the relationship to means of protest', paper presented at the South African Research Chair in Social Change Workshop on Concept and Evidence, University of Johannesburg, 2–4 July 2011.

Antentas, Josep María, 'Resistance to neoliberalism', *IV Online Magazine*, IV380 (July–August 2006), www.internationalviewpoint.org/spip.php?article1088 (accessed 15 July 2011).

Apollis, John, 'The political significance of August 31st', *Khanya*, No. 2 (December 2002).

——, 'South African social movements: Where are we now?', *Khanya*, No. 5 (April 2004).

Arendt, Hannah, *On Revolution*, New York: Viking Press, 1963.

Ballard, Richard, Adam Habib and Imraan Valodia, 'Social movements in South Africa: Promoting crisis or creating stability?', in V. Padayachee (ed.), *The*

Development Decade? Economic and Social Change in South Africa, 1994–2004, Cape Town: HSRC Press, 2006.

——, *Voices of Protest: Social Movements in Post-apartheid South Africa*, Scottsville: University of KwaZulu-Natal Press, 2006.

Barchiesi, Franco, *Classes, Multitudes and the Politics of Community Movements in Post-apartheid South Africa*, CCS Research Report, No. 20, Durban: Centre for Civil Society, 2004.

Barker, Colin and Laurence Cox, '"What have the Romans ever done for us?" Academic and activist forms of movement theorizing', paper presented at the Alternative Futures and Popular Protest Eighth Annual Conference, Manchester Metropolitan University, Manchester, 2002.

Baskin, Jeremy, *Striking Back: A History of Cosatu*, Brooklyn and London: Verso, 1991.

Benford, R., 'Frame disputes with the Nuclear Disarmament Movement', *Social Forces*, Vol. 71, No. 3 (1993).

—— and D. A. Snow, 'Framing processes and social movements: An overview and assessment', *Annual Review of Sociology*, Vol. 26 (2000).

Bénit-Gbaffou, Claire and Laurence Piper, 'Party politics, the poor and the city', *Geoforum*, Vol. 43, No. 2 (2012).

Bilchitz, David, 'Is the Constitutional Court wasting away the rights of the poor? *Nokotyana v Ekurhuleni Metropolitan Municipality*', *South African Law Journal*, Vol. 127, Part 4 (2010).

Blaug, Ricardo and John Schwarzmantel, *Democracy: A Reader*, Edinburgh: Edinburgh University Press, 1988.

Blumer, H., 'The field of collective behavior', in A. M. Lee (ed.), *Principles of Sociology*, New York: Barnes and Noble, 1951.

Böhmke, Heinrich, 'The branding of social movements', *Dispositions*, Vol. 1 (1 May 2010).

Bond, Patrick, *Elite Transition: From Apartheid to Neoliberalism in South Africa*, London: Pluto Press, 2000.

——, 'Power to the people in South Africa: Operation Khanyisa! and the fight against electricity privatization', *Multinational Monitor*, Vol. 23 (January/February 2002).

——, *Unsustainable South Africa: Environment, Development and Social Protest*, Pietermaritzburg: University of Natal Press, 2003.

——, *Against Global Apartheid: South Africa Meets the World Bank, IMF and International Finance*, Cape Town: UCT Press, 2003.

——, 'Capitalism, the privatisation of basic social services and the implementation of socio-economic rights: Challenges and advocacy strategies for human rights and social justice actors, learning from the Johannesburg Water defeat', paper presented at the International Commission of Jurists Southern Africa Socio-economic Rights Camp, 31 August 2010.

——, Ashwin Desai and Trevor Ngwane, 'Uneven and combined Marxism within South Africa's urban social movements: Transcending precarity in community, labour and environmental struggles', paper presented at the conference Beyond Precarious Labor: Rethinking Socialist Strategies, City University of New York Graduate Center, May 2011.

Booysen, Susan, 'With the ballot and the brick: The politics of attaining service delivery', *Progress in Development Studies*, Vol. 7, No. 1 (2007).

——, *The African National Congress and the Regeneration of Political Power*, Johannesburg: Wits University Press, 2011.

——, 'The "ballot and the brick" – enduring under duress', in Susan Booysen (ed.), *Local Elections in South Africa: Parties, People, Politics*, Bloemfontein: Sun Press, 2012.

Borer, T., 'A taxonomy of victims and perpetrators: Human rights and reconciliation in South Africa', *Human Rights Quarterly*, Vol. 25, No. 4 (2003).

Brown, W. and J. Halley (eds), *Left Legalism/Left Critique*, Durham: Duke University Press, 2002.

Buhlungu, Sakhela (ed.), *Trade Unions and Democracy: Cosatu Workers' Political Attitudes in South Africa*, Cape Town: HSRC Press, 2006.

——, 'Upstarts or bearers of tradition? The Anti-Privatisation Forum of Gauteng', in Richard Ballard, Adam Habib and Imraan Valodia (eds), *Voices of Protest: Social Movements in Post-apartheid South Africa*, Scottsville: University of KwaZulu-Natal Press, 2006.

——, *A Paradox of Victory: COSATU and the Democratic Transformation in South Africa*, Scottsville: University of KwaZulu-Natal Press, 2010.

——, Roger Southall and Edward Webster, 'Conclusion: Cosatu and the democratic transformation of South Africa', in Sakhela Buhlungu (ed.), *Trade Unions and Democracy: Cosatu Workers' Political Attitudes in South Africa*, Cape Town: HSRC Press, 2006.

Burger, J., 'Institutional schizophrenia and police militarisation', Institute for Security Studies, 2010, www.iss.co.za/iss_today.php?ID=1024 (accessed 5 November 2010).

Callinicos, Alex, 'Toni Negri in perspective', *International Socialism*, Vol. 92 (2001).

——, *An Anti-capitalist Manifesto*, London: Polity Press, 2003.

Carey, S., 'Dynamic relationship between protest and repression', *Political Research Quarterly*, Vol. 59, No. 1 (March 2006).

Cassiem, A., *The Role of Law and its Ability to Protect Poor Families Facing Evictions in the Western Cape, 2005*, RASSP Research Report, Vol. 1, No. 6, Cape Town: University of the Western Cape, 2005.

CDE (Centre for Development and Enterprise), *A Fresh Look at Unemployment: A Conversation among Experts*, Johannesburg: CDE, 2011.

Ceruti, C., 'African National Congress change in leadership: What really won it for Zuma?', *Review of African Political Economy*, Vol. 35, No. 115 (2008).

——, 'Striking against a politically explosive background: Hidden possibilities in the 2005–2007 South African strikes', paper presented at the How Class Works conference, SUNY, Stonybrook, 2010.

——, 'The hidden element in the 2010 public-sector strike in South Africa', *Review of African Political Economy*, Vol. 38, No. 127 (March 2011).

Chatterjee, Partha, *The Politics of the Governed: Reflections on Popular Politics in Most of the World*, New York: Columbia University Press, 2004.

City of Johannesburg, 'Context', n.d., www.joburg-archive.co.za/2008/sdf/soweto/soweto_statusquo_context.pdf (accessed 3 August 2011).

Coalition Against Water Privatisation and Anti-Privatisation Forum, *Lessons from the War against Prepaid Meters: The Struggle against Disconnections Continues*, Johannesburg: Anti-Privatisation Forum, 2006, http://apf.org.za/IMG/pdf/Final_PPM_Research_Report_-_102006-2.pdf (accessed 1 August 2011).

Cock, J., 'Introduction', in J. Cock and E. Koch, *Going Green: People, Politics and the Environment in South Africa*, Cape Town: Oxford University Press, 1991.

——, 'Engendering lesbian and gay rights in South Africa: The equality clause in the South African Constitution', *Women Studies International Forum*, Vol. 26, No. 1 (2003).

——, 'Sustainable development or environmental justice? Questions for the South African labour movement from the Steel Valley struggle', *Labour, Capital and Society*, Vol. 40, No. 1 (2007).

Connell, R., *Masculinities*, Cambridge: Cambridge University Press, 1995.

COSATU (Congress of South African Trade Unions), 'On emerging social movements', Resolution No. 3, *Resolutions of the 8th National Congress, 2003*, www.cosatu. org.za (accessed 29 October 2010).

——, 'The Alliance at a crossroads – the battle against a predatory elite and political paralysis', political discussion paper, September 2010, www.cosatu.org.za/docs/ discussion/2010/dis0903.pdf.

——, 'Declaration of the Civil Society Conference held on 27–28 October 2010, Boksburg', Politicsweb, 28 October 2010, www.politicsweb.co.za/ (accessed 13 November 2010).

Cottle, Edward, 'The failure of sanitation and water delivery and the cholera outbreak', *Development Update*, Vol. 4, No. 1 (2003).

Crehan, Kate, *Gramsci: Culture and Anthropology*, London: Pluto Press, 2002.

Croteau, D., 'Which side are you on? The tension between movement scholarship and activism', in D. Croteau, W. Haynes and C. Ryan (eds), *Rhyming Hope and History: Activists, Academics and Social Movement Scholarship*, Minneapolis and London: University of Minnesota Press, 2005.

Currier, A., 'Decolonising the law: LGBT organising in Namibia and South Africa', in A. Sarat (ed.), *Studies in Law, Politics and Society, Vol. 54*, London: Emerald, 2011.

Daniel, John and Roger Southall, 'The Zuma presidency: The politics of paralysis', in John Daniel et al. (eds), *New African Review 2: New Paths, Old Compromises*, Johannesburg: Wits University Press, 2011.

Davis, Mike, *Planet of Slums*, New York: Verso, 2007.

Dawson, Marcelle C., 'Social movements in contemporary South Africa: The Anti-Privatisation Forum and struggles around access to water in Johannesburg', DPhil. thesis, University of Oxford, 2008.

——, 'Resistance and repression: Policing protest in post-apartheid South Africa', in J. Handmaker and R. Berkhout (eds), *Mobilising Social Justice in South Africa: Perspectives from Researchers and Practitioners*, The Hague: ISS and Hivos, 2010.

——, 'Phansi privatisation! Phansi!: The Anti-Privatisation Forum and ideology in social movements', in William Beinart and Marcelle C. Dawson (eds), *Popular Politics and Resistance Movements in South Africa*, Johannesburg: Wits University Press, 2010.

—— and L. Sinwell, 'Ethical and political challenges of participatory action research in the academy: Reflections on social movements and knowledge production in South Africa', *Social Movement Studies*, Vol. 11, No. 2 (2012).

Day, Richard J. F., *Gramsci is Dead: Anarchist Currents in the Newest Social Movements*, London: Pluto Press, 2005.

Dean, Jodi, *Democracy and Other Neoliberal Fantasies*, Durham and London: Duke University Press, 2009.

DefenceWeb 2009, 'Police to revert to military ranks from April', 26 February 2010, www.defenceweb.co.za/index.php?option=com_content&view=article&id=688 9:222&catid=3:Civil%20Security&Itemid=113 (accessed 7 November 2010).

De Lange, J., 'The second reading: Constitution Twelfth Amendment Bill', National Assembly speech, 15 November 2005, www.justice.gov.za/m_speeches/sp2005/2005_11_15_secondreading.htm (accessed 4 November 2010).

Della Porta, Donatella, 'The policing of protest', *African Studies*, Vol. 56, No. 1 (1997).

——, *The Global Justice Movement: Cross-national and Transnational Perspectives*, New York: Paradigm, 2006.

—— and Mario Diani, *Social Movements: An Introduction*, Oxford: Blackwell, 1999.

Department of Labour, 'Farm workers' minimum wage increases 2007/8', 2 March 2007, www.labour.gov.za (accessed June 2007).

Department of Social Development, *Transforming the Present, Protecting the Future: Report of the Committee of Inquiry into a Comprehensive System of Social Security for South Africa*, Pretoria: DoSD, 2002.

Desai, Ashwin, *We are the Poors: Community Struggles in Post-apartheid South Africa*, New York: Monthly Review Press, 2002.

——, 'Vans, autos, kombis and the drivers of social movements', Harold Wolpe memorial lecture, 28 July 2006, http://ccs.ukzn.ac.za/files/DN072006desai_paper.pdf (accessed 1 August 2011).

——, 'Rejoinder: The propagandists, the professors and their poors', *Review of Radical Political Economy*, Vol. 35, No. 116 (2008).

——, 'The state of the social movements', paper presented at the CCS/Wolpe lecture panel Social Justice Ideas in Civil Society Politics, Global and Local: A Colloquium of Scholar-activists, Centre for Civil Society, Durban, July 2010.

—— and A. Habib, 'COSATU and the democratic transition in South Africa: Drifting towards corporatism?', *Comparative Studies of South Asia, Africa and the Middle East*, Vol. 15, No. 1 (March 1995).

—— and R. Pithouse, 'Sanction all revolts: A reply to Rebecca Pointer', *Journal Asian and African Studies*, Vol. 39, No. 4 (2004).

Dirsuweit, T., 'The problem of identities: The lesbian, gay, bisexual, transgender and intersex social movement in South Africa', in R. Ballard, A. Habib and I. Valodia (eds), *Voices of Protest: Social Movements in Post-apartheid South Africa*, Scottsville: University of KwaZulu-Natal Press, 2006.

Dugard, Jackie, 'Courts and the poor in South Africa: A critique of systemic judicial failures to advance transformative justice', *South African Journal on Human Rights*, Vol. 24, No. 2 (2009).

——, 'Civic action and legal mobilisation: The Phiri water meters case', in Jeff Handmaker and Remko Berkhout (eds), *Mobilising Social Justice in South Africa: Perspectives from Researchers and Practitioners*, Pretoria: Pretoria University Law Press, 2010.

—— and Malcolm Langford, 'Art or science? Synthesising lessons from public interest litigation and the dangers of legal determinism', *South African Journal on Human Rights*, Vol. 27, Part 1 (2011).

Duncan, Jane, 'Thabo Mbeki and dissent', in D. Glaser (ed.), *Thabo Mbeki's World*, Johannesburg: Wits University Press, 2010.

Dwyer, P. and D. Seddon, 'The new wave? A global perspective on popular protest', paper presented at the 8th International Conference on Alternative Futures and Popular Protest, Manchester Metropolitan University, 2–4 April 2002.

——, 'The role of popular movements in Africa today', paper presented at the 5th International Conference on Alternative Futures and Popular Protest, Manchester Metropolitan University, 29–31 March 2010.

Dwyer, P. and L. Zeilig, *Social Movements and Anti-globalization in Africa*, Chicago: Haymarket Books, 2012.

Edwards, Bob and John D. McCarthy, 'Resources and social movement mobilisation', in David A. Snow, Sarag A. Soule and Hanspeter Kriesi (eds), *The Blackwell Companion to Social Movements*, Oxford: Blackwell.

Eisinger, P., 'The conditions of protest behaviour in American cities', *American Political Science Review*, Vol. 67, No. 1 (1973).

Ellis, S. and I. van Kessel, 'Introduction: African social movements or social movements in Africa', in S. Ellis and I. van Kessel (eds), *Movers and Shakers: Social Movements in Africa*, Leiden: Brill, 2009.

Equal Education, 'Presidency retracts ban on "protests" at Union Buildings', 2010, www.equaleducation.org.za/bday-march (accessed 28 October 2010).

Fantasia, Rick, *Cultures of Solidarity: Consciousness, Action and Contemporary American Workers*, Berkeley: University of California Press, 1989.

——, 'From class consciousness to culture, action, and social organization', *Annual Review of Sociology*, Vol. 21 (1 January 1995).

Ferguson, James, *The Anti-Politics Machine*: *'Development,' Depoliticization, and Bureaucratic Power in Lesotho*, Minneapolis and London: University of Minnesota Press, 2000.

——, *Global Shadows: Africa in the Neoliberal World Order*, Durham and London: Duke University Press, 2006.

——, 'The uses of neoliberalism', *Antipode*, Vol. 41, No. S1 2009 (2009).

Fiil-Flynn, Maj, *The Electricity Crisis in Soweto*, Johannesburg: Municipal Services Project, 2001.

Fine, Robert and Denis Davis, *Beyond Apartheid: Labour and Liberation in South Africa*, Johannesburg: Ravan Press, 1990.

Fleury-Steiner, B. and L. B. Nielsen, 'Introduction: A constitutive perspective of rights', in B. Fleury-Steiner and L. B. Nielsen (eds), *The New Civil Rights Research: A Constitutive Approach*, Aldershot: Ashgate, 2006.

Forgacs, David, *A Gramsci Reader*, London: Lawrence and Wishart, 1988.

Foster, J. B., *The Ecological Revolution*, New York: Monthly Review Press, 2009.

Foucault, Michel, 'Governmentality', in G. Burchell, C. Gordon and P. Miller (eds), *The Foucault Effect: Studies in Governmentality*, Chicago: University of Chicago Press, 1991.

——, *Power: Essential works of Foucault, 1954–1984*, ed. James D. Faubion, trans. Robert Hurley et al., New York: New Press, 2000.

Freedom of Expression Institute, 'FXI welcomes commencement of trial in Landless People's Movement torture case', press statement, 24 August 2005.

Friedman, Steven and Shauna Mottiar, 'Seeking the high ground: The Treatment Action Campaign and the politics of morality', in Richard Ballard, Adam Habib and Imraan Valodia (eds), *Voices of Protest: Social Movements in Post-apartheid South Africa*, Scottsville: University of KwaZulu-Natal Press, 2006.

Fullard, M. and N. Rousseau, 'An imperfect past: The Truth and Reconciliation Commission in transition', in J. Daniel, A. Habib and R. Southall (eds), *State of the Nation: South Africa 2003–2004*, Cape Town: HSRC Press, 2003.

Gabel, P. and D. Kennedy, 'Roll over Beethoven', *Standard Law Review Law*, Vol. 36, No. 1 (1984).

Gamson, W. A., *Talking Politics*, New York: Cambridge University Press, 1992.

Gaventa, John, 'Triumph, deficit or contestation? Deepening the "deepening democracy" debate', IDS Working Paper, No. 264, Brighton: Institute of Development Studies, 2006.

Gibson, Nigel (ed.), *Challenging Hegemony: Social Movements and the Quest for a New Humanism in Post-apartheid South Africa*, Trenton: Africa World Press, 2006.

Gilkerson, Christopher P., 'Poverty law narratives: The critical practice and theory of receiving and translating client stories', *Hastings Law Journal*, Vol. 43 (1991–92).

Goldstone, J. A., *States, Parties and Social Movements*, Cambridge: Cambridge University Press, 2003.

Goodwin, Jeff, James M. Jasper and Francesca Polletta, 'Emotional dimensions of social movements', in David A. Snow, Sarah A. Soule and Hanspeter Kriesi (eds), *The Blackwell Companion to Social Movements*, Oxford: Blackwell.

Gramsci, A., *Selections from the Prison Notebooks of Antonio Gramsci*, New York: International, 1971.

Greenberg, Stephen and Nhlanhla Ndlovu, 'Civil society relationships', in *Development Update*, Vol. 5, No. 2 (2004).

Greenstein, Ran, 'Civil society, social movements and power in South Africa', unpublished paper presented at Rand Afrikaans University sociology seminar, 2003.

Gumede, Vusi, 'Poverty, inequality and human development in a post-apartheid South Africa', paper presented at the conference on Overcoming Inequality and Structural Poverty in South Africa: Towards Inclusive Growth and Development, Johannesburg, 2010.

Habib, Adam, 'Is economic policy likely to change under Jacob Zuma?', Polity. org, www.polity.org.za/article/is-economic-policy-likely-to-change-under-jacob-zuma-2009-03-25, 25 March 2009 (accessed 4 November 2010).

—— and Rupert Taylor, 'Parliamentary opposition and democratic consolidation in South Africa', *Review of African Political Economy*, Vol. 26, No. 80 (1 June 1999).

—— and Imraan Valodia, 'Reconstructing a social movement in an era of globalisation: A case study of COSATU', in Richard Ballard, Adam Habib and Imraan Valodia (eds), *Voices of Protest: Social Movements in Post-apartheid South Africa*, Scottsville: University of KwaZulu-Natal Press, 2006.

—— and P. Opoku-Mensah, 'Speaking to global debates through a national and continental lens: South African and African social movements in comparative perspective', in S. Ellis and I. van Kessel (eds), *Movers and Shakers: Social Movements in Africa*, Leiden: Brill, 2009.

Hall, Stuart, 'Gramsci's relevance for the study of race and ethnicity', *Journal of Communication Inquiry*, Vol. 10 (June 1986).

Hardt, M. and A. Negri, *Empire*, Cambridge, Mass.: Harvard University Press, 2001.

Harris, Jessica, 'Towards a movement of the poors? A survey of Durban activists' views on struggle, unity, and the future', unpublished paper written for the School for Development Studies, University of KwaZulu-Natal, Durban as part of the School for International Training South Africa, www.abahlali.org/node/848#attachments.

Harrison, G., *Issues in the Contemporary Politics of Sub-Saharan Africa: The Dynamics of Struggle and Resistance*, Basingstoke and New York: Palgrave Macmillan, 2002.

Harvey, D., *A Brief History of Neoliberalism*, New York: Oxford University Press, 2005.

——, *The Enigma of Capital*, New York: Oxford University Press, 2010.

Harvey, Ebrahim, 'The commodification of water in Soweto and its implications for social justice', PhD thesis, University of the Witswatersrand, 2007.

Harvie, D. et al., *Shut Them Down: The G8, Gleneagles 2005 and the Movement of Movements*, West Yorkshire and New York: Dissent! and Autonomedia, 2005.

Hassen, Ebrahim-Khalil, 'Unsatisfactory strike outcome: Public service agreement', *South African Labour Bulletin*, Vol. 34, No. 5 (5 December 2010).

Heinecken, L., 'Ban military unions, they're a threat to national security! So where to from here?', *Strategic Review for Southern Africa* (November 2009), http://findarticles.com/p/articles/mi_hb1402/is_2_31/ai_n55089500/ (accessed 3 November 2010).

Heller, Patrick, 'Moving the state: The politics of democratic decentralisation in Kerala, South Africa, and Porto Alegre', *Politics and Society*, Vol. 29, No. 1 (March 2001).

——, 'Democratic deepening in India and South Africa', in Isabel Hofmeyr and Michelle Williams (eds), *South Africa and India: Shaping the Global South*, Johannesburg: Wits University Press, 2011.

Helliker, Kirk and Peter Vale, 'Fanon's curse: Re-imagining Marxism in South Africa's age of retreat', paper presented at the Twelfth Annual Conference of the International Association of Critical Realism, Rio de Janeiro, July 2009.

Heywood, M. 'Social movements: Challenging the state', paper prepared for the Harold Wolpe Memorial Seminar, presented at The Edge Institute, 4 May, www.the-edge.org.za/seminars.htm, 2005.

Hickey, S. and G. Mohan, 'Towards participation as transformation: Critical themes and challenges', in S. Hickey and G. Mohan (eds), *Participation from Tyranny to Transformation: Exploring New Approaches to Participation in Development*, London and New York: Zed Books, 2004.

Holloway, John, *Change the World Without Taking Power*, London: Pluto Press, 2002.

Holston, James, *Insurgent Citizenship: Disjunctions of Democracy and Modernity in Brazil*, Princeton: Princeton University Press, 2008.

Houston, G., *The National Liberation Struggle in South Africa: A Case of the South African United Democratic Front 1983–1987*, Brookfield: Ashgate, 1999.

Houtart, F. and F. Polet (eds), *The Other Davos: The Globalization of Resistance to the World Economic System*, London and New York: Zed Books, 2001.

HSRC (Human Science Research Council), *IEC Voter Participation Survey 2010/11: An Overview of Results*, Pretoria: HSRC Press, 2011.

Hyde, Sandra, *Eating Spring Rice: The Cultural Politics of AIDS in Southwest China*, Berkeley: University of California Press, 2006.

IEC (Independent Electoral Commission), *Results Summary, Local Government Elections 2011*, 2011, www.elections.org.za (accessed November 2011).

——, *Local Government Elections 2011: Information Brochure*, Pretoria: IEC, 2011.

——, 'Turnout and spoilt details, local government elections, 2011', 2011, www.elections.org.za (accessed November 2011).

Invisible Committee, *Call*, self-published, 2007.

Jakopovich, D., 'Uniting to win: Labour–environmental alliances', *Capitalism, Nature, Socialism*, Vol. 20, No. 2 (June 2009).

Jenkins, J.C. and B. Klandermans (Eds.), *The politics of social protest: Comparative perspectives on states and social movements*. Minneapolis: University of Minnesota Press, 1995.

Johnson, K., 'Framing AIDS mobilization and human rights in post-apartheid South Africa', *Perspectives on Politics*, Vol. 4, No. 4 (2006).

Johnston, S. and A. Bernstein, *Voices of Anger: Protest and Conflict in Two Municipalities*, Johannesburg: Centre for Development and Enterprise, 2007.

Jones, Lynn, 'The haves come out ahead: How cause lawyers frame the legal system for movements', in Austin Sarat and Stuart A. Scheingold (eds), *Cause Lawyers and Social Movements*, Stanford: Stanford University Press, 2006.

Joseph, Miranda, *Against the Romance of Community*, Minneapolis and London: University of Minnesota Press, 2002.

Kazis, R. and R. Grossman, *Fear at Work: Job Blackmail, Labour and the Environment*, New York: Pilgrim Press, 1982.

Kimani, Simon, *Surviving below the Margin: Recent Trends in Collective Bargaining and Wage Settlements*, Naledi, 2007, www.naledi.org.za/index.php?option=com_rokdownloads&view=file&Itemid=267&id=115:survivingbelow (accessed 23 November 2011).

Kirshner, J. and C. Phokela, *Khutsong and Xenophobic Violence: Exploring the Case of the Dog that Didn't Bark*, research report commissioned by Atlantic Philanthropies, Johannesburg: Centre for Sociological Research, University of Johannesburg, 2010.

Kitshelt, H., 'Political opportunity structures and political protest: Anti-nucleur movements in four democracies', *British Journal of Political Studies*, No. 16 (1986).

Klandermans, B., 'The demand and supply of participation: Social-psychological correlates of participation in social movements', in D. Snow, S. Soule and H. Kriesi (eds), *The Blackwell Companion to Social Movements*, Malden: Blackwell, 2004.

Kovel, J., *The Enemy of Nature*, London: Zed Books, 2002.

Khulumani Support Group, *Khulumani! Speak Out!*, 2006.

Lambert, Rob and Eddie Webster, 'Global civil society and the new labour internationalism', in R. Taylor (ed.), *Creating a Better World: Interpreting Global Civil Society*, Cape Town: Kumarian Press, 2004.

Larmer, Miles, 'Social movement struggles in Africa', *Review of African Political Economy*, Vol. 37, No. 125 (September 2010).

——, P. Dwyer and L. Zeilig, 'Southern African social movements at the 2007 Nairobi World Social Forum', *Global Networks*, Vol. 9, No. 1 (2009).

Lazzarato, Maurizio, 'From biopower to biopolitics', trans. Ivan A. Ramirez, *Pli: The Warwick Journal of Philosophy*, Vol. 13 (n.d.), www.generation-online.org/c/fcbiopolitics.htm.

Lehulere, Oupa, 'The new social movements, COSATU and the "new UDF"', *Khanya*, No. 11 (December 2005).

Lenin, 'The trade unions, the present situation and Trotsky's mistakes', speech, 30 December 1920, www.marxists.org.

Lichterman, P., 'Seeing structure happen: Theory-driven participant observation', in B. Klandermans and S. Staggenborg (eds), *Methods of Social Movement Research*, Minneapolis: University of Minnesota Press, 2002.

Liebenberg, Sandra, *Socio-economic Rights: Adjudication under a Transformative Constitution*, Cape Town: Juta, 2010.

Lipton, Merle, *Liberals, Marxists and Nationalists: Competing Interpretations of South African History*, New York: Palgrave Macmillan, 2008.

Lodge, T. and B. Nasson, *All Here and Now: Black Politics in South Africa in the 1980s*, Cape Town: David Philip, 1991.

Lundy, P. and M. McGovern, 'Whose justice? Rethinking transitional justice from the bottom up', *Journal of Law and Society*, Vol. 35, No. 2 (2008).

Maddison, Sarah and Sean Scalmer, *Activist Wisdom: Practical Knowledge and Creative Tension in Social Movements*, Sydney: University of New South Wales, 2006.

Madlingozi, Tshepo, 'Post-apartheid social movements and the quest for the elusive "New" South Africa', *Journal of Law and Society*, Vol. 34, No. 1 (2007).

——, 'Good victims, bad victims: Apartheid beneficiaries, victims and the struggle for social justice', in W. le Roux and K. van Marle (eds), *Law, Memory and Apartheid: Ten Years after AZAPO v President of South Africa*, Pretoria: Pretoria University Law Press, 2007.

——, 'On transitional justice entrepreneurs and the production of victims', *Journal of Human Rights Practice*, Vol. 2, No. 1 (2010).

——, 'Human rights, power and civic action in developing societies: South African organisational study – Abahlali baseMjondolo', background paper for Rights, Power and Civic Action, Leeds University, 2011.

——, 'The role and impact of socio-economic rights strategies on social movements', in M. Langford et al. (eds), *Socio-economic Rights in South Africa: Symbols or Substance?*, Cambridge: Cambridge University Press, 2013.

Maduna, Penuell, 'Declaration to the United States New York District Court', 2003.

Malabela, Musawenkosi, 'The African National Congress (ANC) and local democracy: The role of the ANC branch in Manzini-Mbombela', MA research report, School of Social Sciences, University of the Witwatersrand, 2011.

Mamdani, M. and E. Wamba-dia-Wamba (eds), *African Studies in Social Movements and Democracy*, Senegal: CODESRIA, 1995.

Marais, Hein, *South Africa: Limits to Change: The Political Economy of Transition*, London: Palgrave Macmillan, 2001.

——, *South Africa Pushed to the Limit: The Political Economy of Change*, London and Cape Town: Zed Books and UCT Press, 2011.

Marshall, A., *Confronting Sexual Harassment: The Law and Politics of Everyday Life*, Aldershot: Ashgate, 2005.

Marx, Karl, *Preface of a Contribution to the Critique of Political Economy*, 1859, www.marxists.org.

——, *The 18th Brumaire of Louis Bonaparte*, 1852, www.marxists.org.

Maseko, J., 'Transcript of post-cabinet briefing', 10 September 2009, www.gcis. gov.za/newsroom/releases/cabstate/2009/090909_transcript.htm (accessed 2 November 2011).

Matlala, Boitlumelo and Claire Bénit-Gbaffou, 'Against ourselves – Local activists and the management of contradicting political loyalties', *Geoforum*, Vol. 43, No. 2 (2012).

Mbeki, Thabo, 'Statement of the president of the ANC, Thabo Mbeki, at the ANC Policy Conference', Kempton Park, 20 September, 2002, www.anc.org.za/docs.

McAdam, D., 'Political opportunities: Conceptual origins, current problems, future directions', in D. McAdam, S. Tarrow and C. Tilly, *Dynamics of Contention*, Cambridge: Cambridge University Press, 2001.

—— and Sidney Tarrow, 'Ballots and barricades: On the reciprocal relationship between elections and social movements', *Perspectives on Politics*, Vol. 8, No. 2 (June 2010).

——, S. Tarrow and C. Tilly, *Dynamics of Contention*, Cambridge: Cambridge University Press, 2001.

McCann, Michael W., *Rights at Work: Pay Equity Reform and the Politics of Legal Mobilization*, Chicago and London: University of Chicago Press, 1994.

McCarthy, J. D. and M. N. Zald, *The Trend of Social Movements in America: Professionalization and Resource Mobilization*, Morristown: General Learning Press, 1973.

——, 'Resource mobilization and social movements: A partial theory', *American Journal of Sociology*, 82 (1977).

McDonald, David, *The Bell Tolls for Thee: Cost Recovery, Cut offs, and the Affordability of Municipal Services in South Africa: Special Report of the Municipal Services Project*, 2000, www.queensu.ca/msp/.

—— and Laïla Smith, 'Privatizing Cape Town', Occasional Papers, No. 7, Johannesburg: Municipal Services Project, 2003.

McEvoy, K., 'Beyond legalism: Towards a thicker understanding of transitional justice', *Journal of Law and Society*, Vol. 34, No. 4 (2007).

McKinley, Dale, *The ANC and the Liberation Struggle: A Critical Political Biography*, London: Pluto Press, 1997.

——, 'Democracy, power and patronage: Debate and opposition within the ANC and Tripartite Alliance since 1994', in Roger Southall (ed.), *Opposition and Democracy in South Africa*, London: Frank Cass, 2001.

——, 'The Congress of South African Trade Unions and the Tripartite Alliance since 1994', in Tom Bramble and Franco Barchiesi (eds), *Rethinking the Labour Movement in the 'New' South Africa*, Aldershot: Ashgate, 2003.

——, 'Democracy and social movements in South Africa', in V. Padayachee (ed.), *The Development Decade? Economic and Social Change in South Africa, 1994–2004*, Cape Town: HSRC Press, 2006.

——, 'South Africa's third local government elections and the institutionalisation of "low-intensity" neo-liberal democracy', in Jeanette Minnie (ed.), *Outside the Ballot Box: Preconditions for Elections in Southern Africa 2005/6*, Johannesburg: Media Institute of Southern Africa, 2007.

——, 'Xenophobia and nationalism: Exposing the South African state for what it is', *Khanya*, Special Edition No. 19 (July 2008).

——, 'The crisis of the left in contemporary South Africa', paper presented at the Decade of Dissent symposium, University of Johannesburg, 2010.

——, 'South Africa's social conservatism: A real and present danger', South African Civil Society Information Service, March 2010, http://sacsis.org.za/site/article/440.1.

——, 'Brief notes for input to Khanya College Winter School workshop on Law and Organising', Johannesburg, 2 August 2010.

—— and Prishani Naidoo, *Mobilising for Change: The Rise of the New Social Movements in South Africa*, Development Update Series, Johannesburg: Interfund, 2004.

—— and A. Veriava, *Arresting Dissent: State Repression and Post-apartheid Social Movements*, Braamfontein: Centre for the Study of Violence and Reconciliation, 2005.

——, 'Transition's child: A brief history of the Anti-Privatisation Forum,' in *Transition's Child: The Anti-Privatisation Forum (APF)*, Braamfontein: SAHA, 2012.

Meister, R., 'Human rights and the politics of victimhood', *Ethics and International Affairs*, Vol. 16, No. 2 (2002).

Melucci, Alberto, 'The symbolic challenge of contemporary movements', *Social Research*, Vol. 52, No. 4 (Winter 1985).

Mertes, T., *A Movement of Movements: Is Another World Really Possible?*, London: Verso, 2004.

Meyer, D., 'The South African experience in dealing with communal violence', *African Security Review*, Vol. 8, No. 1 (1999).

——, 'Protest and political opportunities', *Annual Review of Sociology*, Vol. 30 (2004).

Ministry of Agriculture, Western Cape, 'Statement by Cobus Dowry, minister of agriculture Western Cape: Road forward for Jonkershoek', unpublished document, 2006.

Miraftab, F., 'Feminist praxis, citizenship and informal politics', *International Feminist Journal of Politics*, Vol. 8, No. 2 (2006).

—— and S. Wills, 'Insurgency and spaces of active citizenship: The story of the Western Cape Anti-Eviction Campaign in South Africa', *Journal of Planning Education and Research*, Vol. 25, No. 2 (2005).

Morton, A. D., 'The antiglobalization movement: juggernaut or jalopy', in H. Veltmeyer (ed.), *Globalization and Antiglobalization: Dynamics of Change in the New World Order*, Aldershot: Ashgate, 2004.

Municipal IQ, 'Municipal IQ's updated protest hotspots', 13 April 2010, www.bvm.gov.za/bvmweb/images/News/1%20december%202010.pdf (accessed 2 November 2011).

Nagy, R., 'Transitional justice as a global project: Critical reflections', *Third World Quarterly*, Vol. 29, No. 2 (2008).

Naidoo, Prishani, 'Struggles around the commodification of daily life in South Africa', *Review of African Political Economy*, Vol. 34, No. 111 (2007).

——, 'Subaltern sexiness: From a politics of representation to a politics of difference', *African Studies*, Vol. 69, No. 3 (2010).

National Institute for Economic Policy, 'From RDP to GEAR', Research Paper Series, Johannesburg: NIEP, 1996.

Ndletyana, Mcebisi, 'Municipal elections 2006: Protests, independent candidates and cross-border municipalities', in Sakhela Buhlungu et al. (eds), *State of the Nation: South Africa 2007*, Cape Town: HSRC Press, 2007.

Nefale, Michael, *A Survey on Attitudes to Prepaid Electricity Meters in Soweto*, Johannesburg: Centre for Applied Legal Studies, 2004.

NeJaime, D., 'Convincing elites, controlling elites', *Studies in Law, Politics and Society*, Vol. 54 (2011).

Neocosmos, M. 'From people's politics to state politics: Aspects of national liberation in South Africa', in A. Olukoshi (ed.), *The Politics of Opposition in Contemporary Africa*, Uppsala: Nordic Africa Institute, 1998.

——, *Civil Society, Citizenship and the Politics of the (Im)Possible: Rethinking Militancy in Africa Today*, 2007, http://abahlali.org/files/Neocosmos%20 2007%20citizenship%20and%20politics.pdf (accessed 1 August 2011).

Ngwane, Trevor, 'The Anti-Privatisation Forum (APF)', *South African Labour Bulletin*, Vol. 27, No. 3 (2003).

——, 'Ideologies, strategies and tactics of township protests', in B. Maharaj, P. Bond and A. Desai (eds), *Zuma's Own Goal: Losing South Africa's 'War on Poverty'*, Trenton: Africa World Press, 2010.

——, 'We, the protesters', *Amandla*, No. 14 (May/June 2010).

Ngyuen, Vihn-Kim, 'Antiretroviral globalism, biopolitics and therapeutic citizenship', in Aihwa Ong (ed.), *Global Assemblages: Technology, Politics and Ethics as Anthropological Problems*, Malden: Blackwell, 2004.

Notes from Nowhere, *We Are Everywhere: The Irresistible Rise of Global Anti-capitalism*, London: Verso, 2003.

NPA (National Prosecuting Authority), *Prosecutions Policy and Directives Relating to the Prosecutions of Offences Emanating from Conflicts of the Past and which Were Committed on or before 11 May 1994*, Pretoria, 2005.

Nzimande, Blade, 'The class question in consolidating the faultline in the National Democratic Revolution', *Umsebenzi Online*, Vol. 5, No. 57 (7 June 2006), www.sacp.org.za/main.php?ID=1858 (accessed 2 November 2011).

Omar, B., 'Crowd control: Can our public order police still deliver?', *SA Crime Quarterly*, No. 15 (March 2006).

——, *SAPS's Costly Restructuring: A Review of Public Order Policing Capacity*, Institute for Security Studies Monograph, No. 138, Pretoria: ISS, October 2007.

Ong, Aihwa, *Neoliberalism as Exception: Mutations in Citizenship and Sovereignty*, Durham: Duke University Press, 2006.

Opp, K. and W. Roehl, 'Repression, micromobilization and political protest', *Social Forces*, Vol. 69, No. 2 (1990).

Panitch, L. and C. Leys (eds), *Coming to Terms with Nature: Socialist Register 2007*, London: Merlin Press, 2006.

Papadakis, Konstantinos, *Civil Society, Participatory Governance and Decent Work Objectives: The Case of South Africa*, Geneva: International Institute for Labour Studies, 2006.

Parliamentary Monitoring Group, 'South African National Defence Force Union grievances', minutes of the meeting of the Portfolio Committee on Defence and Military Veterans, 18 March 2008, www.pmg.org.za/report/20080318-south-african-national-defence-union-grievances (accessed 5 November 2010).

Petryna, Adriana, *Life Exposed: Biological Citizens after Chernobyl*, Princeton: Princeton University Press, 2002.

Pichardo, N. A., 'New social movements: A critical review', *Annual Review of Sociology*, Vol. 23 (1997).

Pieterse, Marius, 'Eating socio-economic rights: The usefulness of rights talk in alleviating social hardship revisited', *Human Rights Quarterly*, Vol. 29, No. 3 (2007).

Pillay, Devan, 'Cosatu, alliances and working class politics', in Sakhela Buhlungu (ed.), *Trade Unions and Democracy: Cosatu Workers' Political Attitudes in South Africa*, Cape Town: HSRC Press, 2006.

——, 'Globalization and the informalization of labour: The case of South Africa', in Andreas Bieler, Ingemar Lindberg and Devan Pillay (eds), *Labour and the Challenges of Globalization: What Prospects for Transnational Solidarity?*, London: Pluto Press, 2008.

Piven, F. F. and R. A. Cloward, *Poor People's Movements: Why They Succeed and how They Fail*, New York: Vintage Books, 1977.

Pointer, Rebecca, 'Questioning the representation of South Africa's "new social movements": A case study of the Mandela Park Anti-eviction Campaign', *Journal of Asian and African Studies*, Vol. 39, No. 4 (2004).

——, 'Questioning the representation of South Africa's "new social movements": A case study of the Mandela Park Anti-Eviction Campaign (MPAEC)', mimeo, 2004.

Polanyi, Karl, *The Great Transformation: The Political and Economic Origins of Our Time*, Boston: Beacon Press, 2001 [1944].

Polet, F. and CETRI (eds), *Globalizing Resistance: The State of Struggle*, London: Pluto Press, 2004.

POPCRU (Police and Prisons Civil Rights Union), 'Memorandum to the ANC on re-militarisation of SAPS', 30 April 2010, www.popcru.org.za/press%20 statements_10_memorandum.html (accessed 4 November 2010).

Prince, Crystal, 'Conditions on farms: A draft paper', Unit for Social Research, Western Cape Department of Social Services and Poverty Alleviation, 2004.

Radebe, Jeff, 'Speech by minister of public enterprises', Workshop on Service Delivery Framework, Gauteng, 2001.

Rancière, Jacques, *Proletarian Nights*, trans. Noel Parker, Radical Philosophy series, Vol. 31 (1982), www.scribd.com/doc/65081569/Ranciere-Preface-to-The-Nights-of-Labour-1981.

——, 'Ten theses on politics', in Steven Corcoran (ed. and trans.), *Dissensus: On Politics and Aesthetics*, London and New York: Continuum International, 2010.

Regan, P. and E. Henderson, 'Democracy, threats and political repression in developing countries: Are democracies internally less violent?', *Third World Quarterly*, Vol. 23, No. 1 (February 2002).

Renton, D., D. Seddon and L. Zeilig, *Congo: Plunder and Resistance*, London: Zed Books, 2006.

Republic of South Africa, 'Government notice: Determination of upper limits of salaries', 18 December 2010.

Robins, S., *From Revolution to Rights in South Africa*, Pietermaritzburg: University of KwaZulu-Natal Press, 2008.

Robnett, Belinda, *How Long? How Long? African-American Women in the Struggle for Civil Rights*, Oxford: Oxford University Press, 1996.

Roithmayr, Daria, 'Transition towns: Using the commons to dismantle racial inequality', paper presented at a University of Southern California workshop, 15 October 2010.

Routledge, Paul, 'Voices of the dammed: Discursive resistance amidst erasure in the Narmada valley, India', *Political Geography*, Vol. 22, No. 3 (March 2003).

Santiago, I., 'A fierce struggle to re-create the world', in J. Sen et al., *World Social Forum: Challenging Empires*, New Delhi: Viveka Foundation, 2004.

Sarat, A. and S. Scheingold (eds), *Cause Lawyers and Social Movements*, Stanford: Stanford University Press, 2006.

Saul, John S., *The Next Liberation Struggle: Capitalism, Socialism and Democracy in Southern Africa*, Durban: University of KwaZulu-Natal Press, 2005.

Scheingold, Stuart A., *The Politics of Rights: Lawyers, Public Policy and Political Change*, Ann Arbor: University of Michigan Press, 2004.

Scott, James, *Domination and the Arts of Resistance: Hidden Transcripts*, New Haven: Yale University Press, 1990.

Seddon, D. and L. Zeilig, 'Class and protest in Africa: New waves', *Review of African Political Economy*, Vol. 32, No. 103 (2005).

Seekings, Jeremy, *The UDF: A History of the United Democratic Front in South Africa 1983–1991*, Cape Town: David Philip, 2000.

——, 'Poverty and inequality after apartheid', CSSR Working Paper, No. 200, Cape Town: Centre for Social Science Research, University of Cape Town, 2007.

Segodi, Siphiwe, 'Thembelihle Crisis Committee contesting elections through Operation Khanyisa Movement', 2011, http://tinyurl.com/3u2w46x (accessed 9 August 2011).

Sen, J. et al., *World Social Forum: Challenging Empires*, New Delhi: Viveka Foundation, 2004.

Shah, Purvi and Chuck Elsesser, 'Community lawyering', *Organizing Upgrade: Left Organizers Respond to the Changing Times* (1 June 2010), www.organizingupgrade.com/2010/06/social-justice-lawyering/ (accessed August 2011).

Simon, Roger, *Gramsci's Political Thought: An Introduction*, London: Lawrence and Wishart, 1982.

Sinwell, Luke, 'Defensive social movement battles need to engage with politics', *South African Labour Bulletin*, Vol. 34, No. 1 (March/April 2010).

——, 'Is "another world" really possible? Re-examining counter-hegemonic forces in post-apartheid South Africa', *Review of African Political Economy*, Vol. 38, No. 127 (2011).

——, 'Asserting political biography: Highlighting the interface between militant black movements in Soweto and the Democratic Alliance', paper presented at the South African Cities Conference, University of Cape Town, 9 September 2011.

——, 'Transformative Left-Wing Parties and Grassroots Organizations: Unpacking the Politics of "Top-Down" and "Bottom-Up" Development', *Geoforum*, Vol. 43, No. 2 (2012).

Siyabengana: Socialist Civic Movement Newsletter, Vol. 1, Issue 1 (16 April 2011).

Smelser, N. J., *Theory of Collective Behavior*, New York: Free Press, 1962.

Snow, D., 'Framing process, ideology and discursive fields', in D. Snow, S. Soule and H. Kriesi (eds), *The Blackwell Companion to Social Movements*, Malden: Blackwell, 2004.

—— and R. D. Benford, 'Ideology, frame resonance, and participant mobilization', *International Social Movement Research*, Vol. 1 (1988).

——, 'Clarifying the relationship between framing and ideology', *Mobilization: An International Journal*, Vol. 5 (2000).

——, 'Master frames and cycles of protest', in C. Mueller and A. Morris (eds), *Frontiers of Social Movement Theory*, New Haven: Yale University Press, 1992.

Solnit, D., *Globalize Liberation: How to Uproot the System and Build a Better World*, San Francisco: City Lights Books, 2004.

South African Cities Network, *State of the Cities Report 2006*, 2006, www.sacities.net/knowledge/research/publications/395-socr2006.

Southall, Roger and Edward Webster, 'Unions and parties in South Africa: COSATU and the ANC in the wake of Polokwane', in Bjorn Beckman, Sakhela Buhlungu and Lloyd Sachikonye (eds), *Trade Unions and Party Politics: Labour Movements in Africa*, Cape Town: HSRC Press, 2010.

Southall, Roger and Geoffrey Wood, 'COSATU, the ANC and the election: Whither the Alliance?', *Transformation*, Vol. 38 (1999).

Southern, Neil and Roger Southall, 'Dancing like a monkey: The Democratic Alliance and opposition politics in South Africa', in John Daniel et al. (eds), *New African Review 2: New Paths, Old Compromises,* Johannesburg: Wits University Press, 2011.

Starr, A., *Global Revolt: A Guide to Movements against Globalization*, London and New York: Zed Books, 2005.

Stats SA (Statistics South Africa), *Mid-year Population Estimates, 2011*, Pretoria: Stats SA, 2011.

——, *Quarterly Labour Force Survey, Quarter 2, 2011*, Pretoria: Stats SA, 2011.

Stoecker, Randy, 'Community, movement, organization: The problem of identity convergence in collective action', *Sociological Quarterly*, Vol. 36, No. 1 (Winter 1995).

Suttner, R., 'The UDF period and its meaning for contemporary South Africa', *Journal of Southern African Studies*, Vol. 30, No. 3 (2004).

Sweeney, S., 'How unions can help secure a binding global climate agreement in 2011', 4 March 2011, www.sustainlabor.

Sylvester, Justin and Sithembile Mbete, 'The 2011 LGE: Separating the reality from the spin', unpublished paper for IDASA, Cape Town, 2011.

TAC (Treatment Action Campaign), *Fighting for Our Lives: The History of the Treatment Action Campaign 1998–2010*, 2010, www.tac.org.za/community/files/10yearbook/index.html (accessed 1 August 2011).

Tankiso, 'Comrade', 'Beyond dreadlocks and demagogy', *Umrabulo* (June 2003).

Tarrow, Sidney. *Collective Politics and Reform: Collective Action, Social Movements, and Cycles of Protest*. New York: Cornell University, 1991.

——, *Power in Movement: Social Movements, Collective Action and Politics*, Cambridge: Cambridge University Press, 1998; 3rd edn, 2011.

Taylor, T., 'Foreword', in Earthlife Africa, *Climate Change, Development and Energy Problems in South Africa: Another World is Possible*, Johannesburg: Earthlife Africa, 2009.

Thompson, Lisa and Chris Tapscott, *Citizenship and Social Movements: Perspectives from the Global South*, London and New York: Zed Books, 2010.

——, 'Introduction: Mobilisation and social movements in the South – the challenges of inclusive governance', in Lisa Thompson and Chris Tapscott (eds), *Citizenship and Social Movements: Perspectives from the Global South*, London and New York: Zed Books, 2010.

Tilly, Charles, 'Models and realities of popular collective action', *Social Research*, Vol. 52, No. 4 (1985).

——, 'When do (and don't) social movements promote democratization?', in Pedro Ibarra (ed.), *Social Movements and Democracy*, New York: Palgrave Macmillan, 2003.

——, *The Politics of Collective Violence*, Cambridge and New York: Cambridge University Press, 2003.

Tiqqun, *Introduction to Civil War*, Los Angeles: Semiotext(e)/MIT Press, 2010.

Touraine, Alain, 'An introduction to the study of social movements', *Social Research*, Vol. 52, No. 4 (1985).

Tregenna, F. and D. Masondo, 'Towards a new growth path', *African Communist* (September 2010).

Trotsky, Leon, *History of the Russian Revolution*, London: Gollancz, 1965.

United Nations Development Programme, *Human Development Report 2009: Overcoming Barriers: Human Mobility and Development*, New York: Palgrave Macmillan, 2009.

——, *South Africa Human Development Report: The Challenge of Sustainable Development in South Africa: Unlocking People's Creativity*, London: Oxford University Press, 2003.

University of South Africa, *Projection of Future Economic and Sociopolitical Trends in South Africa up to 2025*, Research Report No. 351, Pretoria: Bureau of Market Research, 2004.

van Kessel, I., 'The United Democratic Front's legacy in South Africa: Mission accomplished or vision betrayed?', in S. Ellis and I. van Kessel (eds), *Movers and Shakers: Social Movement in Africa*, Leiden: Brill, 2009.

van Marle, K., 'Laughter, refusal, and friendship: Thoughts on a "jurisprudence of generosity"', *Stellenbosch Law Review*, No. 1, Vol. 18 (2007).

Vavi, Zwelinzima, 'SA still moving in apartheid direction', Irene Grootboom memorial lecture, Site B Hall, Khayelitsha, Cape Town, 18 October 2010.

——, 'Speech of Cosatu general secretary to the 8th National Congress of NEHAWU', Tshwane, 26–29 June 2007, www.wftucentral.org/?p=830&language=en (accessed 15 November 2011).

——, 'Address of the COSATU general secretary to the SACP 12th Congress', 13 July 2007, www.cosatu.org.za/show.php?ID=1437 (accessed 15 November 2011).

Veriava, Ahmed and Prishani Naidoo, 'From local to global (and back again?): Anti-commodification struggles of the Soweto Electricity Crisis Committee', in David A. McDonald (ed.), *Electric Capitalism: Recolonising Africa on the Power Grid*, Cape Town: HSRC Press, 2009.

von Holdt, Karl et al., *The Smoke that Calls: Insurgent Citizenship, Collective Violence and the Struggle for a Place in the New South Africa*, Johannesburg: Centre for the Study of Violence and Reconciliation and Society Work and Development Institute, 2011, www.swopinstitute.org.za.

Wainwright, Hilary, 'Transformative resistance: The role of labour and trade unions', in D. McDonald and G. Ruiters (eds), *Alternatives to Privatization: Public Options for Essential Services in the Global South*, New York: Routledge, 2012.

Wallis, V., 'Beyond green capitalism', *Monthly Review* (February 2010).

Walsh, Shannon, '"Uncomfortable collaborations": Contesting constructions of the "poor" in South Africa', *Review of African Political Economy*, Vol. 35, No. 116 (2008).

Westaway, Ashley, 'Rural poverty in South Africa: Legacy of apartheid or consequence of contemporary segregationism?', paper presented at the conference on Overcoming Inequality and Structural Poverty in South Africa: Towards Inclusive Growth and Development, Johannesburg, 2010.

White, Fiona, 'Strengthening democracy? The role of social movements as agents of civil society in post-apartheid South Africa', PhD thesis, University of London, 2008.

——, '2009 elections', *South African Labour Bulletin*, Vol. 33, No. 3 (2009).

Williams, R. H., 'The cultural contexts of collective action: Constraints, opportunities, and the symbolic life of social movements', in D. Snow, S. Soule and H. Kriesi (eds), *The Blackwell Companion to Social Movements*, Malden: Blackwell, 2004.

Wilson, R., *The Politics of Truth and Reconciliation in South Africa: Legitimizing the Post-apartheid State*, Cambridge: Cambridge University Press, 2001.

Wilson, Stuart, 'Litigating housing rights in Johannesburg's inner city: 2004–2008', *South African Journal on Human Rights*, Special Issue on Public Interest Litigation, Vol. 27 (2011).

——, 'Constitutional jurisprudence: The first and second waves', in M. Langford et al. (eds), *Socio-economic Rights in South Africa: Symbols or Substance?*, Cambridge: Cambridge University Press, 2013.

—— and Jackie Dugard, 'Constitutional jurisprudence: The first and second waves', in M. Langford et al. (eds), *Socio-economic Rights in South Africa: Symbols or Substance?*, Cambridge: Cambridge University Press, 2013.

—— and Jackie Dugard, 'Taking poverty seriously: The South African Constitutional Court and socio-economic rights', *Stellenbosch Law Review* (2011).

Wolfe, Tom, 'Radical chic', in *Radical Chic & Mau-Mauing the Flak Catchers*, New York: Farrar, Straus and Giroux, 1970.

Wolford, Wendy, *This Land is Ours Now: Social Mobilization and the Meanings of Land*, London: Duke University Press, 2010.

Worthington, R. and L. Tyrer, *50% by 2030: Renewable Energy in a Just Transition to Sustainable Energy Supply*, Johannesburg: World Wildlife Fund, 2010.

Zeilig, L. (ed.), *Class Struggle and Resistance in Africa*, Cheltenham: New Clarion Press, 2002.

——, M. Larmer and P. Dwyer, 'An epoch of uprisings: Social movements in post-colonial Africa, 1945–1998', *Journal of Socialist History* (forthcoming 2012).

Zuern, Elke, 'Elusive boundaries: SANCO, the ANC and the post-apartheid South African state', in Richard Ballard, Adam Habib and Imraan Valodia (eds), *Voices of Protest: Social Movements in Post-apartheid South Africa*, Scottsville: University of KwaZulu-Natal Press, 2006.

——, *The Politics of Necessity: Community Organizing and Democracy in South Africa*, Madison: University of Wisconsin Press, 2011.

About the Authors and Editors

Peter Alexander holds the South African Research Chair in Social Change hosted by the University of Johannesburg. In a former avatar he was active in anti-Nazi, anti-apartheid and socialist politics in Britain. His doctorate is from London University, and he has held positions at the University of Oxford and Rhodes University. His books include *Racism, Resistance and Revolution* (1987), *Racializing Class, Classifying Race* (2000), *Workers, War and the Origins of Apartheid* (2000), and *Globalisation and New Identities* (2006). He is researching class identity in Soweto and South Africa's rebellion of the poor.

Fiona Anciano is a senior research associate at the Centre for the Study of Democracy at the University of Johannesburg. She is a social science researcher with a special interest in the relationship between civil society and democracy. She completed her PhD at the Institute of Commonwealth Studies, University of London, examining the link between social movements, democracy and socioeconomic inequality. She also worked for several years at the Johannesburg-based Centre for Policy Studies as a senior researcher and researcher. She has produced numerous publications, including several book chapters such as the chapter on South Africa in F. Polet (ed.), *The State of Resistance: Popular Struggles in the Global South* (2007). She has also written journal articles for the *Journal of Southern African Studies, South African Labour Bulletin* and *Journal of Geography in Higher Education.*

Claire Ceruti is completing a doctorate in sociology at the University of Johannesburg through the South African Research Chair in Social Change. Her thesis focuses on the development of class identities in recent public sector strikes, but she has also researched a number of other strikes over the same period. She has published in the *Review of African Political Economy* and *South African Review of Sociology.* Prior to taking up a doctoral fellowship, Claire worked as a researcher at the South African Research Chair in Social Change, where, among other publications, she co-authored a book on class and class identities in Soweto. She has been an entirely participant observer of various social movements in South Africa since the 1980s.

Jacklyn Cock is professor emeritus in the Department of Sociology at the University of the Witwatersrand. She is the author of numerous publications on environmental, gender and labour issues. Her best-known book is *Maids* *and Madams: A Study of the Politics of Exploitation* (1980) and the most recent is *The War Against Ourselves: Nature, Power and Justice* (2007). She has been an activist in the environmental justice movement in South Africa for the past 30 years.

Marcelle C. Dawson works as a senior researcher at the South African Research Chair in Social Change at the University of Johannesburg. She obtained a DPhil. in Politics from the University of Oxford in 2008 under the supervision of William Beinart with whom she co-edited *Popular Politics and Resistance Movements in South Africa* (2010). She is currently working on a monograph based on her thesis on the Anti-Privatisation Forum and grassroots struggles against the commodification of water in South Africa. She is an executive board member of the International Sociological Association's Research Committee 47 (Social Classes and Social Movements) and convened a working group on social movements and popular protest for the South African Sociological Association from 2009 to 2012.

Jane Duncan is Highway Africa Chair of Media and Information Society in the School of Journalism and Media Studies at Rhodes University. Before that she worked at the Freedom of Expression Institute (FXI) since its establishment in 1994 and was its director from 2001 to mid 2009. She was also coordinator of the FXI's predecessor organisation, the Anti-Censorship Action Group. She also worked at the Funda Centre in Soweto and then at the Afrika Cultural Centre in Newtown. She obtained a BA, Honours and MA degrees at the University of the Witwatersrand, and completed a PhD through the Wits School of the Arts in 2007.

Malose Langa is a lecturer in the School of Community and Human Development at the University of the Witwatersrand, South Africa. He is currently the coordinator of the MA Programme in Community-based Counselling Psychology. His career began as an intern psychologist at the Centre for the Study of Violence and Reconciliation's Trauma Clinic (2004), where he provided trauma counselling and debriefing services to victims of violent crime. He has published book chapters and journal articles on violent crime, substance abuse, problems facing former combatants and masculinity. His recent journal articles have been published in the *South African Journal of Psychology, Psychology in Society* and the *British Journal of Substance Abuse*. He is currently completing his PhD entitled 'Becoming a Man: Exploring Multiple Voices of Masculinity amongst Adolescent Boys in Alexandra Township, South Africa'.

Tshepo Madlingozi is senior lecturer in Law at the University of Pretoria and currently a DPhil. candidate at the University of London. His main research interest focuses on how legal strategies and human rights discourse constitute the political subjectivity of social movements. He is co-editor of *Socio-economic Rights in South Africa: Symbols or Substance?* (2013). He has published articles in *Journal of Human Rights Practice* (2010), *Constitutional Court Review* (2009) and *Journal of Law and Society* (2007), as well as chapters in books.

Dale T. McKinley is an independent writer, researcher and lecturer based in Johannesburg, South Africa. He is a long-time political activist and has been intricately involved in social movement, community and political struggles since the late 1980s. He obtained a PhD in Politics-African Studies from the University of North Carolina-Chapel Hill. His main areas of research centre on the contemporary political economy of South and Southern Africa, the strategy and tactics of the ANC, popular oral histories, and the struggles of poor communities for basic services and democratic participation. His publications include: *The ANC and the Liberation Struggle: A Critical Political Biography* (1997), *Arresting Dissent: State Repression and Post-apartheid Social Movements* (2005) and *Forgotten Voices in the Present: Alternative, Post-1994 Oral Histories from Three Poor Communities* (2009); twelve chapters in edited book collections on democracy in the 'new' South Africa, international social movement struggles, South African labour history and South African sports/mega events; and numerous articles in popular magazines and labour and academic journals on a wide variety of topics.

Trevor Ngwane was born in Durban in 1960. He was at high school when the 16 June 1976 student uprising broke out in Soweto. He studied Sociology at Fort Hare University and was involved in student protests and later expelled with many others in 1982. He became a socialist in the late 1980s, helped organise the civic movement in Soweto and worked for the Transport and General Workers' Union in the early 1990s. He was elected an ANC councillor in 1995 and was later expelled by the party for opposing the privatisation of services. He helped found the Soweto Electricity Crisis Committee and the Anti-Privatisation Forum. He is currently completing his MA in the Centre for Civil Society at the University of KwaZulu-Natal and is a member of the Democratic Left Front, an attempt at left regrouping in neoliberal South Africa.

Carin Runciman received her PhD from the University of Glasgow in 2012. Her doctoral research explored the internal dynamics of community politics within the Anti-Privatisation Forum through ethnographic methodologies and considered the counter-hegemonic potential of the forms of insurgent citizenship that were mobilised within the grassroots spaces of the movement. She is currently undertaking a post-doctoral fellowship at the University of Johannesburg and is working with Professor Peter Alexander on a project entitled 'South Africa's Rebellion of the Poor'.

Luke Sinwell completed his MA and PhD at the University of the Witwatersrand in Johannesburg, South Africa. He is currently a Senior Researcher at the South African Research Chair in Social Change at the University of Johannesburg. His research interests include the politics and conceptualisation of participatory development and governance, social movements and housing struggles, non-violent and violent direct action as a method to transform power relations, ethnographic research methods, and action research. He is involved in a project called 'The Voices of the Poor in Urban Governance: Participation, Mobilization and Politics in South African Cities' and is currently leading a project that seeks to create a workers' history of the recent struggle and massacre in Marikana, near Rustenburg, South Africa.

Kate Tissington is a senior researcher at the Socio-Economic Rights Institute of South Africa (SERI), which provides socioeconomic rights assistance to individuals, communities and social movements. She was previously a researcher at the Centre for Applied Legal Studies (CALS), based at the University of the Witwatersrand. She has published research reports on informal trading in inner city Johannesburg, challenges around water services provision, housing waiting lists and allocation, and informal settlement upgrading in South Africa. She has also written two comprehensive resource guides on housing and basic sanitation in South Africa, and has published in the *South African Journal on Human Rights* and in a number of popular journals. She is interested in the role of civil society in the conceptualisation and implementation of socioeconomic policy and programmes, particularly around land, housing and basic services; the opportunities and limitations of rights-based and legal strategies to achieve social change; and the practice of participatory democracy in South Africa more generally.

Karl von Holdt is a professor and director of the Society Work and Development Institute at the University of the Witwatersrand. Previously he was at the COSATU-linked policy Institute, NALEDI, and before that editor of the *South African Labour Bulletin*. He has published *Transition from Below: Forging Trade Unionism and Workplace Change in South Africa* (2003), and *Beyond the Apartheid Workplace: Studies in Transition* (2005) co-edited with Eddie Webster. His current research interests include the functioning of state institutions and the health system, collective violence and associational life, and civil society. He started his working life teaching literacy to trade union members in the hostels and informal settlements of Cape Town in the early 1980s. He has also served as the coordinator of COSATU's September Commission on the Future of Trade Unions (1996–97), and as a director on the board of the South African Post Office (1997–2003).

Shannon Walsh is a filmmaker, researcher and writer. Her documentaries engage vital social issues, such as the devastating effects of oil-sands exploitation in Alberta in the award-winning *H2Oil* (2009), or the diverse stories that make up contemporary urban life in *St-Henri, the 26th of August* (2011). She received her PhD from McGill University, where her research investigated the complex processes of power in post-apartheid South Africa through engaged pedagogy and ethnography of everyday practice. She has published journal articles in *Review of African Political Economy*, *Gender and Development*, *Sex Education*, *Agenda*, and *Feminist Media Studies*. She is currently a post-doctoral research fellow in the Research Chair in Social Change at the University of Johannesburg.

Index

Compiled by Sue Carlton

Page numbers in *italics* refer to authors' contributions, page numbers in **bold** refer to illustrations, page numbers followed by 'n' refer to notes